A FUTURE WITHOUT HATE OR NEED

"Written with the right mix of respect, compassion, and critical reflection, this heartfelt history of the fascinating cultural world of the mostly Yiddish-speaking Jewish left in Canada and the talented and committed women, men, and children who lived it, brims with stories that will sadden, anger, inspire, enlighten, and, above all, stay with you. Through narratives relayed in oral interviews, journals, poems, political and folk songs, plays, women's readings, summer-camp performances, and more, we glimpse the heart and soul of an extraordinary cultural movement for social justice and social change."

> – **Franca Iacovetta**, Department of History, University of Toronto, author of *Gatekeepers: Reshaping Immigrant Lives in Cold War Canada*

"*A Future Without Hate or Need* offers a deep examination of the culture and personalities of the Toronto Jewish radical left during its efflorescence. The Yiddish material, much of it drawn from *Der Kamf*, is superb. Passages translated from the original Yiddish are rarely-used sources that add strongly to Reiter's argument that the principal focus of this movement was social/cultural rather than strictly ideological/political. This book is written with warm sympathy and penetrating insight."

> – **Gerald Tulchinsky**, Department of History, Queen's University, author of *Taking Root: The Origins of the Canadian Jewish Community*

"In her tenderly rendered recovery of the history of Canada's secular Jewish left, Ester Reiter excavates the contradictions and complexities that shaped Jewish identities and underpinned the Jewish left's rich cultural life. Her inspiring account of the women, men, and children in the secular Jewish left immerses us in the radical vision of a 'more beautiful, better world' that informed the activities, organizations, and culture of these twentieth-century Jewish radicals. Poetry, music, and theatre went hand in hand with politics in a movement that demonstrably challenges the bifurcated view of left/right divisions and reductive assessments of left movements. This book's nuanced perspective on the Jewish ethnic left and its many contributions to North American society offers valuable insights on our collective past and makes an important contribution to the new scholarship on left history."

> – **Julie Guard**, Departments of History and Labour Studies, University of Manitoba

"Warm-hearted, intimate, sometimes critical and always courageous, *A Future Without Hate or Need* offers twentieth-century Canadians a fresh understanding of the stalwart men, women, and children who championed and lived their own version of *sotsyalizm* (socialism). In summer camps and orchestras, city councils and schools, left-wing parties and cultural centres, Jewish leftists created a remarkably diverse and successful movement—one that, through personal memoirs, skilful archival digging, and beautiful photographs and cartoons, Ester Reiter lovingly recreates for us—in all its complicated glory."

> – **Ian McKay**, Wilson Chair of Canadian History, McMaster University

Ester Reiter

A FUTURE WITHOUT HATE OR NEED

The Promise of the Jewish Left in Canada

Between the Lines
Toronto

A Future without Hate or Need

First published in 2016 by
Between the Lines
401 Richmond Street West
Studio 277
Toronto, Ontario M5V 3A8
Canada
1-800-718-7201
www.btlbooks.com

Library and Archives Canada Cataloguing in Publication

Reiter, Ester, author

A future without hate or need : the promise of the Jewish left in Canada / Ester Reiter.

Includes bibliographical references and index.

Issued in print and electronic formats.

ISBN 978-1-77113-016-5 (paperback).—
ISBN 978-1-77113-017-2 (epub).—
ISBN 978-1-77113-018-9 (pdf)

1. Jews—Canada—Politics and government. 2. Judaism and politics— Canada—History—20th century. 3. Socialism and Judaism—Canada— History— 20th century. 4. Communism and Judaism—Canada— History— 20th century. 5. Jews—Canada—History— 20th century. 6. Jews—Canada— Social life and customs. 7. Canada—Emigration and immigration—History— 20th century. 8. Jews—Migrations. I. Title.

HX550.J4R45 2016   335.0089′924071   C2015-908225-0
C2015-908226-9

Text and cover design by David Vereschagin/
    Quadrat Communications
Cover art by Avrom, courtesy Anna Yanovsky and
    UJPO Archives
Printed in Canada

We acknowledge for their financial support of our publishing activities the Government of Canada through the Canada Book Fund, the Canada Council for the Arts, which last year invested $153 million to bring the arts to Canadians throughout the country, and the Government of Ontario through the Ontario Arts Council, the Ontario Book Publishers Tax Credit program, and the Ontario Media Development Corporation.

Canada Council **Conseil des Arts**
for the Arts **du Canada**

Canadä

ONTARIO ARTS COUNCIL
CONSEIL DES ARTS DE L'ONTARIO
an Ontario government agency
un organisme du gouvernement de l'Ontario

Shelfie

An **ebook** edition is available for $2.99
with the purchase of this print book.

CLEARLY PRINT YOUR NAME ABOVE IN UPPER CASE

Instructions to claim your eBook edition:
1. Download the Shelfie app for Android or iOS
2. Write your name in **UPPER CASE** above
3. Use the Shelfie app to submit a photo
4. Download your eBook to any device

FSC
www.fsc.org

MIX
Paper from
responsible sources
FSC® C103567

GCC/IBT

To my family
not all of whom are biological relatives
and many of whom remain alive only in my heart:

the people I love and who love me back

Contents

Acknowledgements

The writing of this book has been a long journey, one with an arbitrary, not a clear ending. There is always more to learn. It is also very personal, as this history embodies many of the ideals that I hold dear. Along the way, there have been encounters with people, places, and writings that have enriched me.

This is a work that has relied on many people, contributing in many different ways. Roz Usiskin's pioneering work on the history of Jewish radicalism in Winnipeg established a standard of thorough, thoughtful research that set a very high bar. She has helped in so many ways: advice, materials from her collection, and a contribution to the chapter on Democracy and Dissent, part of which we first presented together at a Canadian Jewish Studies conference. Maxine Hermolin, the executive director of the United Jewish People's Order, supported this research by providing complete access to the extensive UJPO materials in Toronto's Winchevsky Centre. Ruth Grossman, a trained archivist, prepared visual PowerPoint histories of the community for several events we co-presented to the UJPO community. She is also organizing the materials for the UJPO Archives. Shlomit Segal helped with some of the images and made suggestions for the book. A special thanks goes to Drs. May (Lipshitz) Cohen and Gerry Cohen for the donation of May's parents' materials to the Clara Thomas Archives at York University. The Cohens also worked with the archivist Michael Moir in organizing the extensive collection of Sam and Manya Lipshitz.

A number of researchers contributed to this project. Michelle Cohen gave me the idea of studying and writing about a community I know well. She interviewed people from Naivelt as a summer project back in 1994. Mel Cederbaum, the executive director of the Workmen's Circle in Toronto, provided materials from the early history of the WC. Amy Katz collected background materials on the Canadian Jewish community from the *Globe and Mail*. Sylwia Szymanska, who I met at YIVO's Yiddish seminar at Columbia University, helped organize and translate some of the materials in the Lipshitz archives. Sarah Pinder did some interviews in Montreal and transcribed many of the interviews that I had done. Sharon Power did many translations of *Der Kamf* from Yiddish, which she then arranged by topic and summarized in ways that were most helpful. She is a fine scholar, careful in her research, with outstanding organizational skills. A special thanks to the Ross family, Oscar, Honey, and Lisa, for providing photos of their family's involvement in dance, theatre, and the Naivelt summer camp, and Maiyán for her pride in her grandparents. Some of Olga Eizner Favreau's drawings based on her mother's UJPO activities are included in the book. Esther Podoliak provided pictures and some background on her father, Philip. Anna Yanovksy was very generous in allowing the use of her late husband Avrom's art and family photos. Ruth Howard, the producer of Jumblies Theatre, made the interviews I had collected come alive in her play *Oy di Velt*, in ways that brought the history of this community home in an accessible, beautiful way, involving many of the Naivelt community of all ages.

Gerry Tulchinksy offered to read the manuscript when it was still in pretty rough shape. His generosity was a tremendous encouragement in actually completing the work. That also gave me the notion of approaching Ian McKay, and he too was encouraging with many helpful suggestions—not all of which I was able to follow up on. I very much appreciate the kind words of Paul Buhle. Although my views often vary from those of Bryan Palmer, he is an excellent editor and made suggestions for reorganizing the manuscript to make it more coherent. Franca Iacovetta included my earlier work on the summer camps in the edited collection *Sisters and Strangers*. I value her encouragement of my research. Julie Guard read the manuscript and made helpful suggestions. A few of the chapters were presented to the Labour Studies reading group, and I appreciated their input. Susan Berlin read a draft of some of the chapters. Meg Luxton read a draft, helping with grammatical changes. Jane Springer did the original, rather challenging edit of the book. Cameron Duder did a careful and respectful copyedit of the book and the captions for the pictures. A special thanks to Between the Lines and editor Amanda Crocker for their early support for this book.

Several funding bodies provided financial assistance. The Centre for Jewish Studies at York University provided small grants that were particularly important in the initial stages of this research. The Friends of Yiddish in Toronto helped support my attendance at YIVO's Yiddish program at Columbia University. The

YIVO summer program in New York and the Yiddish program in Vilnius, Lithuania were both wonderful for improving my Yiddish and deepening my understanding of the roots of secular Yiddish culture. The Secular Yiddish Schools of America collection at Stanford established by Gela Fishman was very useful. I also received a fellowship from the Fishmans to spend one month in the archives there, which provided an important context for my research. I was the recipient of a SSHRC scholarship, which enabled me to hire researchers, several of whom continued their involvement with secular Yiddish culture.

Archivists have been a great help. Thank you to Stan Carbone and Ava Block of the Jewish Heritage Centre of Western Canada Archives, Janet Rosen of the Canadian Jewish Congress Archives, and the Ontario Jewish Archives. I also benefitted from the assistance of Montreal Jewish Public Library archivists, in particular Eiran Harris and Shannon Hodge, the staff of the Clara Thomas Special Collections Library of York University, the reference librarians in the Ontario Archives, in particular Peter Salvatore, the reference librarian at the Tamiment Library of New York, the staff of the American Lincoln Brigade Association (ALBA), and the Thomas Fisher Rare Books librarians at the University of Toronto.

Unfortunately, a number of key founders of the community were no longer living by the time I began this work, and so I relied on the work of others. The interviews Karen Levine did back in the 1970s were important in preserving this history. She also painstakingly went over the hundreds of photos in the collection of Joshua Gershman, noting who the people in these historic photos were. Mercedes Steedman shared the interviews she did for her book, *Angels of the Workplace*. Doug Smith loaned me his interviews with Joe Zuken, which he used in his book, *Joe Zuken: Citizen*. I had a wonderful afternoon interviewing Ruth Borchiver about her experiences and then she allowed me to photocopy her hand-written transcribed interviews of the major players in the Jewish left, all of whom were her friends. She used them as the basis for her Ph.D. thesis. Sadly, Ruth died not long after. Cheryl Tallan did interviews with her mother, Becky Lapedes, and shared the tapes with me, thus providing the kind of information only possible in the relaxed intimacy of a mother-daughter relationship. Gloria Bruner shared the translations she did for Benita Wolters-Fredlund's Ph.D. dissertation on the Toronto Jewish Folk Choir. The Velvl Katz Yiddish reading group of the UJPO consisted of several people born in Poland; the readings provided invaluable information about the world they had grown up in. Lillian Butovsky, a Canadian-born member of our reading group, recognized the importance of documenting the stories of their lives in pre-Second World War Poland and interviewed some of the members in their beautiful native Yiddish.

I would like to express my appreciation to the many people who shared their stories with me. They include:

Irving Abella	Mildred Gutkin
David Abramowitz	Maxine Hermolin
Freda Akerman	Gerry Kane
Abe Arnold	Francine Korotzer
Bertha Arnold	Aaron Krishtalka
Gerry Bain	Dovid Kunigas
Rita Bergman	Jim Laxer
Sherry Bergman	Gord Meslin
Ronnie Biderman	Claire Benzwi Miller
Barbara Blaser	Mollie Myers
Pearl Blazer	Rae Orlan
Jeanette Block	Claire (Klein) Osipov
Ruth Borchiver	Esse Potash
Galya Chud	Lillian (Milton) Robinson
Gerry Cohen	Dora Rosenbaum
May Cohen	Judee Rosenbaum
Mitzi (Sid) Dolgoy	Honey Ross
Reva Dolgoy	Oscar Ross
Nettie Farber	Frederika Rotter
Olga (Eizner) Favreau	Barbara Belman Segal
Rose Field	Evelyn Shapiro
Helen Fine	Bella Shek
Izzie Fine	Ben Shek
Brenda Fishauf	Bess Shockett
Nathan Fishauf	David Silverberg
Shirley Fistell	Madeline Simon
Marion Frank	Marsha (Fine) Solnicki
Mark Frank	Al Soren
Sylvia Freedman	Elsie Suller
Esther Gartner	Sandy (Fine) Traub
Itche Goldberg	Roz Usiskin
Mollie Klein Goldsman	Mary Winer
Bessie(Chikovsky)Grossman	Anna Yanovksy

In recent years in North America, we have seen an attempt by the dominant forces in the Jewish community to erase from our collective consciousness the awareness of an important part of our not so distant past, the materially challenged but spiritually and culturally enriched life of our parents, grandparents, and great-grandparents. When identity is reduced to bagels, lox, and gefilte fish, and/or uncritical support for the government in power in Israel, what gets lost is the sense of social justice and universal brotherhood and sisterhood exemplified in the work of a Sholem Aleichem or a Peretz expressed in Yiddish. This book can only touch on the many ways that secular progressive Jewish Canadians lived their ideals. It is this author's intention to begin to document this rich and compelling heritage.

INTRODUCTION

In July 2008, a group of Toronto children and teenagers at Camp Naivelt, on the outskirts of Brampton, Ontario spent a week re-enacting the lives of children who in 1920 were part of the Twelfth Jewish Children's Work Commune in Vitebsk.[1] The commune was one of the efforts of the new Soviet regime to deal with the "demographic earthquake" they faced in the aftermath of the First World War, the civil war following the Bolshevik Revolution of 1917, and the resulting epidemics and famine. An estimated seven million children roamed the streets of Russia's towns and villages. The government evacuated as many children as they could, placing about five hundred thousand in abandoned and confiscated estates. The communes emphasized hard work, responsibility, and children's initiative, reflecting the social philosophy of a collective upbringing.

Adopting the personas and the biographies of these children, the Naivelt participants approximated as closely as they could the conditions in the commune and the children's lives.[2] Like the original communards, they had the advantage of resource people to assist with art, music, and dance, but what they created was based on their own initiatives. For a week, they lived with no running water, no electric lights, no washing machines, no beds, and a limited amount of food. They dressed in one set of clothes, cooked, cleaned, slept in one room, ran meetings, learned Yiddish songs and dances, created art, and, in the spirit of the journals written almost ninety years ago, made their own hand-bound journal, writing stories about their experiences. Here is what one young woman, Shifra Cooper, then sixteen, wrote about the experience:

> Through the week, we achieved many things: we learned to bake bread, to mend benches, read about Yiddish writers, sing folk songs and debate period political ideas.... One of our huge accomplishments was the publishing of our

Manya (Margolia Kantorovitch) in the fourth Jewish Children's Commune, Vitebsk, USSR, 1920. Manya is in the centre of the top row, wearing a kerchief. The teacher, Doroshkin, is in the first row, third from the left.

York University Libraries, Clara Thomas Archives & Special Collections, Sam and Manya Lipshitz fonds, F0444.

journal, Kommunar, organized by the Editorial Board. Just like the journals of the real Twelfth Commune, our journal was comprised of the daily writings of all the children, including such topics as "Dancing and Singing," "The River" and "How Children Can Change the Future," as well as poetry and art…. I find myself homesick for a place to which I never "really" went, a place that we re-created that hasn't existed for almost 100 years…. One great teaching of the week is the importance of dreams. From a building with hay all over the floor to a finished flower embroidered on a pocket, it was a week full of realizing our hopes—both in character and out—through our work together. That is a lesson that is relevant even 88 years later, as it teaches us to believe in our own strength, and in the power of deep friendships, however unusually formed.

The young people at Naivelt learned about the Vitebsk commune from a talk I gave at one of our Sunday bagel brunches at Camp Naivelt, a cottage community with a history that dates back to 1925. Sitting in lawn chairs in front of one of the modest cottages under the trees, I tried to convey the idealism of the founders of our left Jewish community through describing the memoir written by Manya Lipshitz, who had been a member of the Vitebsk commune and, for many years, a teacher in our shules. I was pleased that the teenagers stayed around for the lecture after the bagels, but there was something about the notion of a children's republic that interested some of them. And one of the Naivelt community cottagers, Ruth Howard, is the artistic director of Jumblies Theatre, a community arts organization. She was able to provide period costumes, music, art, and dance teachers as resources to assist these young people in making the commune happen.[3]

Manya's Memoir

In 1920, in the midst of the hardships and chaos of the civil war following the Bolshevik Revolution, the teen-aged Manya Kantorovitch was separated from her family who were living in Bialystok. She joined the Twelfth Jewish Children's Work Commune in Vitebsk, then part of the Soviet Union. The new regime provided the children

Camp Naivelt re-enactment of the Vitebsk Commune, summer 2008, Brampton, Ontario.
Jumblies Theatre photo by Michaela Otto.

with a broken down two-storey house. One of the children described it as dirty and cold, with cracked windows and the wind wafting in. Before they could make straw mattresses for themselves, they slept on bare wooden beds that were used as dining tables in the daytime. There were serious food shortages and high inflation. The commune was given food from a government store, but the children collected rations themselves with a cart in summer and a sleigh in winter. Their diet consisted of coarse barley three times a day, which was par-ticularly disastrous for the very young children. When they washed the floors, the water froze. However, the young people took charge. In a short time, the commune was a model of cleanliness; the children made mattresses and clothes and planted a garden. With the help of teachers from Leningrad they organized a full schedule of activities, including nature study, culture, and art, in addition to the work of cooking, cleaning, and mending clothes. Everything was planned by the children.

By this time, Manya's brothers had made it to Canada. In a letter Manya wrote from Vitebsk to her brothers, she insisted that she was not in a *priyut* or orphanage but a commune, which had a new form of socialist education, with thirty friends from eight to fifteen years of age. Even the teachers were not to be thought of as supervisors but simply older friends. She told them: "We were

Shifra Cooper reading Manya's memoir, *Bletl fun a Shturmisher Tsait,* translated as Time Remembered. Shifra played Margolia, as Manya Lipshitz was known as a young girl. Camp Naivelt, 2008.

Source: Jumblies Theatre photo by Katherine Fleitas.

completely independent, responsible for our own lives, which we ourselves were shaping." The children produced hand-made journals with poems and stories describing their lives that they presented as a gift to a visiting Yiddish poet.

Some five decades later, in the 1970s, reading an article in the Yiddish magazine *Yiddishe Kultur* (Jewish Culture), Manya rediscovered the journals she had edited as a girl. This prompted her to write a memoir describing her life and her experiences in the commune. The idealism and the importance of collectivity, which the young people in Manya's commune would have described as building socialism, is expressed differently by the young people of the twenty-first century. However, the message expressed by one of the young participants in the commune re-enactment remains a timely one: "As individuals, we may not change the world, but by creating the world we want to live in, at the commune together, we encourage others to do so as well."[4]

The Secular Jewish Left

Naivelt, where the re-enactment took place, is connected to the United Jewish People's Order (UJPO). The UJPO is part of the Jewish left in Canada, the subject of this book. I am a member of the Toronto organization and spend a good part of my summers at my cottage in Camp Naivelt. The left Jewish community in Canada was one of a variety of movements of secular Jews, all with different understandings of how to build a better world for Jews. All the movements had strong connections to similar organizations in the United States.

I distinguish the Jewish left from other secular Jewish movements by referring to their politics as pro-Bolshevik and, until 1956, friendly to the Soviet Union. They are often described as the "communist Jewish left" which I believe is misleading. While the Jewish left was communist-led, participants explained that being part of this broader organization was quite a different experience than being a member of the Communist Party (CP). In the policy known as Democratic Centralism, CP members undertook to follow directives once party policy was decided. UJPO members had no such constraints in the views they held or their actions. A UJPO person could hold a view quite at odds with the leadership, but one could not be ousted from the organization. While members often shared a belief that the USSR was the model of a socialist country, particularly in the late 1930s and 1940s, others came to enjoy the rich cultural and social activities the left offered. It was a "scene" that many young people wanted to be part of. Most (one former leader estimated 95 percent) of the progressive Jewish left were not communists, and a good part of their activities had nothing to do with Communist Party policies for Canada.[5] They are also referred to as *di linke* or the left; they called themselves "progressive Jews." When Jews from this community speak of the "old country," they mean Eastern Europe, usually Poland or Russia.

I grew up in the sister community in New York, the Jewish People's Fraternal Order of the International Workers Order. Born in 1941, I did not know any of my grandparents, three of whom perished in the Holocaust; one grandmother died when my father was a child. I inherited the grief over the loss of those murdered in the Second World War from my parents. I also was imbued with the hope and idealism of an earlier period, which sustained my friends and me through the threat of the Cold War. A few of our friends' parents had lost their jobs as teachers, refusing to sign affidavits swearing they did not belong to any "subversive" organizations. In the midst of the fearmongering around the "evil" Soviet empire, my left-wing friends stuck together. We knew that the exercise in school of hiding under our desks away from the windows would not really help in the event of nuclear war. Peace, not stockpiling weapons would protect us, and we celebrated the birth of the United Nations, the international forum for resolving conflict. We sang its praises:

> Everywhere the youth is singing freedom's song
> We rejoice to show the world that we are strong
> We are the youth and the world proclaims our song of truth.
> United Nation on the march with flags unfurled
> Together fight for lasting peace, a free, new world.

Like the children in Manya's commune, I grew up with a firm belief that my experiences and my history as a Jew were a route to an understanding of international solidarity. And like the children in Camp Naivelt, I believe in the power of collectivity. My education taught me that my Jewish identity is to be used to try to understand what it is like for an African American in Mississippi,

פון לינקם צו רעכטס:
שולמית ריבאלאוו, אסתר רייטער, נעאמי ריבאלאוו, מעינקע (לערער).

Kings Highway Shule Graduation, Brooklyn, New York, 1953. From left to right: Shulamis Ribolow, Ester Reiter, Naomi Ribolow, Menke Katz (Teacher).

Brooklyn Committee for Jewish Education, Almanac of the Jewish Children's Schools. *Personal collection of the author.*

a child in Vietnam, a First Nations survivor of the residential school system, a Palestinian separated from family, or a refugee from any number of countries in the world today. There is no hierarchy of oppressions. Each tragedy is specific and unique, but the lesson I learned from those years linked a strong commitment to my history with respect for all those who struggle for social justice. I do not react with dispassion to those who would use the Holocaust as justification for oppressing other people, and I find it upsetting when the significance of this history is diminished through the facile equation of every wrong being "just like" the Holocaust or the Warsaw Ghetto. It's through valuing the specificity of my own history that I can connect with others.

As a child growing up in New York in the 1950s, I attended the Kings Highway *shule* (Jewish secular school) in Brooklyn and the *mittlshul* (high school) after my regular school day. I went to the elementary shule three times a week. It was part of the Jewish People's Fraternal Order (JPFO) of the International Workers Order (IWO) and called an *Ordn shule*. The IWO, organized in 1930, comprised fourteen language groups, with the Jewish section the largest. It offered benefits such as health and life insurance and medical and dental clinics.[6] The IWO was placed on the Attorney General's list of subversive organizations in 1947. In 1953, the IWO lost its insurance charter. Although it was financially healthy, the New York State insurance examiner found its activities "unpatriotic" and a "moral hazard" and the IWO was forced to disband. My shule continued, reconstituted as part of the Jewish Cultural Clubs and Societies. My graduating class from the *elementar shule* (Jewish elementary school) consisted of a class of three—the Ribolow twins and me. The rest of the children had been withdrawn, their parents afraid of the repercussions of an association with a leftist school. The poet Menke Katz was our teacher. Meyer Eisenberg, who I later learned was part of the ARTEF collective of radical Yiddish proletarian artists, directed the Yiddish plays we performed for parents and friends. The year I graduated, 1953, was also the year Ethel and Julius Rosenberg were put to death for conspiracy to steal the secret of the atom bomb. My Aunt Anna was a communist and an active member of the Emma Lazarus clubs of the IWO; she regularly went to demonstrations, even as an old lady with sore feet. She was unable to get my mother to join her, with one exception—all of us attended demonstrations to save the Rosenbergs.

Camp Kinderland, 4th group, Hopewell Junction, New York, 1949. Ester Reiter is third from the left in the second row. The banner reads, "Cleanliness flag."

Photo by Itzkowitz. Personal collection of the author.

After graduating from the elementary shule, I attended the mittlshul, which was held all day Saturday. By then, the Yiddish high schools had amalgamated because of declining enrolment. Students from Brooklyn, the Bronx, Manhattan, and Queens travelled to 14th Street in Manhattan each weekend. Our teachers were dedicated intellectuals, their commitment to Yiddish keeping them in a profession where they could earn very little. We kids, on the other hand, were unruly teenagers determined to have fun. It's a miracle that we learned anything, but we did, especially respect for the classical Yiddish writers and sweatshop poets whose songs we sang.

I spent summers in Camp Kinderland in Hopewell Junction, not far from Peekskill, New York. My first year as a camper was 1949. September 1949 was the date of the Peekskill Riots, when vigilantes attacked Paul Robeson's benefit concert for the Civil Rights Congress. He was defended by the left, many of them Jewish, including the counsellors from Camp Kinderland. I was eight, and I knew how our hero, Paul Robeson, had been targeted in a riot aided and abetted by the police. Several years later, when HUAC, the US House Un-American Activities Committee, was still going strong, the children's camp was investigated. One of the charges ostensibly proving "communist affiliation" against Edith Segal, the dance teacher at Camp Kinderland, was that she wrote poems and songs in honour of Julius and Ethel Rosenberg.[7] But we benefited from the Cold War in a perverse way. We were privileged to have Pete Seeger, Earl Robinson, Harry Belafonte, and some of the eminent blacklisted stars of the theatre such as Morris Carnovsky and Hershl Bernardi perform at our camp and at the small venues related to the shules where they were able to find work. It seems that for Senator McCarthy and the HUAC, Jews and communists were virtually identical.[8]

As a New Yorker by birth, the names of many of the people I came across in my research on the Jewish left in Canada were surprisingly familiar. They were known by their last names: Davidovich, Yakhnes, Korn, Kamenetsky, Eisenberg. Many of them had been my teachers in the shules of New York. Itche Goldberg, Rabbi Bick (the Marxist Rabbi), and Aaron Bergman—all teachers based in New York—were frequent visitors and lecturers in the Canadian communities of the left. I learned that the philosophy and the teaching materials in the Canadian schools were identical to what I knew. As a New Yorker, I was less familiar with Jewish life in Canada than Canadians were with the New York Jewish community. I moved to Winnipeg, Canada in 1968 as a young mother with two sons and became active in Voice of Women and *Canadian Dimension* magazine. It was only after I moved to Toronto in 1978 that I became involved in the Jewish left here in Canada.

I believe that the left Jewish community has often been misrepresented in the literature on the Canadian Jewish experience. In my view, the Yiddish left is often approached anachronistically, allowing the experience of the later years—when those holding pro-Soviet sentiments were viewed as "dupes" and mindless followers of "Moscow"—to cloud an understanding of the early years. What Paul Buhle has termed a "grizzled anti communism"[9] dominated scholarship on the communist-led left for many years. This approach obscures a much more varied history.

Fortunately, this is changing, at least in Canadian historical scholarship. Women historians such as Mercedes Steedman, Ruth Frager, Andrée Lévesque, Joan Sangster, and Julie Guard have pioneered new paths in understanding the contributions of left Jewish women. Ian McKay, in a paper presented to a Canadian Jewish Studies seminar in honour of Gerald Tulchinsky, maintained that even in the 1930s, when narrow dogmatism was at its height, Communist Party members were hardly "soldiers of the international." The reality, he argues, was far more dynamic, complicated, and interesting.[10] Gerald Tulchinsky's biography of Joe Salsberg, a labour activist and member of the Ontario Legislature from 1943 to 1955 who remained in the leadership of the Communist Party throughout his career from 1926 to the late 1950s, presents a view of a warm-hearted, intelligent man responsive to the needs of the Jewish community with an egalitarian vision that encompassed all people.[11]

Thanks to access to the Communist International archives available from Library and Archives Canada, scholars are discovering that some of the Canadian Communist Party's most significant achievements were realized in spite of, not because of, Moscow's directives through the Comintern. The Comintern, originally a collective of all Communist parties worldwide, became under Stalin an instrument of Soviet politics.[12] In the mid-1920s, the Comintern, enacting a policy known as Bolshevization, attempted to minimize the role and activities of the ethnic organizations. When the party attempted to impose this reorganization it lost almost half its membership. The ethnic organizations not just survived but flourished, quite in opposition to Moscow's plans. While some historians of Canadian communism are exploring the relationship between the Canadian party and the Comintern, the international organization, the concerns of this book are different. The focus is on the varied political and cultural activities of those who were part of the secular Jewish left. It is worth keeping in mind that the violent purges that characterized Stalin's policies never crossed the ocean. No CP member or sympathizer was murdered because of holding the "wrong" views. The left admired CP people because they saw them as "American radicals committed to a program of social and political change that would eventually produce what they hoped would be a better society." Neither CP members nor sympathizers viewed party people as "soldiers in Stalin's Army."[13]

The bifurcated view of the world as divided between the "free" world and the "evil" Soviet empire led many on the left to accept what needed to be challenged. It was a terrible disillusionment to learn that the Soviet Union did not embody the kind of society communist Jews were working to create in North America. We still don't really know why some of the prominent communist Jewish leaders who had been in the Soviet Union numerous times stayed silent so long.

However, the ending obscures the hope that inspired leftist Jews in the early 1920s. What gets lost is how they were acting subjects, why they became radicals, and the many ways they worked to build a *shener un beserer velt* (more beautiful, better world) in Canada, in accordance with deeply felt ideals. This was reflected in the organizations they formed, the activities they participated in, and the valuable contributions they made to North American society in pursuit of this vision. I do not see the question of "are you now or ever were a communist" as central to this story. This book is about left-wing Jews and how their Jewish identity led to their political and cultural activism.

The movement that secular socialist Canadian Jews created consisted of different, sometimes fluid aspects, depending on the time and place. At times, there were left groups throughout the country—in Hamilton, Windsor, Calgary, Edmonton, with the strongest ones in Montreal, Toronto, and Winnipeg. In the 1920s and 1930s, the Montreal left organization was called the Canadian Worker's Circle, in Yiddish the Kanader Arbeter Ring. In Toronto, it was the Labour League and in Winnipeg, the Freiheit Temple or Liberty Temple Association. The Jewish Workers' cultural centres were affiliated with these mass organizations as well as with the IKOR (Yiddish Kolonizatsiye in Rusland) supporting colonization in Russia, and the YKUF, the Yiddish Kultur Farband or Yiddish Cultural League. The main left organizations also supported groups such as choirs, sports leagues, mandolin orchestras, Jewish schools, and summer camps, which were sometimes part of the organization, and at other times, closely affiliated. While many participants in these activities were members of the mass organizations, not all were. In 1945, the left organizations in Montreal, Toronto, and Winnipeg joined to form the United Jewish People's Order.

This community was at its strongest from the 1920s to the 1950s. I explore several themes: why people joined the socialist Jewish left; women's participation in this community; and the importance of Yiddish in their lives. This involves exploring various facets of the community: the organization of the Yiddish shules for children; the choirs, originally the Freiheit Gezang Fareyn (Freedom Singing League); the summer camps; the dance troupes; drama groups; sports leagues; and union activism. I explore some of the reasons for the community's decline in the late 1950s, including the Cold War and the expulsion of all "left-leaning organizations" from the United Jewish People's Order, the Twentieth Party Congress of the USSR and its revelations of Soviet anti-Semitism, and the emergence of a new Canadian-born generation removed from the struggles of their parents.

Jewish ethnic identity in this community was not based on religion. Support for inter-ethnic and interracial alliances and anti-racist politics were unique for the period, indications of a multicultural approach before such a policy was articulated. The left Jewish community's notion of ethnicity encompassed a universal vision of social justice and human mutuality—what we all as human beings share in common. The Jewish left emphasized translocal solidarities that celebrated difference as a path to what Gilroy calls a universal, responsible humanism.[14] The issues of striking Irish silkworkers in Paterson, New Jersey, the execution of Sacco and Vanzetti, the violence of lynching, and the effects of colonization in Africa were all deeply felt in this community. For them, class was the unifying factor for solidarity.

This was a community of Jewish internationalists, a seeming contradiction in terms. Indeed, the left Jewish community's criticisms of Israeli government policies and sympathy for the plight of Palestinians have been criticized as traitorous sentiments of "self-hating Jews." But the notion of a fixed, immutable identity, whether it is racial, ethnic, or national identity, which sets one group apart from others becomes not an affirmation of individual agency but rather a fixed destiny in a closed culture.[15] It is also historically inaccurate. Over time, a Jewish identity with Yiddish as the mother tongue that was once a given for members of this community has changed. The Jewish identity is no longer in the air that they breathe, and so it has to be consciously inculcated. Religious observances such as Rosh Hashanah and Yom Kippur, which the founders either defied or ignored, are now celebrated in a non-religious fashion. The Jewish schools prepare young people for a coming of age ritual, the Bar Mitsvah or Bat Mitsvah, which had been rejected by an earlier generation. These rituals are secularized, to be sure, but the new generation, many of whom come from mixed Jewish and non-Jewish families, need to be taught a Jewish identity.

While the effects of the Cold War were felt most directly in the United States, members of the pro-Bolshevik left in Canada also suffered during the Cold War. One of the significant events in its onset in Canada was the notorious Padlock Law in Quebec, which declared that any house or institution containing what the authorities considered "subversive material" could be closed without charges, evidence, or even a clear definition of what constituted subversive material. The Montreal Winchevsky Centre was padlocked in 1951, and in 1952 the community was barred from participation in the Canadian Jewish Congress (CJC). The United Jewish People's Order and related left organizations were expelled from the CJC for forty-four years, until 1996. I maintain that with the weakening of the voice of this community, we have lost an important alternative vision of an ethnic identity, which, while respecting difference, was not absolutist.

My connection with the left community is not only from my early life in the United States but also through my activities in Canada. As a member of the UJPO, I have access to all of its materials but am not confined to expressing any particular viewpoint. Using interviews and autobiographical accounts wherever possible, I aim to convey how commitment to this community and its activism were people's heartfelt responses to the conditions around them and to convey some sense of the lives that lie below the surface of "politics."

When I began this project, a few of the original founders of the secular Jewish left organizations who came to Canada from Eastern Europe in the early years of the twentieth century were still alive. I interviewed some of them and drew on oral histories available from archival sources. This was supplemented with dozens of individual interviews with members born in the 1920s and after (including those who left the UJPO in the late 1950s and those who remained); a review of the documentation, including the movement's weekly newspaper, *Der Kamf* (The Struggle); and many other primary and secondary materials primarily found in the Winchevsky Centre in Toronto, the Archives of Ontario, and the Lipshitz archives at York University. Much of the material is in Yiddish and has not been previously researched or translated. Political life, cultural life, and women's activism were all interconnected. Because the chapters are organized thematically, there is some overlap in chronology, as well as participants. The "People" and "The Communist Party and the Jewish Left" appendices offer an outline of some of the main people and events profiled in the book.

PART I

A REVOLUTIONARY DIASPORA

Jewish Immigrants and
What They Brought to Canada

1 ORIGINS:

The Making of Jewish Socialists

In the late nineteenth century, in the midst of terrible poverty and virulent anti-Semitism, the old way of life for Jews in Eastern Europe was crumbling, along with the hegemony of the rabbis and the well to do. Jewish families were driven from their homes in Russia, Poland, and Romania by anti-Semitic pogroms and poverty. As the *shtetlekh* (small towns or villages) disintegrated, many people, driven by economic need, left for larger cities in search of jobs and freedom from restrictive village life. The developing Jewish working class faced both anti-Semitism and class exploitation.

Yiddish culture and its progressive politics were developing in the midst of political upheavals in Eastern Europe and Russia. In Russia, the unsuccessful attempt to overthrow the Tsar in the 1905 revolution and its aftermath led to repression and terrible pogroms targeting Jews. On "Bloody Sunday," January 9, 1905, crowds of workers from St. Petersburg gathered to present a petition of their grievances to the Tsar and were fired on by troops guarding his winter palace; over fifteen hundred people were killed. This massacre unleashed a wave of anti-tsarist strikes, demonstrations, and social unrest in Russia. A constituent assembly, the Duma, was set up, but both the Bolsheviks and the Jewish workers' movement, the Bund, rejected the moderate reforms proposed as too limited and boycotted the elections. The reaction to the worker unrest was fierce as the right-wing opposition reassembled and targeted Jews. By the end of October 1905, the Black Hundreds—reactionary, anti-revolutionary, and anti-Semitic—instigated a ferocious wave of pogroms, with murderous mobs attacking Jews inside the Pale, where most Jews were forced to live, along with intellectuals and students. The pogroms in Kishinev (1903), Kiev (1905), and Bialystok (1906) drove thousands from their homes to seek a safer life in North

Chava Rosenfarb (1923–2011) was born in Lodz, Poland and came to Canada in 1950. She published in Yiddish *Der Boym fun Lebn* (The Tree of Life), a three-volume epic of historical fiction chronicling the destruction of the Jewish community of Lodz during the Second World War. It was one of the few novels written by an actual survivor of the Holocaust. She later wrote two novels, *Bociany* and *Of Lodz and Love*, describing life in shtetlekh before the Holocaust.

Photo courtesy of the Montreal Jewish Public Library Archives JPL Photograph Collection (1235), pr000622.

America. As the revolutionary momentum collapsed, there was widespread political disillusionment and economic depression.[1]

Conditions worsened during the 1914–18 war. The Russian Revolution of 1917 and the civil war that followed produced political and economic chaos, and millions left for the United States and Canada. Many of those who arrived in the new world were people who had been radicalized in the dying days of the old tsarist empire. They brought their passion for learning and their politics with them. They were the founders of the secular Jewish left, connecting the emergence of a Jewish working class in Eastern Europe with the development of a Jewish workers' movement in Canada.

The Old Country

For several years, from 2005 to 2008, the seven or eight members of the Velvl Katz Leyen Krayz (Willie Katz Reading Circle), most of them in their nineties, met weekly in Toronto's Winchevsky Centre to read aloud the work of Chava Rosenfarb, a Yiddish writer.[2]

Rosenfarb, born in Lodz, Poland was a survivor of the ghetto and the camps who later migrated with her husband, Henry Morgenthaler, to Montreal. Her books describe a world that was disappeared by the Nazis, bringing to life the Eastern European milieu in which the secular movements began. For the older members, the readings evoked memories of Eastern Europe, where they were born. For the *higer geboyrene* (those born in North America) such as myself, the older members' comments and discussion provided an invaluable opportunity to learn about their world—and the milieu in which the secular movements developed—firsthand.

Chava Rosenfarb's books, *Bociany I* and *Bociany II*, about a fictitious village just outside Lodz, and the three-volume *Der Boym fun Lebn* (The Tree of Life) offer an unsanitized version of *Fiddler on the Roof*.[3] Our reading group relished every word, and sometimes the older members interrupted the reading to comment on Rosenfarb's descriptions. The narrowness, the superstition and the cruelty of a Jewish father in Bociany who, out of ignorance rather than malice, mercilessly beat his youngest daughter was not exaggerated. Our group agreed: "That's the way it was. People didn't know any better," they said.

Rosenfarb describes how Jews in Poland were surrounded by an anti-Semitic Gentile world which could and did turn on them regularly. In the second volume of *Bociany*, translated into English as *Of Lodz and Love,* the miller, *Reb* (Yiddish for Mister) Faivele, has guests from the town for the Sabbath. They are the town "intelligentsia": the barber-surgeon, called "the Doctor" and the landowner's bookkeeper, *Pan* (Polish for Mister) Faifer, the "writer," also referred

Brenda Fishauf's birthday party, 2008. This is our Yiddish reading group with the staff of the Winchevsky Centre, Toronto, 2008. Brenda is seated in the centre. She is about 94 in this picture.

Photo by Lisa Roy. UJPO Archives.

to as "Pumpkinhead" because of his bald head. Pan Faifer's wife, dressed in the latest Paris fashion, considered herself a superior being. Rosenfarb says: "She was even more educated than the doctor's wife (who read German and Russian) since she did not understand a word of Yiddish. Like the doctor's wife, she considered Yiddish a vulgar language, a jargon, the knowledge of which was a sign of inferior education."[4] Rosenfarb, a staunch *Yiddishist* or lover of the Yiddish language, was poking fun at her character's disdain for Yiddish.[5]

Pan Faifer's wife's view of Yiddish reflected a rather diluted version of the Enlightenment as it moved east from Western Europe. Displaying her ignorance, her "advanced thinking" consisted only of her admiration for the latest European fashions and her negative view of Yiddish culture—nothing more. Known as the *Haskalah*, the Enlightenment was a class-based movement of the Jewish bourgeoisie and intelligentsia, who looked to Western European culture and the ideals of Russian liberalism. It was decidedly paternalistic, exemplified by the slogan, "let us bring light into the dark hovels of our people, Israel." *Maskilim* (literally the enlightened) took the path of what they called "enlightened assimilation" and felt that educated people should communicate in Hebrew and Russian. Yiddish, the language of everyday life, was seen as the inferior, servant girl's language.[6] It was to be left behind, eradicated.

Another powerful force emerging at that time in Eastern Europe joined the Enlightenment ideals of learning with the development of a working-class

I. L. Peretz, Mendele Mokher Sforim, and Sholem Aleichem. The three writers credited with the use of Yiddish in classical literature.

UJPO Archives.

consciousness. It was called *veltlekher* (secular) *Yiddishkayt,* or a Jewish identity centred on culture rather than religious observance. The promise of a better world emerged, a young person's dream. Young people were full of hope and creativity, with a commitment to enlarging life through a shared involvement, their personal lives enormously enriched by engaging in the collective enterprise of changing a world that badly needed changing. And language became central to this project.

In the last quarter of the nineteenth century, three giants of Yiddish literature emerged—the authors Mendele Mokher Sforim (Mendele the Bookseller, pen name of Sholem Yankev Abramovich), I. L. Peretz (Yitzhok Leyb Peretz), and Sholem Aleichem (Sholem Rabinovitsh)—beginning a cultural renaissance. They provided a picture of the lives of ordinary people, challenging an ossified tradition of learning based solely in the Torah or scriptures. Their work exemplifies how one can treasure a culture that includes a religious heritage without accepting its literal beliefs. When Jews immigrated en masse to Canada in the early years of the twentieth century, they brought this *veltlekher* or secular culture with them.[7] For these Yiddishists (people committed to the language), Yiddish was the medium both for the perpetuation of a people and social transformation.[8] Yiddish became known not just as the everyday language of women and the uneducated, but also as the language of those committed to change.

Yiddish and Secular Jewish Culture

The Yiddish language is approximately one thousand years old and is closely related to medieval German, Hebrew, and Aramaic.[9] It became the vernacular of Jews in Central Europe. Yiddish is written in the ancient Hebrew alphabet known as the Ashuri alphabet, taking most of its words and grammar from medieval German. Jews living in Central and later in Eastern Europe were known as Ashkenazim. As they settled in Eastern Europe, Slavic words also entered the language. Hebrew, known as Loshn Kodesh (the holy tongue), was used for study and prayer and was understood by a small number of men. Aramaic, required for advanced inquiry in the Talmud, was studied by even fewer male scholars. The commonly spoken tongue, the language of everyday life, was Yiddish. It was the language in which one raised one's children and provided the necessities of life. As these were the responsibilities of women, the language itself became associated with women and the proste (or ordinary folk).[10] While women were not supposed to study the holy texts, they were permitted to enjoy literature, theatre, and singing in Yiddish, as were men.[11] Books in Yiddish date from the sixteenth century but the cultural explosion of Yiddish as serious literature dates from the late nineteenth century.

Language was a political battlefield. Ideological commitments were expressed in how one dressed and worked, what a person read, but especially the language used. For the followers of *Haskalah*, Yiddish epitomized everything to be discarded in traditional Jewish life. In the late nineteenth century, the revival of the use of Hebrew in the vernacular was a part of the Zionist project aimed at migration to Palestine and the creation of a Jewish state in the Middle East. Yiddish, however, was associated with *do i kayt* (literally here-ness), the desire to build a socialist internationalist secular culture wherever Jews lived.[12] Its proponents celebrated how Yiddish remade its Semitic, Germanic, and Slavic sources into an exciting, joyous, powerful language.[13]

Yiddishists were attempting to navigate a space somewhere between Russian imperialism and Jewish nationalism, fusing the development of a national but stateless culture with an internationalist inclusiveness. Their leaders were what Gramsci termed "organic intellectuals," people who came from the working class and shared the suffering of the poor and exploited.[14] They were socialists and had a deep desire to make people "socially aware"; they loved the Yiddish language, the language in which people lived. These two social forces, the emergence of secular enlightenment and socialism, were connected. A generation developed that was passionate about learning and devoted to Yiddish. It was a period of rising nationalist sentiment and a difficult time for Jews.

There were physical symbols of the revolt against religious orthodoxy. Young men started to shed the long *kapotes* (coats) of their religious elders

Yeshiva boys. Yeshiva students on Nalewki Street, Warsaw, 1928.

Menakhem Kipnis, Raphael Abramovitch Collection. Courtesy of YIVO.

Chaim Ber, Brenda's friend, is on the left. Notice the short jacket, which marked him as breaking away from orthodoxy. Staszow, circa 1928.

Courtesy of Brenda Fishauf.

and go around in short jackets, a sign of a different way of thinking. Brenda Fishauf, the mainstay of our early 2000s reading circle, described how her parents disapproved of her beloved, Dov, in Staszow, Poland. The way he dressed, in a short leather jacket, was suspect; it meant he was throwing off the old ways. Young women such as Brenda yearned for an education, not the confining *kheder* (religious education) that restricted her brothers, but exposure to the treasures of European literature. Through the political movements, young people gained access to a life of the mind. Parents' approval was important, but as happened in Sholem Aleichem's *Tevye and His Daughters*, many daughters, like Brenda, followed their hearts, not their parents'.[15]

Thus, Yiddish culture and its progressive politics were developing in the midst of political upheavals in Eastern Europe and Russia that directed a massive exodus of Jews to North America, where they dreamed of a better life. However, they found that the promise of the new world was not as bright as they had hoped.

Settling in Canada

The Jewish exodus from Eastern Europe in the first decades of the twentieth century was extensive, and the distinctions between the United States and Canada were not very clear; Jews were going to "America." Unless there were family connections, New York was the preferred destination. Between 1880 and 1924, when the United States border closed to immigration from Eastern Europe, about two million Jews immigrated to the United States.[16] Although immigration to Canada was much smaller, there was an 872 percent increase in the thirty years between 1901 and 1931. In 1901, there were 16,401 Jews in Canada; by 1931, there were 156,726 Jews in Canada, three-quarters of them in Montreal, Toronto, and Winnipeg.

1931 Jewish Population in Canada[17]

Greater Montreal	57,997
Greater Toronto	45,751
Greater Winnipeg	14,427
	118,275
Other communities	38,451
Total	156,726

"The Ward," where many Jews first lived when they arrived in Ontario in the first decades of the twentieth century.

City of Toronto Archives, Subseries 32, item 253.

Jews lived everywhere in Canada, in small communities as well as large. Left groups gathered in places such as Windsor, Hamilton, Niagara Falls, Calgary, and later Vancouver. In the larger communities, there was always a class line between the "uptown" Jews (most of Sephardic origin—originally from Spain or Portugal) and the newly arrived immigrants from Eastern Europe. This division was marked geographically as well. Not much love was lost between the two, although a modicum of communal assistance was provided to the less fortunate *griner* or greenhorns.

The majority of Jews in all three cities were desperately poor, but what is remarkable is that in the midst of their horrendous living conditions, a thriving market developed along with a rich and varied cultural life. Storekeepers typically spoke several European languages to serve a diverse clientele. Newspapers, literary associations, drama societies, sports clubs, schools, music, mutual aid societies, and radical politics of various kinds thrived amid the poverty.

Montreal

In the 1920s and 1930s, Montreal had the largest Jewish population in Canada, and a clear division existed between the "uptown" Jews and the newly arrived East Enders—between the wealthy and the poor. The city's Jewish immigrant population suffered from extensive poverty. Wages were low. Average male wage earners' annual income was well below the poverty line in the 1920s, and women earned much less—and this was before the Depression. Along with the poverty came poor housing, crowding, accommodation with poor lighting—rooms with no windows at all or basement dwellings—and disease. Tuberculosis, smallpox, and diphtheria were widespread. Infant mortality was high.

The newer and poorer arrivals lived east of Mount Royal in an area known as the Main, a district bordered by Sherbrooke Street to the south, Mount Royal Avenue to the north, Esplanade Avenue and Bleury Street to the west, and Saint-Denis to the east. Of St. Laurent Boulevard, known as the Main, novelist Mordechai Richler wrote:

> One street would have seemed as squalid as the next. On each corner a cigar store, a grocery, and a fruit man. Outside staircases everywhere. Winding ones, wooden ones, rusty and risky ones. Here a prized lot of grass splendidly barbered, there a spitefully weedy patch. An endless repetition of precious peeling balconies and waste lots making the occasional gap here and there.[18]

Wealthier Jews lived in Westmount and Notre-Dame-de-Grace in the western part of the city, above the hill. Many of them were Sephardic Jews who had been born in North America, Great Britain, or Holland and moved to Montreal for economic opportunities. They were viewed as pompous and arrogant. One prominent person was Clarence de Sola, of Sephardic origin, whose family had arrived in Canada in the mid-nineteenth century. He was the prime organizer of the Federation of Zionist Societies of Canada.

Toronto

Toronto's Jews originally gathered in what was known as the Ward, Toronto's worst slum. It encompassed the area between College Street, Queen Street, Yonge Street, and University Avenue. The Ward, whose name is derived from the old St. John's Ward electoral district, consisted of narrow lanes packed with ramshackle cottages and dingy storefronts. Muddy alleys were cluttered with garbage, wash-baskets, and clothes hanging to dry. Families lived in abysmal rooms in dank cellars. Overcrowding and unhealthy living conditions were common. In a 1913 report, Health Department head Charles Hastings noted that there were three thousand houses, each occupied by between two and six families. Jewish immigrants lived side-by-side with Italians, Poles, Macedonians, Lithuanians, and Chinese. In these congested conditions, the public arena was where one "lived." Joe Gershman described the importance of these collective spaces: "The movement, no matter which movement you belonged to—left or right—became a second home."[19]

By the 1910s and 1920s, the Jews began to move out of the Ward into the Kensington Market neighbourhood, which became known as the "Jewish

Market." Jewish merchants operated small shops as tailors, furriers, and bakers. Around sixty thousand Jews lived in and around Kensington Market during the 1920s and 1930s.

Winnipeg

In Winnipeg, as in the other cities, the class divisions were also geographical divisions. The North End was literally on the other side of the railway tracks. Worker exploitation, slum housing, and high infant mortality characterized the North End, which was known as the

Jewish Market Day, Kensington Avenue, Toronto, 1923.
Toronto Public Library, Reference no. TRL X 65-64.

"Foreign Quarter" or "New Jerusalem."[20] In 1904 and 1905 there were more deaths from typhoid recorded in Winnipeg than any other North American city. A 1913 study by Woodsworth found that a normal standard of living required wages of $1,200 per year; many in the North End were earning less than half that. Most people were working; they just didn't get paid enough. Others worked seasonal jobs on farms or railway construction and endured cold, hungry winters in Winnipeg.

Only a handful of Jews made it to the South End. If they did, they were regarded as "being almost traitors, because they were deserting the Jewish community."[21] In a novel set in Winnipeg during this period a young Hungarian immigrant describes the North End where he lives in "a mean and dirty clutter ... a howling chaos ... a heap seething with unwashed children, sick men in grey underwear." In the South End, mostly inhabited by the Anglo-Saxon elites, on the other hand, "the boulevards ran wide and spacious to the very doors of the houses. And these houses were like palaces, great and stately, surrounded by their own private parks and gardens."[22]

Woman examining a chicken.
Drawn by Joe Rosenthal, described by Adele Wiseman, Old Markets, New World (Toronto: Macmillan Canada, 1964).

In 1931, of the 16,400 Jews in the city, 93 percent lived in the North End. Ten years later, the numbers were only slightly different: there were 113,300

Main Street, Winnipeg's North End, 1910.

Library and Archives Canada, PA 020567.

Mr. Grozny's store on Selkirk Avenue, 1930s. Grozny was an active member of the Liberty Temple in Winnipeg. Jeanette Block, his daughter, recalls that her dad opened and closed stores in a number of places in the North End. As a child, she helped in the store. She doesn't recall it as a deprivation: "It was what a lot of immigrant families did."

Jewish Heritage Centre of Western Canada Archives, JM 864.

Jews in the city, with 90 percent still living north of the railway tracks. Jews from the North End would say of those who lived south of the Assiniboine River that, for them, the "snow falls up," meaning they were snobs.[23]

Living One's Politics in the Old Country and the New

Many on the Yiddish gas or "Jewish street" in Canada celebrated the Bolshevik Revolution. It looked like a new day was beginning in Russia. Soviet policy under Lenin's leadership supported ethnic minorities in a fusion of socialist internationalism and anti-colonial nationalism. In these revolutionary times, a Soviet Jewish intelligentsia developed, experimenting with avant-garde forms of modernism and expressionism. Russian Yiddish writers and poets such as Dovid Bergelson, Isaac Babel, Peretz Markish, and Dovid Hofshteyn were considered world-class artists. They travelled to and lived for a while in places such as Berlin, Palestine, and New York but returned to live in the Soviet Union. In the 1920s, it was the place that appeared most promising for the development of Yiddish culture. Jews in Canada and the United States read and admired the work of these distinguished artists.

The letters from Pauline (Pesel) Wolodarsky and her mother Chaye Rivke to Joseph (Yosl) Wolodarsky document the terrible difficulties they faced until their family reunited in Winnipeg in 1922.[24] Pesel was born in Rizhe in the Kiev district of Ukraine in 1900. Her stepfather thought a girl "shouldn't have to learn too much." But Pesel's cousin offered to give her private lessons in the basement of their little grocery store. The conversations were supplemented by Pesel's reading—books by authors such as Pushkin, Turgenev, Guy de Maupassant, and Emile Zola. By the time of the Bolshevik Revolution, a group of young people left the village of Rizhe for the bigger cities of Odessa and Kiev. They returned each summer, bringing "enlightenment and excitement"—organizing a library, a cultural club, and a Yiddish drama group.

After the Bolshevik Revolution, an estimated one hundred thousand Jews perished in pogroms in the "White Terror" led by Deniken, the general heading the counter-revolutionary White Army. In Rizhe, orphans wandered the streets as their parents had been killed or had perished from the epidemics rampant in the country. Pesel, with her group of young people, decided to organize a children's home. With the help of resources provided by the authorities, Pesel and her friends found an unused house, and carpenters made the beds, tables, and chairs. They brought in sewing machines and, using materials from America sent to the Kultur League, sewed sheets and pillowcases. Pesel was seventeen.

Pesel (Pauline) Wolodarsky and her aunt, circa 1922.

Personal collection of Roz (Wolodarsky) Usiskin.

At nineteen, Pesel married her cousin Zaidel; at twenty she was a widow, her husband murdered in a pogrom. Pesel, stricken with typhoid fever, came very close to death in the winter of 1921. Her brother, Yosl (Joseph) had arrived in Canada in 1913 and had arranged for the rest of the family to come soon after. They were en route to Canada when their passage was interrupted by the outbreak of the First World War and they had to return home. Joseph was able to raise the money and obtain the papers necessary to reunite what remained of his family in 1922, after a separation of eight long years. In Winnipeg Pesel (now called Paula) became a communist and a union organizer with the Industrial Union of Needle Trades Workers. Blacklisted in Winnipeg because of her activities, she moved to Toronto and finally settled in New York, remaining active in progressive causes her whole life.

The early experiences of Sam Lipshitz, who became a leader in the Canadian Communist Party and the Jewish left, help explain his leftist politics. Born in Radom, Poland in 1910, he recalled the terrible hunger and misery at the end of the First World War:

> Food was rationed and you had to go to stand in line in front of the bakery, four, five o'clock in the morning in order to be sure that you may get a loaf of bread. The bakery opened about seven. Now I was eight years old. I went to the bakery—there was already a huge line-up. But I stood in line. And when I came almost to the door, a big husky Pole grabbed me by my neck, threw me out of the line and I had to go back to the end of the line. When I reached the window where they handed out the bread, there was no bread left.[25]

Sam's daughter recalled that despite his prominence as a leader in the Jewish left and the Communist Party, his pay amounted to about fifty dollars a month. The family depended on the earnings of his wife, Manya, who as a shule (secular Jewish school) teacher was also not paid very well. But both were intelligent, learned people; not having money did not prevent either of their children from becoming respected professionals—the son, an academic, and the daughter, a medical doctor.

Sam Kagan, a sculptor, was one of the founders of the Labour League in Toronto and a lifelong activist in the secular left Jewish community. He was born in a village in the district of Mogilev, Belarus around 1906. His father and an uncle traded in lumber. The family was not desperately poor, but because the business was not large enough to support them all, his father went to Canada in 1914, leaving a wife and six small children, including Sam. Thanks to the help of an uncle with whom they shared a house, they did not starve. When the tsarist army disintegrated, the Germans occupied his town for about a year, until 1919.

During this period, Sam was sent to live with an aunt and attended a technical school in Mogiliev, the capital of the area, where he was initiated into radical ideas. Freed from paternal rule because of his father being in Canada, he engaged in radical activities when he returned to his shtetl: "When I came home because I was one of the few fatherless boys, I could do things that others couldn't. I and another friend of mine, also without a father, were the two organizers of the Komsomol [Young Communist League] in my shtetl." When the German army left, the

Red Army organized a Soviet and the first Yiddish shule, and Sam was one of the few enrolled: "This, together with the help from the political leaders of the Red Army gave us a start in organizing the Komsomol. It was not a sudden conversion. The whole atmosphere that existed at the time—the air was full of agitation, meetings, speeches."

It was a generational revolution as well: "The membership was mostly close friends, people from the Yiddish shule, young people who weren't afraid of their parents. Then it became 'kosher.' The older generation was certainly not encouraging." The town was too small to have its own police force, so the army entrusted the Komsomol members to help keep order:

Sam Kagan as a young man, 1920s.
Archives of Ontario, F1405 23.

> One of the people we knew was arrested for committing a crime [theft] and it was left to the Komsomol to bring him to the police. It was my luck to stay up all night, commandeer a horse and buggy, and take him over to the police. We became old at a very young age.[26]

Sam Kagan described how during that period, Lenin's position on the National Question led to support for Jewish culture. Yiddish-speaking shules were set up, although Sam recalled that he didn't really learn Yiddish history until he came to Canada. In the shule in his village "it was as if Jewish life began with the revolution, in 1918."[27]

> Who attended? Some who could not afford to pay tuition to the Melamed [Hebrew teacher], young girls, and a number of children whose parents were away.... It's not clear whether I joined the Komsomol because I went to the Yiddish shule, or I went to the shule because of the Komsomol.

Brenda Fishauf's life similarly exemplifies the intertwining of a commitment to learning and radicalism. Brenda was born in 1914 in Staszow, Poland, although her birth was never registered.[28] She is not old enough to remember the First World War, but she too suffered through the terrible poverty that followed. Her family had a dry goods store and, not untypically among Eastern

European Jews, it was her mother, not her father, who was the businessperson. But during the war one couldn't travel to get things to sell, so business was terrible. After the war, Staszow, which had been Russian, became part of Poland. The drawer of rubles her father had painstakingly collected, reluctant to invest in something like a house in case they would have to flee, was worthless.

Brenda has some vivid childhood memories. When she was about six, she was given a plaid dress from the American Joint Distribution Committee. She put it on and felt like a princess. But then the night came, and she worried it was the only dress she had. What if she wrinkled her dress? She recalls how she cried herself to sleep that night.

Her family was too poor to afford schoolbooks, but Brenda memorized everything and did well enough to earn a scholarship to the gymnasia (high school). Her mother and older sister refused to give permission for her to go—what's the point, they said, what kind of a position could a Jewish girl hope to get even if she got her teaching credentials? But for Brenda, "life had no meaning if one couldn't study."[29] It was as necessary as breathing. She was part of a generation thirsty for knowledge.

Over half of the population of Brenda's shtetl were Jewish.[30] Brenda recalled that every kind of Jewish *bavegung* (political movement) existed in Staszow. Brenda's account of privation, radicalism, and hunger for knowledge reflects the experience of a generation of young people. Moses Kligsberg, a sociologist and researcher at the Polish Yiddish Scientific Institute (YIVO), estimated that the 450,000 young Jews of Eastern Europe between the ages of fourteen and twenty during the interwar years (1919–1939) read about fifteen million books. That is an average of one book a week, but many devoured several books in a week.[31] For many of these young people reading and learning offered a route to a different life.[32] When Brenda arrived in Canada, she brought with her this passion for learning. She joined the choir and participated in a reading circle.

Manya Lipshitz (her birth name was Kantorovitch) was born in Sukolki in 1906, then part of Poland. Her father died when she was very young, and the burden of supporting the family fell to her mother, who had given birth to nine children. The family moved to Bialystok. In the aftermath of the failed 1905 revolution an older brother was arrested, but their mother managed to bribe the authorities and he was released from jail. He fled to British Mandate Palestine, followed by his sister Hannah. Both were members of the Poale Tsion, the left wing of the Zionist movement. Hannah returned just before the First World War because she was ill with malaria.

When the Germans occupied Bialystok during the war, the language of instruction was German. Shortly after came the 1917 revolution and the newly established Soviet regime was at war with Poland. The Red Army advanced to Bialystok, and Manya's sister, Hannah, who spoke Russian, obtained work with the Bolsheviks. But the times were fluid and violent. With the assistance of the French Army, the Poles forced the Red Army to retreat, and there was panic in Bialystok. Hannah, together with her husband, their new baby, and an orphan girl Dvoyra, who helped with the child, ran for their lives. At the last minute, Manya boarded the train with them east to Minsk.

Manya and Dvoyra at first went to the Seventh Jewish Children's Commune in Minsk where her sister was a teacher. When she and Dvoyra were both young teenagers, they were recruited to the Twelfth Jewish Children's Work Commune in Vitebsk described in the introduction. Manya remembered the extraordinary beauty of the Vitebsk landscape. The commune was given a twelve-acre estate that had belonged to a wealthy landowner. By 1922, times in the Soviet Union were a little better but her family still worried about her future. She reminded them that there were Jewish technical schools and Jewish universities. The plan for Vitebsk included the opening of a seven-year Yiddish school for the two hundred children in the district. By 1923, some of the older children went away to continue their education. Manya attended the Esther Frumkin Pedagogic Academy in Vitebsk, a training institute for Yiddish teachers. As a student, she was able to travel throughout the Soviet republic free of charge. In September 1926, one year before graduation, Manya left to join her family who by 1922 had made their way to Canada. By this time she had become a *farbrente communist* (a burning or staunch communist). She eventually became a teacher at the Morris Winchevsky shule in Toronto. When she saw the children's commune journals in *Yiddisher Kultur* a half century later and recognized a number of the stories she had written under her name at the time, Margolia Kantorovitch, she was inspired to write her memoir.

Radicalization in Canada

Adele Wiseman's novel *The Sacrifice* tells the story of a Jewish family who fled the Ukraine after they emerged from hiding and found their two older sons, en route home for Pesakh, lynched in a pogrom in their town. The father, Abraham, "felt that [his] soul was gone." It's a long and difficult journey to Canada and Abraham decides that the family, who have been travelling for fifteen months and eleven days, will get off the train headed west at the next stop, wherever it is: "The important thing now … is that we must stop running from death and from every other insult."[33]

The place the family settles in is clearly Winnipeg's North End, where Wiseman grew up.[34] They move into what they can afford: a furnished room with a bed, a couch, a bureau, a chair, a big window, and a talkative landlady, Mrs. Plopler, who invariably plunks her kettle on the one available burner on the stove in the shared kitchen just when the wife, Sarah, is about to cook dinner for Abraham and their son Isaac: "Nowhere was it said that it would be a honeyed life—not here in these alien lands. But how strong the gall had been, how bitter when it came. Still there had been the miracle, the reiterated promise. How would he have stood it else?"[35] The son, Isaac, decides to drop out of school to help the family. His father, Abraham, is proud of his son's determination and intensity but "felt a bitterness arising in him again. After all his plans his son was to become a tailor in a sweatshop."[36] Isaac becomes a radical.

As the characters in Wiseman's novel learn, it was not a "honeyed life" in Canada. Many found work in the garment industry, most often working in substandard conditions for too little money. In 1931, Jewish men formed the majority of all male workers in the readymade clothing industry and comprised 40 percent of male workers in the hats and caps industry. Jewish women formed over 20 percent of all women workers in women's clothing, men's clothing, and hats and caps.[37] Other Jewish immigrants, particularly in Western Canada, became pedlars and, if they could, eventually opened a general store. Each small town in Manitoba, Saskatchewan, and Alberta typically had a restaurant run by a Chinese family, in addition to a grain elevator, a gas station, and a general store run by a Jewish family.

Sid Bagel's family arrived in Winnipeg from Lvov, the Ukraine (Lemberg in Yiddish) around 1929. The Bagel family lived in a two-storey building with a basement in Winnipeg's North End, at the corner of Selkirk and McKenzie. All three levels had suites. The Bagels lived on the third floor. Sid's parents, his younger sister and Sid shared one bedroom with a bathtub located between the bedroom and the kitchen. Four families shared the communal toilet in the building. During the height of the Depression, Sid's unemployed uncle Israel also lived with the family. He slept and ate in the kitchen. As the senior Mr. Bagel had trained as a baker in the old country, he found work at a bakery known as the Workingmen's Bakery. It later became known as City Bread and still exists.[38]

Lil Himmelfarb Ilomaki of Toronto describes what led her to devote herself full-time to "rabble rousing":

My parents were employed seasonally in the
needle trades. They would work three months and
be off for three months and get into debt—with
the grocer, the butcher, and with the milkman.
Then they would pay back the debts they owed.
The rent, of course, had to be paid every month,
and that was hard at times. We lived in seventeen
different flats until I was twenty-eight. I remember
every flat—seventeen—I counted them up.
Either it was cold, or people wanted the rooms.
We lived seven years at 71 Sullivan Street, the
longest period.[39]

Lil Himmelfarb Ilomaki on Brunswick Avenue,
1990s. Lil's difficult early years contributed to
a life of left activism. She was honoured on the
50th anniversary of the On to Ottawa Trek.
Lil was also invited to Spain honouring those
who worked to defeat fascism in the Spanish
Civil War.

Photo by the author.

Becky Lapedes arrived in Toronto in 1904 from Eastern Europe at the age of six. She says, "We ourselves
moved into a cellar—the cellars were not a basement
apartment, they were cellars. Two or three families occupied them. It was on Centre Ave." Her father had a junk
store and when he needed to get merchandise, he would
keep Becky out of school to mind the store, so she fell
behind at school.

Becky's father reasoned that a girl's education was of no concern because
she would get married. However, Becky had an older sister who had become radicalized in Russia and who used to "go to the forest where an agitator from Kiev
would come and explain how to better conditions." After her mother died and her
father remarried, Becky went to live with this sister, who had become a socialist.
Becky remembers, "Wherever she went she took me with her. I remember there
was a strike in Eaton's. On Church St. in the Labour Temple they would have
public speakers. We had a parade with badges that said 'we don't patronize the
T. Eaton company'."[40] Sadly, her sister died in childbirth, but when Becky was
old enough to get a job at age sixteen, she met her friend Ethel Roder and her
political and intellectual life began: "She was so much like me. She didn't care
about clothes. I didn't know it then, but she was mingling with the Jewish Russian intelligentsia. Itche Levine, Mr. Golden, and others would tell me what to
read. They told me the good books: Upton Sinclair, Sinclair Lewis, Jack London."

Becky Lapedes came to her radical politics from an experience of poverty
and a sister who learned about socialism in the old country. For many Jews born

CORNER YORK & RICHMOND STS., ABT. 1922 Z...

in Eastern Europe in the first decades of the twentieth century, Yiddish culture and radical politics were intertwined. Becoming a socialist was informed not just by reading and thinking but also by the lived experiences of these activists. They knew about anti-Semitism first hand, just as they knew about poverty. Their radicalism emerged from their idealism, their conviction that their difficult situation could be changed and not just for themselves but others as well. Thinking, learning made life worthwhile, and by understanding one's situation, one develops the tools to make social change.

2 REVOLUTIONARY VALUES AND THE JEWISH LEFT

The upheavals in Eastern Europe in the first decades of the twentieth century led to an intense search for how to ensure Jewish survival and the emergence of different strands of Jewish radicalism. For example, in Staszow, Poland, where Brenda (Diamond) Fishauf lived, her parents remained observant Jews, but the younger generation participated in a variety of radical movements. One brother and a sister were Bundists, and Brenda, her older sister and younger brother were members of Hashomer Hatzair (the Youth Guard), a socialist Zionist youth organization, who dreamed of creating a classless society in Palestine where Arabs and Jews would have equality. In Staszow, Hashomer Hatzair was the largest secular movement. Brenda recalled that they provided lessons in reading and writing Polish to the boys whose kheder education was limited to Hebrew. In the 1930s, it was virtually impossible to get to Eretz Yisroel [the land of Israel] and many of the left Zionists she knew transferred their allegiance. They decided that Zionism would not solve the Jewish question because there wasn't room in Palestine for all Jews. The world where they were living now had to change and so in Staszow, many of the Hashomer Hatzair socialist Zionists became communists.[1]

Like Brenda, many new immigrants arrived in Canada as committed radicals. They were Bundists, Zionists, territorialists, anarchists, and socialists, with many different factions within each movement. The Bund, the labour movement of Jews in Eastern Europe organized in 1897, was secular and non-Zionist but devoted to Yiddish cultural autonomy. Some Bundists opposed the Bolshevik Revolution, whereas others moved to the left and became pro-Bolshevik. Zionists, or Jewish nationalists, supported the establishment of a Jewish state but

Florence Litman Wolodarsky and her best friend Clara (Hirsh) Cooperstock, Winnipeg, 1915–16. They were both active members of the Winnipeg Jewish left.

UJPO Archives. Roz Usiskin informed the author that this was a photo of her mother.

could be on the left or right, secular or religious. Poale Tsion (Workers of Zion) were socialist Zionists, divided between the Marxists and the social democrats. The kibbutz-based Hashomer Hatzair was linked to Poale Tsion, and both were influenced by the writing of Ber Borokhov, a Marxist Zionist. Organized in 1905 in the United States and Canada, they supported the development of a Jewish proletariat in Israel. The group split over support for the Bolshevik Revolution and varying views of the importance of Yiddish culture. Territorialists, founded by Israel Zangwill in 1903, sought a homeland for Jews but not necessarily in Israel. Zangwill supported the offer of a Jewish settlement in British East Africa. Jewish anarchist groups had a variety of views on Zionism. The anarcho-syndicalists, following Emma Goldman, viewed the state as oppressive, rejecting the ballot box as a means for social change. In Goldman's words,

Syndicalism aims at, and concentrates its energies upon, the complete overthrow of the wage system. Indeed, Syndicalism goes further: it aims to liberate labor from every institution that has not for its object the free development of production for the benefit of all humanity. In short, the ultimate purpose of Syndicalism is to reconstruct society from its present centralized, authoritative and brutal state to one based upon the free, federated grouping of the workers along lines of economic and social liberty.[2]

While a variety of groups were Jewish, secular, and identified as socialist, the focus of this book is the pro-Soviet community, which includes the predecessors of the United Jewish People's Order (UJPO), the related cultural, political and shule organizations, and the UJPO. In the 1940s, the umbrella group was called the Council of Progressive Jewish Organizations. It included the IKOR (Yiddish Kolonizatsiye in Rusland), the Yiddish Kultur Farband, or Jewish Cultural League (YKUF), the shules, and the summer camps. I also include discussion of the union involvement in this community, as so many members viewed their union activism as central.

The first coalition of socialist-Jewish groups in the new world was the *Arbeter Ring* (Workmen's Circle), organized at the turn of the century in New York. The Workmen's Circle was an umbrella organization, a coalition that brought together all the secular Jewish groups, united by a commitment to social justice, an end to anti-Semitism, and their rejection of the obscurantism and dogmatism so dominant in the shtetlekh where the Orthodox held sway. Like the *landsman-shaftn*—societies based on the shtetl community where people were born—the organization provided mutual aid in the form of assistance with healthcare, life insurance, unemployment relief, and burials. Originally, the Arbeter Ring was decidedly radical. Its membership principles stated, "The spirit of the Workmen's Circle is freedom of thought and endeavor towards solidarity of workers, faithfulness to the interests of its class in the struggle against oppression and exploitation."[3] When the Bundists arrived in North America, most joined the Arbeter Ring, bringing to it a strong commitment to Yiddish culture. By 1910, there were Arbeter Ring branches in Montreal, Toronto, and Winnipeg. In Winnipeg, they were able to purchase a building of their own in 1918, located on Pritchard Avenue in the North End. They called it the Freiheit Temple, or Liberty Temple.

The idea for the Arbeter Ring was that all those opposed to the existing economic system would join without taking sides among any of the political factions—Bundist, anarchist, labour-Zionist, or revolutionary Marxist.[4] However, the divisions within the Arbeter Ring became increasingly bitter after the Russian Revolution and the formation of the Communist Party. Matters came to a head at the Workmen's Circle convention in Toronto's Massey Hall in 1923, when Moyshe Olgin, the editor of the New York pro-communist Yiddish paper *Der Freiheit,* was denied speaking rights and two resolutions condemning the Russian Revolution were introduced.[5] This was followed by a wave of expulsions of left branches and the re-classification of members as "members at large," depriving them of voting rights.[6] The *rekhte* (right wing) or social democrats were determined to maintain control of the organization. The early militant socialist principles gradually weakened and by the 1930s the Workmen's Circle had become much more moderate.

But for many Jews identified as the *linke* or left, events in the Soviet Union seemed to be a living example of the egalitarian world they dreamed of. According to Isaac Deutscher, the anti-Stalinist biographer of Trotsky, in the early years of the post-revolutionary era under Lenin, despite Bolshevik opposition to Zionism or any form of nationalism, a monolithic party was unthinkable. The *Poale Tsion* (Workers of Zion, a Socialist Zionist Party) existed legally in Russia

Winnipeg
Kultur Farband
(Cultural League)
members, 1923.

Archives of Ontario,
F1412 I-1 #315.

until 1925. In those early years, there was a deliberate attempt to eradicate Great Russian chauvinism and grant all small nations and national minorities equality. Jews published in Yiddish and developed Yiddish theatre, and indeed the first great Hebrew theatre, the Habima, was established on the initiative of Anatoly Lunacharsky, the commissar of education.[7]

The revolutionary perspective made sense to Itche Goldberg, a teacher of Yiddish and later Cultural Director of the Jewish People's Fraternal Order (JPFO), the American version of the Canadian left organization, the UJPO. Itche was born in Russia in 1904 and arrived in Toronto in 1920. His decision to join the left was reinforced by personal connections—his friendships with Philip Halperin, the editor of *Der Kamf* and J. B. Salsberg, later elected to the provincial legislature. Both were originally left-labour Zionists who became communists.[8] Itche was director of the Toronto Workmen's Circle camp *Yungvelt* but left in 1927 to join the pro-communist movement. Shortly after, he moved to New York where he became director of the left shules.[9] Itche recalled:

> The split in the Socialist ranks was very powerful and harmful, and it was
> about attitudes to the Soviet Union. There was no question about our

Jewishness or Jewish consciousness, and the Jewish consciousness led us very naturally to the Soviet Union. Here was Romania, anti-Semitic; Poland, which was anti-Semitic. Suddenly we saw how Jewish culture was developing in the Soviet Union. It was really breathtaking. You had the feeling that both the national problem was solved, and the social problem was solved. This was no small thing. It was overpowering, and we were young.[10]

Winnipeg Labour Temple activists, circa 1926. Note the background, "Workers of the World Unite." A picture of Marx is on the right, Lenin to the left of the banner.

UJPO Archives.

In 1923, when the pro-Bolshevik faction in Canada was fighting a losing battle for control of the Arbeter Ring, the Toronto women withdrew to form their own organization, the Yiddishe Arbeter Froyen Fareyn (Jewish Women's Labour League). The Montreal women organized in 1926. They had the encouragement of the newly formed Canadian Communist Party, which also supported the organization of Women's Labour Leagues in the Finnish, Ukrainian, and English-speaking communities.[11] Inspired by the Zhenotdel or Women's Commission, set up in the USSR after the revolution, a women's labour league was a logical way for women to act on their pro-communist sentiments within their ethnic community.

When it was clear that control of the Arbeter Ring would remain in the hands of those critical of the revolution, the pro-Soviet men also withdrew and formed the Labour League in 1926. Similar events took place in Montreal, where the left called themselves the Canadian Labour Circle or the *Yiddisher hilfs fareyn* (the Jewish Mutual Aid League). The Winnipeg Arbeter Ring held together a few years longer but split in 1932. The left maintained control of the Liberty Temple Association, later called the Winnipeg Order, and the right withdrew.

The Jewish Left and the Communist Party

The relationship of the Jewish left to the Communist Party (CP) was always complicated, as it was in the Finnish and Ukrainian left communities. When the CP was organized in 1922, the Arbeter Ring was divided between those who embraced the 1917 revolution and those who remained social democrats. Those

Jews who became part of the CP in the early years did so as individuals and comprised a minority in the party. This was not the case in the left Finnish and Ukrainian communities. The dues they paid through the Finnish Organization of Canada (FOC) and the Ukrainian Labour Farmer Temple Associations (ULFTA) funded the CP. Thus members of the FOC and the ULFTA were considered CP members through their membership in their ethnic organizations. Together they accounted for 77 percent of the CP membership in Canada.

In 1929, the Executive Committee of the Comintern (the Central Committee of Communist parties internationally) ordered the Canadian party to reorganize—the policy known as Bolshevization. Class alone, not ethnic culture was valued. Membership in the language federations was no longer to be considered the equivalent of CP membership. The mass ethnic organizations were now to be recruiting grounds for party membership. This caused dissension within the left Finnish and Ukrainian ethnic communities in particular. Their language associations had formed the backbone of the CP, and they valued the retention of their language and culture, along with their commitment to class politics. The immediate effect of Bolshevization on Ukrainian and Finnish ethnic organizations was the loss of 50 percent of their Party members. While the situation of the Jewish left in Canada is less explicitly documented, there were similar tensions in the United States in the relationship of branches of the International Workers Order (the US sister organization to the left Jewish organizations in Canada) to the CP there.

In the same year, Arabs murdered sixty-seven Jews in Mandatory Palestine in what became known as the Hebron massacre. While the massacre was originally condemned as a pogrom, the Comintern shortly afterward took the position that the deaths were a result of an Arab revolutionary uprising, which was to be lauded. Some Jews left the CP at that time, and the Jewish ethnic organizations found their numbers remained stagnant until the mid-1930s.

For some Jewish socialists, however, the issues were not so clear. The Shek family, who had been living in Palestine at the time, were dismayed by what they saw. Bella Shek and her husband, Sol Shek, socialist Zionists who had immigrated to Palestine in the 1920s, returned to Poland disillusioned by the Histadrut (the Jewish labour union) treatment of Arabs as second-class citizens. Their son, Ben Shek, who was born in Palestine, tells his family's story:

> In 1926, there was an economic crisis in Palestine. The policy of the Jewish
> agency, the slogan was—"they work for us." If Jews had hired Arabs, they were

to lay them off as a solution to the economic crisis. My father had worked with Arab workers as a longshoreman, and in the Rothschild orange groves as an orange picker. Both of my parents picked up Arabic. So we went back to Poland in 1929 and were there for five years.[12]

Bella Shek and her family remained committed socialists and became active members of Toronto's Labour League (which became the United Jewish People's Order) on their arrival in Canada in 1934. She drew on family tradition to explain why a radical organization made sense to her. Interviewed in her nineties, she traced her development as a "left-winger" to the "big hearts" of her grandparents. Along with learning (Torah), another fundamental value in Judaism was the notion of *tsedekah* (righteousness or justice), which Bella assimilated from her grandparents. Her grandmother would cook and bake for *Shabbos* (the Sabbath) every Friday and her grandfather would collect wood to share with people who did not have sufficient heat. Each Shabbos, she and her sister would be sent by their grandmother to collect food and other things: "this one would give a piece of fish, this one would give a khalleh, and we would bring it home." People would come to the door to take what they needed so that they would be able to make their Shabbos meal a joyous occasion. Bella's version of socialism could be viewed as Judaism secularized. Linked to *tsedek* (justice), this Jewish emphasis on tsedekah was easily turned to a socialist purpose.[13]

In the 1920s and early 1930s, the left Jewish organizations, following the CP, put their emphasis on proletarian politics. Communist Party policy of that period was known as "class against class," denouncing all leftists who did not support them. But Jewish left-wingers felt that they were promoting Jewish interests through their participation in an organization that identified with the Soviet Union and Comintern policies (see Appendix B for a brief outline of these policies). They were working for an international transformation of society. Leftists also faced state oppression. Under section 98 of the Criminal Code, anyone deemed to be a member of an unlawful organization could be imprisoned or deported. The fear was that such a vague definition meant that any radical or labour group could be targeted. In the 1930s, the CP was declared illegal, the leadership imprisoned, and hundreds deported.

Although the left Jewish organizations were influenced by CP policy, particularly in the 1920s and 1930s, belonging to a group with pro-Soviet views and actual party membership were quite different. In a 1931 history of the International Workers Order (IWO), Moissaye Olgin laid out in Yiddish the relationship between

Prominent members of the Toronto Labour League, circa 1930s.
From left to right: unknown, unknown, Harry Holtzman, Sol Shek,
Jacob Milton, Israel Strashuner, unknown, Izzy Fine, Morris Biderman.

UJPO Archives.

the party and the IWO. Olgin, who was the editor of *Der Freiheit*, explained that while members of the IWO were not under party discipline, the CP was the only true party of the working class. However, this alliance was a challenge because the members of the Jewish left did not necessarily fall into line. Olgin cautioned that while the IWO had the right to establish policy independent of the CP, a modus vivendi had to be established at the local level, and "One can't allow an opposition from a local branch to a local committee of the Communist Party."[14] Olgin's book reflected the tension between the attempt of Party members to control the Jewish organization and members' insistence on their own priorities. Communist Party influence was both accepted and contested.

Later in the 1930s, after Hitler came to power, positions in the CP and the Jewish left shifted (chapter 4 goes into more detail on this). Where economic issues were foremost in people's minds in the 1930s as people tried to cope with the Depression, a new danger loomed—fascism. In response, the earlier emphasis on proletarian and class alliances as the dividing line between who was a friend and who was a class enemy was superseded by the imperative of a new alliance. The "popular front" emphasized the need for all those opposed to fascism to unite, and those in the Jewish left attempted to make alliances across the Jewish community. Jewish leftists felt it important to look at the common interests of Jews across the ideological spectrum, which included the religious community, the social democratic Workmen's Circle, and the various Zionist groupings. This came with a new appreciation on the left of what it meant to be Jewish.

In 1945, buoyed by a surge in the popularity of the left because of the Allied-Soviet alliance in the Second World War, a national left Jewish organization became possible. The Toronto Labour League joined with sister organizations throughout the country in Hamilton, Windsor, Calgary, Vancouver, Montreal, and Winnipeg and became the United Jewish People's Order (UJPO). The aims of the new national organization were markedly more inclusive than the dogmatic politics of the early 1930s, reflecting an emphasis on a broad popular front. By 1947, the UJPO numbered close to 2700 members, over 600 of them women participating in both mixed-gender and separate women's branches.[15] The branches in Toronto, Montreal, Hamilton, Windsor, Winnipeg, Calgary, and Vancouver were active and growing.[16]

The articles prepared for the first UJPO convention in 1945 stressed unity in the organization and its goals and activities. And Harry Guralnik, editor of the journal prepared for the first convention, promoted unity among the ten cities with participating branches as well as within the broader Jewish community. Most of the UJPO members were workers, but Guralnik made clear that all strata of the Jewish community were welcome to be part of the traditions of progressive struggle and to help a forge a democratic unity.[17]

Although these left Jewish groups were never Zionist, they changed their views of a Jewish state after the Holocaust. Faced with the tragedy in Eastern Europe and refugees languishing in camps, there was strong support for the need for a homeland, and for the establishment of the state of Israel. They backed the founding of a state that would be both socialist and democratic—for Jews and Palestinians alike. The UJPO continued to take pride in the socialist history of the founding groups and carried on their strong support for trade unions and organized labour, and for antiwar/anti-fascist/anti-racist social legislation. They hoped that the wartime alliance in the Jewish community would continue under the aegis of the Canadian Jewish Congress, a place where all Canadian Jews could come together around a common set of objectives and activity. This alliance is linked to an emphasis on Canada as a nation state. Left Jewish groups saw themselves as assisting in the fight for "Canadian independence," which goes hand in hand with democracy.

Until the 1950s, when the revelations of the Twentieth Party Congress made public the vicious anti-Semitism of the Stalin regime, this community remained sympathetic to the Soviet Union. The progressive Jewish Organizations in Montreal, Toronto, and Winnipeg are often referred to as the "Jewish communist" movement. However, while the leadership of the UJPO and its predecessors were CP members, the rank and file was not necessarily so politicized. They considered themselves "progressives" rather than communist as their organizations were independent of the CP, and members were not subject to the demands of the party. Roz Usiskin of Winnipeg described the relationship:

> I think it was a very subtle kind of connection. I was never a party person,
> but the kind of programs we had. The worldview that was presented to

United Jewish People's Order Second National Convention, 1947. The words translated from the Yiddish read (from the top) Benefits – fraternal help; Shules – Kindergarten – Youth club; Camps – teacher's seminar; Choirs, Drama circles, Orchestras.

us—equality, social justice, socialism, and the new world order. We became so imbued with it and accepted it that there didn't have to be a directive from some higher up. It was something within the culture in which we were immersed. There were people who debated—didn't go along with this or that policy. We'd have intense debates. Not everyone would accept verbatim what was the party line. When it came to politics or elections, there was no doubt of who you would support. When it came to support [for] Joe Zuken, everyone was out working for him, simply because there was no one else like him. It wasn't only the left that supported him, either. We felt there was an integrity there, and an honesty that you didn't find with others.[18]

The secular Jewish left attempted to wed commitment to Yiddish and Jewish particularism with their internationalism. While valuing their ethnic roots, they wanted to extend the struggles for justice, anti-racism, and an end to exploitation to include all peoples. This was at times a complicated negotiation, particularly in the 1930s, and was not necessarily synonymous with the demands of membership in the Communist Party of Canada. Even in the 1930s, characterized by the sectarian politics of the Communist Party, pro-Soviet Jews were unwilling to part with their identity as Jews. In a letter written to his sister Pauline (Pesel) in the early 1930s, Joseph Wolodarsky, a Winnipeg trade unionist, explains that he is an internationalist when it means supporting better working conditions for all people, but in response to anti-Semitism, he is a proud Jew.[19] Such ideas were widely held and deeply felt. People expressed their hopes and principles, retaining a strong emphasis on a secular Jewish identity within an internationalist, socialist perspective.

The following table presents a brief outline of some of the important dates that affected the Jewish left:

	General	Jewish Life
1890		Organization of the Workmen's Circle (Arbeter Ring) in New York
1910		Organization of the Arbeter Ring in Canada
1910–14		Radikaler shuln (radical secular Yiddish schools) organized in Montreal, Toronto, and Winnipeg
1917	Bolshevik Revolution	
1919	Winnipeg General Strike Section 98 of Criminal Code introduced, giving the government freedom to deport "enemy aliens"	
1921	Organization of Communist Party	
1922–25		Battles within the WC over support for the Bolshevik Revolution
1923		Women of Toronto and Montreal form the Jewish Women Labour Leagues
1926		Canadian leftists leave the WC to form the Labour League in Toronto and the Kanader (Canadian) Labour Circle in Montreal

	General	Jewish Life
1928		Left secular Yiddish shules in Canada organized
1929	Reorganization—third period (class against class) position of the CP	
1929–31	Toronto Police Chief Dennis Draper's edict against speaking a foreign language in public places	
1929–34	Industrial Union of Needle Trades Workers	
1931		Split in Winnipeg Freiheit Temple Association—the left remains in control
1933	Hitler comes to power	
1935	Popular Front period of the Communist Party	
1936–39	Spanish Civil War	
1938	Kristallnacht and the escalation of the Nazi genocide	
1939–41	Nazi-Soviet Pact	
1939–45	Second World War	
1943		Jewish Anti-Fascist Committee tours North America. The left becomes part of the Canadian Jewish Congress
1945	Gouzenko—beginning of the Cold War	Left organizations in Canada come together to form the United Jewish People's Order
1950	Stockholm peace petition	Winchevsky Cultural Centre in Quebec padlocked

	General	Jewish Life
1951	Padlock Law in Quebec used against Jews	Left Jewish organizations expelled from the Canadian Jewish Congress
1953	Stalin's death	

3 CULTURAL INITIATIVES AND THE POLITICS OF EVERYDAY LIFE

Cultural life and political activism were inseparable. The rich cultural life of the secular Jewish left reflected and nurtured a socialist, internationalist, and proudly Jewish heritage. From the first years of their arrival in Canada, in the first decades of the twentieth century, secular Jews, like their left-wing Ukrainian and Finnish counterparts, demonstrated a profound determination to keep their language, politics, and culture alive, a commitment that continued into the twenty-first century. Their cultural life, emerging from its East European roots, was central to transforming all aspects of their new life in Canada. Jewish radicals established theatre groups, musical groups, dance troupes, a significant literary milieu, and popular education initiatives along with and linked to trade unions and political organizations.

Most members of the Jewish left were workers or small shopkeepers and barely scraped by.[1] The hours of work were long, the earnings poor, the living conditions cramped, but the focus of their lives was the community halls of the left. The centres provided an opportunity to take part in cultural activities, and to be defined not by how one earned a living, but as a singer, a poet, or an artist. For both children and parents, creativity fed the soul. A love of "culture" fostered in the old country went beyond the left and was important throughout the Jewish secular community in Canada. All the secular Jewish movements shared this high valuation of a life of the mind. Despite the ideological differences, they

Three women members of Yiddisher Arbeter Kultur Farband (Jewish Workers' Cultural League) in Winnipeg. Left to right: Bertha Dolgoy, Ray _____, Dora Tissenbaum. Bertha worked in the needle trades and was a militant trade unionist. Her friends were most likely also trade union organizers. Dora was a seamstress.

Archives of Ontario, photo collection of Joshua Gershman, F1412 JI-1 #281.

shared a common history of Eastern European shtetl life in transition. David Rome explained:

> In those days [the immigrants] bore a high cultural vision of an educated Jewish populace with access to knowledge, united in enlightenment. Back home, where the orthodox banned secular reading very firmly, every village had a bookcase or two which the dissidents in the community cherished as a people's library and sometimes had to defend physically against the religious.... These immigrants who brought with them the ideals of the shtetl in revolution sought to establish people's libraries.[2]

How did this happen? Gramsci explained that hearts and minds are won not just through ideas but also through participation. The dominant class manipulates the culture of a society, imposing a worldview that justifies the status quo. Gramsci called this concept hegemony. But cultural practices and institutions at variance with that of the dominant classes—a social movement with a different conception of the world, or an alternative hegemony—can develop.[3]

These Jewish radicals negotiated a terrain between self-identity, the preservation of language and culture that meant a great deal to them, and an equally profound internationalist revolutionary commitment. They exhorted those participating in cultural activities also to engage in left political activism. On the other end of the spectrum were some Jewish communists who stressed internationalism and did not view their Jewish heritage as significant. They were affiliated with the Communist Party (CP) and did not participate in the broader left Jewish organizations. The radicals who were active in the Jewish left rejected assimilation, while not embracing the nationalist, conservative forms of identity of more mainstream Jews. These leftists called themselves "progressive" and attempted to wed their proletarian values with an internationalist ethnic awareness that included reaching out to other ethnic groups and races.[4] At times, particularly in the early 1930s, when CP ideology criticized the attachment to ethnic loyalties as "nationalism," this proved difficult. In the 1930s, when popular front politics were embraced, Yiddish identity was seen as vital for survival and an important tool in the fight against fascism. In that period, the synthesis of a Jewish identity and revolutionary commitment was an easier one.

The forms that cultural "work" took varied in time and place. In the early period, the 1920s and early 1930s, Yiddish was the common language of the new immigrants from Eastern Europe. Yiddish leftists in the 1920s proudly proclaimed their ties to the newly formed Communist Party. They saw the Soviet Union as leading the way in the development of a Yiddish proletarian culture in an egalitarian society. Yiddish was the vehicle through which revolutionary sensibilities were learned and maintained. Whether it was Yiddish singing, drama, art, or sport, the idea was to impart revolutionary Bolshevik sentiments to participants. Those committed to creating a Yiddish proletarian cultural movement distinguished it from other Jewish secular movements such as the Labour Circle or the left Zionist groups, which they saw as too moderate, lacking a militant activist approach to social change.

As late as 1939, 96 percent of Jews over ten years of age in Canada, whether foreign or native-born, listed Yiddish as their first language.[5] Yiddish was also a way for the community to preserve its history and identity. Moishe Nadir, a member of Proletpen, the Proletarian Yiddish Writers Organization in the United States in the 1920s, explained that "we are for culture in Yiddish, with all the beauty, vitality and richness of our cultural treasures."[6] He felt that active participation in cultural production could lead to a different outlook on the world. But what did left-wing Jews mean by culture?

As Raymond Williams explains, culture is one of the two or three most complicated words in the English language. He notes that culture designates different systems of thought.[7] The Jewish left used culture as a way of emphasizing traditional culture (folk culture). Emil Gartner, the conductor of the Toronto Jewish Folk Choir, described it as "the sum total of all of a people's achievements as well as its mode of living."[8] But these Jewish leftists meant the term to include the classics of European civilization, the achievements of "high art"— music, literature, painting, sculpture, theatre, dance and film—which they viewed as transcending class. The Jewish left rejected cheap entertainments pandering to commercial interests, which they called *shund* (trash).

The centrality of cultural activities is striking in all of the left movement's material—newspapers, anniversary books, personal reminiscences. Harry Guralnik, at various times the editor of *Der Kamf*, the director of the shule, and the national chair of the United Jewish People's Order Culture and Education

Mandolin Orchestra of the Labour League, 1932. The conductor, Philip Podoliak, had recently arrived from Mezrych in Poland.

Photo courtesy of Ester Podoliak.

Committee, described the committee's function "as the social conscience of our fraternal movement."[9] The notion of culture and of "conscientization," a term later used by Paulo Freire in *Culture, Power and Liberation*, goes back to early Marxist notions that we are not just "in" the world but "with" the world. Freire, the Brazilian educator known for his work in critical pedagogy, maintained that our humanity is defined by our ability to understand that we can act in the world. In the process of transforming the world, it is possible to humanize the world, and ourselves.[10] Freire argues for a literacy that is an active, not a passive process, one that involves our right and our capacity as human beings to change the world.[11] Thus, one can see the connection between active engagement in cultural efforts and a critical political perspective. Stuart Hall, the British cultural theorist of Jamaican descent, emphasizes the constant change and development in what defines a national culture. It is "the whole body of efforts made by a people in the sphere of thought to describe, justify and praise the action through which that people has created itself and keeps itself in existence." For Hall, the production of identity is a fluid process, the re-telling of the past. Individuals position themselves in the narratives of the past through memory, fantasy, and myth. Meaning is not a static essence but unfolds as identity that is produced and reproduced anew.[12] So these left Jews reshaped what a Jewish identity meant. For them, it was culture rather than religion that defined them.

They were also building the larger community. In *The Cultural Front*, Michael Denning argues that the fraternal organizations of the left, particularly the International Workers Order (IWO) in the United States, made important cultural contributions with their network of lodges, camps and schools that were cultural centres. As a movement of people committed to ethnic identity and social change this movement was much broader and went well beyond the dictates of any political party.[13] The politics of the Jewish left in Canada were virtually the same as those of the IWO. The Canadian Jewish organizations considered themselves part of a North American progressive Jewish movement. But unlike the IWO, the various Canadian left Jewish organizations remained distinct in each city and did not unite with other left ethnic federations, although they maintained close fraternal ties with left Ukrainians from the United Labour Farmer Temple Association (ULFTA) and the Finnish Organization of Canada (FOC). They sang in each other's choirs, visited each other's summer camps, and sometimes married each other.

Kunst Tsenter (Artists Centre), Toronto, 1929–1930. For these new immigrants, Yiddish, art, and politics were a unified whole. Sam Kagan is on the lower right.

Archives of Ontario, F 1405 MSR 8439 #1.

Culture on both sides of the border was central, and cultural "work"—not theorizing, but active participation—was key. The prominent Yiddishist Moissaye Olgin, a founder of the Communist Party in the United States in the 1920s and the first editor of *Der Freiheit*, the communist Yiddish paper in New York, defined cultural "work" as the effort to strive for more knowledge:

> Doing cultural work means doing work so that people will begin to think about humanity and will live a more humane life. To do cultural work means to feel

Shule play. The teachers are Yakhnes (on the left) and Basman in the centre.

Archives of Ontario, B115710.

that people in other parts of the world, can, by uniting their wills overcome all temptations in nature or in their social life and arrive at a higher level. To do cultural work means, in other words, to open up horizons for people.[14]

While many on the left read *Der Freiheit*, the Canadians felt that they needed their own newspaper. *Der Kamf* (The Struggle), the Yiddish newspaper of the left, was first published in Montreal in 1924, then moved to Toronto, where Philip Halperin, a labour Zionist turned communist, became editor in 1925.[15] Originally closely tied to the Jewish section of the Communist Party (the editors were all party members), the paper reflected CP policy but also considered itself an integral part of the left Jewish organizations. In early issues, readers were assured that they were getting the "correct" position, vetted by the Party.[16] In the 1920s, each issue featured a column called "Di Arbeter Froy"—The Woman Worker—which offers a glimpse of the exciting ideas discussed at the time (chapter 5 explores the thoughts and activities of these militant women).

However, the sectarianism of the Canadian Communist Party during what is known as the third, or class against class period, from 1928–33, affected the pro-communist left organizations and their cultural activities. The emphasis was on the creation of a proletarian Jewish culture. Maintaining that there is

Masthead of the newspaper *Der Kamf*, which began publication in 1926. On the right, it reads "Workers of the World Unite." Under that, "all power to the working class."

Courtesy of Roz Usiskin.

no such thing as an "impartial" culture in a classed society, *Der Kamf* writers criticized mainstream (Jewish) culture in Canada as bourgeois, working to support the dominant regime.[17] *Der Kamf* articles stressed that it was impossible for culture to be impartial. M. Pearlman, director of the Montreal Cultural Centre, expressed this view:

> Our approach is a Marxist one—in a classed society there is not and cannot be any impartial culture. All the beliefs of our "culturalists" that knowledge is impartial, "objective," are no more than a means of covering the eyes of the masses in order to support the current regime.[18]

Der Kamf changed its name to *Der Veg* (The Way) briefly in the late 1930s. It then became *Der Vochenblat* (Canadian Jewish Weekly) in the 1940s. The articles reflected what was going on in the left Jewish community and read much like a national community newspaper. As well as reporting on international concerns, contributors provided detailed accounts of community activities, including local labour struggles, celebrations, women's issues, sports, and youth organizations. In addition to poetry, stories, and critical reviews of the many cultural performances in the left community, *Der Kamf* published reports of activities in the children's shules along with policy analyses and constant exhortations to do more and be more active in other parts of the movement.

Der Kamf provided the most comprehensive source of information for left events, sensibilities, achievements, and shortcomings (in the form of self-criticism). It has been an invaluable resource for this book, although limited by an editorial policy that was always aligned with formal CP positions. One must read between the lines to tease out dissenting views. The paper survived until the 1970s through constant fundraising by the left organizations and the efforts of its long-time editor Joshua Gershman.[19] He travelled the country soliciting money to support the paper. Gershman's friendships were not restricted to the pro-Soviet Jewish left. Fayvl Simkin, the non-communist publisher of Winnipeg's *Dos Yiddishe Vort* (The Israelite Press), says that he and Gershman were

Joe Gershman at work, 1977, *Der Vochenblat* office. Gershman was the paper's editor for most of the time since 1936. His fundraising kept the paper going.

Archives of Ontario, F 1405 MSR 8439 #1.

good friends, even though they did not see eye to eye politically. Fayvl did not go to Gershman's lectures when he visited Winnipeg because he didn't want to irritate Gershman or be provoked by him.[20]

With the rise of Hitler came the attempt to unite with all those opposed to fascism in what is known as the Popular Front period of the late 1930s and 1940s.[21] The popular front was an attempt to organize a coalition of all working-class and middle-class parties in defence of democratic forms. In the Jewish community, this meant supporting alliances with the entire Jewish community, a marked change in the left community's cultural policies and activities. In 1937, the writer Chaim Sloves of the Culture Front organized the Jewish International Cultural Congress, held in Paris. It was a popular front effort, supported by a mix of socialists, communists, left Zionists, and Yiddish secularists, a coalition of like-minded groups. The Congress was a determined attempt to put aside the internecine battles among the various ideological factions and come together to protect secular Jewish culture. Chaim Zhitlovsky, one of the organizers of the first Yiddish language conference held in Czernowitz in 1906 (discussed in chapter 7) and prominent in the world of Yiddish culture, strongly supported the conference. The participants and supporters were a distinguished collection of writers and poets, including Joseph Opatoshu, Peretz Hirshbein, H. Leyvik (pen name of Leivik Halpern) and the communist writers Moyshe (Moissaye) Olgin, Moyshe Katz, and Kalman Marmor. At the last minute, the Soviet authorities did not allow major Soviet Jewish writers Itzik Feffer, Dovid Bergelson, and Izzy Kharik to attend.[22]

The Canadian secular Yiddish left reached out, seeking to unite with other Jews from different ideological streams as well as develop closer connections with similar left Jewish organizations throughout Canada. Left cultural activities, many under the aegis of the Yiddish Cultural League (the YKUF) set up by the conference, grew in popularity. YKUF reading circles, developed in the late 1930s and 1940s, were devoted to anti-fascism and cultural continuity and concerned with nonpartisan culture rather than ideology. Gerry Kane, born in 1935, recalled that his mother, a member of Branch 6 of the United Jewish People's Order, was part of a YKUF reading circle most of her life:

> I used to sit at the top of the stairs, listening to my mother and a group of women read and discuss a book. What did they read? [Yiddish] novels— romance novels, lousy culture? No! ... I remember hearing my mother and the women discussing Sinclair Lewis in Yiddish.... Sometimes there was a leader; usually they each read. Sometimes someone prepared something. It depended. In my mother's Leyenkrayz [reading circle], some were more argumentative, some were more passive—just ingesting what they heard. But these were women who never went to school.[23]

The language, which in the 1920s and early 1930s had stressed the Jewish left's contributions to proletarian culture, changed. In the 1940s, it highlighted Canadian patriotism as well as respect for Yiddish and Jewish national culture. Olgin described a range of activities that were part of cultural "work"—from learning about history and the struggles of working people to reading stories such as those by Mendele Mokher Sforim (Mendele the Bookseller) to understand how Jews once lived.[24] It encompassed looking at contemporary contributions of Jews to American music and history, learning Yiddish poetry, or seeing a Yiddish play, a lecture about Gershwin's music or a Picasso exhibit to appreciate the contributions of great artists of all origins, particularly those with left politics. The definition of "the people" became far more inclusive. It now included all who work in one way or another to earn a living: the factory workers from large and small establishments, the counter server who is called a "white collar slave," the small and middle size proprietors, grocers—all who do not and can not identify with the ruling class.[25]

This theme of emphasizing one's Jewishness as well as one's Canadianness was reiterated by Emil Gartner, who became the director of the Freiheit Gezang Fareyn (Freedom Singing League) in Toronto in 1939. He wrote that "we shall be better Canadians by being conscious Jews, offering unique cultural contributions to the Canadian mosaic: a beautiful color in the rainbow of the world's cultural beauties." Gartner emphasized the importance of a multicultural repertoire, singing the "songs of other nations" as a political act: "The spiritual kinship to other peoples enables us to sing their songs too, and with conviction!" He envisioned the choir's work as "sing[ing] the great song of Canada."[26]

The left took the lead in anti-fascist activities at a time when the Canadian Jewish Congress was unwilling to alienate Canadian officialdom by seriously challenging government policies.[27] Support for the left declined during the period of the Nazi-Soviet Pact of 1939 but became more popular than ever when the Soviet Union became Canada's ally in 1941. In the 1940s and early 1950s, the cultural productions, dance troupes, and choirs of the left were reviewed in the civic newspapers, and known and applauded throughout the wider community.

The effects of the Cold War and the repression that accompanied it, followed by the 1956 revelations of Stalin's murder of prominent Yiddish poets and artists, weakened the community. Coupled with the growing prosperity of many of Canada's Jews, the left became less popular. All in the Jewish secular community faced a struggle to keep Yiddish alive. However, the lasting contributions of the Jewish left to theatre, graphic arts, the folk music revival of the 1970s, and dance remain impressive.

The Jewish left was the equivalent of a university for working-class women and men. When one sang in the choir or belonged to a branch or lodge, one became part of a strong community where people had a sense of fitting in. One did not just go to rehearsals or meetings: there were dances, concerts, dinners, lectures, and for the young, romances—the works.[28] The fraternal groupings also provided needed social service benefits—health care, cemetery plots, credit—along with support for the choral groups, dance troupes, mandolin orchestras, wind orchestras, sports leagues, and literary study circles.

PART II

POLITICAL STRUGGLES AND THE JEWISH LEFT

4 FIGHTING CLASS EXPLOITATION AND FASCISM

In the 1920s and 1930s, two major issues, one national, the other international, preoccupied the secular Jewish left. One was class exploitation. Although they believed that the overthrow of capitalism and the creation of a new social order were necessary, the Jewish left was not about to wait for a revolution. The immediate challenge was organizing unions in Canada to improve pay and working conditions. The other concern that grew during the 1930s was the rise of fascism. These two concerns linked their experiences as workers and their identity as Jews. Nazi Germany and fascist Italy were both providing arms and manpower to the dictator Franco and his Nationalist forces. If the people of Spain could defeat the Nationalist forces in the Spanish Civil War, this was the opportunity to contain Hitler. Sadly, as we know, Hitler grew in strength. The secular Jewish community in Canada then had to deal with Stalin's pact with Hitler, followed by the war years. The Holocaust against the Jews of Europe destroyed not only people's lives but also a history. For Canadian Jews, the communities where they came from in Eastern Europe disappeared—and along with them went a vibrant secular culture in Yiddish.

Working Conditions

The Jewish left was a community of workers. They grappled with low wages and often with unemployment. Canada's Federal Department of Labour estimated that a family needed between $1200 and $1500 a year to maintain the "minimum standard of decency." In the early 1930s, 60 percent of men and 82 percent of women made less than $1000 a year.[1] By 1933, 30 percent of the

In the mid-1930s an estimated 45 percent of the township of East York was on the dole. These students were trying to induce their friends to stay away from school.

Toronto Reference Library Picture Collection, Can-On-Toronto-Hist.

Regina, 1934. People lining up at a clothing depot.

Thomas Fisher Rare Book Library, University of Toronto, Kenny Collection, MS Coll 179.

labour force was out of work, and one-fifth of the population was dependent on government assistance.

All around were signs of widespread destitution. Toronto, for example, was in crisis with a welfare bureaucracy in disarray. In early October 1930,

> hundreds ... were sleeping in parks ... brickyards and the benches and floors of rest rooms. People went door to door begging for bread and more than a thousand men lined up for hours to receive wrapped lunches prepared by some of the city's philanthropic women. In 1932 3,000 families were dependent on outdoor relief from the city's House of Industry for their survival.[2]

The Canadian Consumer Council in 1938 found that 60 percent of the Canadian population was suffering from malnutrition. These statistics were gathered by family. Adult women and children were at even greater risk of malnutrition because when food was available, the male breadwinner got a larger share.[3]

Conditions in the garment industry, where most Jewish women and many Jewish men found employment, were terrible. Even when the economy was doing well in the 1920s, it was not easy to make a living as a clothing worker. In the Depression years, shops closed, and even for those fortunate enough to keep their jobs, a shorter working season and wage reductions reduced clothing workers' earnings to just above or below abject poverty.[4]

An article in the *Winnipeg Free Press* in 1934 described the difficulties. All the experienced cutters and machinists as well as the young girls learning button sewing "work hard and monotonously. Employers admit that working in their shops is a severe and steady grind." Employers responded to the competitive nature of the industry by slashing wages, intensifying the work and cutting costs with no consideration for the impact on working conditions. For example, bosses saved on rent by setting up textile plants in abandoned warehouses. These factories, designed for storing goods, had poor air circulation and unsanitary facilities. Workers were crowded into tight spaces.[5]

Commercial clothing factory, St. Hubert St., Montreal.
Maurice Laniel, Bibliothèque et Archives nationales du Québec, P48S1P06570.

Letters to *Der Kamf* offer an idea of the conditions workers faced, even in the relatively more prosperous 1920s, when the economy was doing well. A department store sales clerk described her "slave-like situation":

> We work 52 hours a week, from 8:30 in the morning to six at night we must stand on our feet.... Whether it is busy or slow, the saleslady is always at fault. When business is slow, the manager says you have to be able to sell when everyone doesn't want to buy.
>
> And for this slave-like labour, a saleslady gets twelve dollars a week and a stock lady six dollars. And you are never secure with this wretched job.... In the firm where I work, salesladies who have worked 10–15 years were fired without any prior notice. It is time to organize these slaves for a struggle for humanitarian working conditions.[6]

Employers could intimidate their workers, especially because the workers thought they had no recourse and no alternatives. Women workers were particularly vulnerable. A letter in *Der Kamf* described an incident in the letter writer's workplace. A young red haired woman was ordered by the boss to stay late after the other workers had left. She was in tears but had to stay if she valued her job. The writer makes clear what the boss had in mind. She stayed and, it is implied, the boss did what he wanted with her. The next day, he was shouting at her once again. It was not uncommon for women workers to have to sell themselves as well as their labour to keep their jobs.[7]

These firsthand accounts of sexual harassment, intimidation, and payment of illegally low wages underscored why unionization was so needed. One writer to *Der Kamf* described the conditions in her shop. The workers were divided into two sections, and the foreman managed to manoeuvre a war between one section and the other. His relatives worked in one section, and he gave them the more lucrative work, which gave rise to arguments. The biggest trouble, the writer said, was the absence of consciousness:

> I speak to my shop sisters about our situation, and they reply that it doesn't trouble them as they believe in the world to come. They go to church and there all is well. How can one make the blind see? In the shop, it is filthy, disgusting. In the washrooms, the sinks are overflowing so much that one can float a little boat in there. And there are only three towels for forty women. When we light the flatirons, the gas goes off in all the rooms. That is the environment of the cloakmakers—it's dark and filthy where we spend our best years.[8]

In the 1920s, the members of the communist-led Trade Union Educational League (TUEL) worked inside the mainstream unions. Left activists were particularly important in the formative years of the International Ladies Garment Workers Union (ILGWU).[9] In Quebec, the Catholic unions were known to be less militant and employers often manipulated conflicts between unions to undermine union strength.

Mike Buhay, a union activist, editor of *Der Kamf* when it was founded, and on the Central Committee of the Communist Party in the early 1920s, described the divide and conquer tactics of Jewish bosses in Montreal when organizers were trying to unionize the open (i.e., non-unionized) shops. In Samuel Hart and Society Brand, two of the largest factories, the pay was lower than in the union shops, so many of the workers wanted to unionize and went on strike. What did the boss do? He couldn't prevent unionization, so he decided to draw on religion and nationality. The owner Samuel Hart, a prominent member of the Jewish community, gathered together the Catholic workers and proposed that they join the National Catholic Union rather than the more militant Amalgamated Clothing Workers. He even arranged for a priest to speak with them. The workers rejected the offer of the company-friendly Catholic union. Then the owners, who with the collusion of the authorities had previously targeted Jewish workers they viewed as the most militant, inflicted violence on all the workers trying to unionize, Jews and non-Jews alike. The law, clearly on the side of the bosses, declared picketing illegal, and workers were attacked and arrested. Clearly, when it came to a conflict between profit and ethnic solidarity, the Jewish bosses had no qualms about choosing the union that would do the least for their workers.

In Quebec, many working in the garment industry were young French Canadian women. The conservative influence of the church presented organizers with particular challenges. Joe Gershman, an IUNTW organizer in Quebec, described an incident where he successfully negotiated a $3.50 a week increase in wages at Diana Dress:

> Monday a week after we settled the strike, five girls with the shop chairlady, a French Canadian girl, beautiful person, came down together with the shop committee. The girls brought me back, brought *me* back, the increase they got in the new pay and said we have been to Church yesterday and we were told by the priest that this is dishonest money and they begged that I should return the money back to the boss…. We had to go visit many parents of these girls and convince them that it's o.k., that it's all right to belong to the union…. Many of the parents agreed with us but the Church really worked against us.[10]

Gershman found that Jewish girls in Quebec would have to don a cross to be hired by a Jewish boss because the bosses suspected that Jewish girls might want to form a union.[11]

Activists and unionists regularly reported instances of violence and intimidation in their attempts at union organizing. But class war didn't always work as planned. Jewish manufacturers hired some gangsters, many of them Jewish, to beat up Gershman and two other union organizers, Frank Breslow and Leo Robin. The problem was that Gershman knew the boys from the neighbourhood. They didn't want to beat him up, but they needed the money. So they arranged a deal. He got some of the girls from the union to call up the president of the Dressmakers Guild and cry on the telephone and berate them for the beatings of Gershman and Breslow. Then Joe Gershman and Frank Breslow showed up on the picket line the next day all bandaged up, with Gershman's arm in a sling. Leo was in another part of the city and so didn't have to appear. Everyone was happy: a few days later, the gangsters collected the money, the unionists took their bandages off, and they even organized a feast at the LaSalle Hotel to celebrate.[12]

The left understood the importance of unity and emphasized support for other ethnic groups and union activists internationally. Bessie Schachter, a leading member of the Montreal Yiddish Arbeter Froyen Fareyn, described participating in a dressmakers' strike in 1926 along with Italian and French Canadian women.[13] Bessie's group was assigned to the Society Brand shop, a place well known for its treachery. The police drove them away and didn't even let them approach. An "older" Italian woman (in her forties) said they must struggle as if they were on a battlefield:

> She yells to us in her language and makes it possible for several women to get near the shop. The police get wild, and begin to hit and arrest us.... It takes five policemen to get the brave Italian woman into the patrol wagon. She calls to the women to "fight bravely, don't be afraid."[14]

The Trade Union Educational League (TUEL) had been set up by the United States Communist Party in 1920. It stressed the need to work within the international unions, pushing for progressive action from inside. In Canada TUEL supporters opposed settling disputes by arbitration, convinced that the arbitrators were not neutral but would always side with the bosses. They called for local control of the unions based on a shop delegate plan and, after 1923, national autonomy for the Canadian trade union movement.

The left had played key roles in the formation of the ILGWU, but the opposition they faced in the union was formidable. By the late 1920s, the international leadership based in New York had pushed the leftists out of Montreal, where they were strong, and closed the local office. The left charged that the American Federation of Labour (AFL) craft unions would collude with the employer to prevent unionization if there was a communist leadership.

In response, in 1928 the CP ordered workers to withdraw from mainstream unions and organize separate revolutionary unions. Leftists in the needle trades unions such as the ILGWU and the Amalgamated Clothing Workers of America (ACWA) joined the newly organized Industrial Union of Needle Trades Workers (IUNTW), which became part of the Workers' Unity League (WUL). These unions were communist-led and militant. While the union activists tended to be CP members, workers joined unions that would fight the hardest for them; whether or not the union was run by communists or had communists in it was not their major concern. Many IUNTW members were not communists. Under the aegis of the IUNTW, the drive to organize unions was led by dedicated workers with some impressive results. The rival ILGWU was not doing well in the midst of the Depression. They made little headway in the face of falling wages, bosses imposing cost-cutting measures in piecework, and workers suffering from increased exhaustion, strain, and fatigue.

J. B. Salsberg, the national organizer for the needle trades union, announced the new executive—Max Shur, Annie Buller, Joshua Gershman, and Max Dolgoy—all of whom were part of the secular left Jewish organizations, the Labour League in Toronto and the Liberty Temple Association in Winnipeg. As the IUNTW focus was on organizing the lower paid workers, in practice this meant paying attention to the women, who were the majority of poorly paid wage earners. In contrast to the ILGWU, whose efforts on behalf of women had been half-hearted, by 1935, IUNTW had had some successes in Toronto and Montreal.

Khane Novinsky Kleinstein, Gertie Blugerman, and Rachel (Rae) Watson were three union organizers from Toronto who were also active members of the Jewish Women's Labour League. They worked with Annie Buller in the struggle to organize the dressmakers. Left activists had a three-pronged battle: they confronted the manufacturers and the Canadian state, which supported the bosses, but also had to deal with the international and craft-based unions. During the 1930s, the battles inside the needle trades, a predominantly Jewish terrain, between the pro-communist forces and the Co-operative Commonwealth Federation (CCF) democratic socialists, were bitter. The left cultural and fraternal organizations followed the lead of the CP in union politics. When the rival federation, the IUNTW, was set up in the Bolshevization period, all those in trades where union struggles were going on supported the left unions.[15]

The struggle between the international unions and the communist-led unions is a complicated story, and none of the leadership had completely clean hands. On the one hand, the shop floor democracy in the left unions was more extensive than in the bureaucratic ILGWU, run from the head office in New York. But there was pressure on the IUNTW leadership to abide by the dictates of the CP. One prominent IUNTW official, Max Dolgoy, lost his position and his membership in the CP when he refused to organize a strike that he thought was not winnable. His wife Annie remained a member of the Party, and they both continued their membership in the Labour League.[16] However, there is also documentation of collusion between the bosses and the more conservative international unions who were quite willing to sacrifice the interests of the workers to defeat the communists.

The international garment unions affiliated with the Trades and Labour Congress did very little in this period to challenge manufacturers' impositions of wage cuts and layoffs. While left Jewish unionists from the IUNTW were often involved in the secular left Jewish organizations, the ILGWU and Amalgamated Clothing Workers (ACW) joined with the Arbeter Ring to form the Jewish Labor Committee. The mainstream unions responded to the depression and hard times of the 1930s with resignation, fearing that activism among starving workers was bound to fail. The IUNTW, on the other hand, engaged in escalating levels of militant protest. These left labour activists felt that radical unionization was the only means through which workers could gain some control over their lives. Despite the threats of unemployment and poverty in an oppressive state that protected the interests of employers, workers engaged in fierce battles.

The press was not sympathetic to strikers. An article in the *Toronto Star* described the arrest of women involved in the 1931 dressmaker strike in Toronto, ignoring the issues of the strike and depicting the women as wild and out of control. "One man," the newspaper reported, "claiming to be an innocent bystander was pounced upon by some half dozen irate females who grabbed him by the hair, then pushed him head first through a plate glass window." These women, dressmakers organized within the IUNTW, allegedly mobbed policemen and strike breakers until they were arrested:

> The first patrol car was so crowded with the arrested fighters that the police had to push them in like sardines in a can. One woman kicked and screamed furiously. She was hard to handle. She gave the police all they could do to shove her into the wagon. Another fellow was held down on the sidewalk by a bunch of women . . . the policeman was checked by six or eight women. They clung to his coat, his arms, his belt, anything in reach . . . but the big fellow shook the women off.[17]

Of the ten arrested, at least three of the women and one man were from the Labour League of the Jewish left: Rae Watson, Becky London (later Lapedes), Diane Bisgold (later Meslin), and Ben Biderman.[18] Joe Gershman and Meyer Klig of the IUNTW executive reported that they were planning to extend the strike to other shops.

Becky described how the women who went to jail kept up their morale by singing. Her description of one incident is most likely the strike at 127 Spadina described in the *Toronto Star* article:

There was a whole bunch of us taken in that day. Spadina and Adelaide, I think. They told us not to call them scabs … they put us in the Black Maria, and they took us to Richmond to search us. Then they took us into the city hall … we were singing and singing, making a disturbance. They put us in a wagon and took us to the Don jail. Then we had to have lunch … they gave us some soup that looked like it had just washed the floor. We were laughing and laughing.… At the same time there were two prostitutes. We all were searched and they took out of the hem of their skirts some cigarettes or maybe drugs. They knew each other.… There was a woman in a cage—she had shot her husband. She couldn't mingle with us.

As the hours went by, we didn't laugh so much. I couldn't understand why we weren't taken out. We had a special organization to help us, the Canadian Defence League. They bailed people out. It's getting later and later. Finally, we didn't know but we found out afterward that at five o'clock, the judge came, and our people were there to bail us out. Which they did. In the meantime they took our fingerprints and this and that. We probably paid ten dollars.[19]

Like Becky Lapedes in Toronto, Paula (Pesel) Wolodarsky, Bertha Dolgoy Guberman, and Freda Coodin of Winnipeg were union organizers in the needle trades as well as active members of the left in Winnipeg's Labour Temple Association. Bertha had migrated to Winnipeg in 1922 as a thirteen-year-old girl. One of six children, she was separated from her father and three siblings who arrived just before the outbreak of the First World War. Her brother, Max Dolgoy, had arrived earlier, and as a representative of the cloakmakers' union had been involved in the Winnipeg General Strike. Bertha quickly integrated into Winnipeg's North End radical Jewish community and got a job in the needle trades at the age of fifteen. She joined the IUNTW in 1929.[20] Bertha expresses the connections between international events, political struggles, workplace struggles, and culture:

The Winnipeg General Strike played a very important role for us and also the question of what was going on in Europe was important. The immigrants that came at that time were a more idealistic type, more desirous of knowledge. We started building schools, we started building cultural organizations. After the strike in 1923, the ILGWU was practically defunct. The shops were all unorganized and it was like that all over Canada, not just here in Winnipeg, in Toronto in Montreal too. So most of the organized were under the left-wing

Freda Coodin, a victim of bitter class struggle. "Died in Winnipeg. From Belilevker, Kiever Province. Through the influence of the Soviet Revolution from her early years she showed a deep sympathy for the struggle of the oppressed. With a profound belief in the triumph of social justice, she gave her young life for the struggle. Honour to her memory."

Sholem Aleichem Shule, 25th Year Jubilee Book, 115.
Collection of Roz Usiskin.

leadership. We were ourselves, a sacrificing bunch. We worked for practically nothing and went around ragged and organized the workers. We were the ones who were idealistic and you needed to be in order to do all that work.[21]

The contradictions between Canada's claims to be a democratic country and the lived experience of the suppression of workers was something these women knew firsthand:

The main exploiter found out that I am active in building the Industrial Union amongst the needle trades and that I am a member of the Communist Party. The manager of the shop has forgotten that we live in a land of "democracy," even though he needs my labour, he fired me because I saw that the workers need to be united.[22]

Freda Coodin of Winnipeg was an organizer for the IUNTW,[23] honoured as a martyr for her activism. A slender and frail woman, under five feet in height, she was charged with threatening a scab with death in the 1933 strike at Hurtig furs: "According to victim Pauline Furer, Coodin had terrorized her home and had promised to break every bone in the strike breaker's body if she continued to scab." The mainstream press described Coodin as a "lawless monster," although witnesses testified that Coodin had not been at Furer's home, and they themselves had issued the threats to Furer.[24]

Freda Coodin charged that one strikebreaker at Hurtig Furs, Simon Lesternick, had slapped her in the face while she was picketing outside the plant. Although several witnesses independently confirmed these allegations, the judge concluded that the charge was "very little short of absurdity." Coodin's lawyer Solomon Greenberg argued that the charges against her were a frame-up while the man who had assaulted her in plain view of the police "was given a seat of honour at crown counsel's table." Even the owner testified on her behalf! Adolph Hurtig, co-owner of the fur manufacturing plant, stated that "he had seen Miss Coodin parading up and down outside his store on several occasions, but at no time had she misbehaved herself." But the judge dismissed all evidence that would have vindicated Coodin. He found her guilty of nine charges of assault, intimidation, and unlawful assembly and sentenced her to nine months in jail. Coodin contracted tuberculosis in Stony Mountain Penitentiary. She was released to hospital and died two months later, at the age of twenty-three. Her death was mourned by all of Winnipeg's North End, and the funeral procession went on for miles. Her brother Mottl had her tombstone engraved with the inscription in Yiddish "A Victim of the Hurtig Furrier Strike, August 1933." The day after it was erected, the word "Hurtig" was scratched out of the inscription; it is not clear whether the family was threatened, or whether Hurtig or the cemetery were responsible.[25]

Freda Coodin's grave in North Jewish Cemetery, Winnipeg. Notice how the name Hurtig is erased at the bottom: "A victim of the_____ Furrier Strike."

Jewish Historical Centre of Western Canada Archives.

In August 1934, the Industrial Union of Needle Trades Workers declared a general strike in Montreal. They demanded a forty-four-hour week and a minimum wage of $12.50 a week, at a time when in some shops, workers were putting in as many as seventy hours a week and earning as little as $5.00 a week.[26] The strike turned violent when, as the *Montreal Herald* reported, the strikers were attacked by "a group of men armed with bludgeons, lead pipes and rubber hoses filled with sand, goons imported from the United States to break the strike. Twelve strikers were arrested, ten women and two men."[27] Among them were Eva Shanoff and Rose Myerson.[28]

While most women withdrew from the labour force when their children were very small, many returned when the children were of school age. Eva Shanoff of Montreal took on paid labour during the Depression to stave off hunger. Her husband, a presser, had a hard time finding work. As an operator with less skill and paid less, Eva was able to get jobs more easily than her husband.[29] In a period when approximately 30 percent of the population was out of work, sometimes it was the women, working for very low wages in exploitative conditions, who became the breadwinners for their families. This did not deter Eva from union activism.

Repression rather than collective bargaining seemed to be the strategy of choice of the federal and provincial governments in response to the unrest. In these difficult times, the communist-led unions were ones most likely to take up the challenge of attempting to limit employers' power through unionization. Although the dedicated union representatives encouraged militancy, spontaneous workplace revolts were also frequent. Grievances included unfair dismissals and wage cuts. IUNTW organizers were paid very little, if at all, and so they too were working in the shops.

Work in the needle trades was the most common occupation for both men and women in Toronto's Labour League. Of those employed in wage labour, 60 percent were in the clothing industry. The Labour League at the time had a total of 803 members, and most of them were young, 82 percent being under forty years of age.[30] The total Jewish population in Canada numbered less than 170,000. In Toronto, the Jewish population was about 58,000, so the community was not large numerically.

Main Occupations of Toronto Labour League Members, 1936

Cloakmakers	128
Tailors	87
Furriers	34
Dressmakers	40
Operators	37
Pressers	44
Cap and Millinery	38
Shoe and Leather Workers	47
Housewives	139
Other occupations*	209
Total	803

*These included small business people (e.g., butchers, grocers, bakers); tradespeople (e.g., carpenters, painters, electricians); professionals (e.g., doctors, lawyers); bookbinders; pedlars.

Lil Himmelfarb Ilomaki, born in Toronto in 1912, was arrested no fewer than ten times from the time she was sixteen to twenty-four (1928–36). She was part of the Canadian Labour Defence League (CLDL), which gathered people together to stop evictions, putting the furniture back in people's homes. Often, the CLDL would initiate actions and then the neighbours would join in, remaining in people's homes until there was some solution. Because she could speak loudly, she often became the spokesperson and was known as "Red Lil." Lil also loved to sing and write poetry and was an active member of the Labour League, later the United Jewish People's Order (UJPO). Lil described how in 1935, she became the spokesperson for the women on the On to Ottawa Trek from eastern Canada that took place after the Royal Canadian Mounted Police (RCMP) instigated a riot in Regina. In June 1935, 831 men from work camps where they were paid twenty cents a day for their labour gathered in Vancouver and travelled on boxcars east to Ottawa to meet with Prime Minister Bennett to ask for relief for the unemployed and destitute. Under orders from the federal government, the trekkers were stopped in Regina. The RCMP and the police attacked the people with guns and bullets, lashing out at anyone in their path. They arrested 120 of the trekkers, and hundreds were injured. Lil Ilomaki recalled that as soon as news came of the assault on the strikers in Regina the Workers Unity League (WUL) started to mobilize people for a trek from Toronto to Ottawa. On July 15, 350 people gathered including a contingent of women. They walked about 30 kilometres a day, singing "Hold the Fort" and "Solidarity" and shouting slogans like "no 20 cent a day camps" and "down with Bennett." Farmers and business people contributed food. A Finnish woman named Ann Scott was the leader of the women, but Lil was the speaker. "I was the one who made the noise," she said.[31]

The members of the Jewish left organizations combined labour activism with other activities. Izzy Fine, a cloakmaker, president of his union and later the president of the United Jewish People's Order, explained:

> The Labour League wasn't just an organization of left-wingers. It was people
> from the unions that used to come in because it was a cultural organization....
> But at the same time, if there was a strike for instance, the cloak and
> dressmakers used to have a strike every year. Because the manufacturers
> didn't hold to the contract we made with them. When we were on strike,
> members from the Labour League came to the picket line to help out. The
> women did the same thing. That's what was progressive ... to help people who
> need help![32]

Eva Shanoff recalls the social life that went along with union membership for the Jewish Women, who were also part of the Kanader (Canadian) Labour Circle (Kanader Arbeter Ring): "We had meetings, we had parties, we had all kinds of things.... I really enjoyed myself." There was also a deep commitment

In 1929, Joe Gershman became an organizer for the Industrial Union of Needle Trades Workers.

Archives of Ontario, B115601.

to building organizations and institutions to foster and promote socialist ideals.

Left activists in different provinces knew each other and considered themselves part of a national community. Participation in union activities was not separate from the shule, the cultural activities, and the summer camps. When Leybl Basman (teacher and later camp director at Naivelt) first came to Canada from Wilkomir, Lithuania in 1930, his first stop was the home of trade union activist Max Dolgoy in Winnipeg. When the Dolgoy family moved to Ontario in 1932, they first lived in camp Kindervelt in Rouge Hills. Max Dolgoy was busy as an organizer in the dressmakers' union. Annie worked in a dress shop in the winter and as a waitress at Camp Kindervelt during the summer to pay fees for their sons Sid and Lenny. Sid recalled, "We were brought up in Kindervelt, we lived in tents."[33]

Several men in the leadership of the left organizations began their careers as union organizers. Joe Gershman, for example, worked as a fur dresser and dyer in Winnipeg then became an organizer in the needle trades in Montreal and a member of the IUNTW executive. He edited the Jewish left newspaper, *Der Kamf*, later the *Der Vochenblat* (Canadian Jewish Weekly), for almost forty years, from 1936 until it ceased publication.

In those years most Jews, whatever their political leanings, understood that one didn't cross a picket line. Ruth Frager writes, "By the interwar period, the pro-labour current within Toronto's immigrant Jewish community was so deep that a Jew who was a strike-breaker may well have found himself spurned by neighbours and friends." In Joe Salsberg's words, a "scab" was almost to be outlawed.[34]

Despite widespread agreement on the importance of collective action, the dissension between the left and the social democratic unions hurt all workers during that period. Ruth Frager holds the communist policy of dual unions responsible for the detrimental inter-union rivalry.[35] However, both Mercedes Steedman and Jodi Giesbrecht argue that the model of bargaining in the left needle trade unions was far more responsive to rank and file control than the

ILGWU-dominated craft unions, which by the 1930s had become more bureaucratic.[36] The language of the left at that time, however, was of a narrow sectarianism. During the Bolshevization, or third period, from 1929 to 1934, the slogan "class against class" meant that there was little distinction made between social democrats, deemed "social fascists" and reactionaries in collusion with the bosses. The compliment was more than returned in insults hurled by the social democrats to "go back to Russia"—accusing all pro-Bolshevik groups of being mindless pawns of Moscow.

A multifaceted workers' movement required establishing a physical location, a place where people could meet. In Winnipeg, the Liberty Temple on Pritchard Avenue in the North End was the home of the left, who stayed in control after the Arbeter Ring organization divided. In Toronto, Branch 2, the first Toronto Labour League Branch managed to buy a house on 414 Markham Street in 1928, shortly after they left the Arbeter Ring. They supported the establishment of a shule as well as mobilizing support for union struggles.

> The enthusiasm of the membership was so great that they allowed no obstacles or hardship to stand in their way.... Our organization from the very beginning put itself forward with its face to the working class. They not only raised the money for their own house, but responded to every action of the workers' movement. It's only to wonder at the spirit of the Labour League members who managed to raise five hundred dollars to support the important cloak makers' strike then taking place in New York.[37]

Survival and improving working conditions in Canada were difficult enough, but by the mid-1930s, attention was drawn to the international arena. Jews across the ideological spectrum were alarmed by the threat of fascism.

Anti-Semitism on the Rise

After Hitler gained power, anti-Semitism in Canada increased. It had been a concern since the arrival of Eastern European Jews at the beginning of the twentieth century. Admissions into medical and dentistry programs were limited, and Jews were banned from many resorts and private clubs with signs such as "no Jews or dogs allowed" or "gentiles only." Even living in certain urban areas was forbidden. In Quebec, the *Achat Chez Nous* campaign, which began in the 1920s, grew stronger in the 1930s, urging French Canadians to boycott Jewish-owned stores. In Toronto in 1933, the "Pit Gang," a group of Anglo toughs

Telegram, August 1, 1933.

Clara Thomas Archives, York University.

Ste Agathe sign, 1930s.

Anti-Semitism: Social, 1. TCTH Artefact Pages. Vancouver Holocaust Education Centre. www.vhec.org

shouting "Heil Hitler," unfurled a banner with a swastika in Christie Pits. A four-hour battle followed between hundreds of Jewish youth, assisted by a few Italians and Ukrainians, and the Anglo gang. In Toronto's East End members of swastika clubs with Nazi badges and shirts harassed Jews and other minorities.[38]

The streets of Canada were full of anti-Semitic propaganda. In *Cabbagetown*, Hugh Garner's book set in the 1930s depression in Toronto, one character organizes a demonstration to rid the beaches and parks of Jews, in particular from Kew Gardens where people would come to picnic:

> We are tired of our Christian wives and girlfriends being leered at by every Abie and Izzy who ogles them on the boardwalk as they pass by. The sight of big fat Jewesses calling to Rachel and Sammy around our neighbourhood has got to stop.[39]

The Canadian Union of Fascists had branches in Manitoba, Ontario, British Columbia, and Saskatchewan.[40] A number of measures were used to harass communists and labour organizers. Section 41 (enacted in June 1919) of the Immigration Act allowed officials to deport any alien or Canadian citizen not born in Canada for advocating the overthrow of the government by force. Under this provision, hundreds of activists opposed to government policy or business interests were deported. Section 98 of the Criminal Code, liberally applied to socialists, Jews, and other ethnic minorities, prohibited unlawful assembly of anyone the authorities deemed were threatening to use coercion for economic or political purposes. The act was interpreted broadly enough to include anyone who was a member of the CP, making Canada the only democracy banning CP membership. When popular mobilizations finally resulted in throwing out Section 98 in 1935, it was followed by the notorious Padlock Law of Premier Duplessis in Quebec, which gave the authorities the power to padlock for one year any place they considered "subversive."[41]

As Hitler and his National Socialist party gained power in Germany in 1933, the Jewish community was deeply concerned about events in Europe. The left began to support a united opposition to fascism rather than a continuation of the sectarian politics of the early 1930s. The left women, in their protests against higher meat prices, had successfully involved many people in the wider community. The youth section of the CP began to drop the practice of branding social democrats "social fascists" in 1934, and a popular front began to emerge. By 1935, support for a popular front was official CP policy.

The 1930s was a difficult time for working people, for young people, for Jews. Many North Americans were still suffering from the ravages of the Depression, which had left so many unemployed, hungry, and homeless. For some, the question was not why one became a radical, but rather given the conditions, how one could not be a socialist. As Celia Ceborer, an American nurse who volunteered her services in the Spanish Civil War said, "It was in the air. Social consciousness was wedded to the Depression.... There was union activity. May Day at that time was a tremendous event."[42]

The importance of May Day, the workers' holiday, is illustrated by a story I was told by a friend. She was visiting her elderly father, a left socialist all his life, in his nursing home on the Jewish holiday, Yom Kippur, the Day of Atonement, which generally falls in September. She asked him if he knew what day it was and helpfully hinted that it was the most important day of the year. It didn't look like spring outside, and confused, he asked her, "Is today May Day?"[43]

In 1935, the demonstrators marking May Day filled Maple Leaf Gardens in Toronto. The Mandolin Symphony of the Labour League led by Philip Podoliak performed, along with the Workers' Sport Association, a choir with three hundred Ukrainian, Jewish, and German singers, and the Ukrainian wind orchestra. Two parades, one from the West End and one from the East End, joined at Queen's Park. The headline of *Der Kamf* indicated that workers from fourteen nationalities demonstrated in unity against hunger, fascism, and war. The union locals from the left Workers' Unity League included painters and decorators, carpenters, bricklayers, the shoe workers' industrial union, furniture and woodworkers, the Food Workers Industrial Union, fur dressers and dyers, window cleaners, textile workers, house workers, needle trades and industrial workers, shirt and overall makers, and leather jacket makers. The Workers' Sport Association had a float. *Der Kamf* proclaimed "It was impossible to count the forest of banners and slogans" waving in the air. The *Globe* headline reported "10,000 Radicals in May Day Parade: Good Humor Mingles with Socialism as

These women were gathering in Riverdale Park for a longer march. They would be among the 10,000 radicals who gathered on May 1, 1935 at the new band shell in Queen's Park. The *Globe* article indicated, "Good humour mingles with Socialism as orderly throng gathers in Queen's Park. Police present only to regulate traffic."

Toronto Reference Library Picture Collection S13, 685.

Orderly Throng Gathers in Queens Park—Police present only to regulate traffic." The newspaper called it the "the largest gathering of labor in the history of the city."[44] The enthusiasm workers showed for May Day reflected the attractiveness of the popular front, the strong support for unions, and the fight for better pay and working conditions. It also indicated the concern for a grim international situation as Hitler was building concentration camps in Germany. The marchers were worried about Canada's official response to Hitler as well as the rise of fascism at home, where it was increasingly dangerous to be a Jew or a leftist. Internationally Mussolini and his fascists were consolidating their control in Italy, and the Italian army had marched into Ethiopia.

Anti-Fascism and Aiding the Republic in the Spanish Civil War

In the midst of the rise of fascism in Europe and its popularity in England, the United States, and Canada, Spain was a shining exception. In 1931, the Spanish government implemented the Republican constitution with guarantees of freedom of speech and association, separation of church and state, women's rights, procedures for nationalizing land, railroads, banks, and public services, and autonomy for the regions. For the first time since their expulsion in 1492, Jews were officially welcomed back to Spain. In 1933, Albert Einstein accepted an invitation from the University of Madrid to become a member of its faculty.[45] Spain's wealthy elite and powerful Catholic Church—stripped of public subsidies and schools—were determined to regain power. The left was fractured, which made it possible for the right to regain control of the country, but the country was exploding with workers' movements and struggles for serious land reform. Frustrated by the slow pace of reforms, the miners in Asturias in northern Spain revolted in 1934–35 and were brutally suppressed by the army, led by Franco, who was dubbed "the butcher of Asturias."

The left Jewish community in Canada began to organize against fascism. The "class against class" name-calling from the left ended and social democratic groups were invited to join the Canadian League Against War and Fascism. However, the Canadian Jewish Congress (CJC) remained adamant in its refusal to cooperate with the left organizations. The deep divisions in the community undermined the struggle against fascism.

Did the pro-communist movement pose a threat to the CJC leadership because its left ideology was at odds with that of the dominant anti-communist Zionist groups? Or was the CJC leadership afraid that mobilizing an anti-fascist movement would fan the flames of anti-Semitism in Canada? Perhaps both. Despite the Congress's refusal to participate in the popular front coalitions, some prominent members, such as Mrs. Ida Segal of Toronto and Rabbi M. N. Eisendrath of Toronto's Holy Blossom Temple joined the Canadian League Against War and Fascism.[46] The Congress also found it difficult to silence the noted Winnipeg Labour Zionist Alter Cherniak, leader of the Winnipeg Peretz School and, since 1924, vice president of the Hebrew Immigrant Aid Society. He headed the Canadian Zionist Congress from 1933 to 1936. Despite the disapproval of the CJC, Cherniak accepted the leadership of the Winnipeg Committee Against Anti-Semitism and Racism and represented Canada at the 1937 Paris Congress of the International Federation Against Racism and Anti-Semitism (Federation internationale des ligues contre le racisme et anti-Semitism).

Anti-fascist mobilization was a popular cause but in the eyes of the leaders of the CJC, it was a communist movement. The Youth Conference against War and Fascism proved to be another challenge for the CJC, as many youth organizations and women's groups joined. The Talmud Torah, Folks Schools, and Peretz

Schools were warned by the Congress leadership that to deserve continued support they "must fundamentally revise the programs and enforce a more militant point of view of Judaism as opposed to the reactionary baseness of communism."[47]

David Rome, the CJC archivist, thought the left was misguided: "The Jewish community [by which he means the Canadian Jewish Congress] from the beginning kept these Communists in Coventry. It rejected their cooperation and the United Front with their committees against war, Fascism and anti-Semitism."[48] When the CJC regrouped in 1934, it made sure that "Jewish communists were carefully excluded." When the primarily Jewish students in the Students League at Montreal's Baron Byng High School struck, Rome denounced them: "What do the Young Communists care if by their criminal provocation they contribute to a wave of anti-Semitism and hatred? What do they know of elementary responsibility and decency?"

The CJC wrote to the Young Men's Hebrew Association and Young Women's Hebrew Association and warned them that the anti-fascist organization was under communist influence and therefore a liability. It seems that Rome equated belonging to any group where there were communists with aiding fascism. H. M. Caiserman, a Labour Zionist and an official in the CJC, held the same views. Writing to his friend Rabbi Eisendrath in Fort William, Ontario, he said,

> I will be happy if your community will not be represented at the conference of the League because to be identified with the Communists at the present temper of Canadian politics is a vital danger for the Jewish population and plays into the hands of Nazi agents from coast to coast.[49]

The eyes of the world continued to focus on developments in Spain. In 1936, the left-wing parties in Spain put aside their differences and a popular front government of socialists, communists, trade unionists, and anarchists won the election. Supporters of the regime were known as Republican loyalists. The victory was short-lived, however, as Franco quickly turned to his friends Hitler and Mussolini, who were only too happy to assist with troops, weapons and funding to support the overthrow of the new democratically elected regime. Fearful of provoking Germany and Italy into a war, France, Great Britain, Belgium, Russia and allies (twenty-seven countries in all) agreed to a non-intervention pact. Canada followed the lead of Britain and the United States in isolationism; it was not a signatory of the pact but abided by its terms. The allies refused to allow the shipment of arms to the Republicans. However, left-wing radicals in Spain, including German and Italian refugees fleeing their oppressive regimes, joined the Spanish militias. Word of the internationals helping the Republicans spread throughout Europe. Russia had contradictory interests. A third fascist power in Europe was a serious threat, but Russia did not want to provoke the allies into attacking them by supporting a revolution in Spain. Stalin would help defend the democratic Republic but also ensured that a real revolution would not take place.[50]

With the encouragement of the Comintern, Communist parties throughout the world recruited volunteers to fight on the side of the loyalists. Approximately 2600 men from the United States took up arms, mostly fighting in the American Lincoln Battalion, and about 1600 Canadians, who formed the Mackenzie-Papineau Battalion, joined the fight. Over 40,000 volunteers, many of whom had no home to return to after the war was lost, came from over 50 countries, the largest number coming from Germany and Poland. A disproportionate number of these were Jewish, the majority of them from Poland and the United States. Albert Prago, an American volunteer, wrote:

el generalisimo

Anti-fascist poster showing the collaboration of Franco, Mussolini, Hitler, and the Catholic Church.

Junta Delgada de Defensa de Madrid, Delgacio n de Propaganda y Prensa, circa 1936.

> The 7,000 Jews who fought in Spain were usually not known as such. We were Americans, Germans, English, French, Poles and so forth. The Palestinian Jews, some 250–400 of them were quite aware of their identity. The others were communists, antifascists, progressives, socialists, trade unionists and identified with the country of origin.[51]

Left Jewish women throughout Canada were actively involved in organizing support for the embattled Republic. When the Montreal women who had become part of the Canadian Labour Circle (the Montreal equivalent of Toronto's Labour League) reported their activities, the campaign for Spain was clearly their highest priority.[52] In fundraising for Spain, they reached 150 percent of their goal.

Although Spanish anarchist women in the early days of the war had taken up guns to fight, the Communist parties in the United States and Canada did not permit the recruitment of women for battle. There was, however, a critical need for doctors and nurses to provide medical help and to bring medical supplies. From Canada, Doctor Norman Bethune set up his famous blood transfusion service, which was then turned over to the Spaniards. We know the stories of only two of the handful of Canadian women who went to Spain: a reporter, Jim (Myrtle Eugenia) Watts, who became an ambulance driver, and Florence Pike, who died in England in the 1940s.[53]

The US medical contingent was the largest and the best documented, thanks to the extensive research done by Frederika Martin, the head nurse.[54] More than half, forty-six of the United States nurses, were Jewish, mainly from the New York area. Most came from poor immigrant families. They were socialists and secular Jews and emerged from a radical milieu where, for many, volunteering in Spain was an extension of their activism for progressive causes in the United States. Esther Silverstein (Blanc) talked about why she volunteered:

> I had followed the whole issue of the Jewish question in Germany.... I was a committed anti-fascist, as was every Jew I knew.... I believed in "to each according to his needs, from each according to his abilities." It seems to me that's a strikingly marvelous notion.[55]

In both the United States and Canada, committees sprang up to send aid to the Spanish Republic and to support the volunteers. The Communist Party recruited fighters, not all of whom were communists, but the aid committees had broader support. The left in both countries clearly saw Spain as the last bulwark against Hitlerism. They felt that they were both helping a beleaguered democracy and protecting democracy in their own countries. Half of the Americans who volunteered to fight with the Loyalists in Spain were from the New York area. They had the help of an extremely popular anti-fascist coalition that included communists, socialists, democrats, the African American community, who were concerned about the fall of Ethiopia to Mussolini, and unions and diverse ethnic communities. Money for aid to Spain was raised on street corners, on subways, through soccer matches and baseball games. A triple-header game was held at the New York Hippodrome on February 19, 1937. Two women's locals of the ILGWU held a basketball match, followed by the Furriers' Union facing off against the International Workers Order (the American sister organization to the Jewish left groups in Canada). Then the all-star ex-collegians played the all-star non-collegians (the people who didn't go to college) with all proceeds to the Spanish Republic.

Artists, writers, and performers contributed their creativity and some— including Ernest Hemingway, Martha Gellhorn, Dorothy Parker, Lillian Hellman, Langston Hughes, and John Dos Passos—went to Spain. Even the famous stripper Gypsy Rose Lee (born Rose Louise Hovick) supported the Spanish Republic. Moneyed liberal socialites from New York held gatherings for relief aid; community groups and unions raised funds for ambulances, medical needs, and civilian needs, including milk, wheat and flour, beans, sugar, shoes, coats, and raincoats.[56] The relief ship for Spain that left New York Harbor in September 1938 included five thousand tons of food, clothing and medical supplies, including one thousand tons of wheat donated by Canadians and a fully equipped ambulance donated by Harlem African Americans. In total, United States aid organizations donated about two million dollars in aid in cash and materials. Equally important were the calls to boycott shipping of military supplies to Franco and demands that the embargo of aid to the Republic be ended.

There were massive support efforts in Canada spearheaded by the Jewish left organizations, which did everything in their power to help the Republicans. The Committee to Aid Spanish Democracy formed in the fall of 1936, several months after the fascist coup. It was a broad organization of social democrats, communists, trade unionists, ethnic organizations, prairie farmers, and others, with branches throughout Canada. One of the first tasks was to equip a medical unit for Spain and to recruit Dr. Norman Bethune to head it. He left for Spain in October 1936, organizing the Mobile Canadian Blood Transfusion Unit that pioneered a way of getting blood to the front lines using refrigerated ambulances.

When the blood transfusion unit was transferred to the Spanish authorities, Canadian Communist Party officials had to convince Dr. Bethune, a brilliant but irascible surgeon, that his efforts to help the Spanish cause were better served by fundraising in Canada. To co-ordinate fundraising to support Dr. Bethune's work, the Spanish Assistance Committee in Montreal organized a conference in May 1937, calling together a number of Montreal Jewish organizations, all of which pledged to meet a quota of money raised. Several branches of the left Canadian Workmen's Circle, the left Jewish Cultural Centres, the Junior Council of Jewish Women, the Borokhov League, the Poale Tsion youth (labour Zionist), the Women's Cultural Club and others came together and pledged support. The Canadian Jewish Congress did not endorse any of these efforts.[57]

While women were not the only participants in the aid work, they played a central role. Jewish, Finnish, and Ukrainian women leftists in Canada were particularly prominent in these efforts.[58] On October 21, 1936, a large reception

Mural of the
Spanish Civil War
by Avrom. Nor-
man Bethune
is in the centre.
On the left are
the progressive
forces, and on
the right are
the reactionary
forces, including
a figure holding
a padlock, repre-
senting Quebec's
Padlock Law.

*Courtesy of
Anna Yanovsky.*

and mass meeting was held in Toronto in the Mutual Street Arena to welcome a delegation from Spain. Over ten thousand people came. The women's branches of the Labour League and representatives of other women's organizations marched into the hall along with trade unions and other leftist groups, banners held high, to officially greet the delegation. Palensia from the Spanish delegation addressed the crowd in the name of tens of thousands of women heroes of Spain, saying "We particularly appeal to the women's organizations [of Canada] to make all the preparations to greet the heroic woman leader [Dolores Ibárruri, known as La Pasionara] of the Spanish People's Front."[59]

Supporting the overthrow of Franco and the return of the Republican loyalists to power took many forms. The Canadians who volunteered for the Mackenzie-Papineau Battalion were called the Mac-Paps; the Friends of the Mac-Paps organized in May 1937. Soon eighty women's committees throughout Canada were knitting and in December 1937 Becky Buhay Ewen, the head of the Friends of the Mac-Paps, reported that they had provided seven hundred pairs of woollen socks, mufflers, sweaters and mitts to support those who had volunteered. One returned vet explained, "Cigarettes, cigarettes and cigarettes, then soap and the odd pair of sox for a more frequent change—that's what we wanted in the trenches and behind the lines."[60] The contributors ranged from children such as Shirley Silverman of Cornwall Ontario, who saved up her spending money to send seven packages of cigarettes, to an elderly woman in British Columbia who knitted three pairs of socks. Girls' Brigades sprung up in various parts of the country and children joined in the fundraising effort.[61] The

Nurses who were part of the Medical Brigade fighting for the Republicans in Spain. Ambulance donated by Canadians, circa 1937.

New York University, I. Tamiment Library, ALBA Series, Edward K. Barsky Photograph Collection.

money raised was not from rich people—working people contributed what they could ill afford.

The casualties in the International Brigades were horrific.[62] By the end, over half of the International Brigades were either dead or missing. One American volunteer nurse described her feelings: "The U.S. watched when the Spanish Fascists were supported in every way and the Republic was left with empty hands because of the so-called non-intervention pact. There is no neutrality! An honest human being must take sides."[63]

In 1939, the graduation class of the Bronx mittlshul (the Yiddish high school of the International Workers Order) devoted their class project to those who went to Spain. They contacted volunteers who went to Spain and the families of four who did not return. The students then composed stories in Yiddish, a composite of their interviews. Virtually all of them knew some volunteers, and some had an older sister or brothers who had fought in Spain. The book, published in Yiddish as *Lebns farn Lebn* or "lives for life," described why people decided to go to Spain and their experiences there.[64] Many had sneaked away from home, as parents, particularly mothers, would not willingly send their children off to such danger. In one account, a young nurse says: "They didn't allow to me to go. I am their only daughter. But I could no longer stay."[65] Some of the young people described in the stories were unemployed; one had to drop out of university when his scholarship was withdrawn. They all felt they were participating in a significant struggle. A mittlshul student said that after talking to a person who went to Spain, "I felt that if fascism won in Spain, not only the Spanish people would live in horror, but also my mother, my father, my sister and my friends."[66]

The Spanish civilian population suffered horrifically during the Spanish Civil War. While there were some reported accounts of murders on the Republican side in the early days of the war, the scale of terror and repression made clear that the object of Franco's nationalist forces was to exterminate an entire liberal culture. Anyone who had benefited from the reforms of the Republic—workers, peasants, teachers, intellectuals, mayors, parliamentary deputies—was a target.[67] Houses were looted, women raped, and people were slaughtered indiscriminately. The destruction of the town of Guernica, made famous by Picasso's painting, remains distinctive as the first time in modern history that the goal of a bombing was the complete annihilation of a town and its population.

The support efforts for Bethune and the Canadian men fighting in Spain were extensive. At a meeting in Winnipeg on August 6, 1937, Harry Guralnik, editor of *Der Kamf*, talked about the importance of the struggle and the Canadian volunteers in Spain that he knew personally. They needed cigarettes, soap, razors, combs, toothbrushes, toothpaste, and warm socks, which the women collected to send to Spain. The Jewish Women's Committee was set up as a part of the Manitoba committee to help Spain and planned a mass meeting with Bethune, recently returned from Spain.[68] In Hamilton, the Workmen's Circle, the IKOR (Yiddish Colonization in Russia), and the IKOR women's branches listened to Joe Gershman report on the Congress against Anti-Semitism and Racism held in Paris. They immediately raised money for the Spanish delegation touring North America. They were particularly proud of the IKOR women's branch, which was the first to collect money. Thirty volunteers from Hamilton were on the Spanish battlefields.[69]

On his return to Canada in 1937 Bethune wrote passionately about the need to provide assistance to Spanish children—but in Spain, rather than have them adopted outside the country. Mansions of the wealthy were taken over and given to the children. Jean "Jim" Watts, a Canadian reporter for the *Clarion*, visited a children's home in Barcelona and another in Valencia supported by Canadians. She said the form of education was very much a children's collective, where the children were given as much responsibility as possible for running the homes.[70] Social workers such as Constance Kyle, working with the Children's Commission with its headquarters in Paris, strongly supported this approach.[71]

In an unsuccessful attempt to win support from the French and British governments, the Spanish Loyalist leadership asked the International Brigades to leave Spain in 1938. By that time, Franco's fascists were winning the civil war and the support organizations' concerns shifted to raising money to alleviate the desperate situation in Spain. Over a million orphans were wandering the streets, and the wounded Canadian volunteers were returning home. The Canadian Committee appealed for money for orphanages, to provide food, milk, and clothing for children and, for five dollars a month, to adopt the care of an orphan.[72]

After the Mackenzie-Papineau veterans had returned home, a weekend carnival was planned at the Labour League's Camp Naivelt, in Brampton, Ontario to welcome the veterans and hear about their experiences. The events included a concert, a dance, and a picnic. Some of the volunteers dug trenches in the camp to give the children an idea of the life they had led in Spain.[73]

The casualty rate among the volunteers was high, and many others returned sick or wounded. Of the seventeen hundred Canadian volunteers, more than four hundred died or were missing; others returned wounded or ill.[74] When the last group, including twenty-eight sick or wounded, was to arrive in February 1939, *Der Kamf* appealed to people to take in and care for a volunteer.

Fears about the rise of fascism proved accurate. To this day, many believe that it would have been possible to stop Hitler in the 1930s had the allies joined forces in opposing Franco in Spain and supporting the democratically elected government. This would have meant defeat for Hitler and Mussolini. Despite the activities of the Jewish left, which paid such a key role in the mobilization of support for Spain, Canada and the allies remained "neutral" and Hitler grew stronger. In 1939, Stalin's signing of a non-aggression pact with Hitler, the worst enemy of Jews was a shock. The left Jewish community, which had been mobilizing against the rise of fascism since the 1930s and which had seen the Canadian Communist Party as a strong ally in this struggle, felt betrayed. To oppose the Nazis and their anti-Semitic policies was not just a political position, but also one that affected the lives of friends and relatives abroad. The situation changed only after Canada entered the war, with the Soviet Union as its ally.

The Second World War and the Holocaust

The rise of Nazism was a personal threat to many Jews who still had close ties to Eastern Europe. The Nazi-Soviet Pact signed in 1939 horrified people and many Jews parted ways with both the CP and the Labour League. Sam Lipshitz, a member of the Central Committee of the CP and a leading figure on the Yiddish left, recalled that period long after he had severed his affiliation with the CP and the Jewish left. In the 1990s, he remembered how he had felt at the time:

> The Hitler Stalin Pact was a big blow and a lot of people started to have doubts. But there was this reasoning—Chamberlain's appeasement policy allowed Czechoslovakia to be given to the Nazis, with Spain, the western powers didn't do anything.... The Soviet Union is trying for a pact and Poland says that they'll never allow a Soviet soldier on Polish soil.... Everybody feels that there is the danger that the English and French are trying to appease Hitler in order for him to go east. If Poland prevents the Red Army from passing, how can you have a coalition?
>
> The idea that what's good for the Soviet Union is good for the whole world is absolutely fallacious, but at that time we weren't prepared to accept it. The first week of the Pact, in September 1939, the Party had adopted a wonderful resolution saying that the Soviet Union for its own interests concluded a Pact with Hitler and that stopped Hitler from initiating a war with the Soviet Union, but we have to organize in the battle to defeat fascism. But two weeks later a directive came from Dmitrov and the Communist Internationale and suddenly overnight we said that it is an imperialist war.... I remember we had to drop a leaflet off explaining the situation and it was absolutely impossible—how do you explain it? The third international had openly become an instrument of Soviet foreign policy.... This crisis was overcome by the fact that in June of 1941 the Soviet Union was attacked and there's the big alliance.[75]

The Jewish left became very popular once the Soviet Union entered the war alongside the allies. The pro-Soviet Jewish left once again was central in a broad coalition supporting the war in the fight against fascism. The cultural organizations of the Yiddish left throughout the country were thriving, as the Soviets were key to the war effort. Stalin organized the Jewish Anti-Fascist Committee (JAFC) in 1943 to raise support for the war. The Soviet Yiddish poet Itzik Feffer and Shloime (Solomon) Mikhoels, founder, director, and star of the Moscow Yiddish Art Theater, were sent on a tour by Stalin to elicit support for the war effort. This was an important occasion, and Lipshitz travelled to New York to report on the JAFC visit there for the Canadian Jewish Review. He described how, despite the punishing heat, forty-seven thousand New York Jews left their workbenches, offices, and stores. Most of them came direct from the factories. They ate no supper and went to the Polo Grounds, somewhere in the Upper Bronx. For some, it meant two hours travel after a day's work. All of them sat there for five solid hours, from seven to midnight. It was not an ordinary mass meeting. Lipshitz described it as a convention of the people. It was a "get-together" with "long-awaited, long-unseen brethren." There were many inspiring speeches. B. Z. Goldberg, the son-in-law of Sholem Aleichem, declared: "You can't be a Jew unless you are an anti-fascist."[76] Lipshitz wrote:

Left to right: Itzik Feffer, Paul Robeson, Shloime Mikhoels. They met in New York on July 8, 1943 during a JAFC visit to North America.

Montreal Jewish Public Library Archives, Solomon Mikhoels and Itsik Feffer Album (1300).

> It was a historic gathering. All Jews: "Zionists and non-Zionists, Orthodox and free-thinkers, Conservatives and Communists, prominent leaders from all walks of life were there to greet the delegation." Mayor LaGuardia greeted the delegation. The celebrated Yiddish writer Sholem Asch was standing before the microphone. "His silvery grey hair and his dominating personality attracted everybody's attention." Asch's speech moves the audience and the whole gathering cheers: The evil of fiery hatred has kept us divided, but the happy moments of brotherly understanding and love are here again, and we say to you "Acheinu Atem"—you are our brothers.

Performer Eddie Cantor also spoke: "Before I became Eddie Cantor, I was called Itzik Cantor. And tonight, seeing the huge crowd that came to pay tribute to Itzik Feffer, I hereby give you notice, that from tomorrow morning on, I am to be called Itzik Cantor again." Rabbi Luckstein said, "You heard the delegation representing Jews without 'Yarmelkes.' I am here to greet them in the name of the Jews with 'Yarmelkes'."

Lipshitz reports that "In the most beautiful Yiddish, Itzik Feffer gave an inspiring speech, greeting the American Jews, hailing the achieved unity and promising the people that just as Hitler could not take Moscow and Leningrad, just as he could not take Stalingrad, so he would never be able to fulfill his promise to destroy the Jewish people." At the end of his speech, Feffer read his "magnificent" poem: "My vineyards will yet grow beautiful. Of my fate I will be my own master, on Hitler's grave I shall dance. I am a Jew."[77]

The JAFC also travelled to Montreal and Toronto, accompanied by Sholem Asch. In Montreal, Sholem Shtern, a poet, writer, frequent contributor to *Der Kamf*, and director of the Winchevsky shule in Montreal, was one of the organizers. Years later, he described overhearing Sholem Asch's conversation with Itzik Feffer in an elevator just before the mass meeting in the Montreal Forum: "Oy, Itzikl—they will punish you! They will punish you for the poem Ikh Bin a Yid [I am a Jew]." Feffer laughed: "Sholem Asch, you are a great writer and know that we are not punished."

Shtern described his troubling interaction with Feffer in the corridor that same day: "I would like to know why you didn't stand up for Izzy Kharik?" (Kharik was a Soviet Yiddish poet who was murdered by Stalin in 1937.)[78] Feffer became pale and whispered these words: "A fire was burning around him and I did what I could. Did you want that I myself should jump into the fire?"[79] Shtern writes that he didn't let up: "Feffer, it was printed in the Yiddish and non Jewish press here that Tsinberg was arrested. Why? Can you explain?" His [Feffer's] voice trembles, the words were quiet and secretive—"it is a misunderstanding. I assure you, he will be released shortly."[80] These disturbing recollections, written years after Mikhoels and Feffer were murdered by Stalin, raise questions. If Shtern suspected something was amiss in the late 1930s and early 1940s, who else on the left was questioning what Stalin was doing at the time?

The events in Montreal's Forum and Toronto's Maple Leaf Gardens were packed with Jews and non-Jews. And, as in New York, the events were profoundly moving. Shtern remembered Sholem Asch's speech in Montreal: "his voice full of tears, trembling, and the dread went deep into the heart.... [He] spoke for about ten minutes. He sat down, tears running down his face, and he murmured, 'Woe is me, what will happen to my Jews?'"[81] In Toronto, Lieutenant Governor Albert Mathews was one of the honorary patrons.

For the first time in its history, the coalition supporting the visit of the Jewish Anti-Fascist Committee included the Canadian Jewish Congress, which was a co-sponsor. Ben Lappin, a Zionist and employee of the CJC, recalled that "the summer of 1943 was no time to cast aspersions on the Soviet Union."[82] As Zilbert, a leftist described by Lappin as a left-wing thorn in the side of the Farband Labour Zionists and the Workmen's Circle, said to Lappin, "Supposing they are Communists? Nu, is it so terrible? Is Shlomo Mikhoels a bank robber or a great Jewish actor? Is Itzik Feffer a murderer or a first-class writer, a poet?"[83]

Maple Leaf Gardens, the largest hall in Toronto, was filled for the occasion on September 9, 1943 and Lipshitz described how "one important dignitary after another got up to greet the guests and the Jewish Community in the name of the city, the provincial government, the churches, the armed forces, the labour unions and so forth." For the UJPO, this event was important, because the visit of the JAFC presented "living proof of a flourishing Jewish life in the Soviet Union." The contact that the Labour League and its counterparts had with Mikhoels and Feffer became imprinted on the hearts of all who were part of the left. (It also made very personal Stalin's later betrayal of these men.) Lipshitz reported:

Itzik Feffer in Toronto, 1943.
York University Libraries, Clara Thomas Archives & Special Collections, Sam and Manya Lipshitz fonds, C1 FO444.

> Itsik Feffer got up to speak … and when his energetic voice came calling out over the loudspeakers, "Brider, Yidn fun Canada, zayt bagrist" (Brothers, Jews of Canada be greeted), the audience rose as though sprung from their seats. They came back with a stupendous roar, which reverberated through the arena and went on and on for what seemed like an eternity.[84]

Mikhoels spoke about what he had seen. Lipshitz said, "His bizarre glowing face and his hissing voice gave him the ominous appearance of a prophet bringing the frightful story of a people's doom."[85] Mikhoels chided the audience for expressing only token concern for what was happening in Europe: "you are not doing enough to save our sisters and brothers. You eat chickens and shed tears."

For those in the Jewish community in Canada, and particularly for the left Jewish community, many of whom were born in Eastern Europe, the Second World War was a deeply personal tragedy. Despite the ban on Jewish immigration in 1937—the period of "none is too many"—Brenda Fishauf had managed to get papers to come to Canada through her aunt who had a friend in parliament.[86]

Brenda's experiences illustrate the anguish people faced. Born in Staszow, Poland, she and her beloved, Dov, had lived together in Lodz, but she could not find work and so they returned to Staszow. When Brenda left for Canada, she and Dov hoped soon to be reunited, but war broke out in 1939. She received

Brenda Fishauf (1914–2015) and her friends, Staszow, 1926. First row (right to left) Brenda (Brayndl Diamond) Fishauf, Khaye Wagner; middle row, Alte Goldberg, ?, Bayltshe Kestenberg; top row, Bina Segal, Malke Vitenberg. This is the only picture Brenda had of her friends from her life in prewar Poland. She described what happened to each of them during the Holocaust when most of the Jews in Staszow perished. Bayltshe kept a store for her parents. During the war, a Pole took the money she gave him to hide her, but he killed her. Bina sold eggs and salt in her parents' store and so had contact with Poles. She arranged to hide in a bunker under a Polish woman's floor. One of the women in the bunker became pregnant and had to give the baby to the Polish woman, who strangled the child. Alte Goldberg lived in a bunker with 14–15 people during the war and made it through the war. Malke also survived. She had returned to Staszow from Lodz during the war with her child. She was able to give the baby to a Polish family, but Malke was sent to Auschwitz. A guard in the camp would walk outside each day. She watched, and when he went out, she grabbed his coat from the hook, put it on, and walked out. She found her child and was taken in by a Polish family she knew from school along with two other girls.

Photo and recollections courtesy of Brenda Diamond Fishauf.

a postcard from him, written before the war. He wanted to go to Russia because his two brothers were there. Brenda responded, "You should see to stay alive." Dov thought that perhaps he could get away from Nazi-occupied Poland by going east, through Iran to Palestine, the route taken by the Polish army. Some seventy years later, Brenda cannot forget how she felt: "I still remember that day, 1939. I heard on the radio: Warsaw was bombed.... I heard this and I was distraught."

Brenda wanted to return to Poland, but that was impossible because there was no transportation. It took her until 1942 to become a citizen and get a passport. The very next day, she enlisted in the army and volunteered to go to England and work as a seamstress. She kept trying to get to Poland, but the answer was always the same: "No we cannot do it. It's a war zone, we can't do it." At the end of the war, she again tried to connect with Dov through the Canadian Red Cross, the English Red Cross, and the Swiss Red Cross. She said, "After the war, the Canadian Jewish Congress in Toronto had lists of survivors. I went there every day to find out if someone survived. That's the story. Nobody knows.... I can't talk about it. When I see people talking about what happened, I live through it again."[87]

In early 1945, the Red Army entered Warsaw. It was clear that Hitler would be defeated. The victories of the

Red Army came at a huge cost—in the twenty-three days following their entry into Warsaw, the Red Army suffered 194,000 casualties. Almost nine million Russian soldiers were declared dead or missing between 1939 and 1945. The Nazi siege of Leningrad lasted 872 days. Nearly one-third of the population in that city starved to death.[88]

The Jewish community supported the war effort in every way they could. In February 1944, the Jewish People's Committee, headed by Fred Donner, a left Jewish activist in Winnipeg, donated $2200 to the Department of National Defence for the purchase of an ambulance. In February 1945, as the war was drawing to a close, the small Jewish community of Winnipeg held a fundraiser. They wrote messages in "Dos Goldener Bukh" (the Golden Book) to present to the "Heldisher felker in Sovietn–Farband" (the heroic peoples of the Soviet Union). The Mayor of Winnipeg and the Premier of Manitoba signed the book. Premier Garson expressed "profound appreciation to the wise statecraft of Soviet leaders, the skill and judgment of Russian generals and the unexcelled valour of Russian soldiers and people." The book was signed by another four hundred people, and one can read the heartbreak in many of the entries. Written in Yiddish, Russian, and English, people congratulated and thanked the Red Army and the Russian people for defeating fascism. But then many of them asked about missing friends and relatives. Here is an example written in Yiddish:

> A heartfelt greeting to the Red Army and to All Soviet peoples. I, Yetta Furman (my maiden name is Ayesha Heshl Munstshnik) from Kudnia near Berditchev and Zhitomir. I am looking for my three brothers and sister Yankl, Chayim and Pinye Munstshik and Menstiya Munstshnik. The brothers lived in Zhitomir, the sister in Koretin, I am also looking for my husband's six sisters and their old mother from Zhitomir.
>
> Mrs. Furman, 477 Dufferin Winnipeg.[89]

Poland after the War

Sam Lipshitz was the chair of the Council of Progressive Jewish Organizations, which included all the left Jewish organizations in the country. He was a founder of the Labour Progressive Party, which the Canadian Communist Party was called in 1945. Through Lipshitz's CP connections, he learned that the officials of the Polish ministry representing the Central Committee of Jews in Poland were travelling to New York and would be willing to facilitate a delegation of

Canadian Jews to Poland. The Canadian Jewish Congress agreed to sponsor such a delegation. H. M. Caiserman would go, representing the CJC. Sam Lipshitz was the other member of the delegation, which was endorsed by twenty-five Jewish organizations. They arrived in Warsaw in December 1945.

Lipshitz and Caiserman were the first Jewish delegation from North America to visit Poland after the war and what they found was "indescribable." Out of a prewar population of 3.3 million Jews in Poland, approximately sixty-five thousand were in Poland in early 1945. For a full week in Warsaw, they did not meet one Jewish child. When people met, they didn't say "How do you do" but "Who survived in your family?" Some survivors who had fled to Russia were expected to return.

Lipshitz lost his entire family from Radom, Poland. Out of seventy family members, only one uncle survived. His mother, a witness told him, was shot. His father, older sister, younger sister, nephew, brothers-in-law—all were killed. His uncle had a skilled trade of some sort and had a labour permit, which is how he survived. He had managed to obtain a permit for his younger sister, a very talented young woman of twenty-two, but the Germans came and took her away before he managed to get it to her.[90]

The reality of the situation facing the Jews in Poland was devastating. Lipshitz wrote several letters from Warsaw to his wife, Manya.[91]

> Warsaw, Dec.25
>
> My dear Manya,
>
> …One has to be here in the country to understand how little we in Canada know about Europe and about Poland. The tragedy of the Jews is indescribable. Whatever we read is nothing compared to what one learns here. The destruction of Warsaw is so big that it surpasses human imagination. House upon house are destroyed. The great wonder is, how people live here, and so many people. But however destroyed Warsaw is, it is nothing compared to the destruction of the ghetto. An enormous grave. Mountains upon mountains of bricks under which tens of thousands of people lay buried who didn't manage to save themselves from burning houses. But maybe those people were the happy ones because those who saved themselves were later tortured and burnt in Majdanek or in Treblinka.
>
> I can write and write for days and still it will all remain to be told. I spoke to a Jewish captain of the Red Army and this alone was a great and unforgettable experience. I spoke to a girl who was thrown alive to a "sewer" in

the Warsaw ghetto and she saved herself. She was caught again and sent to Oswiecim [Auschwitz] where she spent three years. I spoke with a man who, for three months, was hiding in the swamps, where a human foot had never stepped before. I spoke to a mother whose child was taken to a crematorium in front of her own eyes and the child begged the Nazis that the meal that they gave him before burning they should give to his elder brother whom they let live. I spoke to a person who was bricked into the wall for two years. I saw an 11-year-old girl who together with her mother hid in a grave at the Jewish cemetery for two years and survived, but her legs are thin as sticks. But the girl has a terrific talent. The world will soon hear about her. So many experiences and such stories that my blood becomes frozen in the veins.

On the other hand, I was in the children's home in Otwock where 120 children—complete orphans—are being brought up in a wonderful way. It is easy to be moved in Poland. But in Otwock I cried for the first time, cried from joy and sorrow. I was in a nursery and saw a child of 20 months who was born in a forest among the partisans. The mother lay down on the bare ground, a German tank drove over her. The woman was killed but the child survived, saved by the partisans and now is being raised in the Jewish nursery in Otwock. I was in a children's sanatorium and heard a cry about lack of money for the holy work that they are doing and I was very ashamed. How we American and Canadian Jews sin against the remnants of tired, hungry, exhausted and crying Jews in Poland.

I miss the children a lot. I hope that they feel well and that everything is Okay.

Be well and give my heartfelt regards to all our comrades and friends. Tell them I am looking forward to the moment when we will see each other. Kiss the children from me and stay well and strong.
Your Sam

During this period, with the wounds so fresh, both Lipshitz and Caiserman saw all Germans as the enemy.

Wroclaw (Breslau), New Year's evening [December 31, 1945]

My dear Manya,
I am writing this letter to you on New Year's eve sitting in a hotel in Wroclaw (formerly the German Breslau). A year ago the "Herrenvolk" here were still in

command and now they are so willing and obedient, as if they weren't guilty in the slightest. When one is in Poland for three weeks, one begins to understand a little the full nature of the Nazi atrocity, the terrible inhumanity of the Germans—all Germans…. People here are very worried whether or not we are too soft on the Germans. Our popularity is not very large among the people who survived the years of Nazi-horror and they hear that we are already starting to demand justice for the Nazis…

The Jews here need massive material help and fast! All who survived expect that if they survived Hitler, they will be received like heroes—as they deserve it. Their disappointment with what they consider an indifferent world Jewry, is in a certain measure not less than the suffering they already went through!

Where does one garner strength in order to hear about so many troubles? Where does one get enough understanding to prove to people what they need so much? On the one hand, where did so much authority come from in the world, and on the other, so much resistance!

Caiserman too was horrified:

What the German Nazi beasts, the Polish Nazi helpers, the Ukrainian Nazi killers and the miserable Lithuanian blood hounds have done to our children, to our little girls of seven and eight years, to our women, to our intelligentsia and the most spiritual leaders of our people in Poland, you might commence to understand the real catastrophe, the true defeat, the true physical torture and liquidation of our people with gas and fire.[92]

Both Lipshitz and Caiserman were impressed with the organization of Polish Jewry so soon after the war that was recognized and partially subsidized by the Polish government. They found rampant anti-Semitism, but also a Polish government committed to eliminating it. The Central Jewish Committee of Polish Jewry consisted of the spectrum of existing Jewish political parties, including the communists, the labour Zionists, the Bund and the partisans. They were operating children's homes, schools, hospitals, shops, cooperatives, and farms. Rabbi Kahane, who represented Orthodoxy, was not part of the Central Committee. However, the Orthodox Jews requested and obtained the same recognition for their religion as Protestants and Catholics, and they organized the Central Religious Committee of Poland.

Jewish children in postwar Poland, under the care of orphanages of the Central Committee of Polish Jews. People viewing the picture are asked to help identify the children.

Children summer camp in Dzierzoniow, ZIH-ZWP-0140 Jewish Historical Institute Collection. Courtesy of the Jewish Historical Institute, Warsaw, Poland.

In his report to the Canadian Jewish Congress, Caiserman indicated that Polish Jewry were disappointed, "convinced that we did not do everything that could have been done to rescue Polish Jewry, insulted by the shipments of used clothing." He then defended the Joint Distribution Committee and its leader against accusations such as the one from the Polish Kattowitz Voyewodisher Yiddisher Comitet (Committee). The Comitet asked the Joint Distribution Committee of North America to "deliver a curse of the Jews on the American continent" for underestimating the woe of Polish Jewry. The Kattowitz Comitet said that it was not charity that was required for the "half naked, broken, and sick Jews returning from Russia, but assistance in becoming productive."[93]

Anti-Semitism had become a crime in Poland, but Caiserman maintained that the "Polish nation is against Jews."[94] In Lodz, the Central Committee told the American and Canadian delegation a similar story: "We will not beg from the Joint [Distribution Committee].... We must maintain with dignity the relief needs of Polish Jewry." Mr. Shaftel from the Labour Zionists in Lodz reiterated the need to "not make of Polish Jews schnorrers" (beggars) and to enable the Central Committee to teach a profession to all those who wanted to stay or leave.

Not surprisingly, the solutions proposed by Caiserman and Lipshitz reflected their ideological leanings. Caiserman, a Zionist, thought that the anti-Semitism was so strong that there could be no future for Jews in their homeland, Poland.[95] Lipshitz, a communist, looked at the strong measures of support the government was taking and felt that it was possible to rebuild Jewish life there, a position supported by the Bund and the PPR (Jewish communist group) in Poland.

On their return to Canada, both Lipshitz and Caiserman were invited to speak about what they had seen. Their public accounts diverged so much that it seemed impossible they were together on the same trip. In a Canadian Broadcasting Corporation (CBC) speech, Caiserman declared how grateful the Polish Jews were for all the assistance the Joint Distribution Committee had offered. Caiserman travelled throughout the country, funded by the Canadian Jewish Congress. When Fred Donner of Winnipeg wrote to CJC Executive Director Saul Hayes to ask that Lipshitz's trip to Winnipeg also be funded, Hayes responded that he was "shocked" that such a request should even be made. This marked the beginning of the end of the short-lived honeymoon between the Canadian Jewish Congress and the progressive Jewish left.

By the late 1940s and the beginning of the Cold War, the Soviet Union once more became the enemy. The Canadian Jewish Congress joined the North American bandwagon of isolating the left, in the process disregarding civil liberties in Canada. The cost they paid to continue the sha shtil policy (literally silence or don't upset the authorities) was silence regarding the rearmament of Germany and the welcome given to known Nazis by the Canadian government.

5 ARBETER FROYEN VAKHT OYF (WORKING WOMEN AWAKE!)

The Jewish Women's Labour League
and Women Activists

Women in the secular Jewish left were involved in labour struggles and anti-fascist mobilizations alongside the men and threw themselves into the work and concerns of the larger Jewish secular left organizations. But they also maintained a separate women's organization in the 1920s—the Jewish Women's Labour League (Yiddishe Arbeter Froyen Fareyn)—and participated in broad mobilizations involving women from many different groups.

The Jewish Women's Labour League organized summer camps for children, which the women considered one of their major achievements. This chapter details the challenges they faced in establishing the camps in Toronto and Montreal in the 1920s. (The growth and popularity of the summer camps and their impact are taken up in chapter 9.) The varied nature of their activities illustrates the connections the left Jewish women made between waged work, domestic life, and national and international political struggles—although the women themselves did not describe their activities in this way.

The radical ideas of the Bolshevik revolution resonated for the women of the Jewish Women's Labour League, particularly in the 1920s.[1] The Soviet Union in the early years promised women a great deal. Equality before the law, civil marriage, legalization of abortions, the abolition of the category of "illegitimate children," and divorce were some of the changes legislated in the aftermath of the revolution. The civil war in the Soviet Union was a time of great scarcity, homelessness, and famine, and millions of children were orphaned in the upheavals of the First World War. Communal domestic work, communal kitchens, and nurseries were instituted as a matter of necessity. The Zhenotdel (women's commission) set up by the Bolsheviks in 1919 originally under Alexandra Kollantai's leadership was devoted to organizing and encouraging the activities of revolutionary women. Kollontai wrote,

> You are young, you love each other. Everyone has the right to happiness. Therefore live your life. Do not flee happiness. Do not fear marriage, even though under capitalism marriage was truly a chain of sorrow. Do not be afraid of having children. Society needs more workers and rejoices at the birth of every child. You do not have to worry about the future of your child; your child will know neither hunger nor cold.[2]

At first, the Jewish women were part of the Jewish Mutual Aid League (Yiddisher hilfs fareyn), which worked to provide relief to the many orphans left destitute by the chaos of the revolution. But the women wanted to be more than an auxiliary of the men; they wanted a broader scope for their activities. Their independent organization, the Yiddishe Arbeter Froyen Fareyn, although affiliated with the communist-led women's labour leagues in other ethnic communities, functioned autonomously.[3]

The Arbeter Ring, although theoretically committed to gender equality, in practice had not been a welcoming place for women.[4] The left was no different. The women needed an organization of their own. The Jewish Women's Labour League provided a place where respect for learning and culture and opportunities for personal growth merged with support for left-wing causes and labour struggles. It combined self-education, singing in choirs, playing in a mandolin orchestra, lectures, organizing a children's camp, fundraising "bazaars" and picket line support. These women were committed to class-conscious activism and used their positions as workers and mothers to revolutionize and transform an understanding of what those two responsibilities involved.

Under Nadezhda Krupskaya's (Lenin's wife) leadership, women were encouraged to become agents for the revolution, with a special emphasis on the welfare of women and children. The program of the Zhenotdel (women's section) headed by Alexandra Kollontai was nothing less than the transformation of the nature and structure of daily life (byt) through socialization of the domestic sphere. The idea was that laundries, dining halls, co-operatives, and daycare centres staffed by paid workers would replace the family, which would gradually "wither away." Partners would be based on choice, not economic dependence. As historian Wendy Goldman puts it,

> the Zhenotdel aimed to change the way women and men lived their lives, organized their families, cared for their children and divided power in every institution from the village to the state. The vision encompassed a complete reconfiguration of family life in every way.[5]

Throughout the 1920s, the Zhenotdel struggled against great odds to implement these revolutionary aims.[6]

The Communist International or Comintern, which was also established in that period, exerted great influence over communist organizations around the world. Internationally, the Comintern established a women's secretariat in 1920 under the leadership of Klara Zetkin. Zetkin was a German Marxist who launched the first International Women's Day in 1910. She was a member of the Comintern Executive until 1933.

Der Kamf and "Di Arbeter Froy": The Woman Worker

In Canada, the new Soviet regime's emphasis on women's issues was reflected in articles in the Canadian Yiddish newspaper, *Der Kamf*. During the 1920s, a special column on the woman worker, "Di Arbeter Froy," was a regular feature. Women's concerns were addressed in every issue of the paper in the 1920s, in articles that were often authored by members of the Jewish Women's Labour League. While some articles in *Der Kamf* were devoted to the praise of the situation for women in the USSR, most dealt with the challenges for women and the vision of women's equality in Canada.

In her autobiography, *Mayn Lebns Veg* (My Life's Path), Rokhl (Rachel) Holtman described her life in Minneapolis, where the men were engaged with political and social questions while the women remained focused on housework, baking "tortes" and organizing parties, a life Holtman found boring. But then, in 1916, Alexandra Kollontai arrived in Minneapolis on a speaking tour of the United States. Kollontai impressed Holtman, not just with her speeches, but also with her appearance. She was beautiful: a tall, tastefully dressed, slender woman with a very expressive face.[7] She spoke Russian, German, French, Finnish, and some English. Kollontai told Holtman about Klara Zetkin, whom she adored, and foresaw the important role Lenin would play in the future. Meeting Kollontai had a huge impact on Holtman. By 1926, Holtman was contributing to *Der Kamf*. Following the ideas of Kollontai, Holtman wrote about how to ease the burden of the woman worker. For Holtman, the solution lay in industrializing housework. Her ideal was to transform the essence of the bourgeois home, where women were expected to create a "haven in a heartless world" for their men, and make it a haven for both women and men.[8] She argued that if the home were to be a place of rest, relaxation, and comfort, the work of women must be lightened by the use of technology and collectivizing activities. She said that, "when weaving, spinning, sewing, baking and brewing were removed from the home, it did not destroy the soul of the home." What remained was cooking, cleaning, washing, and ironing, but "an oven and washing basin is no more vital to a familial happiness than the spinning wheel and weaving stool. And use of machines will lighten the burden of cleaning."[9]

Holtman did not argue for a redivision of responsibilities between men and women. Rather, women's collective effort would make their work much lighter: fifty women in a block prepare fifty breakfasts and lunches and clean fifty kitchens. Five women could do all the cooking and cleaning in one big central kitchen equipped with every kind of machine. "Cooking would be done by professionals with love and commitment to their work, and should be as respected as the work of physicians." With the help of a vacuum cleaner, the task that takes the housewife most of a day will be accomplished in an hour. "Instead of her not having a minute to herself, particularly when there are children, the promise is of a home that is a healthy, friendly, comfortable place for physical and spiritual rest and joy where all will be free to enjoy themselves with their loved ones."[10]

For Rae Watson, one of the founders of Yiddishe Arbeter Froyen Fareyn, the Soviet Union was a "symbolic land where a new life has begun for the working women," whereas in capitalist countries, "the woman is a mother, a cook, an economist, a wage earner, and often a social activist."[11] Watson praised the Soviet Union's abolition of the private system of cooking, washing, ironing, sewing, and child care for many women and its substitution with communal facilities: "The woman in Russia is not burdened with all the problems together: the house, the children, earning a living and social activities. It doesn't trouble her where to leave children."[12]

Watson proposed that a woman had a right to wage labour and to live on her own without a husband "if she wishes to work to ease the economic situation of the family, or if she wants to be economically independent, and eliminate the common complaint, who is the most important member of the family. Or if she wishes to altogether leave her man and live separately."[13] She argued that a woman's economic dependence on a man leads to a situation where "disputes are a frequent guest" exacerbated by the constant stress of making ends meet. She writes: "The man by nature is a bigger egoist and will, at every opportunity, make the woman feel that he puts her on her feet, she is lucky that he supports her and the children (of course)!"[14]

The language is different, but the ideas prefigured those of 1970s feminists who stressed the dangers of women's economic dependence.[15] In the 1920s, women took on wage labour because they had to; the labour-intensive work of maintaining a home made having two sets of responsibilities, home and waged work, very difficult. A position that promoted women's right to work was radical indeed. Unlike many of the 1970s feminists who saw paid work in itself as liberating, the women writing in *Der Kamf* understood that waged work was done under terribly exploitative conditions.

In 1928, and again in 1933 and later these women organized housewives' meat boycotts against rising food prices, in my mind making the links between production and consumption. However, Watson did not see it that way. She echoed Marx in her view that only waged labour is productive. There is not a hint of the later domestic labour debates of the 1970s and 1980s where feminists theorized the linkage between housework and waged work and argued about extending Marx's notion of productive labour to include reproductive work and household maintenance.[16] Watson wrote: "The work in the house is not productive, not visible—so the housewife is simply put, a parasite."[17] She also implies that collectivizing childcare is more than a nice idea—it is necessary if women are to get out of the house and enjoy some independence:

> If a woman wants to go to work to escape from her bondage, but how? Should she leave her children in bourgeois philanthropic nurseries? Aside from their religious instruction, they won't take children with two living parents and even then there is a big complicated history with invasive investigations that any radical person must reject.[18]

Men are left off the hook—technological development, along with women's collective efforts, was the solution to all kinds of difficulties, including women's oppression.[19]

In the early 1920s, before the split in the Workmen's Circle, Rokhl (Rachel) Holtman was known in Arbeter Ring circles as the author of the women's column in the Workmen's Circle newspaper, *Der Fraynd* (The Friend). She emphasized that the plight of the working woman would only be improved through class-based politics and solidarity. Suffrage, she argued, had done little for women of the working class. She said that women must not waste their time in social clubs, "where one spends one's time with a little glass of tea, a little packet of playing cards and occasionally reads a paper about a literary or political question."[20] Holtman's experiences confirmed her view that working women needed to act on the big issues they faced and to reject trivial diversions.

A woman's right to choose was also discussed in these articles in 1926, although most on-the-ground activism tended to be on union picket lines, rather than support for reproductive choice. F. Frumes describes how in Toronto a doctor was jailed for six years, his assistant for four, for performing an abortion where the woman died. Frumes writes:

> Whose business is it that a woman doesn't want children? Who cares that a woman wants a certain number of children and not be a child bearing machine her entire life? The hypocrisy of a system which prohibits the dispensation of birth control information and allows thousands of women to die each year is contemptible.[21]

Not all women suffer equally, however. In the author's view, the rich, who don't need reproductive information as much as the poor, get what they need because they can pay. It is poor women, working in factories and unable to support large families, who are the ones who become pregnant, who are forced to go to doctors who are profiting from an illegal livelihood. Frumes notes in her article that although some capitalist countries, such as Holland, allowed birth control information, the only place abortions were free was the Soviet Union.[22]

Women's appearance was also important. Women with revolutionary views were urged to dress the part, demonstrating their freedom from the constraints of capitalist society by literally wearing their politics.[23] Rae Watson in *Der Kamf* addressed whether women should use makeup. A friend tells her she would look better if she applied a little powder. Watson's response is that "anything that

Women's
Gymnastics,
Workers' Sport
Association.
Alleyway,
Alhambra Hall,
450 Spadina,
1925–26.
Women's
activism
encompassed
sports as well
as politics.
Alhambra
Hall was the
gathering place
of the left. From
left to right:
Fanny Zuckert
Kalinsky, ?, ?,
Sonya Layefsky
Hershman on
bars, Albert
Goldfile, ?, Lil
Carson, Gertie
(Mintz) Radin,
Vera Radin.

*Archives of Ontario,
F1405 23-113, #236.*

is not healthy, necessary or natural is to be put aside. Communist women are obliged to get rid of such things." Her friend asks, "Do you think that in the future, women will not use any powder?" Watson answers that "using makeup is for aristocrats: their face is a mirror of their life: fancy, made up and not natural. But for a working woman, particularly for a radical revolutionary, powder is a sign of being backward." She adds, in sentiments illustrating the limitations of a European Western gaze that we would now consider quite unacceptable, "What's the difference between these women and primitive tribes enslaved by nose rings, earrings and other absurdities?"[24] Given the definitely unladylike actions of these militant women, one can interpret this ideological rigour as a determined effort to proclaim defiance of middle-class norms of respectable femininity.

Comments from personal interviews confirm that radical women were indeed meant to look a certain way. Sam Kagan, who became a member of the Komsomol (Young Communist League) just after the revolution in his home shtetl in Russia, was asked by his interviewer Karen Levine if other members of his family also became Komsomol members. Reflecting some sixty years later on what he sees as his failing, he tells the interviewer that his sister wanted to join, but wearing lipstick disqualified her:

> Mostly, it was my own fault—I didn't feel that she was a suitable person to be in the YCL [Young Communist League]. We figured that it was an honor, and we noticed one day that she had put lipstick on! That was taboo! She was a beautiful girl, and was flirting, and that was not for the YCL! … It was decided that she was not the right sort of material.[25]

Kagan ruefully acknowledged that these absolutist views about appearance were problematic. Bess Schockett of Montreal also recalled the uniform of the communist women:

> My brother used to get together with what they called cells, and the girls who came in, because they belonged to the Party, didn't dress up. They wore straight hair, and didn't wear make-up. They wore a brown leather jacket that came just to the waist. Pants weren't worn at the time—so you wore a straight skirt…. My brother had about four or five women who were part of his cell, and they all looked the same.[26]

Bess, who was twelve at the time she was describing, said, "it was not for me—I was looking forward to the day that I could put lipstick on and have a perm! Not for me!"[27]

Socialist and Feminist?

I would characterize many of these articles from the 1920s as "feminist" because on issues such as reproductive choice, reorganization of domestic work, and prostitution these women were arguing for positions commonly thought of as developed by the women's movement of the 1970s. The history of women's rights advocacy predates the activists of the 1960s and 1970s, many of whom did not realize they had predecessors.

At the time, these women would have considered being called a feminist an insult—it was a bourgeois term, and they were revolutionary women.[28] They believed that formal legal equality wouldn't provide much help to working women in a capitalist society. However, their commitment to class-conscious activism led to an erosion of gender boundaries. Picketing and going to jail did not exactly represent proper "lady-like" behaviour. Political ideals, gender, ethnicity, and class all came together in the goals of their organization. Suffrage and participation in the political system were insufficient, these women maintained; they wanted a proletarian revolution and a socialist society like the one they believed existed in the Soviet Union. Radical women in other ethnic communities, such as the Italian anarchist women described by Jennifer Guglielmo, also criticized bourgeois women for contributing to their exploitation as working women.[29]

Feminist historians have reminded us that what we think of as socialist feminism of the late 1960s and early 1970s had its origins in an earlier period. Annelise Orleck, Jennifer Guglielmo, Julie Guard, and Joan Sangster are some of the women who have examined earlier forms of women's militancy. In *Red Feminism*, Kate Weigand argued that there is a generational connection between American communist women activists of the 1940s and 1950s and the later feminist movement.[30] Yet the work of Orleck on Jewish labour activists in the first decades of the twentieth century, Guglielmo's history of Italian anarchist women in that period, Sangster's research on Canadian communist women in the 1920s, and Julie Guard's work on housewives' mobilization against rising food prices in the 1930s and 1940s in Canada remind us that historians need to look back to see what leftist women were doing in the first decades of the twentieth century. It is in the 1920s that one can see the beginnings of a socialist feminist sensibility that disappeared (or went underground) in the 1930s, a period marked by the narrow "class against class" Communist Party policy. Even in the 1930s, there were high profile women communists such as "Jim" Watts who in their activities and sexual practices challenged any notion of normative behaviour.[31]

Organizing Women

Militant women were a minority even on the left, and it was a challenge for them to organize. Bessie Schachter of Montreal noted the difficulties in organizing women:

> There were the constant pessimistic views of women as backward, assertions that it was not possible to discuss larger social issues with them. It was not easy to build a women's league because of a host of reasons preventing women from being active. But the dedication of a small group of women made this possible.[32]

By the end of 1928, Montreal had around one hundred members, with between forty and fifty attending meetings regularly. Schachter encouraged more contact with the Finnish, Ukrainian, and Russian women's leagues and support for the organizing of women's leagues among English and Francophone women.[33]

As a separate organization, the Yiddishe Arbeter Froyen Fareyn did not have to contend with the predominantly male Labour League.[34] Becky Lapedes recalled that when the women were invited to join the Toronto Labour League after the men formally withdrew from the Workmen's Circle, they remained on their own for a number of years because they wanted to remain autonomous and not be reduced to an auxiliary.[35] As with the Arbeter Ring, the founding members of the Labour League were all men.[36]

Becky Buhay, born in England, was one of only two women, both Jews, in the leadership of the Communist Party.[37] She was a labour organizer and one of the founders of the Labour College in Montreal in 1920.[38] Her articles in *Der Kamf* focused on women, particularly those in waged work.[39] A tireless activist in Toronto, Buhay participated in a successful effort to organize a strike among waitresses and other workers in several hotels to demand a minimum wage for women. In one of the first articles to appear in *Der Kamf* in December 1924, Buhay described a prostitution ring in Montreal. In marked contrast to the suffragettes' concern with protecting the virtue of girls working in factories, she did not speak about "saving" women, but about the economics of prostitution.[40] Buhay noted that the low wages and absence of unions in the textile mills in Quebec make it impossible for young women, 30 percent of Quebec workers, to live on their wages. She wrote that "Between the dark walls of poverty, lurks the curse of prostitution." Prostitution brought in an estimated six million dollars a year, with an estimated three thousand prostitutes in three hundred houses "of ill repute," many of the girls under the age of sixteen. Two hundred to five hundred dollars were paid for each "girl," and the "stock" had to be changed every six months as the "stock" wears out. Buhay connected prostitution and the system that spawns such abuses: "When the system built on profit will be overthrown, human bodies will not be bought and sold, because no one will profit. The overthrow of capitalism means the overthrow of prostitution."[41]

In article after article, Buhay stressed the needs of working women in Canada. She tells us that women made up 22 percent of the workforce in Canada, not including home workers or agricultural workers. In 1919, a prosperous year, women's wages were no more than 55 percent of men's—women earned about nine dollars a week. In Woolworth's and other department stores, women were earning as little as five or six dollars a week.[42]

Faced with the need to alleviate the difficult position of women and the dangerous working conditions, Buhay saw unionization along with support for protective legislation as an important first step in transforming a system.

Only one percent of women were unionized. She called for a forty-four-hour work week and equal pay for equal work. In arguments that were current fifty years later as more and more women took on waged labour, Buhay acknowledged how little unions had offered women and criticized the thinking that women were taking bread out of men's mouths. While the women's movement of the 1970s would stress how women were disadvantaged relative to men, Buhay pointed out that the profit system does not distinguish between women's and men's work, and that women's low wages brought down the entire working class. Unionization was not enough. Buhay urged women to join the (Canadian) Labour Party (the name of the Communist Party at the time) and insist on a raise in the minimum wage, protection for mothers, mothers' pensions, unemployment insurance, and an end to child labour.[43] She concluded: "Neither the boss nor the government will give anything through begging. We must struggle to change things."[44]

While the women of the Jewish Women's Labour League did not succeed in transforming personal and family life in the way Kollontai described, the very act of getting together did change many of the women. Noting the importance of culture as well as politics, the executive of the League described their goal on their fourth anniversary:

> To draw on Jewish working women and elevate them to a higher cultural level and develop their class consciousness.... She [the housewife] cannot and must not remain imprisoned in the four walls of her own kitchen, she must also not be contented with the auxiliaries … where she wastes her energy on trivial "societies," whose main purpose is parties and banquets, and where the richer women have an opportunity to be the leaders and set the tone.[45]

The Jewish Women's Labour League offered lectures, discussions, and study groups: "Our League has in many instances elicited from the members the courage to think independently and to express their ideas. Also the energy to do independent work."[46]

But the gap between membership in the Yiddishe Arbeter Froyen Fareyn and the Party is clear from a report on an International Women's Day event in Montreal in 1930 where the Labour League women were chastised for their insufficient "class consciousness."[47] The event, organized with the Finnish and Ukrainian and English women's leagues and reported in *Der Kamf*, described Becky Buhay's blazing speech.... Herself a Kamf fighter for years, a bold and courageous revolutionary, a talented speaker she stood on the stage like a symbol of the rebelling women.... Mighty rang her voice, which called the women to fight. Full with revolutionary temperament were her movements. So humble, sincere, and deeply penetrating were her words and they inflamed the hearts of the listener. Enthusiastic waves of applause often interrupted her speech. Comrade Buhay scientifically analyzed the situation of global capital and the growing disenchantment with the bourgeois system.[48]

However, it seemed that not all the women were inspired. *Der Kamf* writer B. Berkowitz complained that for the second year in a row, many of the Jewish women left before the speeches were over. Her conclusion? More education was needed to raise the women's level of understanding and increase their class consciousness and commitment.

While many members of the Jewish Women's Labour League could be found on the picket line in support of striking workers in the needle trades, most of the women were unwaged homemakers married to workers. In a 1928 article, Manya Shur, secretary of the Toronto League, indicated that there were seventy Fareyn members. Of these, twelve women were waged workers themselves, while the rest except for three were the wives of workers. The three unspecified were probably wives of professionals or small businessmen. If the Fareyn members' husbands were also activists, as was often the case, the women's activities tended to be strike support through financial contributions, canvassing for Canadian Labour Party candidates in political campaigns, eliciting subscriptions for *Der Kamf*, the *Worker* and *Der Freiheit*, and participating in the actions of the Canadian Labour Defence League. They also supported cultural activities such as the choir and the mandolin orchestra. In 1928, the women had raised money and assembled clothing for the striking coal miners in Nova Scotia and the silk weavers of Passaic, New Jersey, who were primarily Irish. The groups in both Toronto and Montreal also devoted meetings to lectures and discussions "to raise the educational level of our members."

Manya Shur pointed out how women's confidence was increased through involvement in the Leagues: "Women who are embarrassed to put in a word in discussions in other organizations, have learned to speak freely and have become more developed and class conscious."[49] At the conclusion of an article on League activities, Shur addressed herself to the men: "Comrades, you give a great deal of time and energy to the unions and other worker organizations.

Spare a little time for your families." She did not, however, suggest that the men actually help their wives and take on childcare responsibilities. Rather, she urged the men to get their children to become young pioneers and their wives to join the League so that they would be "not just good housewives, but comrades."[50] Some of the women, like Rae Watson and Becky Lapedes, activists in the Toronto Yiddishe Arbeter Froyen Fareyn, were "farbrente communistn" (burning or fervent communists). Becky even left one man for another because the first was not revolutionary enough for her.

Even if a woman wanted to be a good "comrade," men's activities took precedence and the time-consuming nature of family responsibilities made it difficult. There is often a chasm between the Jewish left's theories of women's equality and their actual practice. One letter in *Der Kamf*, written in 1926, was called "A grievance from a woman worker." The writer described her conversation with a friend whose husband "Harry" was active in the movement and was away many nights of the week at meetings. Although she wished that he would spend a little more time with the children, she understands why he is away so much. But she too is interested in the issues, although she doesn't have the opportunity that he does to be knowledgeable about them. Sometimes they converse, as comrades and friends. But here is her heartache: she feels that he is teaching her, that his tone is impatient, that of a "higher sort of person who looks down on someone lower than him." He is polite and attempts to listen, but his distracted attention hurts. The writer comments that she understands because she too has often had the same feeling.[51] The man is the one with the time to read newspapers and the freedom to attend meetings. The emphasis on education to improve women's class consciousness is clearly limited by the failure to address a division of labour that imposes serious time constraints on women.

Summer Camps for Children

The workers' children's camps were started by the Jewish Women's Labour League in Toronto in 1925 in Long Branch, and then in 1926 in Rouge Hills and the Laurentians near Montreal two years later. The women said: "We built a proletarian children's camp in order to provide the children of workers a vacation in the fresh air, in a proletarian collective atmosphere."[52] Becky Lapedes was the secretary manager, and her friend, Rae Watson, the director in the first year in Toronto.

As Becky later commented, "it was very idealistic, but it certainly wasn't practical as they had no money." Only about a dozen women were involved in

Rae Watson, an activist in the Jewish Women's Labour League, was the prime mover in organizing the children's camp in 1925.

Ontario Jewish Archives.

organizing the camp, and the Toronto Jewish Women's Labour League had a membership of about thirty. They rented Sam Green's furnished cottage in Long Branch and operated the camp on donated supplies brought from their own homes: pots, silverware, an ice box, and whatever else was needed. All the members committed themselves to two-week work shifts at the camp without pay. They even paid for their own food and charged from $3.50 to $4.00 a week per child according to age. The higher fee was for the older children who, they reasoned, needed more food. The cottage was filled to capacity with eleven children, but then one night Mr. Belfer showed up with his five children because his wife was giving birth to another baby. "We took care of them somehow," Becky recalled.[53]

After the first year, an appeal went out to the left Jewish community describing the camp. The women radicals presented their project as women's work but with a difference. The charity offered by some of the institutions was not what they wanted for their children. Their article published in *Der Kamf* graphically describes why the women undertook such a difficult task. The focus is on the children, rather than on relieving the challenges faced by women for child care in the summer months:

> With little experience and even fewer financial resources or, to put it more accurately, completely without any means, we, the Jewish Women's Labour League, have undertaken the project of a summer camp. No one believed that it was possible, neither our foes, nor our friends who called us dreamers of beautiful fantasies. They didn't believe we could survive for more than one week, and how could we survive without a cent in the treasury and with expenses of $100 a week? We faced unheard-of obstacles, but our courage kept us moving ahead. We borrowed from one place, and paid in the second, and despite the obstacles, we managed to pull through the enormous difficulties of those first few weeks. And now, with the season over, we can say with full understanding, that we managed to carry this undertaking through successfully. The camp served 50 children over the summer, ages ranging from 3 to 15. All of them were happy and satisfied. They had all the

Camp Kindervelt in Rouge Hills, 1927. Sam Chikovsky, kneeling. Kids in barrel: Bessie Chikovsky, Label Temkin, Max Chikovsky. Left to right: Ben Katz, Becky Lapedes, David Marinas, Tillie Chikovsky, Ethel Temkin, Moishe Shifris.

Archives of Ontario, F1405 23-60 image 15.

conveniences—food, games, etc. We also organized a reading circle, concerts, lectures, and other events from the workers' children's world. And so the children were never bored, and also learned something.

Next summer, we hope to expand this undertaking.... We will explore all avenues in order to create a summer home for workers' children so that they don't have to go to the rich charity institutions who with one hand take the skin from our bodies, and with the other throw us a bone and humiliate. But we, class conscious working women, must not and will not take their charity offerings, we throw them back: we will not kiss the whip that lashes us; we will not send our children to them, where they will be trained to be faithful and obedient slaves of capitalism and exploitation. We must raise our children in a free atmosphere. They must know who are their friends and who are their foes. Creating a summer home for children must be the work of the women workers.[54]

In 1926, the women expanded the camp. After much searching, they rented a farm in Rouge Hills north of Toronto that had a stream running through it and bought tents and beds. The farmhouse was too small, and because they charged so little, they ended up with a deficit. They solved this problem by organizing a banquet under the open sky with an appeal for funds. They also hired Goncharov, a director from New York, who had some camping experience. Virtually the entire camp continued to run on the volunteer labour of the women who did what needed to be done, including cooking outdoors on cookers heated with

Becky Lapedes and Ethel Temkin.
Courtesy of Cheryl Tallan.

coal oil, but they faced many challenges. For instance, there were no garbage services, so the men would bring a clean garbage container when they came to help out on weekends, and take away the full one when they left. There was no running water and no electricity, and only a small house that served as the office and the dining room. The children lived in tents put up in a circle around the field and would go down to the river to wash.

The experience of running a camp presented new opportunities, such as learning to hitchhike, for Becky Lapedes and her friend Ethel Temkin. If they ran short of anything, the women would have to go into town to get supplies, but there was no car and no driver during the week. The town was about three miles away and while Becky and Ethel were walking, cars would stop and offer them a lift. Becky described one incident when she and Ethel were hitchhiking without success. A car came along and stopped for them, but there were two men in it and they usually avoided getting into a car with more than one man. But there had been few cars on the road since it was under construction. In Becky's words:

> I look at Ethel and Ethel looks at me. The way we were dressed. We had a suit, a man's suit with a tie with a cap and I say, "We have to go. We can't help it." We got into the car and the man says, "I bet you two girls are Bolsheviks. I bet you have your party cards in your rucksacks." I was always the spokesman. I said, "What of it? This is a free country, what if I do have my party card?"[55]

Perhaps Becky and Ethel's unconventional dress (knickers and caps) and their unconventional activity (hitchhiking) marked them as political radicals. If a woman had the courage to break the gendered rules of proper womanly behaviour, perhaps it was expected that she also held a strong ideological opposition to bourgeois society. In any case, the driver was like-minded. He started telling them about the divide between rich and poor, and how 20 per-cent live at the expense of 80 percent of the people, and how the rich build the nicest schools, which most children can't attend. One of the men was a labour lawyer.[56]

The women ran the camp near Toronto for three years, from 1925 to 1927. It was an exhausting undertaking. Becky says,

"Comradely well wishes to esteemed comrades Pekerov and Drevin who are travelling to the Soviet Union." March, 19, 1929.
UJPO Archives.

> When we came to Rouge Hills [in 1926] we hired a handyman who carried the water—we had a spring there.... Anyway Ethel Temkin and I were papering the kitchen, how I did it I'll never know because I'm not very handy, but we did it.... So I was supposed to be the manager so am I going to tell somebody "go and clean the toilets"? So I did it myself. I used to clean them twice a week with soda—I cleaned the walls, the toilet, the floor.[57]

One wonders if the contradictions between being a communist and ordering someone else to clean the toilets would have been noticed if there had been a man in charge. Given the traditional division of labour in the home, one suspects not, as communist men like most other men, had wives who "naturally" cooked and cleaned for them.

By 1928, the women decided that they needed more resources to run the camp, which had become incredibly popular, and called on the men's organization. Becky Lapedes recalls that the change was not done lightly:

> In 1928 (the 4th year), we invited the Labour League to be a partner. And we were very afraid because our Women's Organization was so kosher, we were so fanatic and at that time Trotskyism raised its head.[58] And we were afraid some of those people were getting influenced....We weren't sure if we could trust the camp, if it wouldn't get into the wrong hands. But we had no alternative. We came with them one year and in 1929 we said, "It's your baby." We helped them just like they helped us. I was a secretary there.[59]

Women finally joined the Labour League in 1932, with the Yiddishe Arbeter Froyen Fareyn becoming Branch 3, the Ella May Wiggins branch, later renamed

Branch 6, Labour League. Branch 6 was the first women's branch in the Labour League. They called themselves the Rosa Luxemburg branch.

Archives of Ontario, 1405 23-113 #237.

in Annie Buller's honour.[60] Another women's branch, the Rosa Luxemburg Branch 6, had joined the Labour League originally as a women's auxiliary. The Gina Medem[61] branch, a new branch associated with the development of a second shule in Toronto, formed in 1936. In Montreal, the names of the women's branches reflected their continued concern with women's particular issues, honouring their heroes. One was called the Klara Zetkin branch and the other the Krupskaya branch.

In the 1930s, "Di Arbeter Froy" (The Woman Worker), the special column devoted to women's issues, disappeared as Communist Party policy abandoned a specific focus on women's struggles. Many of the women's efforts in the Jewish left continued, however. They devoted themselves to support for the shules, the camps (with the men in charge), and general political causes. They were not silent.

In March 1933, the women's branches of the Labour League in Toronto organized a meat strike when the kosher butchers attempted to raise the price of meat from fifteen cents a pound to eighteen cents. They formed a strike committee of fifty and wrote a leaflet. Two hours later, seven hundred women packed Weinberg Hall. They decide to picket the butcher shops, and they were attacked. The newspaper reported "Drunken gorillas attack the women with knives." The response to the hooligans' attack on the women was tremendous. College Street was covered with thousands of strike sympathizers. One week later, the butchers agreed to continue selling meat at fifteen cents a pound. [62] Although official positions promoting a popular front did not become formal policy until a few years later, the boycotters were a women's popular front, encouraging all women to participate in the name of their common interests as housewives.

In the mid-1930s, Canada was in the midst of what has been called the "dirty thirties." The left organizations were growing as many people, in both Canada and the United States, suffering from the ravages of the Depression, were convinced that change was needed. Manya Lipshitz, in an article written in

March 1936, criticized Prime Minister Bennett's cavalier dismissal of women's pleas for jobs with the answer, "Get married!" She commented that this position was not unlike that of Nazi Propaganda Minister Goebbels, who declared in a speech in 1934 that "the main task for women is to marry and birth children who will be needed for the war."

Manya went on to describe the devastating effect of the Depression and its impact on women, in particular.

> In Toronto four thousand houses where working families lived were declared by a special government housing commission to be substandard. In these poor neighbourhoods, the mortality rate amongst children is twice as high as in the better neighbourhoods. A family of five on relief receives up to nine dollars a week at a time when the minimum subsistence for such a family is almost twenty three dollars a week. Forty percent of school age children have physical defects of one type or another....The situation is no better for women who are employed in industry. On average, women's wages are 30–40% smaller than those of men. The minimum wage for women of $12.50 a week is violated each day by the score. In such times, women cannot remain indifferent. On the shoulders of the poor woman lies the crisis with its full hardship. It is the woman who racks her brain to find a way to pay the butcher, the milkman and the grocery man.[63]

With an unresponsive political system, sometimes direct action was necessary. In 1935, Annie Buller was on her way to speak at an election rally where she was running for school board when she was told about a Mrs. Marchand, facing eviction from her apartment at 6 Andrew Avenue. Mrs. Marchand, a sick woman with a weak heart, was lying in bed in an unheated apartment with three children to care for. Annie Buller used "the only means we workers have." She found the unemployed from the ward who surrounded the house with a picket, and then got the bailiff to agree not to accept the order to throw the family out—for now. *Der Kamf* reported, "The house was in a terrible, dilapidated state. The woman gets seven dollars a month for rent from Relief. The boss, however, decided to demand three more dollars a month rent or he will evict the family if they can't pay."[64]

The left Jewish women who remained active in their separate branches of the left organization in Montreal, Toronto, and Winnipeg were underrepresented and their work largely unacknowledged in the general organization. The

May Day march, Winnipeg, 1930s.

Thomas Fisher Rare Book Library, University of Toronto, Kenny Collection, mss 179.

tenth anniversary book of Toronto's Labour League in 1936 celebrated the proud achievement of the purchase of a huge property in Brampton, Ontario for Camp Naivelt. In recounting the history of the camp, J. Cowan, who later became president of the United Jewish People's Order, fails to mention the role of the women in establishing the camp. He writes: "Outstanding among the Canadian camps was the creation by the Labour League in 1925 of Camp Kindervelt on the Rouge River." He got some of the details right, the exhausting work that was involved, but he "forgot" that the camp was organized by the women, it was not a Labour League camp until 1929, and even then, the work continued to be done primarily by women.

Some men noticed. Moyshe Katz addressed the underrepresentation of women in the Labour League on International Women's Day, March 8, 1935:

> Women are marginalized in their rights, not only through laws, but through custom—bad customs in our own organization. We must help women to exercise their full rights.
>
> Women have already come into our organization and into our assemblies. She brings with her the full enthusiasm of a newly freed people, the full sincerity and commitment to the work and to the idea of which only a woman

is capable. But how are women treated in society and in our organizations? As a citizen of a second class. When it comes to a chairperson, the president, the managers, the important committees, to speakers, to proposals, men occupy all the positions, and the women who often feel that they are more practical, more intelligent, better organizers and better speakers stay sitting at the back mute, far from that which takes place at the front. The men speak, the women listen, the men command, the women follow orders, the men make the plans, the women carry them out. This won't do. This is unjust punishment. This robs not only women of their rights, this robs the movement of fresh energy and initiative. This is an injustice to our female members and to the interests of our movement.[65]

Katz concluded his article with a revolutionary proposal: half of all positions should be occupied by women, even if they are inexperienced or hesitant. He argued that they would learn.[66] However, Moyshe Katz's words promoting the equality of women remained just that—words.

Women and the Formation of the United Jewish People's Order

During the war years, women energetically supported the war effort. In Winnipeg, Anne Ross spearheaded support for the Red Cross canvassing of the entire city to raise funds. Anne and her husband Bill Ross, the head of Manitoba's Communist Party, were both members of the first graduating class of the Peretz School in 1925. Anne actively participated in the Housewives Consumers Movement against rising food prices. In 1948, Anne, a nurse, joined the Mount Carmel Clinic, originally organized to provide care for indigent Jews in Winnipeg's North End. She expanded the clinic's services to serve the entire community in Winnipeg's North End.[67]

In Toronto during the Second World War, the Labour League women organized the Women's Armed Forces Relations Club for parents, spouses, and children of soldiers. They sent packages and cigarettes and letters to overseas soldiers. They also held "showers" where they gathered linens and blankets to send to the victims of the siege of Stalingrad. In 1944, the two women's branches in Toronto came together to form a women's division of the Labour League. Their interests were not limited to relief efforts. As the war was drawing to an end, Annie Buller recorded in *Der Vochenblat* the positive changes the war had brought. Thirty-six percent of all waged workers were women, and in 1942, 95 percent were in the

war industries. So as to facilitate women's work, the government had established nurseries and arranged for the provision of warm lunches in schools and parental supervision after school. There was no unemployment. Annie Buller wondered how women could continue to protect their interests, their right to work, and their right to equal pay, and encouraged support for trade unions.[68]

As the war ended, the alliance with the Soviet Union and the activism throughout the war made the left popular. The mood was celebratory, and the left rejoiced. The women's branches of the new national organization, the United Jewish People's Order (UJPO), were growing but were now commonly referred to by branch number rather than the militant women they were originally named after. There is one woman vice president of the City Committee of Toronto, Mary Harris. The souvenir book produced for the first convention does not include even one article devoted to women or written by a woman. The only significant mention of women's issues is in a caption underneath a group photograph. Annie Eizner, chair of the Women's Council in Montreal, cautions vigilance against the forces of reaction and the dangers they pose in the "propaganda deployed to rob women of the positions and rights which they gained in the course of the war."[69]

In the spirit of a principled United Front and in opposition to great pressure to return women to the home, Eizner continued:

We wish to work together with all bodies to hold onto the economic and social status of the women and secure them further. We demand security and equality for women in industry and in social life—more day nurseries, more play spaces for our children and so forth, in order that women can make their fullest contribution to the welfare of healthy and economically secure families as an expression of a true people's democracy.[70]

Annie Eizner's contribution stands out. Her daughter, the artist Olga Eizner Favreau, described her mother as a devoted communist, a lover of Yiddish, an activist in the Jewish left, and a feminist. Annie Eizner was clearly a woman of formidable energy and intelligence.[71] The daughter of Orthodox parents, Annie was born in Eastern Europe into a very poor family of nine children. Her life-long regret was being forced to leave school to work to help support the family after her father died. She was thirteen. Annie arrived in Canada in 1924 as a teenager. Committed to her heritage as a Jew as well as to her revolutionary politics, she managed to feed her family (she did all the cooking), sew clothes, conduct a business at home making brassieres for large-breasted women, and remain politically active.

International Women's Day in 1946 celebrated the war's end and women's contribution. But the pull back had already started—women's wages were cut while the men's had not risen, and there was pressure for the women to give way to the men. The only thing that had risen was the cost of living. Annie Buller was clear: "The women more than ever will have to be on guard and not allow the union busting employers to use them as rivals against the men and against their families."[72]

By 1947, over six hundred of the members of the new national UJPO were women, but their accomplishments still do not seem to be given any special importance. Women continued their prominent role in supporting the shules, campaigning for the Red Cross, and assisting in hospitals, but they remained largely unrecognized and uncelebrated.

In the postwar period, a new note was heard—women's concern for peace, and the call to support the International Democratic Women's Federation—and mobilization extended well beyond the left Jewish women's organization. Although Canada was not represented at the first international conference held in Paris in 1945, UJPO women raised funds to support Dorise Neilsen's participation in the women's conference for peace in Budapest in 1949.

There was a strong women's presence in the youth branches that developed in the new UJPO. In Winnipeg, Toronto, and Montreal women made up over half the membership and were well represented on the executive for the youth division. Six of the thirteen board members representing all the youth branches were women. They remained underrepresented in the national leadership; only three of the executive were women, and only one, Becky Lapedes, was a member of the resident board, representing the women's division, which consisted of all the women's branches. She wrote a column in the 1947 journal celebrating the UJPO convention entitled "The Order's Women Take Their Place." She reviews the women's efforts during wartime and the need to fight against scarcity. The question of building affordable homes was central.[73]

As always, the women were doing double duty. In addition to supporting the general actions along with the men's branches, they were engaged in special women's actions. All the women's branches of the UJPO were encouraged to join the Housewives Consumer Association, fighting to maintain price and rent controls.[74] But the Cold War was beginning. The challenge facing the Canadian government was, as Julie Guard describes, to turn their broad public appeal as "good Canadian citizens" into "dangerous foreign women."[75] Over three hundred women from all over the country formed a delegation to Ottawa in April 1947. Minister of Finance Abbott refused to meet with them, declaring them a Communist Front organization. The women were enraged and decided to meet with the representatives of their ridings. They continued with their work and organized a "Buyer's Resistance Week," protesting high prices. From June 21 to 27, 1947 the housewives urged a boycott of anything not absolutely necessary and asked people to buy as little as possible of what they could not do without.

The Housewives Consumer Association national delegation planned to gather in Ottawa and meet with the representatives of all parties. They linked preserving the wartime alliance between the Western countries and the USSR with the issue of prices. Becky Buhay explained the connection:

> The mothers and women who have lived with the hope that the high prices will fall and that the promises of the politicians for social security will be kept—these women must be made to understand that the foreign policies of St. Laurent, Drew and Coldwell which is harnessed to American imperialism and is now attached to the North American "suicide pact" [NATO] can only end in a catastrophe for Canada. You cannot have both cannons and butter! You cannot prepare a mass-murder and at the same time expect well-being and prosperity.

She encouraged the women's branches of the UJPO to affiliate with the Congress of Canadian Women and join the struggle to prevent yet another war.[76]

Despite the UJPO's difficulties in Quebec under Duplessis, in 1950 the Montreal women organized a new English-speaking branch focusing on women's rights and the general welfare of families. For the fourth national convention of UJPO in 1951, the women planned a special women's panel.

The Women's Legacy

In the 1980s, nearing the end of her active involvement in the left, Becky Lapedes decided that it was time for a woman to be honoured in the fundraising "banquets" regularly organized for male leaders. The UJPO responded by organizing a banquet for her. She graciously thanked the organization for the honour—saying "not that I don't deserve it"—and then several speakers recounted her activist contributions to the organization over six decades. Then the chair of the UJPO, the "infamous" Cowan, who had "forgotten" who had actually organized the children's camp, spoke. His tribute completely ignored Becky's accomplishments, instead recounting her wonderful husband Sam's activities and describing how brave Becky was not to fold up and disappear after Sam died but rather continue "his" work. This was recorded on tape. Cowan probably stands out in his remarkable inability to acknowledge and respect women, but it is clear that male attitudes in the organization die hard.

The housewives were protesting the rise in prices after the war. Avrom's drawing is from a later period, but the issues remained the same. The protests were targeting the middleman, not the farmer.

Courtesy of Anna Yanovsky.

From the interviews carried out with Becky Lapedes by her daughter Cheryl in the 1980s, one gets the impression of a generous, energetic, principled woman. I would consider her a feminist because of how she lived—hitchhiking and jail were only part of it. A self-educated woman, she grew into an independent, courageous, hardworking and caring person who found a husband who respected and supported her, and did not deter her from her independence, even when it included adventures few other women of her time would consider. This included lots of joy.

Many of these women were exceptional, but they lived in exceptional times, and some of the qualities that distinguish them—a love of learning, a dedication to the hard work of contributing to social change, generosity of spirit, a zest for life—shine through. How to recognize these women, and honour their bravery and activism without glorifying them or glossing over their limitations remains a challenge. Too often, one falls into anachronistic critiques based on second wave feminism's contributions to the broadening of the arenas in which to challenge gender inequality. Although some women had husbands who helped out, there is little indication that anyone felt it was a husband's responsibility to share in domestic tasks. A few of these women were interviewed in the 1980s and 1990s when they were elderly. When asked how they viewed the feminist movement and the challenges to having men take on household responsibilities, one said, "If I was younger, I would probably be involved in it."[77]

These women felt that it was in their hands to build the kind of community they wanted to be part of, to live their socialism, to live a rich, full life of song, dance, literature, culture, politics, concern for working people all over the world, and even to contribute to creation of a just world and lasting peace. Some of their most impressive accomplishments come from their activities in women-only organizations, or in the women's branch of the mixed organization. As Lil Milton Robinson of Toronto said of her experience:

> We were busy all the time. We were on the picket lines, we were out on demonstrations, we were part of something that was really very special. It enriched our lives: the choir, the drama group.... I grew up thinking that capitalism was going to crumble any day now. And I was going to push it.[78]

6 DEMOCRACY AND DISSENT

The mainstream Canadian Jewish community's discomfort with the progressive Jewish left has a long history. For them, the left was (and still is) an embarrassment. Left activism has consistently undermined the community's quest for "respectability." The Canadian Jewish Congress, dominated by those committed to a Zionist ideology, experienced the left as challenging their priority of fostering Canadian government support for the establishment of a Jewish state in Palestine. Their decisions also reflected the anti-communist political climate of the 1950s, the period known as McCarthyism in the United States. The chilly weather travelled across borders.

The Canadian Jewish Congress (CJC) expelled the United Jewish People's Order (UJPO) in 1951. All groups affiliated with the Council of Progressive Jewish organizations, in particular the UJPO, the Morris Winchevsky shules, and the Jewish Cultural League were excommunicated (the Hebrew word for excommunication is kherem), no longer to be considered part of the Jewish community. Declaring that the "views and actions of the left-wing oriented group stem out of an ideology rooted outside of Canadian Jewish life," the CJC executive proposed that "eligibility for their election as delegates to the next plenary session be withdrawn from individuals or groups of known left-wing affiliation."[1] In response, UJPO submissions, documents, and analyses argued that a fully functioning democracy could not exist without including dissenting voices.[2] But by bending their own rules and limiting those who could take part in voting, the CJC succeeded in defining left secular Jews' views as illegitimate and external to the Canadian Jewish community.

Especially in the early years of the twentieth century in Canada, hostility toward the new immigrants from Eastern Europe was racially based, and immigrants were often accused of being dangerous, unpatriotic radicals.[3] However, despite the very different views in the Jewish community—religious, anarchist, socialist, Zionist—they managed to work together. When the CJC first organized in 1919, it was a democratic body. It represented a coup for the newly arrived immigrants, who took power from the "uptown Jews," wealthy men, many of Sephardic (southern European) descent, who had arrived in Canada from England in the nineteenth century.[4] The new immigrants were poor, exploited, faced widespread discrimination, and needed to work together to help each other as well as rescue friends and relatives still in Eastern Europe. They wanted an organization that would focus not just on the colonization of Palestine, the major concern of the Federation of Zionist Societies of Canada, but would address itself to the needs of the Jewish community in Canada, organize help for the war-ravaged Jews in Eastern Europe, and support civil and political equality worldwide.[5] The new democratic CJC organization soon dissolved.

From the start, the Canadian Jewish Congress was anti-communist. Despite the evidence that most Jews did not consider themselves secular, much less socialists of any description, Jews were often associated with communism. David Rome, the archivist of the Canadian Jewish Congress, feared that in the eyes of the Canadian public, Jews and communism were synonymous with slogans such as "Jewish blood is oil on the wheels of the revolution."[6] In response, Rome worked hard to make sure that the Jewish community rid itself of all communist associations. Anti-communist rhetoric by the non-communist left, Rome thought, was based on the "awareness of the need to destroy the semantic and political association of the word Jew and communist [which] led even socialist and labor-oriented men in the community into the anti-communist drive."[7] Even the RCMP knew that this connection was false. Their sources indicated that Jews did not dominate the Communist Party of Canada; fewer than 10 percent of the CPC's membership were Jewish.[8] Pro-Soviet positions were equated with Communist Party membership, something the Jewish left organizations consistently denied.

Canada's Cold War and the Canadian Jewish Community

It can be argued that Canada's Cold War began with the Winnipeg General Strike of 1919. At the time, authorities considered all immigrant Jews "dangerous radicals" responsible for any labour unrest. When the leaders of the Winnipeg General strike of 1919 were arrested, *Dos Yiddishe Vort* (The Israelite Press) in Winnipeg noted that Anglo leaders were let out on bail, while the

Ukrainian and Jewish East European immigrants were kept in jail. The newspaper objected to the unfairness. The hostility directed toward "unacceptable" immigrants, they felt, constituted an attack on all Jews.

The Citizen's Committee, together with local Winnipeg newspapers (most of whose employees were out on strike), blamed the strike on "Bolsheviks," "alien scum," and "bohunks." Papers ran cartoons showing bomb-throwing hook-nosed Jews and the *New York Times* ran the headline "Bolshevism Invades Canada." There were two contradictory anti-Semitic allegations: Jews were Bolshevik provocateurs as well as greedy capitalists. An article in the *Manitoba Free Press* found that "Thrift is [the Jew's] best known virtue and his fatal weakness. [The Jew's] danger is in permitting money to be his god.... Nowhere does life wear so materialistic an aspect as among ... the chosen people."[9]

Rally of the Great War Veterans Association, Winnipeg, June 4, 1919. Great War Veterans Association Parade. The returning veterans were divided. Some feared that the strikers were dangerous revolutionary aliens who would take their jobs.

Archives of Manitoba, N12296, L. B. Foote, photographer.

There was class war in Winnipeg. The War Measures Act gave the government broad powers to arrest, intern, or deport anyone its agents considered enemy aliens. The RCMP raided the Liberty Temple in Winnipeg, smashing desks and seizing documents. Moses Almazov, a student of philosophy and economics at the University of Manitoba, was a member of the Social Democratic Party and known as one of the most active workers in the (Jewish) War Relief Society for War Sufferers. The Royal Northwest Mounted Police had him marked as "an active revolutionary plotter" and arrested him during the strike.[10] When ten strike leaders were arrested, the Winnipeg Jewish community rallied to the support of the five "foreigners" thrown in jail, who were treated quite differently from the anglophone leaders. An editorial in *Dos Yiddishe Vort* declared, "Let every Jew remember that three of the [five] arrested foreigners are Jews. And for this reason it is necessary that every Jew help to free the arrested.... It is your struggle for justice."[11]

During the period in Toronto known by the left as "the terror" (1929–32), Toronto Police Chief Dennis Draper, convinced that foreigners' meetings were

Section 98 of the Criminal Code, rushed through parliament in forty minutes during the 1919 Winnipeg General Strike, made illegal any association the government deemed to be advocating change. Communists and trade unionists were targeted. May 1, 1932.

Jewish Heritage Centre of Western Canada Archives, JM480.

hotbeds of revolution, appointed a "Red Squad" and issued an edict forbidding all public meetings not held in English. He ordered jailed and/or deported as many troublemakers as he could.[12] The silencing of left voices became a free speech issue for liberals as well as the Jewish left, supported by people such as sixty-eight professors from the University of Toronto, church officials from the United Church, and the Fellowship of Reconciliation (a Christian pacifist organization) who maintained that the police commission did not have the right to interfere with civil liberties through licensing of public halls.[13]

While many Jews could unite around issues of anti-Semitism the community held disparate views on virtually all other issues. A bitter rivalry existed for the loyalties of the Jewish working class. Essentially this was a battle between the communists, the non-communists, and the Jewish elites. The left Jewish organizations with their strong emphasis on union activism, racial equality, and solidarity with other victimized peoples had wide appeal. They were a constant thorn in the sides of more moderate Jews.

The debates were passionate and were carried on not only within the community but also within families. Irving Abella's family encompassed the gamut of views from left to Zionist to Orthodox; his uncles would gather each Saturday evening to play cards and argue.[14] My children's grandfather described weekly chess games with political discussions so fierce that often someone would angrily stomp out, only to return the next Saturday evening to continue the argument.[15]

Even the naming of children became part of the struggle. Roland Penner of Winnipeg recalls how strongly people felt about their allegiances to the various movements in the 1930s: Mrs. Cohen of Pritchard Street, who lived down the street from the Liberty Temple, named her first-born son "Liberty." Six o'clock and suppertime, she would stick her head out the little front porch and yell in a voice that reached three blocks either way, "Liberty!" Penner said, "One could almost hear the applause up and down the street!" Penner also remembered how he and his sister Ruthie eagerly anticipated the arrival of a baby in a family who lived across the street. The new baby was named "Ninel May—Lenin spelled backwards, and May for his wife's birthday."[16]

In 1934 after Hitler came to power the Canadian Jewish Congress, which had dissolved in 1919, regrouped in response but the left was not invited to join. The dominant powers in the CJC opposed the leftists for two reasons. To begin with the ideological differences were irreconcilable. The left was internationalist, not Zionist. Second, political strategies were not compatible. In the face of anti-Semitism, the CJC leadership was anxious to prove that Jews, many of whom were new Canadians, were not troublemakers. Militant activity challenging the government was unacceptable to them. Thus, any challenge to existing Canadian government policy was either silenced completely or carried out with the utmost discretion through polite representation by the few Jewish elected politicians.[17] Critics referred to this as the "sha shtil" (hush hush) policy of the CJC.

The Canadian Jewish Congress approach to the Spanish Civil War and the struggle against fascism after Hitler gained power (detailed in chapter 4) provides an example of this "sha shtil" policy. While many Canadians saw Spain as the last bulwark against Mussolini and Hitler, CJC as an organization followed the lead of the Canadian government. It refused to support the struggle against the fascist leader Franco, despite the dictatorship's alliances with Mussolini and Hitler, and it discouraged participation in the popular front organization the Canadian League Against War and Fascism. The International Conference on Yiddish Culture held in Paris in 1937 to defend Yiddish culture pulled together prominent people from many ideological streams as part of the campaign against fascism. However, the CJC, following its counterparts in the United States, didn't support or send delegates to the conference. It seemed that opposition to anything that included communists trumped any consideration of a particular issue, no matter how compelling. Nevertheless, the more activist approach of the left appealed to many within the Canadian Jewish community.

When the Soviet Union became Canada's ally in the Second World War pro-Soviet sympathies became "kosher" and the CJC had to change its views, at least for the duration of the war and shortly after.

With the wartime alliance of the allies and the Soviet Union after 1941, left-wing socialists and communists gained some legitimacy in the wider society. Jewish communists held elected public office in Quebec, Ontario, and Manitoba. Left organizations became part of the now legitimate struggle against fascism.[18] The Canadian government's embrace of the left was limited, however. The veterans of the Spanish Civil War had difficulty enlisting in the armed forces because they were considered "premature anti-fascists," a term used by the Canadian and US governments. Being considered politically unreliable, some were hounded by the RCMP and prevented from signing up to fight while others were assigned to dangerous missions behind enemy lines or sent to special camps.[19]

In December 1943, the umbrella organization that included all the left organizations, called the Council of Progressive Organizations, was invited to join the CJC. Prominent Jewish communists such as Sam Lipshitz, Joe Zuken, Joe Gershman, and Morris Biderman became active participants. They were described by Irving Abella as highly intelligent men, eloquent speakers, but cantankerous.[20]

The Gouzenko Affair

In the late 1940s, the Canadian Jewish Congress' aversion to communists and those with pro-Soviet sympathies began to re-emerge, which the CJC argued was justified by international and national events. In the aftermath of the Second World War, the victors redrew the map of Europe, Asia, and the Middle East. The Soviets established satellite states in Eastern Europe and East Germany, which some considered expansionist while others viewed it as creating a buffer zone to protect themselves against western hostility. Those in Canada with pro-Soviet sympathies were criticized for their views.

The Gouzenko spy affair in early 1946 shocked the nation with charges of espionage and disloyalty on the part of prominent Canadian public service employees, including Fred Rose, a Jewish communist Member of Parliament from the working-class riding of Cartier.[21] Igor Gouzenko, a cipher clerk (a person who encrypts and deciphers codes) in the Soviet embassy in Ottawa, defected to Canada and showed evidence of an undercover Russian spy network in Canada. A royal commission was set up to investigate the matter. Raymond Boyer, a science professor at McGill University, convinced that he was acting in the interests of Canada, expected a sympathetic hearing when he gave evidence to the commission about his role in passing on confidential information to Fred Rose that he believed would then be given to the Russians. The information in question was about an explosive called RDX that Boyer worked on developing. Both Boyer and Rose felt that scientific knowledge should be shared. In *Cold War Canada*, Whitaker and Marcuse detail how the processes for the manufacture of RDX were already known and had been on a list of military technology approved by the British and the Americans to be passed on to the Soviets.[22]

Gouzenko's revelations led to the arrest of Sam Carr, a Jewish immigrant and a national organizer of the Communist Party. He was charged with forging passports. Carr later said,

> While the Russians were bleeding in Stalingrad, the Canadians were developing explosives and hiding it from the Russians and Boyer was outraged.... It's true that it contravened the letter of the law, but were they really spies, because spies presuppose doing it for the enemy—but here we were in a war.[23]

Unlike most of the people named by Gouzenko whose convictions did not hold up in court, Boyer and Carr each received two-year sentences and Rose six years, a sentence that was one day more than required to deprive him of his seat in the House of Commons. Freed after four years, but hounded by the RCMP and in ill health, Rose left Canada for Poland, hoping to return to clear his name. But his citizenship was revoked in 1957.[24] The Communist Party's decision to involve an elected Member of Parliament in such activities was unfortunate (to put it mildly), but the cloak and dagger descriptions of Rose as nothing more than a pawn doing Stalin's bidding seem woefully uninformed.[25] In his tenure as MP Rose had a record demonstrating his commitment to social justice issues; in fact, he was the first MP to propose Medicare and anti-hate legislation.

The charges against Rose made all associated with the Jewish left suspect. The Supreme Court denied a hearing to appeal his sentence.[26] Fred Rose was not fairly treated by either the Kremlin or the Canadian government. He was a victim of a political climate intent on revving up anti-communist hysteria and was abandoned by the Canadian Communist Party and the Russians in their efforts to distance themselves from charges of espionage.[27] Whitaker and Marcuse argue that it was not the abrupt shattering of illusions by Soviet duplicity or Gouzenko's defection that explains Cold War Canada, but rather the striking continuity

RE-ELECT

FRED

Rose

JUNE 11

CANDIDATE LABOR-PROGRESSIVE PARTY

CARTIER

HE WON RESPECT FOR CARTIER

Election poster for Fred Rose who served as MP for Cartier from 1943–46. He proposed the first medicare legislation and the first anti-hate legislation. He was expelled from parliament in January 1957, convicted under the Official Secrets Act.

www.archivespolitiqueduQuebec.com.

of anti-communism throughout the century. The wartime alliance, they maintain, was one of convenience.[28]

Sam Carr, who was also jailed under the Official Secrets Act for passport offences, looking back on his career, said:

> I have had a lot of disappointments, but … I never did anything I didn't want to do. Everybody should have done it because they were our allies, they were fighting the Nazis.… I don't regret it, I'm not ashamed of it, I wasn't betraying Canada, you guys were betraying Canada, after all there was a war on.… We were not accused of helping the enemy, we were helping an ally.[29]

Sam Carr never rejoined the Communist Party but became active in the UJPO after he was released from prison.

The Rosenbergs

In 1945, in the aftermath of the atom bomb devastation of Hiroshima and Nagasaki, the use of nuclear power that had the potential to destroy the entire human race became a major concern of the Jewish left. One strategy supported by the left was to contain the threat of total annihilation through a strong supranational power, the United Nations, and through the sharing of information. Canada and the United States chose another path—pursuing collective security through a military alliance and stocking nuclear arms as a deterrent to communist aggression. While antiwar sentiments had been popular in the pre-Second World War period, postwar the climate shifted.[30] The secular Jewish left wanted peace, not an arms race, but for the Canadian government and the Jewish establishment the enemy was no longer Hitler and fascism, but once again, the threat of communism.

In 1950, a few years after Fred Rose's trial and at the height of the activities of the House Un-American Activities Committee (HUAC), Ethel and Julius Rosenberg, two American Jewish leftists from New York, were arrested and charged with what was called "the crime of the century." Implicated by Ethel's brother-in-law, David Greenglass, they were tried and executed on the charge of conspiracy to commit espionage—stealing the secrets of the atom bomb to give to the Russians. It was the height of McCarthyism, and the trial was about silencing dissent in North America, not about the evil Soviet empire. The Communist Party at first dissociated itself from the case, not wanting to be connected to espionage, but all of the left, especially the Jewish left both in Canada and the United States, mobilized in the Rosenbergs' defence. Although the judge, Irving Saypol, was a Jew, the left saw anti-Semitic forces at work in singling out two Jewish communists. The Rosenbergs were convicted of espionage on March 29, 1951 and executed by electric chair in June 1953.

Many years after the Rosenbergs' deaths, in the 1990s, investigators gained access to decoded Soviet cables. They learned that Julius Rosenberg had indeed been involved in espionage activities but not in atomic secrets. A more recent investigation by Walter Schneir found that in September 1945 when Julius was supposed to have passed on the information about the atom bomb, he was no longer a courier for the Russians. He had been removed six months earlier in 1945 after being fired from his job with the U.S. Signal Corps for his leftist associa-tions.[31] The evidence indicates that Ethel was never involved in espionage.

The struggle to save the lives of Ethel and Julius Rosenberg played a large role in UJPO activities, with picket lines in Montreal and mass protests in Ottawa and at the United States consulate in Toronto to demonstrate against this "legal murder" by the "American imperialists."[32] The secular Jewish left was not alone in protesting the harsh sentence—there was a worldwide response to the Rosenberg death sentence, involving protests by Albert Einstein, Harold Urey, Bertolt Brecht, Pablo Picasso, and even Pope Pius XII.[33] In Canada, the left organized a National Friends of the Rosenbergs Committee and held rallies all over the country. Up until the very final hour, people hoped that the sentence would be commuted. The night of the execution, June 19, 1953, virtually every person connected with the UJPO remembers where they were, assembling in their communities to protest and mourn the grave injustice.[34]

Neither the American Jewish Congress, the American Jewish Committee, nor the Canadian Jewish Congress joined with those petitioning for clemency

The article from the *Ottawa Citizen* of May 28, 1953 quoted in this leaflet says, "The Rosenbergs it is clear are to be executed for refusing to confess.... They seem to be scapegoats of the cold war and victims of mass hysteria."

Thomas Fisher Rare Book Library, University of Toronto, Kenny Collection, ms 179.

Clemency for the Rosenbergs protest, Vancouver, 1953. Virtually every progressive Jew remembers exactly where they were the day the Rosenbergs were killed. On September 28, 2015, the New York City Council honoured the life and memory of Ethel Rosenberg on the 100th anniversary of her birth and declared her wrongfully executed. Three generations of her descendants were present.

Archives of Ontario, F1412, JI-1.

in the Rosenberg case. Jewish historian Lucy Dawidowicz, writing in the *New Statesman*, argued that the Rosenberg defence campaign "serves only one purpose—to intensify the 'hate America' campaign throughout the world" and that commutation of the death sentences would hand the communists an unwarranted propaganda victory. She faulted anti-communist critics of the death sentences for "providing a cloak of legitimacy for communist agitation on the issue."[35] Ignoring the claim by several Jewish organizations that the proceedings were tainted with anti-Semitism, representatives of the American Jewish Committee (AJC) declared that the trial employed the highest standards of fairness and lawfulness. The Anti-Defamation League of B'nai B'rith (ADL) expressed similar views to those of the AJC. In an article published on December 22, 1952 in the *New Leader*, Dawidowicz claimed the communists had used the Negroes' struggle and now in the Rosenberg case, the Jewish issue, as tools in "their war against America." Along with most of the Jewish establishment, she took the position that the Rosenbergs' Jewishness was irrelevant.[36]

Throughout 1952 Jewish organizations in the US such as the AJC, ADL, Jewish War Veterans of the US Jewish Labor Committee, and the Union of American Hebrew Congregations denounced attempts to link the Rosenberg case with anti-Semitism, warning Jews not to take part in the "communist" efforts on the Rosenbergs' behalf.[37] This position was virtually identical to the CJC's fears of the linking of "Jewish" with communism, and so it was not a difficult call for them to heed the warnings of their American counterparts and remain silent. Canada can take credit for beginning the Cold War in 1945 with the Gouzenko affair. Although no one was sentenced to die here, the chill winds had an effect on both sides of the border. In Canada, both the RCMP and provincial police began zealously investigating civil servants, scientists, university professors, and trade unionists.[38]

Quebec and the Padlock Law

The Padlock Law in Quebec, originally enacted by Premier Duplessis in 1937, allowed the Attorney General to close, to "padlock" for a year, any house that officials deemed was used to propagate communism or Bolshevism "by any means whatsoever." Any publications found in the house could be destroyed, and those deemed offenders were subject to imprisonment. What constituted communism or Bolshevism or the criteria used to detect them were never clearly defined. Duplessis was voted out of office in 1939, and the law was not used when he wasn't premier. However, when he regained power in 1944, the "red squads" (as the Quebec provincial police in his administration were called) were once again in action.[39]

On January 27, 1950, twenty-one officers descended on the newly built Morris Winchevsky Cultural Centre of the UJPO on 501 Esplanade in Montreal and padlocked it, carting away several truckloads of office machines, organizational records, files, correspondence, and library books. The Morris Winchevsky Shule was raided by the police, and the children sent home. The police also raided the home of the secretary of the order, Benny Silverberg, and activist Bess Schockett. No charges were made against the UJPO nor were there allegations that any of their activities were unlawful. Bess Schockett recalled that when the RCMP invaded her home, they took all her books that had a red cover![40] Under the terms of the Padlock Law, contentions did not need to

The Padlock Law in Quebec allowed institutions or houses to be shut if the authorities thought they had subversive materials.

Drawing by Avrom, courtesy of Anna Yanovsky.

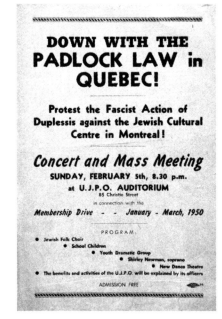

Thomas Fisher Rare Book Library, University of Toronto, Kenny Collection, ms 179.

be proven in court, nor police actions justified.[41] Following the Quebec raid, the Toronto Jewish Welfare Fund discontinued support of the Toronto Winchevsky Shule. Winnipeg soon followed.

The Canadian public reacted to the closure and the Padlock Law in Quebec with protest resolutions across Canada. The issue became one of civil liberties and due process. *Saturday Night* magazine objected to a law that made Duplessis "policeman, prosecutor, judge, sheriff and hangman." In one of several editorials, *Saturday Night* pointed out that not only had the UJPO not been charged with any criminal offence, it had not been proven guilty of anything. "He [Duplessis] is depriving them of their property by his own absolute power, conferred upon him by the Quebec Legislature.... They are of course a minority, but there was a time when Quebec was supposed to be solicitous about the rights of minorities."[42]

Those who spoke up included the Civil Liberties Union in Montreal and Toronto, the Montreal Labour Council, the Ontario Federation of Labour, students at McGill University, the *Ottawa Citizen*, and the Montreal Presbyterian Presbytery. Forty-three clergy and ministers published their petition to Duplessis in the *Montreal Daily Gazette* and called the padlocking a flat contradiction of "our accepted democratic tradition."[43] The UJPO drafted a petition and mobilized its members to canvas for signatures. Thousands signed.

The silence from the Canadian Jewish Congress was deafening, although some organizations affiliated with the CJC passed formal resolutions protesting the use of the Padlock Law. The Jewish Junior Welfare Committee, a member of the Women's Liaison Committee of the CJC, condemned the use of the law "under any circumstances whatsoever" and encouraged the CJC to take a stand, "heartily" endorsing any positive action it might take to undo the wrongs.[44] Saul Hayes, executive director of the CJC replied, asking them to "leave the matter in abeyance" until the Joint Public Relations Committee of Congress met.[45] The CJC Youth Councils in Toronto and Montreal passed protest resolutions. The Winnipeg Jewish Youth Council wrote directly to Duplessis protesting the padlocking of the UJPO and requested the Eastern Division of the Joint Public Relations Committee to take up the matter. Heinz Frank, executive director of the CJC's Western Division, was not pleased. He informed Hayes, who chastised Harold Buchwald, president of the Winnipeg Jewish Youth Council, for taking action without a decision from the National Joint Public Relations Committee. Frank described the incident as "greatly embarrassing."[46]

Some attempted to straddle the issue, taking the position that the left needed to be ostracized, but not by the government. An editorial by Melvin

Fenson, editor of Winnipeg's *Jewish Post*, was titled "It Reminds Us Of Hitler." Fenson urged the National Joint Public Relations Committee to consider this a vital Jewish issue. However, the CJC was faced with a dilemma—how to reconcile its desire to defend civil liberties of "peculiarly Jewish concerns" with its wish to punish left-wing elements. To resolve this dilemma, the notion of community self-censorship was introduced: "Canadian Jewry must have the democratic freedom to voluntarily boycott negative trends in Jewish life: they need no benevolent or malevolent tyrants to make such decisions for them."[47] In other words, silencing dissenting voices in the Jewish community was justified as long as it was done by the Jewish community itself. The CJC's women's and youth organizations that sought to join those denouncing the use of the Padlock Law on a Jewish organization had to be brought into line.

Given the history of anti-Semitism in Canada, the CJC's position in defence of civil liberties was generally strong, but dealing with pro-communist groups in their midst was a different matter. Congress officers decided that they "do not believe that the closing of the United Jewish People's Order is a Jewish issue."[48] The Eastern Division, and subsequently the National Joint Public Relations Committee, followed the wishes of the officers and decided not to issue a statement, arguing that they needed more time for "careful study." UJPO secretary Morris Biderman then sent a letter to members of the Dominion Council, the national body of the organizations belonging to the CJC, asking them to challenge the CJC leaders' inaction:

> Surely it is high time for us to realize that any and all reactionary and repressive legislation which smacks of fascism is first and foremost a threat to the Jewish people. Surely the reactionary anti-Semitic record of Premier Duplessis is too well known to be hidden under a cloak of red-baiting and the cry of "Communist."[49]

The Dominion Council did not respond, and the Canadian Jewish Congress remained silent. It took until 1957 for the Supreme Court of Canada to declare the Padlock Law unconstitutional.

The Drive for Respectability: Expulsion of the UJPO

The uphill decades-long battle faced by the Jewish community in its struggle for acceptance was easing by the early 1950s. Jews were finally becoming white folks. Restrictions were lifted for Jewish entry into professional schools such as

Joshua Gershman protesting Canada allowing Nazis to immigrate to Canada. He is second from the left.

Archives of Ontario, F1412 J I 1.

medicine, law, and dentistry. In Ontario, the Fair Employment Practices bill made it illegal to ask about an applicant's race or religion. In Quebec, anti-Jewish discrimination by a hotel owner was challenged. Restrictive covenants against selling properties to those of "Jewish, Hebrew, Semitic, Negro or colored race or blood" were struck down by the Supreme Court of Canada.[50]

But by 1951, Cold War politics (McCarthyism) had become part of the American psyche and had also permeated Canadian life, threatening the inclusiveness of the Jewish community in which the left had thrived during the war years. The Canadian Jewish Congress, with strong Liberal ties, was increasingly uncomfortable with any challenge or embarrassment to the Liberal government in power. The UJPO organized a campaign against German rearmament. At the same time, Nazi war crime trials in Germany were suspended, and in 1950 restrictions against former Nazis entering Canada were lifted.[51] These issues resonated among Canadian Jews, and initially all CJC branches and the Toronto Regional conference of the CJC supported the UJPO campaign.[52]

The Canadian Jewish Congress appealed to Prime Minister St. Laurent and sent a delegation to meet with Lester Pearson, the Minister of External Affairs. They strongly urged the minister to vote against allowing Germany into the United Nations.[53] Canada, however, supported the position of the United States that German rearmament was an integral part of their Cold War policy and a bulwark against the Soviet Union and its westward expansion. The new enemy was communism and the Soviet Union. Measures against former enemies were suspended. Pearson informed the CJC delegation that the Canadian government supported rearming Germany to contain the expansion of communism.

Following this meeting, National Executive Director of the CJC Saul Hayes recommended abandoning the campaign.[54] However, the UJPO would not agree. They were convinced that German rearmament constituted a critical danger to world Jewry. At the same time, the UJPO took the position that securing peace through international co-operation and an end to fighting wars was the best route. These were the policies of the Communist Party, but they clearly resonated among left Jews, who also supported the Stockholm Peace Petition and vigorously opposed the Korean War, a conflict that resulted in four million casualties, three million of them civilians.[55] The CJC, following Canada's position on both issues, supported the Korean War and opposed the Stockholm Peace Petition. UJPO members maintained that the campaign against German rearmament, the issue most directly in conflict with Canadian government policy, was the real reason for Congress' drastic action in the expulsion of the UJPO.[56]

Stockholm Peace Petition

The Stockholm Appeal, calling for an absolute ban on nuclear weapons, was drafted in Sweden in March 1949 at the First World Peace Congress and approved on March 15, 1950, by the World Peace Council. Drafted by five people, including the Reverend James Endicott, head of the Canadian Peace Congress, it was supported by such figures as scientists Linus Pauling and Frédéric Joliot-Curie, historian W. E. B. Du Bois, and singer Paul Robeson. A group called Partisans for Peace came together at the World Peace Congress with committees in forty-six countries and circulated the petition around the world. It was signed by hundreds of millions of people throughout the world, including a long list of artists and poets.[57] The Jewish Committee of the Canadian Peace Congress was one of the organizations bringing the appeal to Canada. They authored a pamphlet entitled "Shalom Aleichem" (peace be with you). Addressed to the Government of Canada, it stated:

> We, the undersigned petition you to make the following declaration:
> 1. Canada stands for the unconditional banning, by all countries of the atomic weapon as an instrument of aggression and mass extermination of people, with strict international control....
> 2. Canada will regard as a war criminal that government which first uses the atomic weapon against any country.[58]

Many in the UJPO, in particular women and young people, collected signatures.

However, support for the petition went far beyond the left, resonating with those who had been closest to the devastation of the Second World War. It was unanimously endorsed by the French Rabbinate, who declared:

"SHALOM ALEICHEM"

PEACE– IT IS IN YOUR HANDS!

The pamphlet that contributed to the ousting of the United Jewish People's Order from the Canadian Jewish Congress.

Thomas Fisher Rare Book Library, University of Toronto, Kenny Collection, ms 179.

Whoever we are, whatever opinion we have, we must recognize that the Stockholm call to ban this weapon of mass destruction (the atom bomb) means to us the expression of the noblest aspirations and is in full agreement with God's commandments. It is therefore imperative that every Jew sign the Stockholm appeal.

Over half the total adult population of Israel signed the petition, including many rabbis, the vice president of the Israeli Knesset and twenty-two deputies, and Israeli soldiers, including the former Commander in Chief of the Haganah.[59]

The New York Anti-Defamation League office denounced the Stockholm Peace Appeal, characterizing it as a "despicable divide and conquer tactic" and as pro-communist, provoking groups to violence. Ten major US Jewish organizations signed this denunciation: the American Jewish Committee, American Jewish Congress, Anti-Defamation League, Association of Jewish Chaplains in the Armed Forces, B'nai B'rith, Jewish Labor Committee, Jewish War Veterans of the United States of America, National Community Relations Advisory Council, National Council of Jewish Women, and Union of American Hebrew Congregations.[60]

J. B. Salsberg, the popular communist MP from Trinity-Spadina in Toronto, emphasized the particular relevance of the Stockholm Peace Petition for Jews. In response, the Canadian Jewish Congress was urged to make a public statement. In September 1950, the CJC endorsed the US statement denouncing the petition and called on the Canadian Jewish community not to be misled into signing it. The National Executive Committee asked "all individuals and groups affiliated with Congress and urging every member of the Jewish Community in Canada not to sign the Stockholm Peace Petition."[61]

Despite the widespread support the petition received from people and countries throughout the world, it appeared that Soviet support was enough to make the issue subversive in North America. Given the terrible devastation of the Soviet Union during the Second World War, it was clear why the petition had such strong support there. Within a few months of its drafting, millions of signatures were collected, mainly in the Soviet Union, China, and other countries of Eastern Europe and Asia. In Canada, 300,000 signatures were collected, and street demonstrations and street corner meetings were held.[62] Ben Shek recalled the climate of the time when peace supporters faced police harassment and physical threats as they circulated through the community for signatures.

Sam Bronfman, president of the Canadian Jewish Congress, praised Canada's pro-war stance on Korea, supporting American involvement in what the left felt was essentially a civil war between North and South Korea.[63] Bronfman's views received official endorsement by the regional council, and the CJC followed its American counterparts and the Canadian government and supported the war. The National Executive was concerned about a series of articles appearing in the *Canadian Jewish Weekly* (the English section of the pro-communist Yiddish paper), expressing views that differed from those of the CJC and requested that the group abide by Congress' position.[64]

The National Joint Public Relations Committee was outraged by the CJC's inability to exert control over the leftists, who continued their campaigns. This was, they argued, "contrary to the principle of national Jewish unity and the binding force of majority decision." They called on the Executive Committee of the CJC to take disciplinary measures. They felt so strongly about silencing the left and presenting the community as speaking in one voice that they were ready to alter their own rules of who was eligible to vote, and even disqualify representatives from the landsmanshaftn (folk organizations) from voting to ensure that the one view expressed was that of the leadership.

One day before the Executive Committee met, on April 28, 1951, Sam Lipshitz, the president of the Council of Progressive Jewish Organizations, which included the United Jewish People's Order, asked Saul Hayes, the CJC's National Executive Director, whether UJPO would be on the agenda, and was told it was not. Hayes later justified his response: "I answered punctiliously and truthfully that it was not.... In fact it was not on the agenda but it was raised." At the meeting on April 29, 1951, chaired by Sam Bronfman, president of the CJC, the decision was made to expel the UJPO. In justifying this decision, Saul Hayes reported that "verbal and written demands had been received requesting that individuals and groups of known left-wing affiliation be barred from Congress." He added, "There has been a serious violation of publicized Congress policy." The violation in question was identified as the Stockholm Peace Petition, although subsequently National Executive Director Ben Hayes indicated that

that was not the main or only consideration.[65] Congress policy, the minutes of the meeting declared, was

> formulated in an effort to help the Jewish community to take its place with all other elements in the country determined to guard and maintain the fundamentals of our democratic way of living, so seriously imperiled these days. To urge a contradictory course at this juncture in world affairs was not only a threat to the country's security but undermines the position and good name of Canada's Jews at a crucial time when intergroup strife must be avoided. It was obvious that UJPO was behind the distribution of the [Shalom Aleichem] pamphlet.[66]

The minutes continued:

> This break with Congress policy and indeed with the overwhelming majority of Canadian Jewry goes beyond a matter of discipline. Since views and actions of the left wing oriented group stems out of an ideology rooted outside of Canadian Jewish life, the members of the national Executive Committee have to address themselves to the question if it will ever be possible for this group to accept the type of discipline to which the other elements of our community have voluntarily committed themselves.[67]

The unanimous decision of the members was that "no constructive purpose can be served by left-wing elements in their further association with Congress." The executive committee moved that individuals or groups of "known left-wing affiliation" lose eligibility for election as delegates. Before its final ratification, the four regions of the Regional Dominion Council were required to approve the resolution.[68] This process was a significant departure from normal procedure, which was that decisions made by the executive committee needed the approval of the entire Congress plenary. In this instance, however, the executive was concerned that this was too risky because of support of the left among rank and file members. It seemed a safer strategy for each of the four councils to meet separately than risk having the resolution raised at a plenary of the entire Congress where it was likely to fail.

The decision at this point was not about varying positions on current world issues. Rather, there was one concern. Jewish "left leaning organizations" were no longer to be considered part of the Jewish community. Given the UJPO's organizational strength and active presence in the political and cultural life of Canadian Jewry, this was not easy to accomplish. It required careful tactical planning. The Congress archives reveal the flurry of memos, all marked "Personal and Confidential," that passed between Saul Hayes and the presidents of the regions. With a bit of tinkering with the rules of eligibility for voting, the East and Central regions did not present a problem for the leadership. The resolution was presented at carefully orchestrated Dominion Council meetings where a new rule allowed only Council members to vote rather than allowing all delegates a vote at a general plenary. The Eastern Region of the Dominion Council adopted the resolution on May 23. It named the United Jewish People's Order, the Morris Winchevsky School, the YKUF (Yiddish Cultural Organization), and other "like minded organizations." Further, it resolved that these organizations should not be invited to send delegates to the Plenary Session and should be refused permission to participate as electors for the Plenary. The Central Region [Ontario] went a step further. Concerned that left-wingers held elected positions in Congress as delegates from organizations that were not excluded, their resolution specified that such people could not act directly or indirectly as delegates to the forthcoming Plenary Session or serve on the Dominion Council.[69]

Saul Hayes reported to Ben Lappin of the Central Region that there was "surprisingly little opposition" to the resolution in Montreal. Winnipeg (Western Region) and Vancouver (Pacific) proved to be more difficult to convince. Questions were raised in various quarters throughout the country. Ben Shek recalled the meeting of the Toronto Youth Council in which they were asked to support the Central Region's decision. Michael Benazon, the head of the Holy Blossom youth group at that time, voted against the resolution asking for disaffiliation. It wasn't necessarily a sophisticated political analysis that led him to his opposition. He recalled that it didn't make any sense to him to exclude his friends, such as his pal Ben Shek, from the group.[70] The Vancouver Council of Women took a similar position. Judging from the extensive Congress correspondence in the archives filed under "Eligibility," the Winnipeg section presented the greatest challenge and required cautious planning. Correspondence there indicated that the offending Shalom Aleichem pamphlet was not named as the primary reason for expulsion. The left was being excluded, according to the Winnipeg Division of CJC, for its positions deemed a threat to the community. Saul Hayes assured Heinz Frank, executive director of the Winnipeg region, that the real basis was not the pamphlet but the UJPO's antagonism to Jewish life. The strategy they arrived at was to get the Dominion Council to accept new by-laws, one of which gave the National Executive Committee the discretion to exclude members.[71] Frank was concerned that they create some "organizational means to ferret out communists…. Needless to say the Reds … will try every possible means to infiltrate us with their people and bore from within."[72] Several influential people had reservations about the implications of such a move. S. M. Selchen, noted Labour Zionist, editor of *Dos Yiddishe Vort* (The Israelite Press) and president of the Winnipeg Congress Council, thought that it changed the nature of Congress from an inclusive organization to one that would exclude.[73]

The Council of Progressive Jewish Organizations, the umbrella group for Jewish left-wing organizations, held a rally in Winnipeg on June 19, 1951. They stressed that the major issue in the Jewish community was the nature of democracy:

> The Jewish Congress is built on the principles of democracy in Jewish life and all groups and shades of the Jewish community have the right to freedom of thought in Congress. Will you permit that tolerance and democracy be abolished in Congress and that Congress should be transformed into an instrument of a few individuals who want to rule over Jewish life?

All members of UJPO and Congress should not permit "such an undemocratic act, which will only bring in division, bitter fights and demoralization in the ranks of the Jewish life."[74]

The protests failed to change the decision. "All is over but the shouting," H. Frank reported to Saul Hayes on June 24 from Regina. The Western Region, which included Manitoba and Saskatchewan, became the third Congress region to evict the UJPO, YKUF, Morris Winchevsky Schools, and other like-minded organizations from Congress. The vote was eighteen to seven with three abstentions, reaffirming the position of the national office.[75] Only in the Pacific Region, where all the delegates were able to discuss the resolution, was the outcome different. On October 11 they voted against supporting the resolution to expel the left but their decision had no effect on Congress since the support of the other three regions was sufficient to ratify the resolution.

An editorial in Winnipeg's *Jewish Post* headlined "Congress Cleans House" lauded the critical Regina decision of the Western Region. In a somewhat contradictory argument, Melvin Fenson, the paper's editor, explained that external pressure to limit civil liberties wasn't necessary; organizations were perfectly capable of doing it themselves:

> The threat of Communist domination of legitimate Jewish organizations
> was recently met by a local branch of a national body in a way that proves
> "instructively and conclusively" that left to themselves, national Jewish
> organizations know how to clean house without the imposition of any outside,
> coercive or restrictive measure.[76]

The article went on to link events in Canada with the United States where the American Jewish Congress had to send its trouble-shooters from New York to oust a democratically elected left-wing leadership with mass support in a Los Angeles Jewish community. They had to be brought into line with American Jewish Congress policy.[77]

The saga of arbitrary decisions and outright dishonesty continued. A letter from Lipshitz to Samuel Bronfman and Saul Hayes requested that the Council of Progressive Organizations be given an opportunity to appear at the national executive meeting and later at the plenary council to present their case. after several inquiries, the left were to be allowed one half hour during the lunch break to appear before the national executive. There is no evidence that there was any discussion of the expulsion in the minutes or the agenda of the plenary held that fall. Lipshitz argued that the national executive's decision was unconstitutional, the procedure undemocratic, and the vote in favour at the various regional council meetings unrepresentative. He pointed out that only sixty-seven of the three hundred Dominion Council members voted in favour of the recommendation to expel, as changes in the rules meant that not all council members had a say in the decision. Jewish publications in Canada were virtually all against the recommendation. Those opposed included the *Canadian Jewish News* in Toronto, *Dos Yiddishe Vort* in Winnipeg, and the *Hebrew Journal* in Toronto.[78] Morris Biderman, a former president of the UJPO, believed that "the leadership of the Canadian Jewish Congress was caught up in the cold war atmosphere and was pressured by the Canadian government, and particularly by the RCMP to expel UJPO."[79] This analysis was supported by B. Z. Goldberg in a Yiddish article published on May 16, 1952 in *Der Tog* (The Day), a New York newspaper. Goldberg felt the same pressure had been coming from US organizations. *Der Tog* was a middle of the road journal, unlike *Der Freiheit*, the pro-communist paper, or the *Forward*, which was decidedly anti-communist.

In an attempt at an even-handed approach, Goldberg interviewed Michael Garber, for Congress' point of view, Joshua Gershman, editor of the *Der*

Vochenblat, and Sam Lipshitz for the excluded left organizations. He introduced the topic by noting that the Canadian Jewish Congress had always been a more democratic, non-elitist Jewish institution than its American counterpart. Noting that all sectors of Jewish society were included, he stated: "The eighth wonder of the world was how all worked together harmoniously within Congress, despite the sharp ideological differences outside of Congress."

Goldberg held that the Canadian Jewish Congress had followed the example of the American Jewish Congress in expelling its leftists. He said Michael Garber of the Congress had assured him that Bronfman, the liquor magnate, did not exert special influence because of his wealth, but participated in Congress in a democratic fashion.[80] Lipshitz and Gershman were emphatic that neither in Montreal nor Toronto did a majority of members vote for the resolution. They pointed out that in the West and at the last moment, representatives from the folk organizations were not allowed to vote. Gershman indicated that when the left did meet with Congress officials, Garber admitted that Congress was acting undemocratically. However, they would not allow further discussion and debate. After much bitter argument, Goldberg reported, the CJC leadership proposed a concession. If the UJPO would prepare a statement that did not mention freedom, or German rearmament or any dealings with Adenauer, the German prime minister, and if they would allow the statement to be censored, then Congress would decide whether the UJPO would be allowed to read it for Congress to consider. With these restrictions, the UJPO rejected the offer.[81]

What was at stake was not just defending the UJPO's views, but the right to hold views with which Congress didn't agree, and some of the questionable methods Congress used to rid itself of a powerful group. Some felt that only one view should dominate and that Congress had the right to determine what Jewish interests were, others felt that a Jewish community must include everyone and that all views must be tolerated, and still others maintained that many voices, including dissenting ones, enrich community life. What is surprising is the outright dissembling the Congress leadership used to make their view prevail that left secular Jews be seen as external to the Jewish community. For example, when Sam Lipshitz in a letter asked for a copy of a memorandum that was to be read at the national executive of the Pacific Region to discuss the expulsion, he was told there was no such memorandum. But the "non-existent" memorandum is in the files of the CJC![82]

Within the context of Cold War Canada, the situation within the Jewish community was not unlike that of other institutions in the country. Similar processes of ousting pro-communist elements were found in the union movement (the United Electrical Workers, Canadian Seaman's Union, Mine and Mill, and Needle Trades) as well as in other ethnic communities. Any position that challenged Canadian government policies was deemed to be disloyal and un-Canadian. The *Telegram*, a Toronto newspaper, featured eight articles in 1951, republished as a pamphlet under the title *Red Menace in Canada*.[83]

The *Telegram* articles charged that communists were everywhere—in the armed forces, in control of many unions, and in the peace movement: "National security officials call the peace movement 'the most insidious thing' the Communists have yet launched." Enemy number one was Dr. James Endicott, a China-born son of a missionary who, disillusioned with Chiang Kai Shek, returned to Canada and launched the Canadian Peace Congress. James Endicott was one of the drafters of the Stockholm Peace Petition. Also named in the *Telegram* were left

Red Menace In Canada?

Much of the daily news and the literature of three continents is concerned these days with Communism and Communists.

They are a major factor in international politics and a considerable one in the domestic politics of the United States, Great Britain, and most of the Western World.

What about Canada? How serious is the Red menace here?

Who are the people directing the Communist effort in this country?

What are they doing currently? And have they any real hope of accomplishing the revolution they're working for so hard?

The *Telegram* assigned reporters Allan Kent and Clem Shields to investigate the present state of Communist fortunes in Canada and to try and find answers to these questions.

The assignment put them in touch with police, with Communists and ex-Communists, and with students of current history over a considerable area during the last month and a half.

The report on their investigation, which first appeared in a nine-article daily series in The *Telegram*, is reprinted in this pamphlet as a service to the public.

Their report is written in clear, factual style.

It may astonish you, it may disturb you. But whatever your reaction, it will give you the truth of the present Communist activity in Canada.

THE TELEGRAM
DAILY plus WEEKEND
BAY AND MELINDA STREETS   TORONTO 1, CANADA

The newspaper thought these eight articles important enough to reprint as a pamphlet in 1951.

Thomas Fisher Rare Book Library, University of Toronto, Kenny Collection, ms 179.

organizations among the Ukrainians, Russians, Poles, Hungarians, Slovaks, Finns, Lithuanians, Macedonians, the Jews, and the Congress of Canadian Women. Smaller groups such as Negro youth, the Germans, the Romanians, and the Italians were also suspect.

The UJPO Continues its Work

The expulsion created a divided Jewish community, but UJPO activities continued. Young people were involved in the drive to collect signatures for the Stockholm Peace Petition. Many UJPO women who had been active in the housewives' consumer movement against rising food prices turned to an involvement in peace activities in the early 1950s. They connected their mobilization for peace with cost of living issues and the expense of an arms race, enriching those who profit from war.

Some UJPO people remember with pride their participation in the peace movement. Mary Winer was born in 1903 in Lodz, Poland. Interviewed when she was in her early nineties, Mary proudly recalled the many years she marched for peace. As she grew older, her children and grandchildren and eventually great-grandchildren marched along with her. Once a reporter came up to her and said,

"Oh you're four generations marching, since when have you been marching?" Her reply was "Since I understood that I am against war.... I have gone to all demonstrations. All of them. And if I could I would go now too." She noted that the UJPO was the only overtly Jewish presence at these demonstrations.[84]

However, some remember the growing unpopularity of peace activities and how they hoped no one outside the community would know about their left views. Gerry Cohen of Montreal, who became an Oxford professor of philosophy, writes:

> When I was twelve, I made a speech before an audience of a couple of thousand at the Canadian Peace Congress in Toronto; it was duly reported with a photograph of me at the podium, in various low-circulation journals, and I was proud of all that, but I would not have known how to cope if my classmates had learned about it. Later, as teenagers, my comrades and I did quite scary things, like secretly carrying newspapers and leaflets in our bicycle baskets for delivery at sympathetic destinations. When doing so, we were always wary when we saw policemen, who knew how to rough people up without leaving a mark. McCarthyism was less insidious and more brutal in its Quebec manifestation that it was in the United States. Fewer people lost their jobs, but more people were beaten in police stations. I think I might have preferred to be beaten up, just a little bit, than to face classmates who knew what I was doing.[85]

Despite the blow of the expulsion and an overall drop in membership, the UJPO carried on its activities. The expulsion had repercussions on community events. One was honouring the Holocaust and the resistance in the Warsaw Ghetto. For ten years from 1943 to 1953, seventy-five organizations in Winnipeg came together to commemorate the Annual Warsaw Ghetto Memorial Evening and to mobilize the yearly campaign for the United Jewish Appeal.[86] Winnipeg Jewry had learned about the fate of the Warsaw Ghetto uprising two weeks after its final liquidation. On June 1, 1943, a front-page article in *Dos Yiddishe Vort* appeared with the title, "The Battle of Warsaw Ghetto Told by Correspondent." Mr. A. C. Cummings from the *London Tribune* reported in horrific detail the tragedy that had befallen the Jews in the Warsaw Ghetto: "The struggle in the Ghetto began more than a month ago (April 19) with 40,000 Jews still living there." (Three hundred thousand Jews had already been sent to Treblinka.) The remaining Jews "had pledged that it was better to die a hero's death than to be shamed and tortured by the Nazis." In the largest revolt by the Jews during the war, the residents of the Warsaw Ghetto "fought back with smuggled arms but only a handful survived the struggle." This act of resistance by a handful of Jews captured the imagination of the world and set the stage wherever Jews were living for an annual commemoration dedicated to the heroes of the Warsaw Ghetto.

The first memorial meeting was planned for Tuesday, July 20, 1943 at the Talmud Torah Hall. It was organized by Congress Council, the local wing of the Canadian Jewish Congress.[87] The Council in Winnipeg included organizations with diverse interests and ideologies, from the religious factions, the schools, and the Zionists and their divisions to a cross-section of left-wing Jewish organizations. The slogan for the first memorial was Let Their Blood Not Be Forgotten. For many years thereafter, the community united in a two-fold mission, to remember that Jews resisted in the face of tremendous odds and to remember the six million who had perished.

In 1953, after the UJPO and other left-wing organizations were expelled from the CJC, a common commemoration was no longer possible, and two separate memorial evenings were held.[88] The first was organized by the Winnipeg Congress Council and held on April 12, 1953. The second, on April 19, 1953, was organized by the left UJPO, Shalom Aleichem Shule, and YKUF. Both evenings commemorated the fifteenth anniversary of the Warsaw Ghetto uprising. The proceeds of the Yizkor Campaign of the left were used to help establish a community centre in Israel to commemorate the heroes of the Warsaw Ghetto.[89] When the UJPO attempted to broaden Holocaust education by proposing its incorporation into the Winnipeg school system, Congress refused to cooperate. Once again, the issue itself and the common interests were secondary to boycotting anything to do with the organization.

The community continued to feature artistic performances, and some of the performers became nationally known. The choirs in Montreal, Toronto, and Winnipeg, the drama workshop in these cities, and the Vancouver Drama Group continued performing. The UJPO Folksingers, the Youth Singers, the Realist Film Society, the Winnipeg Jewish Folk Choir, the Vancouver Folk Singers, and the Montreal Dance Group all organized in the early 1950s. The singing group the Travellers, all Naivelt campers, became nationally prominent and their Canadian rendition of "This Land" remains widely sung. Older institutions, such as the choir, with Emil Gartner as conductor, stayed strong. However, Cold War politics contrived to undermine the dance troupe, and 1952 was the last time the New Dance Theatre associated with the UJPO participated in the Canadian Dance Festival. Although there is no written documentation, a website describing Canadian ballet festivals notes that festival organizers felt the group's ideals fell "too far left of centre" and grew nervous about their association with a pro-socialist organization.[90]

The repression and Cold War atmosphere hit Montreal the hardest. For young people, coming of age in the 1950s as a child of left parents was not simple. Decades later, Olga Eizner Favreau found out that the principal of her school in Montreal jettisoned one of her teenage romances by warning the boy in question to stay away from her because to be seen with a young woman from a communist family would hurt his prospects. Years later, he told her he was haunted by his cowardly behaviour, but as it turned out she had decided at the same time that he was not for her and felt guilty for dumping him.[91]

Charles Law, director of the youth division of Montreal, revealed some of the pressures facing young people in the 1950s, which he called the "jitters." They feared the menace of the H-bomb and "the creeping threat of a McCarthy brand of fascism." They knew about unemployment and diminishing opportunities for Jewish Canadians, and the rearmament of Germany. He maintained that the Canadian Jewish Congress was trying its utmost to contain the power of the appeal of the left "with the illusion that Israel and Zionism [will] solve all problems for the Jewish People of Canada. Yet their policy is in bankruptcy."[92]

The forcible expulsion of UJPO's youth division from Congress angered many young people, who were upset at the banning of their friends from the organization. The UJPO youth division also encountered hostility from many quarters. When the Montreal group organized a dramatization commemorating the Warsaw Ghetto uprising, the event was shut down by the police. They faced the obstacle of not having an adequate centre since the closure of the Winchevsky Centre, but they continued trying to extend their membership and influence in the wider community.[93] Abe Rosenberg described the difficulties of small cramped meeting spaces and harassment by the police who systematically made it their business to know who the key organizers were, where meetings were held, and who the speakers were.

Despite this, two new branches organized in Montreal after the shutdown of the centre in 1950.[94] The fourth national convention in Toronto in May 1954 was held in grand style. The weekend included a concert in Massey Hall, Toronto's largest theatre venue, with the choirs from both Montreal and Toronto, the New Dance Theatre, and guest artist, actor Howard Da Silva from New York. Ironically, the blacklist in the United States meant that the left Jewish venues were among the few places where blacklisted actors such as Howard Da Silva and Morris Carnovsky could get work.

UJPO women held on to their conviction, expressed in the Stockholm Peace Petition, that an arms race endangered the world. In 1951, Annie Eizner of Montreal expressed support for the goals of the Women's International Democratic Federation (WIDF) in the journal for the second UJPO convention. Together with other left groups in Canada, the UJPO women were involved in the organizing of the Congress of Canadian Women (CCW) and became part of the WIDF.

Annie Eizner, head of the women's council of the Montreal UJPO, addressing the Second National United Jewish People's Order convention. The drawing (circa 2012) is by the artist Olga Eizner Favreau, based on a photograph of her mother from 1951.

Founded in 1945 in Paris, the WIDF was devoted to anti-fascism, international peace, child welfare, and improvements in the status of women. The WIDF saw strengthening democracy as the best strategy for a lasting peace and actively opposed France's involvement in Vietnam. UJPO women were part of each delegation to federal, provincial and city governments presenting petitions to control rising prices in the cost of living, including rent controls, and against using the atomic bomb. The women saw all these issues as interconnected—their desire for women's equality and the need for social supports were integrally connected to peace.

The Jewish left in the 1950s was dealing with the revival of anti-communism and attempts to marginalize leftist views. Influenced by the more drastic events in the United States, they worked to ignore the harassment and hold on to the conviction that an arms race was not a route to security. They were part of the basis for what a decade later became a mass movement to get out of Vietnam, and "give peace a chance."

PART III

CULTURAL FORMS

The Melodies of the
Jewish Soul

7 LANGUAGE AND THE EDUCATION OF A NEW GENERATION

A love of learning and respect for intellectual life were central to all the secular Jewish movements—the labour Zionist shules, the Workmen's Circle, and the left shules.[1] The shules developed from a grassroots movement and were staffed by dedicated teachers committed to the education of a new generation of girls and boys in Yiddish and social justice. In the left shules, Yiddish language, literature, and culture were intertwined with a politics that used the bitter history of anti-Semitism and class exploitation to teach the children that all struggles against oppression were their struggles as well.

Jews have been called the "people of the book." The term literally refers to the study of the Torah, but it also indicates the high literacy rate in the community and the respect for learning. A secular movement dating from the late nineteenth century rejected the limitations of an exclusive focus on religious knowledge and the ways it was taught in the traditional Jewish school or kheder. The kheder was the place where small boys were sent for instruction with a teacher or *melamed,* who was frequently not well paid or even respected. Secular Jews were scathing in their critiques of the traditional Jewish school. Lithuanian philosopher Salomon Maimon recalled his kheder years in his autobiography as "a hell whose name is school."[2] Chava Rosenfarb's novel *Bociany,* which takes place in a Polish village in the early twentieth century, offered this profile of a kheder:

Boys' kheder, Lublin, 1924.

Courtesy of YIVO.

Reb Shapsele [the melamed or teacher] was a hunchbacked little man whose nose continuously ran and whose tiny eyes continuously watered. He sat with his kheder boys at a long, corroded table, a red handkerchief in one hand, the disciplinary whip in the other. The greatest praise for a student was when the melamed did not mock him or shame him in front of the others, or did not give him a going-over with the whip. The kheder itself was located in a moldy, dingy cottage, where the melamed's wife and daughters, their faces powered with coal dust, busied themselves around the black sacks of coal that they were selling. Everything and everyone was smeared with the coal dust, including the boys' clothes and faces. Here in this dark room, its mildewed walls covered with dark blotches, the students spent their days. The melamed's wife and daughters ordered them around or made them do household chores, scolded them, and checked to make sure they did not play cards under the table.[3]

A Yiddish Education

The inspiration for the development of secular Yiddish language schools came from a conference held in 1908 in Czernowitz, then part of the Austro-Hungarian Empire. The conference addressed the challenging question of how to define a people without a state. Conference participants constituted a who's who of distinguished Yiddish writers and scholars, including Sholem Asch, Ester Frumkin, Moyshe-Leyb Halpern, Avrom Reyzen, Chaim Zhitlovsky, and I. L. Peretz. They declared Yiddish to be a unifying language for Jews.

Arriving at this position was not smooth going. There were conflicts between the Hebraists and Yiddishists, the Bundists and the Zionists. In his keynote address, Peretz expressed the view that a nation state can encompass many cultures, foreshadowing a multiculturalism not articulated until more than fifty years later. Peretz outlined three important moments in Jewish history:

The poor Jewish masses, the poor ignorant Jews begin to liberate themselves. They lose confidence in both the Jewish Talmudic scholar, and in the rich man. The rich man's "charity" does not fill his stomach; the Talmudic scholar's Toyre doesn't give him any joy. The masses long, feel, want to live their own poor lives in their own way. And Chassidism emerges. Toyre for everybody.... And this is the first moment.[4]

Yiddish writers at the Czernowitz Conference, 1908. From left to right: Avrom Reyzen, Yitskhok Leybush Peretz, Sholem Asch, Chaim Zhitlovsky, Hersh Dovid Nomberg. Postcard (Warsaw: Verlag Jehudia). Reprinted from the *Pakn Treger* (Fall 2015), 32.

Courtesy of YIVO.

The Jewish woman—the Jewish wife—the Jewish girl awoke and demanded something for herself. Women's books appeared, and out of Judeo-German was born a "mother-tongue." And the Jewish people still has two tongues: a language for the scholars in the house of study—the language of the Toyre, the language of the Gemoreh, and the second for the masses and the Jewish daughter.

This is the second significant movement. The third is:

> Now the Jewish worker appears, the Jewish proletariat, and creates for itself an instrument for its struggle for life, its working-class culture in Yiddish.... He wants to and he must express himself in Yiddish. And the Yiddish secular book in the Yiddish language appears.
>
> The weak, oppressed people awake, and struggle for their language, for their own culture against the nation-state. And we, the weakest, have also joined their ranks.... The nation-state will no longer falsify the cultures of its peoples, no longer suppress individuality and differentness. This is the byword of the multitudes, and we are in their ranks under our own banner and in the name of our own cultural interests.
>
> We don't want to be anyone's handmaiden. A lackey people can-not create cultural riches—and we do! ... We no longer want to be fragmented, and to render to every Moloch nation-state its tribute: There is one people—Jews, and its language is—Yiddish.[5]

Peretz encapsulated the origins and significance of the secular Yiddish movement, and how Yiddish became the instrument for the creation of a people's culture not confined by the borders of a nation state—a development in which he played an important role. Here he was arguing for respecting Yiddish language and culture within and between the borders of multi-ethnic nation states that encompass many cultures and peoples. For Canadians, this respect for difference is an early argument for the value and importance of a multicultural society.

Peretz's advocacy of Yiddish was not immediately accepted by the new immigrants to North America. Many of the early socialists in the Workmen's Circle, who arrived from Europe at the end of the nineteenth century, were committed to a cosmopolitan and assimilationist outlook. In fact, prior to the establishment of the Yiddish shules, the Workmen's Circle established Sunday School experiments in various parts of North America, teaching socialism in English. These schools did not last because people did not readily discard their ethnic language and culture. Jewish radicals felt that they could be both socialists and internationalists and still be committed to their identity as a Jew.

As Peretz indicated, for centuries Yiddish was the language of women and everyday life. Dovid Katz, in his history of Yiddish, *Words on Fire,* discusses how Yiddish was reviled by religious Jews and the educated "enlightened" elite and dismissed as jargon. It was the language ordinary people spoke when they were doing things that weren't important—the everyday business of existence such as raising children and making a living. Hebrew was the holy tongue of the synagogue. Katz argues that while Hebrew was associated with a territorial and nationalist model, Yiddish reflected a humanistic and internationalist model. Yiddish was associated with *sotsyalizm* (socialism), a vision of equitable societies in which there is no unchecked exploitation of workers by ultra-rich capitalists.[6] By the late nineteenth century, this involved sympathizing with those who hoped to overthrow the oppressive regimes of Eastern Europe to establish a new democratic order in a new society. Yiddish was the only language most could read and understand, and it came to be used with "defiant pride" as a political statement. So the use of the Yiddish language among secular Jews became associated with a movement for social justice.[7] One example of this is I. L. Peretz's short story "Sholem Bayis" (peaceful house).

Khayim, an uneducated water carrier, fearing that his ignorance will jeopardize his heavenly chances in the world to come, goes to the rabbi. The rabbi advises him to study after work. But, Khayim asks, what should he do about his beloved wife, Khane, who puts together a Sabbath meal each week like a magician, despite the missing ingredients they are too poor to afford, and who is busy caring for the children? Not to worry, says the rabbi, when Khayim earns a place for himself in the world to come, his wife will be there too, as his footstool. Khayim, the uneducated worker, returns home, thinks it over and says to his wife, "No, Khane, you will have to sit beside me, and God in Heaven himself will simply have to understand!"[8]

Peretz's work illustrates how Yiddish came to be associated with radical thinking, including challenging women's position in the world.

Radikaler Shuln Come to Canada

Following the Czernowitz conference of 1908, the fifth annual left labour Zionist conference was convened in Montreal in 1910. Participants debated a proposal to establish Yiddish radical schools in Canada and the United States.[9] The influential Russian Jewish intellectual, Chaim Zhitlovsky (1865–1943) attended the conference and made an impassioned plea for Yiddish schools in North America, arguing, "if you reject Yiddish, the Jewish proletariat will reject you."[10] The conference decided to support Yiddish instruction. The 1910 Montreal deliberations agreed to develop a community school organization, welcoming girls, introducing social issues and current events, and emphasizing folklore, history, and pedagogical training.[11] The first teachers were labour activists, men who worked in the needle trades and who put a great deal of thought and commitment into the schools.

In the early years the schools, called *Radikaler shuln* (radical schools), were supported by a coalition of secular radicals. These included labour Zionists, Bundists, socialists, anarchists, and territorialists. Despite ideological differences, they had in common their opposition to the capitalist system. These activists established Radikaler shuln in Montreal, Toronto, and Winnipeg to teach the Yiddish language and a critical outlook on the world. The teachers were often workers as well as union activists.

By the early 1920s, teachers who had trained in Yiddish teachers' seminaries in Eastern Europe arrived in Canada. Leybl Basman, who studied in Wilkomir, Lithuania, became perhaps the most well-known teacher in the left-wing schools. He had a career that spanned forty years. Basman saw the establishment of the

Radikaler Shule Winnipeg, 1914. Radical School.
Jewish Heritage Centre of Western Canada Archives, JM 480.

Yiddish shules in Eastern Europe and North America as the coming together of enlightenment ideals of expanding knowledge with a workers' movement.[12] As Jews sought an escape from impoverishment in their small villages by emigration to the cities, and later to North America, they experienced class exploitation and learned about forbidden ideologies such as Marxism, which spoke to the realities of their lives. They became socialists. When they emigrated to Canada and the United States, they hoped to transmit the values that gave meaning to their lives to a new generation through the Yiddish shule. They sought the latest pedagogical methods to educate and develop a generation of Jewish youth.[13]

Writing in Winnipeg's *Der Kanader Yid* (The Israelite) in 1914, A. Glantz laid out why he thought a Yiddish shule was important. He hoped that a Yiddish education would help bridge the divide between North American-born Jewish children and their immigrant parents. Without it, Glantz thought the children would grow up to be

> spiritual cripples, not Jews and not Americans ... the National Radical schools, every part of them are not modernized Talmud Torahs.... The children don't just learn Yiddish. We develop in them the pride of humanity, their humanity, we teach them to love all people, all folk; we teach them to help all the oppressed, we awaken in them a love of all that is beautiful and just.[14]

The Shules and the Larger Canadian Jewish Community

Since the early twentieth century the Jewish community in Canada comprised religious and secular Jews; this included socialists of all varieties, from the radical left to the right; Zionists of all varieties—left and right socialists, radicals, moderates, and reactionaries; Hebraists who belittled Yiddish as the language of the ghetto, and Yiddishists who frowned on Hebrew as the "dead" language of the Talmud and the past. There were numerous divisions in the religious schools, and after it was established the secular shule movement did not remain unified for long.

The religious majority did not take kindly to any of the secular initiatives. In their eyes, these cynics and questioners of Jewish orthodoxy were *apikorsim* or heretics. In Winnipeg, in 1914, the left secular teachers were dubbed "Christian missionaries," threatened with *kherem* (excommunication), and forced out of the Aberdeen Public School, which they had been using in the afternoons after the English school day ended. In Montreal, in 1916, nineteen rabbis and sixty-nine others signed a resolution warning that "we are being robbed of our children" and that the left secular schools "practice the desecration of the Sabbath and our Jewish religious commandments."[15]

The early Radikaler shuln were socialist but in keeping with their Labour Zionist origins they also stressed love for the land of Israel.[16] The passion with which people approached the question of how best to secure a future for Jews soon resulted in the splitting of the secular shule movement. The non-Zionists soon left to form their own schools.[17] (See the box on page 161.) Essentially the differences reflected ideological rather than pedagogical differences. All were secular, but each movement considered it necessary to have its own school. Depending on the size of the city and the political situation in a province, different Yiddish schools developed at different times. For example, in Montreal the public school system was either Catholic or Protestant; there was no non-religious publicly funded public school system. Catholics did not want Jewish children in their schools, so Jewish children attended Protestant schools, where they learned English, not French. The only alternative for a non-Christian education was a religious Jewish school or a Yiddish school, which required money for tuition. Yiddish day schools developed, offering full day education and after-school classes. They were the Yiddish Folk Shule, where Hebrew was taught along with Yiddish, and the Peretz School, which had a greater emphasis on Yiddish. For seven years (1945–52), the left secular Jews in Montreal ran a full day school named after Morris Winchevsky. The full-day shules covered the English curriculum in half the day; the rest was devoted to Jewish subjects. The left Liberty Temple Shule in Winnipeg, which began in 1921, also had a full day school for a few years in the 1930s.

All the secular shules ran after-school classes. Children attending public schools went to Yiddish after-school programs three or four times a week.

In Toronto there were two Zionist shules—the Farband (right wing) and the Borokhov, which was more radical, as well as an Arbeter Ring (Workmen's Circle) Shule, and, after 1928, a Labour League Winchevsky Shule. In Winnipeg, the Radikaler shule was renamed the Peretz School after Peretz's death in 1915 and had a full day school until the 1980s, teaching Yiddish, Hebrew, and English. The many commonalities of the schools—all built and supported by grassroots efforts—were sometimes forgotten in the midst of their fierce ideological debates.

The left-wing schools shules in Canada were connected to the North American Jewish left secular movement. After the International Workers Order (IWO) was organized in the United States in 1930, the left Yiddish shules in Canada used the resources afforded by a larger population concentration and became part of a North American movement. IWO histories even list the Canadian schools as a subsection of the IWO shules.

When the struggles over support for the Bolshevik revolution tore the Workmen's Circle apart, many of the affiliated schools also withdrew. The left branches in both countries were expelled (or withdrew) from the Workmen's Circle in 1926, and the schools followed. Seventeen of the twenty-four schools in New York organized what they called the *umparteyisher shuln* or unaffiliated schools. They became part of the IWO when it was founded in 1930. Independent left shules organized in Montreal and Toronto in 1928 and became "Ordn" shules in 1930, using IWO materials and in some cities recruiting teachers from the IWO in New York. The box provides an overview of the Yiddish secular schools that emerged in three of Canada's cities from the 1910s to the late 1920s. It shows some of the many splits that occurred—between left and more radical left Zionists, between social democrats and pro-communists. In various cities, schools opened, closed, united with other schools. Such divisions were not possible in smaller communities such as Hamilton or Calgary where opposing factions had to work together if they were to be able to support a shule. The shules were often named for writers such as I. L. Peretz, Sholem Aleichem, and Morris Winchevsky. In Winnipeg, the left schools were called the Liberty Temple Shule, later renamed the Sholem Aleichem Shule. In Toronto, the shule was part of the Labour League, and in Montreal the shule was part of the Canadian Labour Circle. In Montreal and Toronto, the shules were named after Morris Winchevsky. They all became affiliated with the UJPO after 1945.

When Louis Rosenberg compiled his extensive study on Jews in Canada in the 1930s, the statistics available to him indicated that students who attended

Development of the Secular Yiddish Shule Movements in Canada

1913–1915 Natsionale Radikaler Shuln (National Radical Schools) were organized in Montreal, Toronto, and Winnipeg. They were established by secular Jews opposed to the capitalist system but often from different ideological movements. Teaching was in Yiddish with some Hebrew.

1914 Yiddish Folkshule or the Jewish People's School opened in Montreal. Yiddish and Hebrew were taught. This school had a stronger emphasis on Hebrew and Zionism than the Radikaler shules and had a full-day school. In Toronto, the left Labour Zionist school was called the Borokhov Shule. The right-wing Zionists organized the Farband Shule.

1916 The Natsionale Radikaler Shuln were renamed the Peretz schools after the famous writer's death. There were Peretz schools in Montreal, Toronto, and Winnipeg. Yiddish was the main language but some Hebrew was taught. In Montreal and Winnipeg, the schools included full-day schools as well as after-school programs.

1918 The Arbeter Ring (Workmen's Circle) began to open schools. In Winnipeg, the Arbeter Ring School dates from 1921 and was located in the Liberty Temple (Freiheit Temple). The Arbeter Ring rejected Jewish nationalism and the slogan of the Radikaler shule, "The Jewish Child for the Jewish People." Their emphasis was more socialist and internationalist.

1920s Day schools developed in Montreal and Winnipeg.

1928 The split in the Arbeter Ring over the left's support for the Russian Revolution motivated leftist Jews in Montreal and Toronto to open their own schools. Called Winchevsky schools, they were affiliated with the left movements. The new schools' motto was "The Worker's Child for the Working Class." The emphasis was on children developing a proletarian anti-racist consciousness. Yiddish was the language of instruction.

1930 After the establishment of the sister organization, the International Workers Order, in the United States in 1930, the schools became part of a North American network and were called the Ordn shules.

1932 The Winnipeg split in the Arbeter Ring took place. The left remained in control of the Freiheit Temple, renamed the Arbeter Freiheit Temple Shule, later the Sholem Aleichem Shule.

1945 The left shules become affiliated with the UJPO

any of the secular shules were a minority. Most of the Jews who gave their children a Jewish education chose to send them to a Hebrew school for religious instruction. In 1931, there were 16,213 Jewish children in Canada between ten and fourteen, the ages when they were most likely to be attending a Jewish school. In the 1930s, 40 percent to 50 percent of Jewish children received some form of Jewish education, generally after English day school. Eighty-four percent of these children lived in either Quebec or Ontario, the two provinces for which Rosenberg was able to get detailed statistics. Of the 8,700 children receiving a Jewish education in Toronto and Montreal, only 1600, or 18 percent, attended the secular Yiddish schools.[18]

In 1937 in Toronto, 22 percent of Jewish children received an education in Yiddish; in Montreal, the number was lower, only 16 percent, but the Montreal figures are only available for 1930, an earlier period. More girls than boys received a secular education in Yiddish because parents tended to want their boys to know Hebrew and have a traditional Bar Mitsvah. In Toronto in 1936, the girl-to-boy ratio in the secular schools was 2:1. In Montreal in 1930, the ratio was 3:1. The ratio between girls and boys was more even only in the left shules where parents did not care about religious training for a boy's Bar Mitsvah.[19]

While the secular shule movement in its entirety was never the majority, the left had an important place in it, although recent descriptions often omit any mention of the size or significance of the left shules.[20] By 1936, Toronto's Labour League shules were in two different locations; they also had a kindergarten with a total shule enrolment of 170 children.[21] In Montreal, the Winchevsky shule had a large after-school program and developed a full day school in the mid-1940s. The Workmen's Circle school almanac compiled statistics for the shule movements in North America. In the spring of 1935, they identified three major shule movements: the Farband or Labour Zionist shules, the Arbeter Ring or Workmen's Circle and the International Workers Order, which included the Canadian left shules. In Montreal, the left schools were part of the *Kanader Arbeter Ring* or Canadian Labour Circle. In Toronto, they were affiliated with the Labour League and in Winnipeg, the Liberty Temple. All were counted as part of the network of IWO shules. Statistics gathered by the Workmen's Circle found that the North American shules affiliated with the IWO had the most students—a total of 6,200 students in 122 schools or 38 percent of the students.[22]

Shule Movements in North America, 1935

	Shules	Students
Jewish National Workers Union or Farband	54	5100
Workmen's Circle	93	5497
Sholem Aleichem Folk Institute	[about] 25	1800
Jewish Worker Shules	2	80
International Workers Order	[about] 122	6200
Left Poale Tsion	5	328
Totals	301	19,005

Source: Herman Frank, *Shule Almanac: The Modern Yiddish Shules throughout the World* (Philadelphia: Workmen's Circle Schools, 1935), 348–64.

It is noteworthy that this list was compiled and published not by the left, but by the Workmen's Circle. Fradle Pomerantz Freidenreich's more recent research has calculated the number of shules and children in the left or IWO schools as even higher than the estimates published in the Workmen's Circle almanac. She estimated 8,000 children in 144 IWO shules in the United States and Canada in 1935, out of a combined total of 19,000 students in all the secular shule networks. Unfortunately, the statistics are not divided by country. As late as 1946 even after the onset of the Cold War, the left, while no longer the largest in the secular shule system, still had 6,000 students. (Arbeter Ring schools had 7,200 students and the Farband, 6,000 students.)[23]

Dedicated Teachers

Virtually all of the teachers in the early years of all the secular Yiddish schools in Canada had been educated in the Yiddish schools that developed in Eastern Europe after the First World War. David Rome described the devotion of the first teachers:

> Many of them were tailors who laboured all day in the shop, but their mind was in the school. The shop was their week day life; the school is Sabbath and festival. They would rush from work to the school with enthusiasm, with Chassidic fire. Once across the threshold they forgot shop and personal life. Their mind was on the children. We had planted a garden of living flowers. We must tend it, guard it.[24]

Morris Winchevsky surrounded by children from the Arbeter Ring I. L. Peretz Shule, 1921—this was before the split between right and left.

UJPO Archives.

Wolf Chaitman, one of the early teachers in the Radikaler shule, was also a labour activist:

> After a long and hard day in the factory where he was one of the "hands" (the want ads in the newspapers referred to "hands" rather than human beings), he would go to his room, wash, shave and dress in his best; and then, like a groom going to meet his bride, he walked to the shule, where he was transformed into a prince. The factory hand was transformed into the man of mind, heart and soul.[25]

The left shules differed from the other secular shules by their stress on internationalism as well as their pro-Soviet socialist outlook. They had a particularly difficult time financially as their left politics did not sit well with the dominant players in the community. For most of their history, the financial assistance offered to all other Jewish schools, including the secular ones, by the municipal Jewish Welfare Funds in each community was denied to them. For a brief period when the Allies and the USSR were fighting in the Second World War, the left schools were also funded. However by 1950, this money was withdrawn with the claim that the schools were not really "Jewish."

These schools attempted to instil the values of anti-racism, anti-colonialism, and pro-unionism in the children. The teachers devoted their lives to Yiddish—not a very lucrative career choice—and maintained a principled opposition to inequality, racism, and greed. Their education model strongly resembled the one developed by Paulo Freire in the 1960s and 1970s. Freire's notion of praxis, which he outlines in *Pedagogy of the Oppressed*, is based on the idea of putting one's learning into practice—or conscientization.[26] Similarly, education in the shules was viewed as a means of consciously shaping the person and the society.

Many of the left shules were named after Morris Winchevsky. Born in 1855 in Kovno, Poland, Winchevsky emigrated first to London and then to New York, where he died in 1932. He was a poet and socialist who edited one of the first Yiddish socialist newspapers, *Der Arbeter Fraynd* (The Workers' Friend). Winchevsky wrote songs that honoured the life of working people and called on them to come together to build a better life. He opposed the First World War as an imperialist war and cheered the victory of the Bolshevik revolution.

One of Winchevsky's poems, *Di Tsukunft* (The Future) was put to music and sung by children in shules and Yiddish choirs all over the world.

O di velt vet vern yunger	Oh the world will grow young
Un dos lebn laykhter gringer	And life, easier, more beautiful
Yeder kloger vert a zinger	Every complainer will become a singer
Vern brider bald	All will soon be brothers
O, di velt vet vern sheyner	Oh the world will grow more beautiful
Libe greser, sine kleyner	Love, greater, and envy smaller
Tsvishn froyen, tsvishn mener	Between women and men
Tsvishn land un land	Between countries

Reading Circles and Women's Support for the Shules

None of the secular Yiddish schools could have functioned without the work of women. With the help of the Muter Fareyn (the Mother's League), the left shules were among the first to introduce kindergarten classes in Canada. (Kindergarten

Kindergarten class in Winnipeg, June 1934. The secular shules had kindergartens well before the public school system.

Jewish Heritage Centre of Western Canada Archives, JM 4298.

did not become part of the public school system in Canada until after the Second World War.)[27]

The women worked tirelessly to fundraise for the shules by holding bazaars and bake sales, and they also sewed costumes for performances. They described their unheralded and often invisible work as a labour of love. Their pleasure in enhancing their children's experience was coupled with how they used the Muter Fareyn to enhance their own education. Most of the mothers had not received any secular Jewish education. In order to promote the schools, they had to know what the children were learning. One would imagine that this was both a reason and a rationale for devoting themselves to their own self-education. With a taste came the appetite and the zest to learn more. The women organized reading circles in virtually all the secular shules, not only those on the left. A preface to a 1939 pamphlet published by the Detroit Reading Circles Council noted that "the Yiddish schools became not just a learning institution for the children, but also for the parents, in particular the mothers.... In general our fathers in the old home worried little about the Jewish education of their daughters."[28] On the left, Yiddish Kultur Farband (YKUF; Jewish Cultural Association) reading circles were established in Montreal, Toronto, Winnipeg, Windsor, Hamilton, and Calgary, an outcome of the International Cultural Congress of 1937.[29] They helped support the journal *Yiddishe Kultur* as well as the shules.

Aided by the efforts of the energetic teacher and actor Leybl Basman, who had returned to Winnipeg from Toronto to teach, the Winnipeg YKUF Youth Group formed in January 1941 and had about thirty-five members aged between sixteen and twenty-three.[30] The group decided to use Yiddish as much as possible, even though some of the members were not Yiddish speakers. They planned to establish a choir, a drama circle, and discussion, literature, and dance groups.[31] Despite continued financial difficulties when the shule was denied funding from the Winnipeg Jewish Welfare Fund from 1939–41, the Winnipeg YKUF held major subscription drives for *Yiddishe Kultur*.[32] Every Sunday evening there were forums with local speakers and visiting speakers from central Canada and New York. The subjects ranged from the work of I. L. Peretz to Yiddish poetry, Freud, the civic elections in Winnipeg, and Soviet Jewry.[33] The Winnipeg YKUF also held an evening for parents to hear their children read their own work in an attempt to involve the parents more in what their children were learning.[34] Interest in Yiddish culture in Canada was strong. Winnipeg had four YKUF reading circles. In 1944, there were eleven YKUF reading circles in Toronto.

Three hundred women from Detroit and Windsor were members of the United Detroit Reading Circles Council first organized in 1934. By 1939, there were twenty-five reading circles in Detroit and Windsor attached to the secular schools from different movements. The gatherings always included tables laden with food and singing. One woman would contribute a reading, another a recitation, someone else a lecture, another a song or story she had written. "We learned what the other reading circles were doing and became closer. We celebrated traditional holidays, national holidays and International Women's Day."

The uniqueness of the United Detroit Reading Council was its inclusiveness at a time when denunciations of other movements were still common. Right and left were included, and the political divisiveness was left behind. Indeed, the women achieved a unity that was a model for others. Poet Kadya Molodovsky, who had visited Detroit from New York, greeted the women with these words: "The work of our finest masters consisted of love for the people—let us hope that this spirit will influence the reading circles and they will bring the unity and love to our cultural life instead of the divisiveness and bitterness that now dominates our cultural life." One leftist reading circle was so inspired by her visit that they named their reading group after her.[35]

A woman from the Workmen's Circle described the Muter Fareyn activities:

A holiday arrives, the first of May, a workers holiday, or Purim, Chanukah—all of the muter fareyn can be found baking, cooking, shopping, running here and there to prepare a beautiful festive holiday for the children in the shule. How much pleasure and joy the women provide through their volunteer work.

The second function is very interesting. Every Tuesday evening eighteen women gather in the shule. After the routine problems are dealt with we begin the study work. We discuss world events … we are also reading Yiddish literature, such as David Pinksi Sholem Asch, I. J. Singer and others. The women's education grows and general knowledge, with pride in the culture and literature of their people.[36]

Mothers' League, Branch One, Winnipeg. Below from left to right: Esther Miller, G. Taylor, H. Boz, F. Moltinski. Sitting: F. Chochinov, A Kirk, Sarah Kligerman, Ellen Tessler (Financial Secretary), Fanny Yanovksky (Chair), Gittl Simkin, Sh. Dorfman, D. Slavin, L. Brussl. Second row: S. Singer, S. Kaminksi, R. Papeski, P. Merkel, H. Bunov, R. Liebkind, A. Dolgoy, A. Handler, H. Bronstein.

25 Year Jubilee Book, 1921–1946. Collection of Roz Usiskin.

Some groups felt the need to extend their activities. For the left women from the IWO schools in Detroit, half of the money they raised went to the shule and the rest was divided between the YKUF, the left Yiddish paper, *Der Freiheit*, and a Yiddish radio show. Another reading circle raised money to support children orphaned in the Spanish Civil War.

In Winnipeg in 1946, Gittl Simkin looked back on her twenty-five years' involvement with the Muter Fareyn of the left-wing Liberty Temple. During the Depression years, the miserable wages the men earned made it a challenge to care for the family. She wondered how she and the other women managed to find the time, money, and strength to help the shule. There were many memorable pleasures—the family suppers, the exhibits of children's work, the concerts, and the teas and bazaars.[37]

Gittl Simkin's husband, Fayvl Simkin, the publisher of *Dos Yiddishe Vort* (The Israelite Press) in Winnipeg, was an anarchist who did not share her views. Fayvl says, "I was against the Communists, and she was a Communist."[38] Asked if that made for a difficult marriage, Fayvl answered with one word, "No." He was involved with the more moderate Peretz School, not the Liberty Temple. Gittl, her father, Noakh Levin, and some of her friends were active in the left. Fayvl adds, "Maybe to spite me too."

Gittl Simkin and the Winnipeg women, like their counterparts in Detroit, found that the fundraising work to support the shule was not enough for them. They wanted more. Gittl wrote that the Muter Fareyn always considered their own education and development of the members. They organized elementary and more advanced study groups, learning a great deal from Bloshtein, the first teacher in the shule. They held reading circles and lectures on many themes—literary, political, medical. During the 1940s, during the brief period when the schools received financial support from the Jewish welfare fund, their work was much easier. They were able to take on other activities such as aid work for European Jews and anti-war efforts and still continue their cultural work.[39] In 1946, on the occasion of the twenty-fifth anniversary of the shule, Nozhnitsky, one of the shule's founders, paid tribute to the women who played such an important role.[40] It is noteworthy because the acknowledgement of women's role was unusual. The Muter Fareyn's efforts in the shule and their self-education can be viewed as translating their socialist principles into concrete realities, the often unglamorous, hard work of social change.

Winnipeg Shules

In Winnipeg in 1921, the Arbeter Ring separated from the Radikaler shule and opened their own Yiddish school in the Liberty Temple, with just eighteen children. Within a few months, Khaver M. Bloshtein arrived from Russia and was installed as principal.[41] Faygl Kirk remembered how strange Bloshtein seemed to the children at first, with his tall fur hat and odd accent. But it didn't take long for them to realize they had not only a teacher but also a friend. For Faygl, shule was not a duty, but the most wonderful part of the day, an environment of love and warmth. It was never too early or late for Bloshtein to listen to the children's dreams and worries.[42] Within three years the shule had 250 pupils in seven grades and a kindergarten. Bloshtein's personal dynamism and devotion drew people to the educational and cultural work of the shule. People competed to participate for the twenty-five places on the advisory board. These volunteer board members were idealists and "did not shrink from any difficulties, of which there were plenty."[43]

Writing in Winnipeg's Yiddish newspaper, *Dos Yiddishe Vort* (The Israelite Press), in 1927, Bloshtein described how creating a Yiddish proletarian shule was the realization of a dream:

> For years the Winnipeg workers' colony dreamed about a school. A school that will educate the young generation in the ideals of the working class; a school that will educate the youth so that they know how powerfully great and lofty is the joy of true brotherly unity … which will unleash the energy to transform one's

entire life on a foundation of brotherhood, of work, of economic equality.... We want to prepare our children so that they will be able to later participate, serve humanity, not the group of people that have grabbed the riches of the world.[44]

The graduation celebration of 1927 celebrating twenty years of the Workmen's Circle and ten years of the Liberty Temple was a joyous event.[45] The Winnipeg Playhouse was rented for the occasion, with a banquet in the evening in Steiman's Hall on Selkirk Avenue.[46] The concert went from two in the afternoon until seven in the evening. At the graduation ceremony Waldman, the teacher, handed out the diplomas and Principal Bloshtein kissed each student. At the evening banquet, the teachers were lifted into the air. Bloshtein's appeal for funding for the Liberty Temple raised $6,000. People danced till late in the evening and for the moment, any divisiveness was forgotten, "everyone feeling that they were part of one family all struggling for a freer world."[47]

The late 1920s and early 1930s were confusing times for the left, and Winnipeg was torn by the battles waged in the Workmen's Circle elsewhere in Canada and the United States. Bloshtein, however, very much wanted the shule and the Liberty Temple organization in Winnipeg to remain united. Addressing the internal crisis of the school, the pro-Bolshevik faction known as di linke (the left) versus the social democrats, called di rekhte (the right), Bloshtein attempted to remind people of what the different movements had in common: "Language and secularism unite them; goals and tasks separate them.... Each type of school has its aims, its spirit, its soul." But his call for moderation could not withstand the volatile politics in the rest of the country. The Liberty Temple split between left and right, although in Winnipeg it was the left who remained in control of the school and the Freiheit (Liberty) Temple building on Pritchard. The Workmen's Circle set up its own school but after a few years joined with the Peretz School. When the Liberty Temple shule divided in 1932, Bloshtein, who had tried to reconcile both sides, could no longer remain as principal in this environment of bitter debates. He moved to teach in Calgary. Bloshtein's departure was a difficult one, and he retained an honoured place in the hearts of those who remained. Mike Usiskin later described the shule as "Bloshtein's holy place," and the students, "his priceless treasures." One of the teachers, Leybl Basman, left as well, to teach in Windsor, then in Toronto and Montreal. Basman returned to Winnipeg in 1941.

With the departures of Bloshtein and Basman, two of Canada's best teachers, the survival of the school was in jeopardy. A series of teachers were sent from the International Workers Order. First came Moyshe Feldman from Montreal, who left a "broken man." Presumably, he was unsuccessful in negotiating the tense divisions that persisted. He was followed by Nathan Kamenetsky, David Laxer, and Hershl Sandler, all from New York. Sandler stayed for four years and helped rebuild the shule. Finally, after a long absence, Basman returned.

A Curriculum Reflecting the Times

The "class against class" politics of the Communist Party (CP) of the late 1920s and early 1930s influenced shule policy and curriculum. Sam Lapedes, writing in *Der Kamf* in 1931, captured the fierceness of the debates in the Jewish left. His article illustrates how the sectarian politics of the CP affected the shules, although it is not clear how closely these policies were followed in practice. Lapedes dismissed the Talmud Torahs for placing youth under the powerful influence of religious ideas and rabbis in synagogues controlled by the rich. He denounced other socialist groups as well, calling the Arbeter Ring and Poale Tsion (Labour Zionist) shules too nationalist for placing "folk" over "class." He said, "Although they call themselves secular and progressive, they are not free of religious education and include religious holidays, legends and stories in their programme." In the Labour League, on the other hand, the goal of the shule was a class-conscious education in Yiddish, rather than just a Yiddish education.[48]

In the early years, there were debates about which should take precedence—the Yiddish language or politics. When the left in Montreal and Toronto decided to open schools in 1928, there were no suitable materials in Yiddish, and *Der Kamf* writers disagreed over the form the schools should take. Was Yiddish the means by which children would receive a political education, or was the language itself of value? Impassioned debates marked a shule convention held in New York's Camp Kinderland in 1929. One faction, led by Jacob Levine, maintained that the shules should be non-aligned: the children should be informed about all the political movements and make up their own minds. This view seems to be the one held by Bloshtein, the principal in Winnipeg's shule. However, the majority prevailed, denouncing this position as "petty bourgeois liberalism." They argued that education in a bourgeois society could never be free. Children are influenced by the street, the movies, the schools, radio, the funnies, the media, the schools. They must be taught class struggle in Yiddish, and the language is the means, not the goal.[49]

The shule convention adopted a model of education based on the Soviet style "project" system, or learning through actual involvement in issues beyond the classroom:

Liberty Temple School play, Winnipeg. The English sign at the back of the room says, "Workers of the World Unite." The Yiddish sign reads, "Our future lies in the emergence of the new Yiddish school." The sign on the right is partly cut off, but it says something about the "Working Class, Brotherhood, and our ideals." The play included opposition to anti-Black racism (see the KKK character at the back).

Jewish Heritage Centre of Western Canada Archives, JM4293.

The instruction should not be one of words but should also be bound to practical work. This practical work will find its expression not only in special school activities but in participating in the life and struggle of the working-class, to the extent that this is possible for children. Help for strikers, delegations to children of other nationalities, assistance in political activities of the revolutionary labor movement, participation in picket lines. The language of our school is Yiddish but the language is utilized for the purpose of developing the internationalist spirit in the children.[50]

For some, the lack of emphasis on Jewish issues was a concern. Itche Goldberg, who was the director of the IWO School and Cultural Division of the Jewish People's Fraternal Order, felt that too little emphasis was placed on the Jewish aspect of this education—in particular, on history.

M. Bakal argued in *Der Kamf* that the non-aligned schools must be proletarian not Yiddishist because Yiddish was a language like other languages; using it, one could learn to be reactionary or influence children to be enemies of the working class. For Bakal, the idea that Yiddish alone was a sign of developing idealism was an illusion.[51] Critiquing Peretz's statement from the Czernowitz conference of "one people—the Jews and their language Yiddish," the poet Sh. Nepom, also writing in *Der Kamf*, sought to de-essentialize the idea of who and what Jews are. He says that Jews are not one people:

> Jewish politicians, Jewish exploiters, Jewish factory owners who incite their Christian workers against the more progressive Jewish workers fighting for bread, Jewish scabs—"one people Jews." Let's do a little dance. They all speak Yiddish and they are all of a relation to "our treasure," our culture.[52]

The raison d'être of the left shules in the early years emphasized the importance of a "proletarian Jewish education to counter the chauvinism, patriotism, militarism promoted in the wider society."[53] While adopting positions consistent with CP policy, Philip Halperin, the well-respected editor of *Der Kamf* until his death in 1932 and a CP member, cautioned that proletarian is not synonymous with communist: "From the other side it is false and vulgar to understand that the left shules will create "little Communists.'" He added that the left shules were not a factory to "make Communists," but they would have a marked emphasis on students' appreciation of the class struggle.[54] Again, while CP politics influenced what happened in the shules, particularly in this period, the left movement was much broader than the Party. Understanding these distinctions, and neither minimizing them nor exaggerating CP influences, is a challenge.

The schools were seen as all-important if the left was to have a future. Although the lessons learned might not have exactly echoed what was taught, the shule became the centre of a community for the children where they met their friends, had fun, and enjoyed music, dance, and singing as well as learning Yiddish and a workers' approach to the world. Many years later, students from the shule recall their delight in the artist Avrom's "chalk talks" in which he developed a story with a message from a squiggle or line drawn by a member of the audience. Neither art nor teaching Yiddish, however, were ways to make a good living.

Financial difficulties and paying the teachers were a constant worry. A letter likely written in the 1950s by American teacher Khaver Gelman to Khaver Stein, manager of his shule in California, complained about not receiving the $300 owed him for twelve weeks' work.

> I don't clip coupons. I work very hard to "make a living." I'm way over my head in debt.... Listen, Khaver Stein, I never sought honors in the shuln but the

Avrom's chalk talks and children of the shule watching with delight.
Toronto, 1950s.

Photos courtesy of Anna Yanovksy.

dishonor of having my wages cut and comparing me to other teachers who cannot even spell well—no not that. This is not our Movement, this is an abomination.[55]

The letter concludes with greetings to Stein's family and solicitous inquiries about his injured back. The financial situation north of the border was no different.

The proletarian emphasis was so pronounced that even the most prominent and beloved teachers, such as Basman and Bloshtein, were criticized for not placing "social awareness" front and centre. The goal was to teach about "hunger, unemployment, strikes, unionization, wage cuts, evictions, demonstrators attacked and heads beaten, miners shot at and bloodied, thousands deported, imprisoned in Canada and around the world" together with presentation of the "possibilities for workers in the Soviet Union," who were busy building a new world. In retrospect, while the struggles here in Canada supported by the left community were important ones, the left later learned how terribly mistaken was the projection onto the Soviet Union as the place where those ideals were being realized.[56]

At the time, in the midst of the Depression, the philosophy of the left schools resonated with many people, and with a strong and energetic leadership, the schools began to flourish. By 1936, the fifteenth anniversary of the Winnipeg school, the Liberty Temple school offered a day school, with English classes up to the fourth grade, after school Yiddish classes through mittlshul (the middle school or about 8th grade), a kindergarten, adult classes, a mandolin orchestra, a dance class, and a chorus. The students also published a children's magazine, wrote for the children's section of *Dos Yiddishe Vort*, and organized masquerade balls and a benefit for the Yiddish shules in Poland.

Rokhl (Cookie) Papeski wrote in 1937:

> The public school teaches us that everyone can benefit from and enjoy the riches of the country. But the shule tells us that isn't true. Thousands of people suffer hunger while the rich capitalists in their factories are wallowing in luxury. In the shule we become familiar with the true cause of the crisis, and of the unemployed. Then it becomes clear why capitalists support anti–semitism. Only in the Soviet Union, where capitalism was defeated, these scourges no longer exist. Can we understand all these problems without a Jewish workers' education? Can we meet our obligations for the future without the help of the Jewish workers' shule? I think not.[57]

Looking back, one former student questioned this emphasis on "workers' education." Moishe Miller attended the Liberty Temple shule in Winnipeg in the 1930s.[58] Moishe asks his elderly mother many years later (in the late 1980s) why all three of her children were sent to "such a political, left wing school?" Mrs. Miller replies: "The simple answer is that we were free-thinkers and believed in a Yiddish education with the language, history, culture and so on—and one can do very well without the influence of Zionism or religion. Do you have complaints about this choice?" Moishe responds: I just mean that the school was extreme. At seven years, we already knew about Lenin, Trotsky, Capitalism." His mother tells him: "Don't dramatize everything so much ... you also studied good literature, and there were gymnastics as well ... not so terrible!" Moishe remembers:

> On one wall of the hall in the Liberty Temple there was a picture of a large man, standing proudly because he had broken the chains which had surrounded his entire body. The children learned that the picture symbolized the workers' struggle against oppression and freeing themselves of the capitalist system. Underneath the picture it was written, "Workers of the world unite." A little further along the wall, was a picture of Lenin.... Every May 1st we marched to show our solidarity with the working class of all the world. We sang the Internationale, "Arise ye prisoners of starvation ..."

The children attending these shules generally came from poor families; some families like Moishe's moved when they did not have the money to pay

A group of young children and teacher from the Freiheit Temple Shule of the International Workers Order, Winnipeg, May 1936. Lenin's portrait is in the background.

Jewish Heritage Centre of Western Canada Archives.

Mir Lernen un Kemfn (We learn and struggle), a children's textbook used in the shules, 1934.

International Workers' Order. Notice the second letter in each word is drawn as a hammer and sickle.

Collection of Ester Reiter, purchased from the Yiddish Book Center.

the rent. Moishe remembered that in seventeen years, he counted twenty-four different houses. His mother corrected him: "No, that's not right. I count only twenty-three." When he asked her why they moved so often, he didn't get an answer. Most likely they were escaping the landlord.

Dora Paul Rosenbaum, who is the same age as Moishe, remembered him well and described one of the places the Miller family lived:

> He lived in the same house as I did—his family in the front, and ours in the back. Upstairs was a fellow who worked nights as a cab driver. Morris (English for Moishe) had been given a trumpet by a visiting uncle and was taking trumpet lessons.... So he'd be practicing during the day, and you'd hear this broom handle. "Quiet! I'm working nights!"[59]

Dora's mother was a single parent who worked scrubbing floors and caring for old people. At times, they lived on relief and like the Millers had to move quite a bit. Because they moved so much, Dora was always the new kid in English school. But shule was the constant in her life. She remembered the excellent art teacher, Harry Goffman. Her memories included how "we would just be obnoxious kids" with the teachers: "Shule was four or five days a week after school with ten or twelve kids in a class. It was Monday to Thursday, and we'd have art, choir, gymnastics" on Saturday mornings and Sunday. The choir director Bronstein taught music in all the Jewish schools in the city:

> I think that every Jewish boy and girl in the North End went through his hands—and I do mean hands,

as he was abusive. Bronstein was THE man if there was a choir … the Peretz school had him, Talmud Torah, and us. He conducted all the choirs, and he did marvellous work. But he used to hit a lot. Poor Morris Miller, in his one and only white shirt, sitting there and minding his own business, and Bronstein came and ripped his shirt and threw him out. It was a major catastrophe.[60]

Dora's reminiscences express both the good and bad memories of shule and how for the children, the content of what was taught did not necessarily take precedence over other events.

Class-Conscious Textbooks

At first, a Soviet-style method was adopted, emphasizing practical work requiring the students to engage in a political project of social transformation. This was difficult to implement in practice, considering the school hours were in addition to the public school day, and there was not enough time.[61] The left shules began to formalize the curriculum once they affiliated with the IWO. The textbooks published by the IWO and used in Canada were called *Arbeter Shule, mir lernen un kemfen* (Workers' School: We Learn and Struggle). In the 1934 editions, political education is prominent, with content discussing class-consciousness, unions, anti-racism, colonialism, and imperialism. The first-year texts, for children learning to read and write in Yiddish, demonstrate they are also learning who are their friends and who are not:

> Pioneer—a comrade!
> Worker—a comrade!
> Lenin—a comrade!
> Boss—a comrade?[62]

Working mothers also appear in the stories, although some of the stories describe a mother alone doing the housework and urge the children to help her.

Some of the stories deal with racism against blacks although, particularly in the simpler stories for first-year students, the black child has a passive role and is "rescued" by the Jewish child. In the stories, race is usually connected with class. In one, Tom, a black boy, is eight years

א בֿאַווער אָן כאָר

פּיאָנער – א בֿאַווער!
אַרבעטער – א בֿאַווער!
לענין – א בֿאַווער!
——— באָס – א בֿאַווער?

From *Mir Lernen un Kemfn* for first-year students. New York, 1934.

Collection of Ester Reiter, purchased from the Yiddish Book Center.

old and the children call him "nigger." Philip, a child from the workers' school, asks the other children, "Who are we, bosses, that we call him 'nigger'? His name is Tom and that's what we have to call him." The children discuss it and understand that not to call a person by name is to treat him as a stranger. From then on they call the black boy by his name, Tom.[63] The left's active opposition to racism against the black community was unique for the 1930s. The anti-racist emphases, however, seemed limited to blacks. There is no mention of the appalling situation of indigenous peoples or the virulent anti-Asian sentiment of the time.

Many children knew firsthand about unemployment and starvation wages. They were taught about unions. In "A Strike," Lena's father comes home angry; his shop is on strike. They tell the boss they can no longer work for such low wages, and the boss yells that he will replace them. Her father explains what a picket line is, and that those who try to work in their place are scabs. The father walks the picket line and comes home with a bandaged head after being beaten up by the police. The next day he returns to the picket line with his wife and daughter and finds that other workers have also brought their families. The boss relents and Lena's father takes her to a hall where there are speeches and singing because the workers have won.[64]

The children also learned about the evil of war and historical events such as the Paris Commune, the brief rule of a revolutionary socialist government in France in 1871. It is a far cry from the Dick and Jane texts children in Canada and the US were reading in English schools. Dick, Jane, and their small sister Sally lived the prototype of the perfect American family. They were youngsters who played amusing pranks, dressed up in their parents' clothes, visited grandmother and grandfather on the farm, romped with their pets and made fascinating discoveries during spring walks in the woods.[65] Instead, children in the left Yiddish schools read "The Santa Klaus Who Fainted" (*Santa Klaus hot gekhalesht*), reflecting the domination of a Christian ethic and Christian holidays. In the story, Mike's father is unemployed, and there is no food in the house. He looks for work each day, but there is none. One day he sees an ad for a job in a store. He leaves very early the next morning to get the job, which is to dress as Santa Claus. Mike's father puts on the white beard and red clothes and stands in the store, hour after hour after hour, very hungry because he has had nothing to eat. He becomes dizzy and falls down. A child, Alfred, sees him. Later he tells all the kids on the street that there is no Santa Claus. He knows because he saw Santa fainting from hunger and his mother explained that Santa was really an unemployed worker, dressed in other clothes.[66]

Children of the Morris Winchevsky Shule marching. One of the signs demands hot lunches. Another in Yiddish opposes militarism in school. The big banner includes words about struggling against fascism. n.d.

UJPO Archives.

The shule curriculum for third-year students introduced heroes such as Lenin and Eugene Debs, the Wobblie labour organizer. One story reflected the activities of the Labour Defence Leagues that protected tenants and offered labour support during the Depression. The story also emphasizes the importance of acting collectively. In it, a young boy, Ralph, gets up early on a Saturday morning and goes to the shule to paint placards for a rent strike. On his way, he sees furniture being thrown onto the street, and Selma, his classmate, sitting with the furniture and near her, her parents and a policeman. He goes to the shule to gather his friends to help her, but the teacher reminds him they must first inform the workers' council. Ralph runs to tell them. Then the children go to Selma's house, and Ralph gives the order to put the belongings back inside the house. One student takes a chair, another some washing, a third a mattress, and in a few minutes all the household things are once again in Selma's house.[67]

Lil Himmelfarb Ilomaki, born in 1914, recalled participating in these kinds of activities with the Canadian Labour Defence League in the 1930s.[68] And Lenny Dolgoy, who was born in 1926, remembered that when the Canadian

The African American singer Paul Robeson and the children of the Morris Winchevsky Shule. The artist Avrom is on the left. Robeson was a frequent visitor before the US took his passport away.

York University Libraries, Clara Thomas Archives & Special Collections, Sam and Manya Lipshitz fonds, ASC 00904.

Labour Defence League organized to help imprisoned revolutionaries, one of their first actions was honouring Sacco and Vanzetti, the anarchists framed on a murder charge and later executed.[69]

The fourth-year book, for children eleven or twelve years old, contained complex and disturbing material. In "Lynching," a powerful story by Joseph Opatoshu, a sheriff convinces a young black man to give himself up to avoid a lynching. He is accused of rape, and the sheriff promises that if he is innocent, he will go free. Buckhart gives himself up, but the sheriff immediately handcuffs him. A mob takes hold of him, and he is burned alive. This was the 1930s, the era of the Jim Crow regime in the southern US that legitimated racial segregation and allowed the violent murder of blacks by mob rule.

The Jewish left's concern with anti-racism extended beyond North America. One entry in the fourth-year book was called "The Life of the Negroes in Africa: The Congo." It reminds the young reader that while playing ball or using their erasers, they often don't think about where these products come from or how they were produced. The story describes how, before colonialism, tribes in the Congo lived peacefully, surviving from cattle grazing and gathering. In the nineteenth century, the Belgian whites appeared. They taught the "Negroes" how to improve their cattle production, how to make bread, and how to extract precious metals such as gold and copper. The Congo became a colony of Belgium in 1884, although Belgium is less than half its size. From a population of twenty million in 1908, by 1911, there were only eight million Congolese. Twelve million people died in a three-year period. What happened? The tale continues, explaining how the Belgians virtually enslaved the Congolese to extract rubber, killing whole families of workers who refused to comply:

> Rubber trees are spread amongst the forest, so that workers can't work together [as they are able to in field work].... If a worker tries to run away, the Belgian overseer punishes not only the family, but the entire village. Children and women are whipped, entire villages burned, in order to frighten the others.... But the Belgian merchants and the Belgian king are the richest in their country ... when children use rubber, they need to remember the life of the black slaves who live so far from us.[70]

It would have been extraordinary for public school children to be learning about colonialist practices in Africa—just as it would be very unusual for today's school curriculum to include a critique of global capitalism. The shules offered such a viewpoint.

The history of slavery in North America was also part of the shule curriculum. At the time, most history in the English schools was taught as the history of Great Men "discovering" countries and conquering them or bravely leading soldiers in war. The pre-adolescent children in the left shules were being taught a critical social history that was not included in North American university curricula until the 1960s. The focus on the evils of racism and colonialism at this time is impressive. Even Washington and Lincoln were not described as heroes: Washington was portrayed as a slave owner who fleeced poor farmers with heavy taxation and Lincoln was seen as opposed to equality for blacks and only forced into the Emancipation Proclamation to bolster northern industrial interests and protect the union.[71]

The fourth-year political education in Yiddish also included discussions of colonialism in other parts of the world, such as in Cuba and India. Students learned about socialist heroes, particularly Karl Marx and Vladimir Lenin, as well as Karl Liebknecht, Rosa Luxemburg, and Joseph Stalin.[72]

Before the Second World War, most of the secular shules shared a basic socialist pro-worker ideology. Hinde Shutzman Friedman, a student from the "apolitical" Sholem Aleichem Institute shule in the Bronx, wrote, "There were many, many *yom toyvim* (holidays). Do you remember where you were each May Day? I was on the Jerome Avenue train, clutching a handwritten placard, on my way to the May Day celebration at Union Square."[73] And Mildred Gutkin, who in the 1930s attended the Labour Zionist Peretz Shule in Winnipeg, could still deliver a flawless rendition of "The Internationale" in Yiddish to an interested audience sixty years later.[74]

Ben Shek, born in Palestine in 1927, was a student in the Toronto Labour League shule in the 1930s and later became a Yiddish teacher while attending university. The left community was a big part of his life. His family had returned to Poland from Palestine and then immigrated to Canada in the spring of 1934. Ben was immediately sent to the shule:

> It was like heaven to go into the organization. My mother worked in the back of a dress shop located somewhere on Yonge Street. It was a very dingy room. I used to drop in to see her sometimes on Saturdays when I went to the movies. But I wasn't really alone … you finished school you went to shule on 414 Markham Street, Monday to Friday. On Sunday, there were clubs. We put on a show for the shule in the Victory Theatre. We had a mandolin orchestra, drama club, we did tsvei brider ["Two Brothers," a poem by Peretz]. We did Dos Meserl, ["The Knife"], Motl Pesah [stories by Sholem Aleichem]. We had very close links with the United States people. It's the same environment, the same values. All my friends were around the organization until I became a teenager and went to university…. It was a tightly knit community, but not narrowly based because of the cultural activities.[75]

Ben's friend Ruth Biderman Borchiver had a difficult experience at first. Although she grew up speaking Yiddish, when she first went to the shule at six years of age in 1934, she was afraid to open her mouth: "I'm listening to this Yiddish that Manya [her teacher] is speaking and thinking 'Holy Cow! Mine sounds horrible!' I spoke street Yiddish. There was nothing wrong with it, everyone spoke it. So I was mute."[76]

The accepted dialect in the secular shules, and considered more literary, was the Yiddish spoken in Vilna, with a Lithuanian accent rather than a southern Polish one. Ruth mastered the accepted way of speaking in a few months but said that it's still "not the way I talk normally." Ruth went to shule every day after school. She remembers, "We had a cultural life to beat it all" and "we gained an outlook on the world that was invaluable."

What was taught and how it was taught—an education in the importance of collectivity and challenging authority sometimes helped in unforeseen ways. I was told about a teacher who was known to "like the girls a bit too much." They didn't tell their parents but dealt with the issue together, by themselves. When this teacher asked one of the girls to stay behind, all of them did![77] These girls were applying an important message: collective action is a protection and can be a solution.

The 1940s

After Hitler's rise to power, while the concerns with social justice remained central, the militancy and rigidity of earlier years diminished and more attention was paid to Jewish history and traditions. Yiddish came to be valued not just as a means to transmit socialist ideals, but as worthwhile in itself. A new generation was emerging whose mother tongue was English, not Yiddish, one whose identity as a Jew was not a given.

As the concern with the rise of fascism deepened, the emphasis in all the secular shules changed. Some of the more moderate shules introduced religious practices. While Oneg Shabbats (Jewish social gatherings on the Sabbath, usually on Friday night) were often part of the practice of the labour Zionist shules, the Workmen's Circle also began to mark the Sabbath and the Borokhov and the Farband (both labour Zionist) celebrated Bar Mitsvahs. The left shules remained completely secular, but they too became much more tolerant of religion. The "red" Yom Kippurim of the anarchist left—banquets held on Yom Kippur to flaunt the left secularist disavowal of religious observance—disappeared entirely. A story in *Yungvarg*, the Yiddish-language youth magazine of the New York Ordn (International Workers Order) indicated how much thinking had changed. "Julius supports his people" tells of a young boy who, sadly, knows no Yiddish but proves that after all he is a "mentsh" (decent person). Julius knows to come to the defence of a religious Jew with forelocks and a yarmulkeh (religious skullcap) who is being mocked: "In our country, everyone has a right to conduct themselves according to their religious ways. We are not Nazis."[78]

By the early 1940s, nationalism was no longer criticized. For example, the chairman of the Labour League, J. Kleinstein, wrote in 1942 "Let us help raise a Jewish generation which should be prepared to uphold the Jewish traditions, which should be nationally proud, which should be class-conscious. A child who learns in the Labour League schools will grow up to be a defender of his class and people."[79]

In the 1940s, anti-Semitism was still quite widespread in Canada.[80] In a major shift from the early period, writers in the *Der Vochenblat* (formerly *Der Kamf*) saw Jewish survival itself to be at stake. The heated denunciations of the early 1930s disappeared.[81] Every Jewish child was urged to attend a Jewish school, regardless of orientation. These writers insisted that children needed to know their history to understand and cope with the discrimination they faced.[82] *Der Vochenblat* even suggested that the various Jewish secular schools (and even non-secular schools) should unite and popularize the schools in the Jewish community in the major cities. A number of teachers and leaders, including M. Feldman, a teacher in Toronto, Jacob Mamelak of Montreal, and Kleinstein, chair of Toronto's Labour League, urged the schools to set aside their ideological differences and form a collective, one-school movement to be supported by a central city-wide funding body.[83]

The left held annual National School and Culture Conferences in the US and Canada throughout the 1940s. *Der Vochenblat* provided extensive coverage of school openings, graduations, and events. The development of mass culture was seen as a threat because "American born parents do not always carry with them the values of an older generation."[84] One writer, Bloomston of Montreal, stated that many of the parents were "uncultured" due to the influences of cheap movies, penny novels, and card games. He maintained that they needed to be culturally enlightened before they could be convinced of the importance of Jewish education for their children.

The destruction of European Jewry meant that this rich secular culture was annihilated along with the millions slaughtered. In North America, the left wanted their children to learn about what had been lost. The postwar curriculum continued the emphasis on reading, writing, and social awareness but also included discussion of the founding of a Jewish state, initially welcomed as a sign of Jewish survival.

In *Delayed Impact: The Holocaust and the Canadian Jewish Community*, Frank Bialystok describes how the wider Jewish community initially silenced discussion of the Holocaust. But in the left schools, as early as 1945, the children were taught about the Holocaust, with the stress on resistance rather than victimization. Each Passover the celebration included lighting candles in honour of the six million Jews murdered by the Nazis, promising "never to forget and never to forgive what was done to us once." The focus was not on privileging Jewish suffering but on identifying with those who are victimized and opposing injustice to all people. At celebrations, people would stand to honour the

Yiddish partisan song "Zog Nit Keynmol" (Never say). It celebrated the determined battle fought in the Warsaw Ghetto when for forty-three days and nights Jews defied the Nazis in an uprising they knew was doomed.

Written by a twenty-one-year-old Yiddish poet, Hirsh Glik (1922–1944), "Zog Nit Keynmol" became the hymn of the United Partisan Organization in 1943. It was sung in all the camps of Eastern Europe as a song of resistance. Hirsh Glik did not survive the war, but his song did. After the war, it reached Jewish communities around the world, where it has been sung as a memorial for Jews martyred during the war.

> Zog nit keynmol az du geyst dem letstn veg
> Chotsh himlen bluyene farshtelen bloye teg:
> Kumen vet dokh undzer oysgebenkte sho,
> S'vet a poyk ton undzer trot: mir zenen do!

> Never say that you have reached the very end
> Though leaden skies a bitter future may portend
> For the hour for which we yearned will yet arrive
> And our marching steps will thunder, we survive![85]

In late 1945, the children's magazine *Yungvarg* (Youth), published by the IWO in New York and distributed in Canada as well as the US, printed fictionalized and non-fiction accounts of children's experiences in the ghetto. Helena Khatskills worked in a children's home in Kovno (Kaunas), Lithuania and published what orphaned children as young as five had told her. They survived because their parents had managed to hide them—often moving from place to place, crouching in an attic for long periods, learning Lithuanian and forbidding the children to utter a word in Yiddish. Khatskills wrote:

> Each one of them could tell of the hunger, cold, fear and heartache they suffered.... They learn in school, and love to dance and sing. A short while ago
> they performed several scenes from Mottl, the Cantor's son. They love Sholem
> Aleichem. They memorized lines from Sholem Aleichem's story *"Dos Meserl"*
> [The Knife] and decided to hold a trial for Shloime, the boy who stole the knife.[86]

Yiddish and Yiddishkayt were connected explicitly with Jewish national consciousness and survival. In *Der Vochenblat* (Canadian Jewish Weekly)

Erdberg wrote that "the only thing which holds us together, that we should feel as one family in our sorrow and joy is our Yiddish."[87]

While the emphasis remained on the core subjects of Yiddish language, literature, culture, and Jewish history, the demographics among Jews in North America had shifted. The children coming to the schools were English-speaking, and more and more of their parents were English speakers, and often Canadian-born. The textbooks published in the 1940s reflected this. By 1946, much of the first grade textbook was in English and the didactic lessons from the 1930s largely absent. They were replaced by lighthearted stories, which were still a far cry from the idealized books in the regular English schools. For example, "Kider Vider" is the story of two young boys who constantly contradict each other, and the Labzig stories are about a dog that learns Yiddish. The more serious stories come from figures in Jewish history, such as Samson, or David and Goliath.

As Canadian nationalism became more widespread, the Yiddish textbook materials published in New York became a concern. They were now "American" celebrating American heroes, but praise for Abe Lincoln and America was inappropriate for Canadian children; Canadian materials were needed. In 1943, schoolteachers and workers from the Montreal, Toronto, and Winnipeg schools came together to coordinate their work and discuss a common ideological framework.[88] The agenda included establishing a national publishing centre for new literature, creating a centralized campaign to bring in new children, and organizing higher-level courses and lectures, readings and clubs for young people who had finished middle school.

A 1948 "letter to the children" in *Der Vochenblat* implores them to speak Yiddish and to encourage their family and friends to learn and use Yiddish. Yiddish is the language of the Jewish people, and Yiddishkayt is not simply a culture, but a progressive ideology and a means of struggle for survival of the Jewish people.[89]

For a time, it seemed that Yiddish had a future. From 1945 to 1952, the Morris Winchevsky Shule in Montreal had a day school. Mornings were in English with subjects such as math, science, and English. Yiddish was studied in the afternoon; the curriculum included Yiddish language, literature, and history. The principal of the school was Sholem Shtern. His nephew Aaron Krishtalka, born in 1950, attended the shule in Montreal. He wrote Yiddish poetry as a child and Yiddishists felt that this Canadian-born youngster gave hope for Yiddish survival in a new generation. He came from a well-known Montreal family—his mother, Shifre Krishtalka, was a Yiddish poet and teacher, and his father, Sholem Kristhalka, was a Yiddish community activist. Aaron Krishtalka recalled that in this family,

> Yiddish was life itself.... Everyone had to write in Yiddish, to write poems, compositions. Depending on how political they were, they were published either in the left newspaper, *Der Vochenblat*, or the more mainstream *Keneder Adler* [Canadian Eagle].[90]

The teachers of the Morris Winchevsky Shule in Toronto. Bottom row, left to right, Faygl Gartner, Harry Guralnik (principal), Manya LIpshitz. Top row, left to right, Gittl Kagan, Brayndl Grafstein, Ben Shek, Ruth Biderman, Esther Weinberg.

UJPO Archives.

However, the Krishtalka family was an outstanding exception as the generation of East European-educated Jews whose mother tongue was Yiddish aged. Even Aaron Krishtalka, although he continued to write poetry in Yiddish into his thirties, went on to become a professor of history and philosophy with minimal involvement with Yiddish literary culture.[91]

The shules decided that it was crucial to develop a new generation of Yiddish teachers. Ruth Borchiver of Toronto recalled,

> When I was fourteen, I was a teacher already. There were five of us—myself, Benny Shek, Gittl Kagan, Ester Weinberg, Braindl Grafstein. Five die-hards that stayed on for what would be comparable to a university undergraduate education in Yiddish studies. We stayed on to be teachers because there was no one to replace the older people who were teachers.

However, none of the five young teachers from Toronto went on to make a career of teaching Yiddish.

Finding new teachers was difficult, but there were other challenges. An earlier generation, raised in traditional homes, had freed themselves from religious observance. The left schools with their commitment to a secular education had not included Hebrew, the language of prayer. Classical writers such as Peretz and Sholem Aleichem had had a traditional education and included Hebrew words in their Yiddish works, disadvantaging those with no knowledge of the language. Whether or not Hebrew should be taught was a contentious topic at the 1945 annual UJPO Culture and School Conferences.

The older generation, while identifying as Jews, displayed their secular beliefs by not celebrating many of the Jewish holidays. But they knew the Jewish traditions very well. For the younger Canadian-born generation, the challenge was how to inculcate an identity as a Jew without the religion. The shules aimed to teach knowledge and respect for Jewish traditions while minimizing or eliminating the religious element. They worried that if these traditions were simply ignored as they had been in the past, the Canadian-born generation would know nothing about them. But others such as Jacob Mamelak argued that making the schools appear religious was a dangerous idea.[92] They discussed how to teach, secularize, and celebrate the traditional Jewish holidays. At the same time, Jews as a group were beginning to do better economically, and facilities that were once considered acceptable were now criticized as inadequate. Classrooms and school buildings needed improvement and organizers realized that to attract and keep students in the shule and the UJPO, they had to offer enjoyable activities and clubs.[93]

Despite these challenges, the schools thrived in the late 1940s. By 1947, attendance was at an all-time high in Toronto, Hamilton, Vancouver, Montreal, and Winnipeg. Under the leadership of Sholem Shtern, the Montreal Morris Winchevsky Shule, which had a day school, introduced three new subjects to their curriculum: a worker's movement history course that included biographies of the movement's leaders, a social awareness course, and elementary Hebrew.[94] Students such as Olga Eizner Favreau and Gerry Cohen remember the Winchevsky School as a warm and welcoming place. Olga loved going there, appreciating that traditions were taught as history rather than as rigid belief systems.[95]

After 1948, the left, along with the rest of the Jewish community, welcomed the establishment of the state of Israel. Leftists hoped that Israel would remain a politically neutral country, with its development benefiting both Jewish and Arab workers. In a cartoon from the 1940s, the artist Avrom depicted the Israeli flag on a UN pole thrusting a sword into Hitler who he called "Hateler" in the cartoon. Avrom saw Israel as a socialist workers' state where workers would challenge the control of the land by western imperialist oil interests and Arab feudal lords.

The left shules enjoyed their connection with the wider Jewish community in the 1940s and hoped that the cooperation would continue. However, these cooperative views were not reciprocated by other secular movements, in particular the Arbeter Ring (Workmen's Circle), and certainly not by the more religious Jewish majority.

A 1949 investigative report by Dr. Uriah Engelmann provided to the Jewish Welfare Fund in Toronto listed the attendance and the philosophies of each of the Jewish schools. The Morris Winchevsky shules had the largest number of students, 255 children, or 32.6 percent of the total number of children registered in the secular Jewish schools. The Farband had 22 children, the Arbeter Ring 169, and the Borokhov, 136. The Winchevsky schools were distinct in another way as well. Many parents not part of the left continued to send sons to the Talmud Torah for a religious education. While only one-fifth of the students in the other secular schools were boys, the Winchevsky schools, which were more committed to secularism, had a proportion of 55.3 percent boys and 44.7 percent girls. Engelmann devoted several pages to describing the curriculum of each of the secular schools but described the Morris Winchevksy Shules in just five lines. He dismissed them, claiming that the "educational philosophy which motivates the leaders of the schools, is not rooted in the historical, cultural and religious traditions of the Jewish people."[96] It is not clear how or why he came to this conclusion. After all, the curriculum for the shules in 1948 included Yiddish language and literature; biographies of historical Jewish freedom-fighters as well as contemporary leaders in the workers' movement; Jewish history and the significance of Jewish holidays, customs, and traditions; Yiddish songs and recitations; and traditional and modern Jewish dance.[97] The knee-jerk anti-communism was back. The Jewish Welfare Fund refused to fund the shule without looking into how it was run or what was taught there. Ruth Borchiver, one of five young teachers in Toronto being trained to carry on Yiddish teaching, was sent to a meeting of the Board who allocated these funds in Toronto to appeal the decision. Many years later, she recalled her frustration:

Avrom cartoon of Hitler.
Collection of Anna Yanovsky.

The five of us went to make an appeal to reinstate the stipend support for the Morris Winchevsky shule for the kids. It was like going to see people on thrones that wouldn't throw you a bone. We were dealing with wealthy, establishment-minded people. People would hardly listen to us talk, about what we do, what we try to teach the children. I knew as we were saying it that nobody was listening.... It was a lost cause.... Big, wealthy names in the Jewish community.... What did they need Communism for?[98]

The Cold War

As the 1950s progressed and the Cold War developed, the shules suffered. Communism once again became a dirty word. The Quebec Padlock Law gave police the power to seal off any property where communist literature or activity was suspected. It was used to raid the shule in 1950. Gerry Cohen recalled what happened when the Quebec Police arrived at the shule:

It was a day of glorious sunshine. On that sunny day, the Anti-Subversive (or, as it was commonly known, the Red) Squad of the Province of Quebec Provincial Police raided the Morris Winchevsky School and turned it inside out, in a search for incriminating left wing material. A quick-thinking teacher managed to protect the children.... Lererin [feminine for teacher] Asher, clapping her hands in a simulated exuberance, announced that "Children the Board of Health is inspecting the school and you can all go home early." ... Lurking at the entrance were four men, each of them tall and very fat ... eyes down and looking sheepish.[99]

The new Winchevsky Community Centre on 5101 Esplanade in Montreal was also raided and shut down that day. The shule remained open because no compromising materials could be found there. However, the Cold War atmosphere had its effect. Many parents pulled their children out of the school so that its full-time operation, which had included English classes, was no longer possible. Olga Eizner Favreau's graduating class in 1952 was the first and last to have the benefit of a full-day school.[100]

The honeymoon with the rest of the Jewish community had come to an end. In April 1951, all the left Jewish organizations were expelled from the Canadian Jewish Congress. Without the Jewish Welfare funding support in any of the cities in Canada, the shules once again struggled to maintain

themselves. By the 1960s, all the secular shules were suffering, not just the
left-wing ones. The Yiddish in the anniversary books grew sparse, and many
after-school Yiddish shules became
Sunday schools, drastically reducing
instruction time to just once a week.
The Sholem Aleichem shule in Winnipeg's Liberty Temple closed its doors in
1963. The folk shule and the Peretz day
schools in Winnipeg amalgamated and
lasted a bit longer but they too finally
closed as the study of Hebrew became
increasingly popular. The Peretz School
in Montreal remained, although it
became more traditional. Some Yiddish is still taught in Bialik, originally

Der Vochenblat, Thursday, February 2, 1950. The headline reads "Mass reaction against the fascistic act of Premier Duplessis goes across the land."

Courtesy of Eiran Harris, Archivist, Montreal Jewish Public Library.

a labour Zionist school in Toronto. As many of the shules became once-a-week
Sunday schools, knowledge of Yiddish was replaced by "love and respect for the
Yiddish language."[101]

In 1968, Dr. Shlome Simon from the Sholem Aleichem Institute in the
United States offered an overview of the history of all the secular Jewish shules:

> We the old generation, lived with our Jewishness. Our roots were in it.… Our
> old generation could have been satisfied with a minimum of Yiddishkeit, we
> were in no need of congregational life, and as a matter of fact, we had an aver-
> sion to ritual, due to our childhood memories. Still we were full Jews. But your
> generation cannot be satisfied with such a shrunken Yiddishkeit, a Yiddishkeit
> reduced to a Sunday School.… The more we observe the Jewishness of all
> denominations the more we see the necessity for a form of secular Yiddishkeit.
> We see that only a fraction believes in the tenets of the religion preached in
> our centers and the synagogues.[102]

Itche Goldberg, a leading figure in Yiddish education in North America
from the early 1930s until his death at age 102 in 2006, described the goal of
Jewish secular education: "It is not sufficient to say that we want our children
to be Jews, we want them to be a special kind of Jew.… Our universalism does

not lessen out Jewishness, just as our Jewishness does not—should not—in the least impair the universal quality of our teaching." Itche's goal was a synthesis between "Yid and Mentsh," between Jew and human being.

Many of the prominent shule Yiddish teachers of the left were immigrants to Canada trained in the teachers' seminaries in Eastern Europe in the 1920s. Leybl Basman, a teacher, dramaturge, and actor, left his mark in Winnipeg, Windsor, Montreal, Toronto, and Vancouver. In 1970, at his retirement speech in Vancouver, Basman looked back on a career that spanned over forty-five years. He had come of age in Wilkomir, Lithuania in the 1920s when Yiddish culture was flowering. He made clear that his love for those promoting Yiddish did not include those Jews who were the "blood suckers, hypocrites, the establishment, the exploiters, war mongers." His first-hand experience of the Russian Revolution in the years 1917 to 1920 developed his commitment to the working class and the progressive Jewish movement. This love grew in Canada. Together with Fred Donner and Dr. I Viktor in Winnipeg, he devoted himself to establishing the United Front Against Fascism in the early 1940s. The horror of the millions who were slaughtered led him to his passion for Israel, although Basman explained that he was never a Zionist. Basman believed that Israel needed to find a way to peace, not through military might, but through the deep longing of all people for freedom. Subsequent events, in particular the 1967 occupation of Gaza and the West Bank made his heart feel "torn."[103] Basman died in the 1980s.

Manya Lipshitz reflected on her career teaching two generations of children in the Winchevsky shule:

> It was my fate to be part of the generation of Jewish immigrants who left the cities and towns of Eastern Europe inspired by the idea of a better and more beautiful world and encouraged by the positive achievements of the October Revolution and by the emancipation of Jewish people and its culture in the early year of Soviet power … idealistic, self-sacrificing men and women who bore the heavy burden of teaching children, and of building the Jewish schools.

Manya treated her students "as though they were my own children or grandchildren."[104] And anyone fortunate enough to have had Manya as a teacher recalled her warmth and her intelligence. She was loved.

The legacy of a leftist shule education is lasting. The Yiddish may have faded, but for many, such as Gerry Kane, the critical view remains: "The young people who came from that movement, who aren't young anymore—there's a distinct personality of Jews who went through that movement. Wherever they go, they leave a positive stamp, because they believed, and they still believe that there's another way to live besides the way we live now."

Left-wing parents, like most parents, wanted their children to "do better" than they themselves had; they encouraged their children to study and become professionals, and many did. Moishe Miller, who attended the Liberty Temple School in Winnipeg, became a professional trumpet player in England. He made a good living, but Moishe's father had hoped he would find a more secure occupation, like his brother who had become a chemistry professor in a renowned institute in Chicago.[105] Many of the people mentioned in this chapter—Olga Eizner Favreau, Ben Shek, Gerry Cohen—received their PhDs and became professors. Manya Lipshitz's daughter May became a physician, marrying Gerry Cohen of Toronto, also a medical doctor.

If Yiddish has virtually disappeared over the years, the values and sentiments associated with it have lasted much longer. Socialist politics were ingested through Yiddish literature, song, dance, theatre, and the respect the teachers showed for students' thoughts and ideas. Students experienced the shules as places that were a lot freer than the English-speaking public schools. Even as young children they learned to recognize the difference. Young people "knew" that what they heard in school and read in the newspapers was not the way things "really" were. They "knew" that the public school teachers did not understand what socialism meant and what the Soviet Union was doing. The USSR, they later learned, was tragically not the place they thought it was, but it was also true that the hysteria of the time was not based on a Soviet threat to "freedom" in North America.[106] Gerry Bain, who grew up in the Toronto shule and the left-wing movement, looks back:

> It was terrible what the Soviet Union was doing, what a tyrant Stalin was and how everything was gilded over.... Despite the errors, the blindness to the atrocities, there was a great emphasis on peace and justice for all of humanity. That's the thing that really emanates for me from that whole experience.[107]

Like the anti-terrorism violation of civil liberties today, a repressive state and fearmongering were the much larger threat. As left-wing kids in the midst of the Cold War, most felt picked on rather than "chosen" as they huddled together with friends in a safe and culturally rich community.[108] What the secular Jewish schools offered the North American community was an identity shaped by the human and social aspects of Jewish history. All imparted a shared respect for the Jewish past and the ideals of social justice, freedom, and peace.[109]

8 CULTURAL LIFE

Sports, Singing, Dancing, Theatre, Making Music

There was nothing for working-class people until we created it.
—Bessie Chicofsky Grossman*
*interview with the author, 2000

When they first arrived from Eastern Europe Jews gathered in ethnic enclaves. Toronto, Montreal, and Winnipeg, the three major centres where Jewish immigrants clustered, soon developed a Yiddish cultural life. Members of the secular Jewish left often lived in the same neighbourhoods and could walk to community halls.[1] Toronto's Ben Shek recalled:

> The community was concentrated in an area. We used to walk everywhere. You lived, you walked to 7 Brunswick Ave. [the cultural centre]. It was only a few blocks, except for a few people who had stores in the east end, they were the exception. The community lived in a very clearly delineated area and the hall was in the centre of that. Their own living conditions were cramped so that they had much more room to move in the building and to do things: a drama group, orchestra, shule, choir, meetings, lectures, credit union, brass band, youth clubs, sports clubs. There weren't public facilities; the public support for these things was lacking. There was a lot less cultural activity in the city in general than there is now. That's why when our choir gave a concert it was reviewed in all the dailies.... We were reviewed in the *Star*, the *Globe* and the *Telegram*.[2]

Emil Gartner drawn by Avrom. Gartner represents the proudest years in the cultural achievements of the Jewish left.

UJPO Archives.

People were neighbours as well as comrades. Molly Myers of Toronto treasured these friendships:

> I made friends with Rae [Orlan] Rose Field, Brina [Harris]. Brina's son is a little older than my son and we used to spend the days together with the carriages going around. This was my life, you know … in the beginning it was 7 Brunswick. I adopted Solly Hermolin's mother, Lucy, who used to sing in the choir. We became so close that sisters couldn't be any closer, till this very day. There wasn't such a thing as taking a bus. We used to walk.

As early as 1914–16 Toronto's Young Socialist Club boasted an array of cultural activities, including a string orchestra, a brass band, and a literary and dramatic group, as well as a choir, singing mostly Jewish folk music, conducted by Hyman Riegelhaupt. The choir disbanded because of conscription during the First World War but when the progressive movement reorganized as the Freiheit Club, the choir came together in 1925 as the *Freiheit Gezang Fareyn* (Freedom Singing League), renamed the Toronto Jewish Folk Choir in 1940.

In the 1920s, Alhambra Hall at 450 Spadina Avenue in Toronto became the gathering place for Jewish left-wingers. It was not much to look at. Philip Halperin, the first Toronto editor of *Der Kamf*, described it as

> a large, stuffy hall without windows with dirty walls and doors and old decrepit floors. New people would turn up their noses. But, to the left, it was a special place. We loved every nook and cranny—every room and every corner was saturated with our struggle, with our hopes. How many dreams were dreamt within these walls…. It was here that the Kamf was born; the first dinners in honour of the Kamf were held. It was here that the Jewish workers' movement, the Labour League was founded; the athletic association forged, the cradle of the Freiheit Gezang Fareyn with the resounding sound of proletarian song.[3]

Alhambra Hall housed the newspaper *Der Kamf*, the Jewish Worker's Library, the Yiddishe Arbeter Froyen Fareyn (the Jewish Women's Labour

Freiheit Gezang Fareyn (Freedom Singing League), 1927, Toronto.

UJPO Archives.

League), the Young Pioneers, the Mandolin Orchestra, the Jewish Drama League, the Progressive Arts Club, the Freiheit Gezang Fareyn (the Freedom Singing League), and the Workers' Sport Association (Toronto Jewish Section Youth Division). Philip Halperin recalled "the passionate discussions, the call to struggle for a new world in song, the proud steps of the worker sports groups, the fiery affirmations of the pioneers" that took place in Alhambra Hall. Singing was especially important because it was in song that the distinction between "true" workers' culture and *shund* (trash) became clear. Joe Gershman wrote:

> It was the choir which helped tear Jewish people away from cheap entertainment.... The choir with its original slogan *"Mit Gezang Tsum Kamf"* (With Song to the Struggle) set itself the task of raising the enthusiasm of the Jewish workers and the common people, to raise them spiritually to a higher level in all the struggles which they encountered along the way to a society of social justice.[4]

Concerts and celebrations were held regularly and were advertised and then reviewed, sometimes critically, in *Der Kamf*. The first concert of the Freiheit

Club, a fundraiser for the newspaper, was held in 1926. In addition to the choir, the concert included fiddling, dancing, the mandolin orchestra, and political speeches by the head of the Communist Party (CP) and the editor of *Der Kamf*— a full evening![5] The second anniversary concert was an even larger affair, with performances by the Children's Orchestra and the Workers' Sport Association, and a staging of Ansky's *Foter un Zun* (Father and Son) by the Drama Section of the Freedom Club. The songs the choir sang included a collection of political and folk songs such as "Unzer Firer" (Our Leader), "In der Kuznye" (In the Smithy), "Arbeter-Brider" (Working-Brothers), "Serp un Hamer" (Sickle and Hammer), and "Bulbes" (Potatoes).[6]

The Jewish Socialist Library dates from 1908 in Toronto and 1914 in Montreal.[7] Sam Kagan recalled his education in the library, in Toronto's Alhambra Hall:

> It was a circulating library and many, many people used it. It was also doing reviews on books, in the form of lectures and get-togethers.... It certainly was one of the influential institutions that helped a lot of the people who had very little secular education, who had very little education period, but acquired knowledge and in many respects became working-class intellectuals through the influence of the various clubs, meetings, lectures, and so on.
>
> My learning was from Oliver Twist on one side, a dictionary on the other side, and each and every word had to be referred to the dictionary ... we read political science books, philosophy, the reformers of the French Revolution, like Voltaire and Rousseau. We didn't go for the small stuff or anything like that. Plus Yiddish literature, and Mendele, that I had studied and read in the first government-sponsored Yiddish shules [in the USSR].[8]

Holdings included not just the Yiddish poets and writers, and Marxist political economy, but Yiddish translations of favourite classical works, including Tolstoy, Nietzsche, Zola, Dostoevsky, Rousseau, Shakespeare, Anatole France, Oscar Wilde, Goethe, and Victor Hugo.[9] An article in *Der Kamf* described the library's importance to the community:

> Here comes the Jewish worker to rest after a day of hard work, to read a newspaper, a journal or a book and through this enriching his intellectual store.... At present our libraries already have a tradition, a past. From saved pennies, they collected book by book, until the mighty libraries developed. In Alhambra Hall,

which was until not long ago the centre of the leftist Jewish Workers, a large, comfortable room was set aside to the library, which also included a reading room. In the evenings the room used to be crowded with Jewish workers reading. Books were given out and borrowed. So was the library, the nicest, brightest corner in Alhambra Hall.[10]

The Jewish Workers Culture Centres (1920s to 1930s)

In the late 1920s and early 1930s, in Montreal, Toronto, Winnipeg, Windsor, and Hamilton, progressive cultural groups came together to form Jewish Workers Culture Centres (JWCCs).

Montreal

The Montreal Jewish Workers Cultural Centre, established in 1926, attracted newly arrived radical European youth after the United States border closed to immigrants. On its fourth anniversary, Pearlman celebrated it as "one of the first attempts of the left wing workers in Canada to organize on the cultural front" against the mainstream bourgeois organizations.[11] For Pearlman clearly culture and politics were not separable, and culture had to reflect a group's politics: "our cultural centres, which come to life in order to satisfy the cultural and social needs of the Jewish masses, have during the time of their existence demonstrated that cultural activities only have substance when they are connected to the general actions of the workers' movement."[12]

The Montreal centre showed great promise. By 1930, the Montreal centre had 225 members, which included Progress, a drama circle, the Mandolin Orchestra, the Freiheit Gezang Fareyn (Freedom Singing League), and the Worker's Library.[13] The centre published newsletters and held frequent lectures, events, and musical-literary evenings.[14]

Young immigrants, such as Sholem Shtern, the writer, poet, and teacher, gravitated to the cultural centre because it reminded them of progressive cultural activities and spaces in their native countries. Shtern, like most Jewish immigrants from Eastern Europe, referred to the villages and towns where they were born as "the old country."[15] When Shtern arrived in Canada in 1927, the familiar atmosphere encouraged workers like him to join the JWCC and through that the revolutionary movement in general.[16] He described arriving in Montreal:

Picnic of Yiddish Kultur Farband (Jewish Culture League), circa 1923.

UJPO Archives.

[All] of us will always remember the organization through which they entered the Leftist Workers movement.… Many of us took the first step in local social life in the Cultural Centre. Our "greenness," our youthful fervor was connected to the Cultural Centre. All the dreams which warmed our hearts and which we brought with us with so much anxiety from the old country found a blessed placed to continue. I remember a winter night, it was snowing outside. I, a "griner" [greenhorn or newly arrived immigrant] sought a corner somewhere where I could hear a familiar word, somewhere to find a movement with which I could identify. I thought this new, strange land was so cold, rigid and alien that one could become paralyzed with longing for a home.

Shtern was told that the centre had a "bad" reputation as a place where troublemakers gathered. However, the centre's "bad" reputation was for him a plus, making him certain that this was indeed the place for him:

The wind surged the snow so much as I wandered around "my street"—I didn't know uptown from downtown. Suddenly I saw a large sign with red lettering

"Yiddisher Arbeter Kultur Tsenter" (Jewish Workers Cultural Centre). In the neighbourhood in which I had found myself, I had heard only bad things about the centre—they were a gang of irresponsible boys and girls, troublemakers who wanted to know nothing about the beleaguered, considerate bosses of today who also were once young, who built synagogues, went on strike and were active.

The most anger was directed against these "griners" who had the nerve to want to put forward new issues and be too militant … this malicious talk had no effect on me … because I knew that the bosses from my village spoke with the same contempt and anger about the workers' library of the young tailors and shoemakers…. This only strengthened my curiosity. This was a good opportunity to learn about the organization and perhaps also for me to find a home, and a friend.

I went up. The location—packed with young people, speaking so informally. In some of them, the "greenness" still sprouts, with their shorn heads like convicts. I felt immediately that I was among my own people. A speaker was replying to questions. I saw myself reflected in all the struggles present and future. It felt like I was back home—I found in some of the comrades such a great similarity to my comrades at home.

So the Cultural Centre received us newcomers. It led into the new land and struggles of the local Jewish workers' community…. We remember well what the Cultural Centre gives us.[17]

Soon after his arrival in Canada, Shtern was diagnosed with tuberculosis and spent almost two years at Mount Sinai Hospital in the Laurentians where he met and later married Sonia Elbaum, a nurse.[18] His poetry book, *The White House*, is a fictionalized account of his experiences in the sanatorium. Although some of Shtern's close friends maintained that Shtern was too much of an individualist to have survived the rigid constraints involved in CP membership, he embraced those ideals and articulated them through one of the characters in the book, Truchanksy. It is a good example of how art can be used to express one's ideals. In the book, as the character Truchansky lies dying, he says:

I am a communist
because we poor are treated like the trash
because it was my lifelong task
To fight against destructive war.

I am a communist
because my ardent dream of love
When I was innocent and younger
Burned to ash in suffering and longing in my heart[19]

Truchansky says to Velvl (who is the fictionalized version of Shtern him-self) and Velvl's beloved, the nurse, Miss Alman (based on Sonia Elbaum, whom Shtern married):

To be a Jew means more
Than only cherishing a way of life
A Jewish poet must abhor
The men who fasten chains upon the poor
Inside the prison-house of penury[20]

For Shtern, the poet and the Jew are obliged to denounce poverty and exploitation. These views, so eloquently expressed in Shtern's poem, eventually presented difficulties for the cultural centres. The demand to always be politic-ally engaged turned off some people. In addition, the tension between ethnic identity and the rigid politics of that period was a challenge.[21] There was a con-tinual struggle among the Jewish left between internationalists who decried nationalism, religion and particularity (including ethnic solidarity) and leftists who sought a space that recognized and celebrated their particular identities (such as Shtern's emphasis on Yiddish language and literature).[22] For some Jew-ish communists, such as Abe Rosenberg of Montreal, the idea was to "Canadian-ize," to attract more Anglo or native-born Canadians to the Communist Party. The CP criticized the immigrant character of the left Jewish organizations in Montreal as a hindrance in developing "proletariat" cultural work.

The communist leadership of the pro-Soviet left organizations did not always easily accept the attempts of the Party to control the mass organiza-tions. Morris Biderman, former president of the Toronto Labour League, indi-cated in his memoirs that he found the Party "arrogant and dictatorial toward the leadership."[23] In the Ukrainian community, the pronounced battles between party stalwarts and Ukrainian communists in the late 1920s and early 1930s are well documented. The leadership in the left Ukrainian community prided themselves on being Ukrainians as well as communists and resisted pressures to minimize the value of their ethnic organization, the Ukrainian Labour Farmer Temple Association (ULFTA).[24]

Proletarian education was not always enthusiastically received in this period. In 1930, the Montreal JWCC developed a worker's university, the Leninist Institute for Proletariat Learning, and in 1932 offered a series of educational courses to raise class consciousness and instruct workers in revolutionary theory and methods of struggle.[25] They supported the Canadian Labour Defence League (CLDL), which had a Jewish Section, IKOR or Yiddish Colonization in Russia, and the Communist-led Industrial Union of Needle Trades Workers (IUNTW) as well as the workers' school.[26] But they faced declining enrolments in the first half of the 1930s and had to cancel some of the classes.[27] Despite efforts to make the lectures more interesting, to start events on time, even a change to more attractive quarters, membership in Montreal's Cultural Centre declined. It seemed there was a conflict about how politically active the centre needed to be, with *Der Kamf* writers continually promoting positions held by the Communist Party.[28] *Der Kamf* articles criticized "elements" within the JWCC working to "destroy" the centre by pulling it away from the CP and revolutionary work.[29]

Sports, however, remained very popular.[30] Initially established in 1927, the Workers' Sport Association of Montreal consisted mostly of soccer players but soon also sponsored light exercise, boxing, wrestling, basketball, table tennis, Ping-Pong, skiing, and skating. The Workers' Sport Association had its own newsletter and a reading room stocked with newspapers and magazines.[31] The soccer team complained that the bourgeois referees' calls were partisan and that their victories were silenced by the mainstream press.[32]

Toronto and the Years of the "Terror," 1929–32

Toronto faced particular difficulties in the face of the "terror," Police Chief Draper's prohibition against speaking a foreign language in public spaces or even rented private locations. When Draper ordered the closing of Alhambra Hall in 1929, the Freiheit Club had to disband, and only the choir remained.[33] At first, the members joined the Jewish People's Club, but this more moderate group prohibited the singing of "The Internationale," the revolutionary anthem sung at every gathering. So these pro-Soviet Jews left the Jewish People's Club and faced tremendous hardships and persecutions.[34] Their locations were regularly closed, members were threatened with deportation by the police, the choir performed on the street because they couldn't hold assemblies, and the orchestra had to rehearse in private homes and secret locations.[35]

Benjamin Katz evocatively described the atmosphere of celebration and perseverance at the JWCC in the face of the difficult living conditions and the excessive police terrorization and persecution:

> Festivity is in our everyday life, festivity is in our struggle.... Day after day we
> sell tickets, we distribute flyers, we prepare holidays.
> The proletariat school is holding a concert!
> The order is organizing a campaign.
> The Workers Unity [League] is collecting funds for a periodical.
> The library is collecting books.
> The miners are on strike!
> We left the People's club, and rented a location. There were packed excited
> meetings, good lectures. Groups are soon playing instruments, rehearsing—
> every evening the location is bright and high spirits rule—the windows are open
> to the noises of the street, but an eavesdropping ear hears and
> Kicked out of the location!
> The organization crushed!
> But a few weeks go by and a new location opens, new impetus, new courage
> and devotion from the male and women comrades....
> A comrade comes with an important mission—a strike in western Canada.
> The comrade speaks loudly, with strength, with enthusiasm. He insists, and lo,
> the money flies to his appeal.... People revel, people make a racket.
> It is a holiday
> We will send greetings to the miners
> We will send them 100 dollars
> It will strengthen and cheer them in their struggle
> It happens like this, not just once, but in every gathering, like this—for an
> entire year!
> We will criticize, point out our flaws, and we will celebrate.[36]

The recently organized Labour League came to the rescue and provided a meeting place for the Jewish Workers Cultural Centre at 7 Brunswick Ave.[37] It was "the place of the young workers in Toronto.... Workers would go there every evening to discuss political and cultural questions."[38] Much of the JWCC's early work focused on gathering and spreading information about world and local events, as well as raising funds and disseminating information for proletariat cultural events, strikes, and campaigns.[39] It also raised money to ensure that *Der Kamf,* which they considered their newspaper, was regularly published.[40]

Just as in Montreal, despite the early upbeat descriptions, there were difficulties. The Toronto Mandolin Orchestra, like the choir, was an important part of the Toronto JWCC throughout the 1930s and drew large crowds. Founded in July 1931 with twenty-seven members under the direction of *Khaver* (Comrade/ friend) Dophy, by May 1932, the orchestra had grown to almost fifty members and was adding guitar and cello players.[41] However, tensions over the level of political activism in some sections of the JWCCs were also played out here. Members of the orchestra were criticized for their lack of involvement in activities of the general worker's movement because they "don't understand the worker's character of the orchestra."[42]

Between 1932 and 1934, the membership in the mandolin orchestra waned to the point where it was in danger of disassembling. The Drama Circle ("Progress") was also in trouble. *Der Kamf* writers complained that the directors did not impress on their members the revolutionary significance of the drama circle; they were not teaching about the "oppression of proletariat drama by bourgeois literary trash." There were undesirable "elements," and the circle improved once these "elements"—members of the circle who wanted the circle to be "above" the general revolutionary movement—were "removed."[43] Critics argued that they needed to serve the working-class movement, and not become a mainstream bourgeois theatre group. Even the Toronto Worker's Library with its proud history was not doing so well in the 1930s; it had "shrivelled" from lack of use. After the closure of Alhambra Hall, a badly arranged, uncomfortable reading room with tiny tables nailed to the wall and the absence of new journals didn't help.[44]

However, some leftist arts groups were growing. The Progressive Arts Club (PAC) in Toronto was attracting some members of the Labour League. The club published the English-language *Masses* in 1932, a journal containing poetry, stories and articles, drawings and linoleum cuts, reviews and letters. Contributors included people familiar to Labour League members, including sculptor Sam Kagan, artist Avrom Yanovsky (known as Avrom), and the poet Benjamin Katz. Avrom, a respected artist active from the 1930s until his death in the 1970s, was well loved among the Jewish left.

In Toronto as in Montreal, there were tensions in demanding that cultural involvement be combined with proletarian activism. Nevertheless, interest and participation in cultural activities remained strong.

Winnipeg

Winnipeg had a smaller left Jewish community than Montreal or Toronto, but it was renowned for its cultural activity. A Workers Youth Club had been organized in 1927 with a sports section, a drama section, a literature section, and a class in Yiddish. Winnipeg developed its own proletarian cultural centre in January 1931.[45] The JWCC's primary goal was to "educate and familiarize their members with the Canadian and global class struggle."[46] Every Sunday the teachers Bloshtein and Waldman would give instruction in Yiddish literature and political economy and discuss the newspaper.[47] Politics, music, literature, and celebrations came together. A banquet organized for *Der Kamf* in January 1933 featured the Mandolin Orchestra along with recitations in Yiddish by Joe Zuken, a classmate of the artist Avrom in the Peretz School in Winnipeg. Fluent in Yiddish, Zuken recited several labour poems at the celebration. It was a great success, both financially and in terms of morale. *Der Kamf* reported on a feast aimed at the stomach as well as the heart and the mind: "In the intermission, we tasted the food on the tables covered beautifully—a corned beef sandwich, or a cheese sandwich with a glass of hot tea, such as is offered at proletarian celebrations. The worker audience felt very celebratory."[48] Zuken recalled:

> I formed a very close attachment to the Yiddish language, to the Yiddish literature and have kept that up.... I spoke before a lot of Jewish organizations.... I ... became quite well known ... for left wing leanings but also for my fluency and adherence to the Yiddish language.[49]

Zuken was also a fine actor and organized the Progressive Arts Club, a community group of Winnipeg leftists. He served on the school board for twenty years, from 1941 to 1961, winning re-elections throughout the Cold War. He then was elected to city council, a position he held until his retirement in 1983. Among the many causes he supported were the establishment of kindergartens, free textbooks, better salaries for teachers, and protection for tenants. He remained a member of the Communist Party.

In Winnipeg, perhaps because of its small size and unique radical history, dating from the General Strike of 1919, there are many examples of co-operation between different secular Jewish movements as well as inter-ethnic solidarity. For example, Zuken recalled Saul Cherniak's fine performances as an actor in the New Theatre, a left-wing theatre group in the 1930s. Cherniak was a prominent social democrat and a member of the Co-operative Commonwealth

Children's Mandolin Orchestra of the Jewish Workers Cultural Centre. Philip Podoliak, the conductor, is in the centre.

Library and Archives Canada, 10752515.

Federation (CCF). He said that "some of us non Communists were glad to be involved in a theatre that did work of social significance.... So I joined it."[50] His wife Sybil Cherniak recalled: "It was a very friendly atmosphere. We did not ask people if they were Communists or if they weren't. Everybody seemed to be working together. None of us had any money." Saul Cherniak later became Minister of Finance in the first New Democratic government in Manitoba in the late 1960s.

Popular Front Movement (Mid-1930s to 1945)

The lines between political movements were not always hard and fast.[51] Even though most of the Canadian Jewish left dismissed "bourgeois" social democracy in the 1920s, there were instances of co-operation between the left and liberals in that period. The movement to get rid of Section 98 of the Criminal Code drew support from many quarters.[52] The Toronto women's meat boycotts organized by the left because of rising prices in the late 1920s and early 1930s were popular and successful protests. Opposition to Police Chief Draper's Red Squad in Toronto became a civil rights issue. The ideological rigidity and the

Melech Ravich, Ida Maza, ?, Rochl Korn, and J. I. Segal, circa 1950.

Montreal Jewish Public Library Archives, pr017727.

invective pro-communists and social democrats hurled at each other in print did not always characterize personal relations. However, after Hitler came to power in 1933, there was an important policy shift which brought many together. Jews were very conscious of the rise in anti-Semitism. As a result, cultural activities and participation in the Jewish left organizations increased.

The cultural centres, after a lull in the early 1930s, were once again busy places. For example, Montreal had two mandolin orchestras, a wind orchestra, a choir, a drama circle (ARTEF [53]), a beginner guitar orchestra, and a sports section. The worker's library, the reading room, and a workers' university sponsoring classes and lectures were also part of the centre as well as union support groups and the Workers International Relief Committee.[54] Concerts and celebrations were held regularly.[55]

The active literary scene in Montreal in that period included the entire secular Jewish left. A number of well-known Yiddish writers focused on issues of social justice. Prominent among them were Shabse Perl, Esther Segal, Avrom Shloyme Shkolnikov, Sholem Shtern, Yudika, and Ida Maza. At the time, virtually all the Yiddish poets and writers were working-class people with leftist leanings. Despite ideological differences, they published in each other's journals.[56] Yiddish poets and artists with many different viewpoints gathered at Ida Maza's place in Montreal. Poet Miriam Waddington lovingly recalled these salons.

> A small, slight woman with her black hair piled up, Maza wore kimono-like dresses with sashes and wide sleeves. She and her husband, a menswear sales agent, lived in an old building, a third floor walk-up on Esplanade, down the street from the Jewish People's library. One entered their home through a courtyard, walking up a narrow, dark staircase. The front room was bright and cheerful, but gatherings took place in the dining room, near the kitchen and the food. Maza served endless cups of tea with lemon, jam and sugar, Jewish egg cookies, marble cake, and home-made walnut strudel. If anyone was really hungry, there was her thick barley soup, bread and eggs. Yiddish writers and painters, including New York visitors such as the well-known poet Kadya

Molodvosky, would gather, read poetry, discuss ideas and no doubt, debate and argue. Ida Maza also wrote poetry herself and published in the *Kamf*.[57]

Waddington, originally from Winnipeg, met Ida Maza when she was fourteen. Maza was extremely well read and steered the teenaged Waddington to a broad range of Yiddish and English poets and writers. In her memoir Waddington writes: "Somewhere Mrs. Maza is still urging hungry poets to have a bite to eat, and turning on the light in her dining room to illuminate a crowd of displaced Yiddish writers. And behind them stretches a larger crowd, the long procession of every writer who ever wrote in whatever language."[58]

Sholem Shtern, poet, author, and director of the Winchevsky Shule in Montreal was a frequent contributor to *Der Kamf*. He urged greater connections within the different Jewish groups locally, regionally, and between Canada and the United States. He proposed setting up a central Canadian bureau to coordinate and provide speakers and foster communication between Canadian Culture Centres. He also encouraged Jewish leftists to attend the Workers' University in New York.[59] In sharp contrast to the left's denunciations of other secular Jewish movements in the late 1920s and early 1930s and his own earlier exhortations to keep class politics central, Shtern now stressed co-operation between groups, such as Montreal's labour Zionist Peretz school, where his brother was the director, and the more traditional folk shule in Montreal headed by Shloime Wiseman.

In Montreal, both Abe Rosenberg and Sholem Shtern expressed regrets for the time and energy secular movements had spent fighting with each other.[60] The politics were changing, and so were the demographics. The Yiddish immigrant generation was growing older, and a new Canadian-born generation was emerging. Rosenberg and Shtern wanted to establish English-speaking sections in the JWCC so that those Jewish workers who did not know Yiddish, now in the thousands, would not be alienated.[61]

As Hitler's power increased, Yiddish life in Europe was threatened, leading to a growing awareness of the need to preserve Yiddish folk culture in Canada. Embracing Yiddish culture came to be understood as a political act, part of the resistance against anti-Semitism. At the same time, with the emergence of a Canadian-born, English-speaking population, the circle of Yiddishists had become narrower. Yiddishists believed it was the responsibility of Jews in free countries like Canada to work to keep and maintain Yiddish as a "living, dynamic people's culture," the language of European Jews for a thousand years, and to create new Yiddish culture.[62] Sholem Shtern, in particular, was an enthusiastic supporter of the planned International Yiddish Cultural Congress in 1937. He urged Canadians to become more actively involved in global Yiddish proletarian culture. The left Yiddish sister organizations in the United States, such as the Jewish Culture Society, the International Worker's Order, the Proletarian Yiddish Writers Organization (Proletpen), and the Peretz Writer's League in New York City were planning to send delegates to the International Yiddish Cultural Congress to be held in Paris in 1937. Shtern wanted Canadian organizations to do the same.

The Congress lasted four days and was attended by four thousand people and representatives from twenty-three countries. Commissions were formed to promote the growth of Yiddish literature, theatre, schools, scholarship, and art. A new cultural organization called the YKUF (Jewish Cultural Association) was created, with a monthly publication called *Yiddishe Kultur* (Jewish Culture). Edited by Nakman Mayzels, the cultural offerings were non-partisan. However, not all were ready to support this effort if communists were involved. The popular New York Yiddish paper *Forvetz* (Forward) denounced the Cultural Congress, as did the Arbeter Ring. Their animosity toward those with communist affiliations proved more powerful than joining this effort to build support for secular Yiddish culture. Neither the Canadian Jewish Congress nor its counterpart, the American Jewish Congress endorsed the event. Nevertheless, the conference sparked a renewed interest in Yiddish.[63]

Socialist Singing

Of all the cultural institutions created by the Jewish left, the choirs were the most popular. In virtually every city where a left Jewish organization existed, people came together to sing. Particularly in the late 1920s and 1930s, the Toronto choir, the Freiheit Gezang Fareyn, symbolized the external, public face of the revolutionary movement. The choir grew from the early days of the 1920s when, after being evicted from Alhambra Hall, the singers went out to "fight on the street for the right to bring revolutionary song to the Jewish workers of Toronto."[64] By the mid-1930s the choir and the mandolin orchestra were performing often and everywhere, including two concerts at Massey Hall in 1935 and 1936 with guest conductor Jacob Schaefer from New York.[65] Schaefer was a composer and arranger of folk songs, who set radical poetry, oratorios, cantatas, and folk operettas into Yiddish.[66] The choir movement he inspired with his compositions spread throughout North America and drew thousands of people into an appreciation of Yiddish secular culture.

The singers, many of whom could not read music, were devoted to the choir. Bella Shek recalled when she first joined the choir in 1934:

> I used to think if I could sing in a choir, I would give anything.... In 1934 we came to Canada and lived with friends in 40 Brunswick Avenue. One night I came from work and I heard voices and I thought what beautiful singing.... As I was listening, someone came out and she said, are you are a singer? I said no, but I just got off my streetcar and I stopped to listen because I love singing so much. That was before a concert in May [1935] when Jacob Schaefer [from New York] came to conduct the choir.... They were singing Wednesday night from 8:30 to 11 and Sunday afternoon from 3 o'clock till 6.... I thought Sunday I'll go and I'll listen.... After the rehearsal [one person] took me over to the conductor and said, this is Bella Shek, and she's got a beautiful voice and I would like you to take her into the choir. Oh, he said, by all means, we need sopranos. And that's the way I came into the choir.[67]
>
> I sang from 1934 to 1990. [When I got older] I used to stand with Rose Field. She was so young, 15 years old when she joined the choir.... Rose was sitting with me till the last minute.... I don't read music. I didn't have time

יעקב שײיפער

אונזער גרינדער פירער און לערער — אין אײביקן אָנדענק

געבוירן דעם 13 טן סעפטעמבער, 1888 אין טערנאָוויץ, ושליץ
געשטאָרבן אין ניו־יאָרק, דעם 1 טן נאָוועמבער, 1936.

Jacob Schaefer (1888–1936) wrote the music for the I. L.
Peretz poem "Two Brothers." The picture, by Avrom, is in the
25th Souvenir Program of the Toronto Jewish Folk Choir.
It says "Jacob Schaefer, our founder, leader and teacher—
remembered forever."

UJPO Archives.

TORONTO JEWISH FOLK CHOIR

EMIL GARTNER, Conductor

SHIRLEY NEWMAN, Soprano   NEW DANCE THEATRE
                                IVY KREHM, Director
LAWRENCE FELTON, Baritone
                                A.U.U.C. FOLK DANCERS
CONTINENTAL STRING ENSEMBLE   WALTER BALAY, Director

PROGRAM

I

A SCHAEFER MEMORIAL

a) Unzer Firer .... Schaefer
b) Un Du Akerst (Folksong) .... arr. Schaefer
c) Oratorio: Di Tzvei Brider — Text: I. L. Peretz .... Music: Schaefer
     Soloists: Shirley Newman, Soprano; Lawrence Felton, Baritone.

INTERMISSION

II

**SONGS OUR AUDIENCE LIKED TO HEAR IN 25 YEARS
OF TORONTO JEWISH FOLK CHOIR**

a) S'Felt a Shnay .... Sheinin
b) Ev'ry Time I Feel the Spirit (Negro Spiritual) .... arr. Smith
c) Pick a Bale O' Cotton .... Negro Work Song
d) Shir Hapalmech (Israeli) .... arr. Goldman
e) El Yivneh Hagalil (Yemenite) .... arr. Chajes

III

a) Creation Hymn .... Beethoven
b) Gloria In Excelsis (from Mass in B Minor) .... Bach
c) Das Beendchen (Trio) .... Mozart
     Soloists: Shirley Newman, Soprano; Melvin McLean, Tenor;
     David Mills, Bass-baritone.

IV

a) Rage On O River (from Yellow River Cantata) ...... Hsu Hsing Hai
b) The Birch Tree (Russian Folksong) .... arr. Alexandrov
     Soloist: Lawrence Felton
c) Hopak (Ukrainian Folk Dance) .... arr. Podoliak
d) Rumbala (Spanish Loyalist Song) .... arr. Gartner
e) Reb Dovid! (Jewish Folksong) .... arr. Zilberts
f) Birobidjaner Freilechs .... Polonsky

FAGEL GARTNER at the piano.

Schaefer was honoured in the 25th anniversary concert. One
can see the diversity of the repertoire in this program, which
includes Yiddish songs as well as classical works, Black spirit-
uals, and songs in Spanish, Russian, and Chinese. Toronto
Jewish Folk Choir, *25th Anniversary Book*, Toronto, 1950.

UJPO Archives.

to learn music. Sometimes they gave us some lessons but I could never be
there because I was too busy. I had a job, and I had to tend the home. Ben was
young, and I had to cook and clean.

Most of the members of the choir, like Bella, were working people. Many of
the songs they sang, the songs of the sweatshop, spoke to conditions they knew
first hand. Singing in a choir was important for reminding people that they were
not just wage slaves, but human beings. Interviewed in her small, one-room
seniors' residence when she was well into her nineties, Bella described the poverty of those early days. A woman singing next to her told this writer, "Don't ask
what things were like. It was terrible times. Kids were sitting hungry. People

didn't have anything to give the kids to eat. When I think about that, it breaks my heart."

Bella showed me a cherished possession, a biography of Jacob Schaefer, the New York-based conductor and influential figure in the North American Yiddish folk choir movement. Bella's son, Ben, told me that when Schaefer was rehearsing with the Toronto choir in 1935 and 1936, people would line up on the street outside 7 Brunswick Avenue to listen.

In 1936, the Toronto choir, with Dubkovksy as its leader, had grown to 115 singers. It continued to flourish, joined in concerts by the orchestra. In 1934, Philip Podoliak, conductor of the JWCC's Wind Orchestra, combined the wind and mandolin orchestras to form the Mandolin Symphony Orchestra.[68] He also started a beginners' class for wind instruments.

The new Mandolin Symphony Orchestra usually performed with the choir and often the drama section and attempted larger, more ambitious works.[69] *Der Kamf* writers credit Podoliak's initiative and "energetic activity," which included raising most of the funding, for its success.[70] Most of the instruments were owned by the orchestra and borrowed by the players. Podoliak emphasized that the orchestra participated in general workers' movement

Philip (Pesel) Podoliak was born in Ratzine, Lublin, Poland in 1900 and came to Canada in 1927. He was an artist as well as a musician and conductor. Podoliak wrote that "we copy all our scores by hand which meant that for every piece we play we have to write over 50 scores."

Personal collection of Esther Podoliak.

campaigns, including raising money for *Der Kamf* and the *Daily Clarion*.[71]

Podoliak's leftist politics got him in trouble with the musician's union. In May 1936, he was temporarily suspended from the union because he marched with his orchestra in the Labour League May Day parade. The anti-communist union claimed that the marching constituted a performance in a non-union venue! Podoliak was not allowed to participate in the grand anniversary concert in Massey Hall. The JWCC drama section, the choir, and the orchestra performed *No Single Step*, an oratorio about revolutionary Soviet struggles written by the Soviet Yiddish poet Peretz Markish and put to music by Jacob Schaefer.[72] Despite a suffocating heat wave, Massey Hall was packed. Jacob Schaefer came from New York as guest conductor. Even though Podoliak couldn't perform as planned because of his suspension from the union, the evening went well. The reviewer for *Der Kamf* declared it "masterfully performed," and the concert received positive reviews from the generally conservative *Mail and Empire* and from music critic Augustus Bridle in the *Toronto Star*. Bridle said:

All of the women knew by heart a work of great difficulty in modern idioms.... To have memorized a long, difficult work was a triumph of concentration. To sing it, mainly so well, with so unusual a mixed orchestra in place of a regular symphony, was a feat of real mastery in performance.... The program closed by a mass performance of "The International."[73]

By October 1937, the orchestra had forty-five members plus another forty in the beginners' classes. The instruments consisted of 1st and 2nd mandolin, mandola, mandocello, and mandobass, and for the wind section, flute, oboe, clarinet, bassoon, French horn, trumpet, and trombone.[74] Podoliak, the conductor, noted how the orchestra had changed: in the early years, the musicians were mostly shop workers who had little time to learn or practice an instrument. By 1937, around 60 percent of the players were students with more time and ability to focus on music. This transition to younger students also allowed the orchestra to develop a higher quality and the ability to take on more advanced pieces. For example, in addition to new socialist-inspired oratorios, the orchestra attempted classical works, including Beethoven's *Coriolanus* Overture and Rimsky-Korsakov's *Scheherazade*, as well as Bach's Suite in B Major and Mozart's A Flat Major Concerto.[75] Podoliak emphasized that the Jewish Workers' Mandolin Orchestra was distinct from other local musical institutions:

> The significance of our orchestra for our worker's and people's organizations, and for the ordinary workers and folk masses, is of course inestimable. Here they are given an opportunity to become familiar with and make use of the classical musical works, which would not be accessible to them in any other way, because of the high price of tickets, and other reasons. Furthermore, you must not forget that our orchestra gives its especial attention to worker's and folk music. No other orchestras take up these areas. We bring to the people their own music, in which they see an artistic reflection of themselves. This, and the fact that the players are one of us—workers from the shops and studying worker-youth—this is of very great cultural significance for our masses. Take the same musical compositions and you will notice that it is a great undertaking for whoever plays it.[76]

Gerry Cohen, who learned to play the clarinet with Podoliak, put himself through university and medical school with his musical skills. He spent summers playing in resorts for vacationers. Sid (Mitzi) Dolgoy was one of the children who learned to play the mandolin with Podoliak. (Originally based in Winnipeg, Mitzi's father Max Dolgoy was a trade union organizer and an activist his entire life.) In his reminiscences, Mitzi talks about the Toronto orchestra's connection with the left Ukrainian organization, the Ukrainian Labour Farmer Temple Association (ULFTA). They sang in each other's choirs and Ukrainians played in the orchestra. To this day, some of the older members of the Shevchenko ensemble (a left Ukrainian orchestra) of the ULFTA come from the left Jewish organizations. Mitzi recalled:

> My mother was musically oriented and had a mandolin group. I studied the mandolin at the Labour League because she wanted me to. Philip Podoliak was my teacher. Anyway, I developed and became pretty good. I joined the

children's orchestra, and as it happened my wife played the mandolin there, too. That's where we met.

A mandolin, at that time, was peanuts! Fifty cents down, and fifty cents a week. Ida [Mitzi's wife] was a concertmaster in the orchestra when we grew up. They needed a mandocello player, so they asked me to take it over. The children's orchestra met at 7 Brunswick Avenue on Sundays.

I was going to shule five days a week after school. My mother was working in a dress place, and my father became an organizer in the dressmaker's union.... We'd sometimes play with the Ukrainian Orchestra. Dophy was the conductor at the time and he liked my playing. Both Podoliak and he agreed that I should go to the Conservatory to study. They went to my parents, to tell them how they felt. My father said no, that I had to learn a trade. So I went to Central Tech, to study electricity. I only went there for two or three years.[77]

A product of the shule, the camp, and the United Jewish People's Order, Mitzi Dolgoy was one of the founders of the folk group the Travellers. One of the original members, Oscar Ross, thought up the name. The group were fans of Pete Seeger, a frequent visitor and friend to the Jewish left community, and modelled themselves after the Weavers; the name came from the Woody Guthrie song "Lonesome Traveller," sung by the Weavers. The Travellers became popular throughout Canada in the 1960s and wrote Canadian words to the Woody Guthrie song, "This Land is Your Land."

Stage sets were created by the artist Avrom. For the choir's twenty-fifth anniversary book, he looked back remembering the challenges of creating a mural for one of the choir's productions, *A Bunt Mit a Statchke* (A Plot and a Strike), which tells the story of a strike in a garment factory in Russia at the turn of the century:

The Toronto Jewish Folk Choir was my school—wherein I learned, the hard way, to design and build stage settings and create costumes. The Statchke setting had to be constructed almost wholly from anything that happened to be lying about at the 7 Brunswick Avenue "stage." The budget allotted for this part of the production was, for practical purposes almost nil.... One acquired the knack of making one stage set do for a number of different productions.[78]

The choir performed two major works: Peretz's *Di Tzvey Brider* (Two Brothers) with original music by Jacob Schaefer and *A Wedding in the Shtetl*, folksongs about shtetl life accompanied by acting and dancing. *Di Tzvey Brider* is based on a poem by I. L. Peretz set to music by Jacob Schaefer. The widely performed cantata is the story of two brothers who love each other dearly and live together harmoniously in a magical land *oyf yener zayt yam* (across the sea). It can be read as a critique of capitalism:

> Their hearts beat as one heart, so tenderly
> Their bread it was coarse, their furniture rough
> Their life was a hard one, but happy and free
> But they shared joy and sorrow, and that was enough

Along comes a snake who convinces one of the brothers that there is a fortune to be made from the sweat of his sibling's work. So the brother begins to amass a fortune from his brother's work and "their rest and their gladness—both vanished alike." His brother's sweat becomes diamonds, the drops of his blood become rubies. Their happiness disappears, and they are both punished:

> One slept not for pain, and the other for fright
> One cries, it's my wealth, my riches, my god
> The other: my tears, my sweat and my blood!
> Ding-dong-day-dee
> Far away across the sea
> There is fighting and tearing their hair.[79]

The poem is clearly an allegory for what happens when class differences divide people who should be brothers, and half of humanity tries to benefit from exploiting the other.

In 1939, Emil Gartner, a Vienna-born classical musician, came to Toronto as a refugee and became the charismatic director of the choir. Ben Shek recalled that "to work with Emil Gartner was a tremendous experience. He was demanding and would sometimes yell at rehearsals. The women were all in love with him."[80] Under Emil's leadership, the choir's repertoire broadened to include classical works in addition to folk songs. Canadian composers John Weinzweig, Louis Applebaum and others were commissioned to write works for the choir and Canadian opera artists such as Lois Marshall performed with it. Gartner's wife, Faygl Freeman Gartner, was the accompanist.

Members did more than show up to sing—they helped collect money to keep the choir going. The songs reflected what people cared about. Some songs, such

Choir singers helping in the ticket office at 7 Brunswick Avenue, 1945/46. Left to right: Goldie Abramowitz, Lil Landau, Rae Orlan, Sylvia Greenbaum.

UJPO Archives.

as "Shnel Loyfn di Reder" (The Wheels Turn Quickly) by Dovid Edelstadt, described life in the sweatshops of the new world, ending with a challenge to working people: "Ven dayn shtarker hant nor vil, shteyen alle reder shtil" (When your powerful hands will it, all the wheels will stop). In the post-Second World War period, they sang the beautiful and sad Vilna Ghetto songs written by Lithuanian poets Shmerke Kaczeginski and Avrom Sutskever. One song, "Shtiler, shtiler" (Quiet, quiet) written by Kaczeginski in the Vilna Ghetto in 1943, described the deportations of tens of thousands of people and mass murders in Ponar, formerly a picnic site just outside of Vilna. The people in the ghetto held a contest to put the poem to music. The winner was an eleven-year-old named Aleksandr Volkovski, and his song was performed by the Jewish chorus in the ghetto. Here is the poem in translation:

Shtiler shtiler music. This song was written in the Vilna (Vilnius) ghetto by Kaczerginski and put to music by eleven-year-old Aleksandr Volkovksi. Volkovski survived the war and moved to Israel where he was known as Tamir.

From Kaczerginski, Lider fi di ghettos un Lagern (New York: Congress for Jewish Culture, 1948).

> Quiet, quiet let's be silent
> Graves are growing here
> They were planted by the tyrant
> See their bloom appear
> All the roads lead to Ponar now
> There are no roads back
> And our father too has vanished
> And with him our luck[81]

Other songs were songs of resistance. The "Yugnt Hymn" (Hymn of Youth) describes how youth is a question not of age, but of conviction. It says that although the enemy stands guard at the gate, young people will work together for a "nayer, frayer tsayt" (a new, freer time). Also based on a Kaczerginski poem, the song was learned by the children in the secular Yiddish schools.

In the Klein family, participation in the choir was a family affair. Claire Klein Osipov of Vancouver, who sang professionally for many years, recalled her family's history with the choir:

My father, Abie Klein, belonged to the choir in the 1930s and was involved in all the activities of the Labour League. He wanted his children to be part of it. My sister Lillian [Klein London] studied the mandolin. I joined the choir in 1949, when Emil was the conductor. In 1950–51 I became a soloist.[82]

Mollie Klein [Goldsman] who was Secretary/Treasurer of the choir recalled:

I started in the choir in 1940. My mother and father had the snack bar downstairs in the building. For most of the twelve years that I sang with the choir I was on the executive. It was my job to present the bouquets at Massey Hall to our guest artists. I would walk up there with my knees shaking.

Emil was a genius with music. In the 1940s, even before it was widely known what was happening in Europe, we were singing the songs from the ghetto such as "Zog Nit Keynmol," the song composed by Hirsh Glik in 1943 that became the anthem of the Jewish left. I remember our performance of the *Di Naye Hagode* [the New Haggadah or the New Narrative] as the best time of my life. We worked very very hard, rehearsing every night of the week to prepare for our two performances. Saide Gerrard choreographed the dance to be performed on a catwalk above the choir.[83]

The performance Mollie remembers was in 1948 with the Toronto Symphony Orchestra and the dancer Saide Gerrard, who had trained with Martha Graham in New York. "Di Naye Hagode" is a dramatic choral tone poem or cantata based on Soviet poet Itzik Feffer's epic Yiddish poem about the Warsaw Ghetto Uprising, "Di shotns fun varshever geto" (The Shadows of the Warsaw Ghetto). The doomed uprising of its inhabitants against the Nazis began the second night of Passover in 1943, and, amazingly, lasted for forty-three days and nights. The title refers to the Haggada, the story of Passover traditionally read at a *seder* (ritual dinner) each year. The Warsaw Ghetto and the uprising epitomized the entire tragedy of the Holocaust. For those who participated in the production as singers or dancers, one can well imagine that they were singing about their collective souls, a powerful and moving experience. Their singing evoked powerful emotions, expressing their grief and determination to ensure that they would not be defeated and that Jewish culture would survive.

The poem tells the story of a young boy who survives the Nazi invasion of the ghetto, but then in the ultimate act of defiance takes his own life:

> Right here, not too long ago, when evening would fall,
>
> He used to ride on brooms with the other boys.
>
> How quickly has his childhood ended! And what are the worldly possessions now left to him? Only two hand grenades, a gun, the torn flag of his people. He climbs up the broken wall of the tower. He wraps his body like a high priest in his prayer shawl, and clinging to its folds in everlasting embers, he fires two bullets and leaps into space.

Itzik Feffer wrote the poem shortly after people learned of the destruction of the Warsaw Ghetto. The poem was published by the YKUF in 1945. Max Helfman, who became the conductor of the Jewish Philharmonic in New York after Jacob Schaefer's death in 1936, put it to music, and it was performed with dancers in the United States, Montreal, and Toronto.

Feffer had visited North America with the Jewish Anti-Fascist Committee in 1943. Tragically, as this moving and beautiful cantata was being performed in North America, Stalin abolished the Committee and denounced its members as "rootless cosmopolitans." Stalin charged Feffer, along with Dovid Bergelson, Dovid Hofshteyn, and Peretz Markish, with treason, and they were murdered in 1952.

The survival of Yiddish culture depended on its successful transmission to a new generation, and the children's concerts were supported by the entire community. In Toronto, Ruth Borchiver, born in 1928, recalled her participation in the war years:

> When I was very young, we performed at the Strand, what was called "the Victory Theatre" during the war, but it was the Strand Theatre. We had sold-out houses because we did plays from Sholem Aleichem. I remember in one play, Bennie [Ben Shek] was Yossel, and I was a good dancer. We were performing his nightmare, because he'd stolen something, and I was a knife! (*Dos Meserl*) The cultural life was … no one was as lucky. There

was a mandolin orchestra, and you could play in it, you could sing in a choir, you could recite, you could appear in plays, free of charge and yet appreciated. We grew up, Bennie and I, in a very privileged atmosphere ... instead of sitting and studying books, we were encouraged to be creative and express ourselves.[84]

A *Kamf* review of a children's concert at the Strand Theatre in May 1940 noted that it was well attended, with an audience who "understands the importance of building Yiddish culture." The mandolin orchestra also performed, with a repertoire that included several popular American songs. Several children recited poetry. The highlight of the evening was a performance of Sholem Aleichem's *Motl Peyse dem Khazns* (Motl the Cantor's son), directed by Moyshe Feldman, the head teacher of the Labour League School. The production involved acting, dancing (taught by Neli Kon), piano accompaniment (Faygl Freeman), and a stage set by Avrom.

Motl the Cantor's Son tells the story of a nine-year-old boy from Kasrilevke, a fictional shtetl, whose father dies after a long illness. Motl is happy to discover that being fatherless confers on him certain social privileges such as the willingness of the adult community to forgive his mischievous pranks. His older brother Elye, recently married, tries to lift the family out of poverty through a series of get-rich-quick schemes he learns from a book. Motl is a willing accomplice. However, their efforts invariably do not work as planned. Together with a group of friends, they depart for America. Readers laugh at the same time as their hearts ache for Motl and his family, and the failed schemes of Elye.

Sixty-five children took part as singers, dancers, and actors. The reviewer said the performances reminded him of children's spectacles in Eastern Europe when students coming home for vacation would share something educational and cultural with the people in their home village.[85]

Cultural Flowering in the Late 1940s and 1950s

During the Second World War, the alliance with Russia made the Soviet Union popular in North America. Even Eaton's department store took out full-page ads supporting "our Russian allies."[86] Mollie Myers, a choir member and activist, described the feelings at the time:

The Soviet Union was an idol of everybody.... If you scratch any bigshot nowadays on the street ... he had some connection with the choir, or with the

Labour League, or with the shule, or whatever it is …. It was a time when it was popular…. The idea was this was going to be good for the working man.[87]

After 1945, when the national organization, the United Jewish People's Order (UJPO) formed, a National Culture and School Committee was established, responsible for organizing and assisting with the cultural and educational work done by the local branches and conducting concerts and lecture tours across the country. Besides political work (campaigns for benefit funds, elections, strike support, fundraising for the constantly struggling left newspapers, the branches engaged in all kinds of cultural work—Jewish schools, nurseries, children's clubs, Jewish folk choirs, drama groups, dance groups, youth choirs and activities to popularize Jewish song, drama and literature in Yiddish and English. The reach was broad, attempting to connect with the non-UJPO members in the Jewish community as well as the broader non-Jewish Canadian society. The UJPO encouraged the establishment of branches for English-speaking immigrant and Canadian-born Jews as well as supporting the development of a youth movement with separate youth branches.[88] The organization grew. Two new secular Jewish schools in Vancouver and Hamilton opened and Jewish folk choirs in Winnipeg and Windsor organized. There was a new camp, Husavik, for children and adults in Winnipeg and a summer seminar for graduates from UJPO schools, as well as national lecture and concert tours.

Toronto's choir remained a high point of left Jewish cultural life in the city. The revered black baritone Paul Robeson was much beloved by the choir, and he gave several concerts in Toronto and Montreal in the late 1940s, until his passport was revoked in 1950 and he was blacklisted.[89] Robeson had a magnificent voice and was celebrated in Europe, but his career in the United States was damaged by racism as well as the unpopularity of his leftist views, especially during the McCarthy period. Robeson became a friend of conductor Emil Gartner. After a 1946 performance Robeson wrote:

> One of the most memorable concerts of my career was on May 24, 1946 in Toronto with the Jewish Folk Choir under the direction of Emil Gartner. This was a choir with not every technical resource but more one of great heart and feeling. I certainly hope it will be my privilege to appear with them soon again. All my best to them.
> Paul Robeson
> November 10, 1946

P.S. Of especial delight and satisfaction was the authentic rendering of the great folk music of the world—including my own Negro music. Here was a fine demonstration of the common brotherhood of man—expressed in beautiful folk idioms.[90]

Robeson was a hero to the left Jewish community in both Canada and the United States. He was honoured for his transnational and transethnic views, his outspoken critique of racism, and his principled opposition to McCarthy's red-baiting. For many on the left, Robeson epitomized the bond between left-wing Jews and Blacks. They were all part of a larger "common struggle" in fighting oppression. Robeson appreciated the diverse repertoire of the choir, which included Black spirituals, labour songs, Yiddish songs, and classical works. In a banquet in Toronto in his honour in 1949, he indicated that he "felt deeply about the choir for many many reasons.... Nothing could be finer than somehow for America to see this kind of a choir of many peoples—Jewish, Irish, Negro, all kinds of people working together and this basic theme of the unity of different peoples."[91] Mollie Klein recalled hearing Paul Robeson sing:

The man was larger than life. He came in the early 1950s, just before they took his visa away at the height of the Cold War. He gave a concert, I think it was in

The Klein sisters, Claire, Mollie, and Lily, who were soloists with the Toronto Jewish Folk Choir.

UJPO Archives.

the Queen Elizabeth Building of Exhibition Place and the entire place was surrounded by Royal Canadian Mounted Police, with their coats and hats, inside and out. Inside, the place was packed. He came out and walked onto the stage. There was a ten-minute ovation. It was unbelievable. He said hello, and the applause once again went and on. He had been told he couldn't speak, he could only sing. When Robeson did "Kol Nidre," that was the most moving thing.[92]

In the early 1950s, under the leadership of Emil Gartner, choir perform-ances were often held in Massey Hall, the largest concert hall in the city, some-times with the Toronto Symphony and soloists from the New York Metropolitan Opera such as Jan Peerce, Jennie Tourel, Igor Gorin, and Regina Resnick.

The 1950 twenty-fifth anniversary concert of the Toronto Jewish Folk Choir was a grand event commemorated by a book published for the occasion. The pro-gram consisted of a Schaefer memorial, a selection of international folk songs, songs from Russia, China, the Spanish Civil War, Yiddish songs and Negro spirit-uals, and works by Beethoven, Bach, and Mozart. Accompanying the singers were a string ensemble, the New Dance Theatre, and a Ukrainian folk dance group. One commentator explained the Toronto Jewish Folk Choir's approach to culture:

There are today in Canada, two cultures, two approaches to the arts. There is the culture that has been purchased (with US dollars), those in our country who stand for everything that is hateful: who seek to use the arts in all their forms to destroy man's revulsion against violence and war and inculcate in him the culture and the ideology of the brute.

There is the emerging culture of the people ... growing and developing in the course of the daily struggles of the people for peace, for democratic rights, for progress and security.... It is to the everlasting credit of the United Jewish People's Order that it stands irrevocably with the people's culture, that it has made such magnificent contributions to the strengthening of that culture in the field of music, drama, the dance and literature.... It is a Jewish choir and a Canadian choir.[93]

The upsurge in Jewish Canadian cultural expression in the 1950s was part of the larger general upswing in Canadian cultural expression. In a shift from prewar left sentiment, marked by the importance of class solidarity, even the class divide between bourgeois and worker was now viewed as less dangerous than Canadian subservience to the United States. Sam Lipshitz, the head of the Council of Progressive Jewish Organizations and a member of the Central Committee of the Communist Party, declared that bourgeois culture, when it is Canadian, "serves objectively in the fight against the American domination of the cultural life of our country." The fight was now against "Second Avenue culture" with its anti-Semitic Jewish stereotypes. Positive signs of the growth of Canadian-Jewish culture included a production of Arthur Miller's *The Crucible* put on by Holy Blossom Temple in Toronto; the "Songs of the Shtetl" concert sponsored by the YMHA and the CJC; a performance of a story by Sholem Aleichem by the Toronto Hebrew Day School; and a Jewish song and dance concert at the "Y."[94] Canadian nationalism had become a central part of the Jewish left's identity, politics, and cultural work by the later 1950s.

In both Montreal and Toronto accomplished dance groups were part of the UJPO—the Modern Dance Group in Montreal, and the New Dance Theatre (formerly the Neo Dance Theatre) in Toronto. The New Dance Theatre participated in the Canadian Ballet Festival. The Toronto group, which formed in 1946, consisted of dancers who were factory workers, housewives, and students. They were taught by people such as the Moscow-trained Boris Volkov.[95] They held

Program cover for the 25th anniversary concert.

UJPO Archives.

Honey Ross and Tommy Lima. "The 1949/50 season of New Dance Theatre at the United Jewish People's Order featured a range of modern dance classes along with ballet and folk dance. Nancy Lima Dent and Cynthia Barrett headed up the modern classes while Betty Oliphant taught ballet and Ivy Krehm taught folk dance. Ten dollars bought you a term of sixteen classes and half that price paid for children's classes." http://www.dcd.ca/exhibitions/limadent/newdance.html#.

Library and Archives Canada, 10752517.

classes for all ages, mostly in modern dance, but also in folk dancing, ballet, and choreography, with fees that ranged from $5–$15 per term.

Teachers included Betty Oliphant, later a co-founder of the National Ballet of Canada, Cynthia Barrett and Ivy Krehm, all three among the most accomplished dancers and teachers in Canada. In 1952, in addition to dance classes, the Toronto UJPO was also running a lecture and discussion series on dance history and dance in relation to society.[96] The dances, called ballets, expressed Jewish progressive, socialist, historical themes. Performances included *Di Naye Hagode* in 1948 with the Jewish Folk Choir and the Toronto Symphony Orchestra and *That We May Live* in 1950, a ballet about the suffering of Jews in Czarist Russia and their liberation upon immigration to Canada. This ballet got excellent reviews from both socialist and mainstream critics.[97] Nancy Lima was recruited to become part of the UJPO after Emil Gartner had seen an anti-war dance, *Heroes of our Time*, she had choreographed with Laya Lieberman and Marcel Chojnacki. It was performed in the Canadian Dance Festival.

In 1952, Faygl Gartner organized a choir, the UJPO Folk Singers, which along with members of the New Dance Theatre toured the country for five weeks, performing in union halls in small cities like Sudbury and community halls in remote prairie farm towns. Claire Klein Osipov, who met her husband on the trip, recalled:

> We sang our way through Canada, rehearsing on the train. We were billeted in private homes, by kind and generous people. Faygl, the moving force in the group, was a magnificent woman to work with. She gave me lots of encouragement. We sang peace songs, anti-war songs, French Canadian songs, and songs from many different lands. We were all very dedicated and committed, and we had a wonderful time. After that, other small groups popped up over Canada. I started a group in Vancouver, and we performed on CBC radio.[98]

Joan Orenstein, one of the singers, who later became a well-known Toronto actor, said that introducing new people to Jewish leftist culture "brings honor to

the Jewish people as a whole."[99] She described their repertoire: "With our songs and dances we spoke about many things, about love and peace, about friendship amongst the nations, about the horror of war and the cherishing of the cultural heritage of the many peoples who have built this country."

The left was sponsoring cultural activities all around the country. Winnipeg had its own choir and brought in musical troupes and speakers from outside the city. The UJPO Youth Branch 36 in Winnipeg, established in November 1946, had twenty members and held social and educational evenings every other Friday or Sunday, which included debates, book reviews, guest speakers, discussions, readings, musicals, dances, and parties. In the summer, they planned outings to the new UJPO camp Husavik, established north of the city. They also participated in the UJPO Choir and had their own Drama Group, which in 1947 put on *Bar Kochba* by Shmuel Halkin, a play about the struggle of the Jews against their Roman oppressors, directed by Leybl Basman.[100] Although the members of the youth club were entirely Canadian-born and English speaking, they presented *Bar Kochba* in Yiddish.

Cultural activities flourished in smaller cities such as Vancouver, Calgary, and Hamilton. The Vancouver branch of the UJPO, Branch 17, had a theatre group, held lectures and recreational activities, and, with the help of the national UJPO office, brought in prominent speakers from Toronto and New York. A children's Chanukah concert in Hamilton drew a crowd of three hundred people.[101]

Marcel Chojnacki, later a member of the National Ballet of Canada, and Honey Ross, circa 1950s.

Courtesy of the family of Honey and Oscar Ross.

The Travellers perform on CBC circa 1950s.

Courtesy of the family of Honey and Oscar Ross.

There were huge political shifts in the post-war period and into the 1950s that changed how the Jewish left was viewed and how they did cultural work. As the Cold War heated up, the left was under attack. Nevertheless, the Montreal Jewish Folk Choir managed to keep going. It celebrated its thirtieth jubilee with a Panorama Concert on February 29 and March 1, 1956. The choir sang songs from decades past, interspersed with dramatizations written by Sholem Shtern. Shtern wrote a social history of the choir's members—from the needle-trades shop and personal difficulties in "the hungry thirties" through the war years—which was dramatized through the stories of two choir members, Berl and Raisel. The director, Nathan Steinberg, composed his own pieces for the choir and Montreal's Modern Dance Group performed *Les Raftsman*, a ballet based on loggers' experiences in the Ottawa Valley in the nineteenth century.[102]

A substantial number of people from the secular Jewish left became renowned for their contribution to cultural life in Canada and the world. In *100 Years of Hebrew and Yiddish Literature in Canada,* compiled by Chaim Fuks, the number of prominent Yiddish writers and artists associated with left causes, particularly in the 1920s and 1930s, is significant. Of the several hundred entries written in Hebrew or Yiddish, and covering the gamut from religious to secular, four dozen were from the left-wing press: *Der Kamf, Der Vochenblat* (Canadian Jewish Weekly), and the American newspaper, *Morgn Freiheit* or *Yiddish Kultur*. Other Yiddish journals such as Winnipeg's *Dos Yiddishe Vort* (The Israelite Press) also published those with left politics. Most of the Yiddish writers were working-class, few could earn a living at their craft, and they were generally left-leaning—the difference was one of degree.

Many musicians, dancers, and actors from the Jewish left community went on to become nationally known in Canada. Examples include the actor Joan Orenstein; the folk singing group the Travellers; Sharon (Trosten) Hampton of the children's group, Sharon, Lois and Bram; and Marcel Chojnacki, who came to Canada as a war orphan and danced with the National Ballet. Gary Cristall, former director of the Vancouver Folk Festival, credits the Jewish left for the popularity of the folk revival of the 1950s and 1960s.[103]

Oscar Ross later performed as a mime in UJPO concerts and at Camp Naivelt.

Photo courtesy of the family of Honey and Oscar Ross.

The strong anti-racist and internationalist sensibilities in the cultural life of the Jewish left show that the support of an autonomous Yiddish culture does not have to be inward-looking or exclusive. Ethnic consciousness can be progressive, revolutionary, and internationalist. While the leadership of the pro-communist Jewish left were party members, and the formal positions up until the late 1950s did not deviate from CP policy, the experience of the participants was quite varied and quite different from official doctrine. Many came to enjoy themselves, to be a part of a community and to reaffirm their identity as Jews. For them, the preservation of Yiddish language and culture was the basis for their sense of themselves and their revolutionary commitments. Those who put their energies into ethnic movements such as the United Jewish People's Order valued their particular identities as Jews and viewed their participation as a way of expressing their principles and values.

The political tides turned in the post-war period, and the community suffered greatly from the anti-communist politics that dominated both the Canadian state and the wider Jewish community. Because of their socialist and secular convictions they were often outsiders. While membership in the Jewish left declined, it is noteworthy that the cultural institutions continued to thrive throughout the 1950s. Those who participated in singing, dancing, and acting found their lives much enriched. They, along with other left ethnic groups such as the Ukrainians and the Finns, pioneered the notion that socialistic politics and a commitment to the working class could embrace a plurality of cultures.

Their vision of liberation took a cultural form.[104] Through artistic expression, they kept alive a powerful vision of human dignity and their hopes for a different, less exploitative society.

9 SUMMER CAMPS

The summer camps of the socialist Jewish left were afford-able places where working people could go for fun, rest, and relaxation among like-minded people, a place where they did not have to explain themselves. They were surrounded by people with shared secular, Jewish, and internationalist values in beautiful green surroundings. The immigrant generation had fled to Canada for good reasons, but the poverty in the shtetlekh of the old country was at least in the midst of green fields, trees, and all the beauty of nature. The new Canadian-born generation might not share their parents' nostalgia for nature, but they had a lot of fun in a non-authoritarian camp, among friends, living a way of life that reinforced what they were taught at home and in the shule. Both the older generation and their children loved the summer camps.

By the late 1920s, the women from the Yiddish Arbeter Froyen Fareyn who had started camp Kindervelt in Toronto decided to hand it over to the Labour League. By 1927, the adults in Toronto began to arrive at the camp, forming the *Royte Kolonye* (Red Colony), and a camp for adults in the Laurentians called *Nitgedayget* (Not to worry) began the next year. The United States equivalent to Kindervelt, a children's camp called Kinderland in Peekskill New York, had opened in 1923 two years before the Toronto camp's first season in 1925. The Montreal camp for children, called Naivelt, opened soon after, in 1927. Many of the directors of the Canadian camps were teachers during the winter months in the New York International Workers Order Schools, the sister organization of the Canadian Jewish left.

Paul Mishler's *Raising Reds* describes the political culture that the Communist Party in the United States developed for children and tried to implement in all the communist-oriented groups, from the Young Pioneers to the radical

Kindervelt, circa 1927.

UJPO Archives.

Red Campers Colony, Camp Kindervelt, Rouge Hills, Ontario.

UJPO Archives.

summer camps of the mass organizations, attended by many children whose parents were not members of the Communist Party. Mishler's research was in the US, but his findings apply to Canada, where members of the secular Jewish left were part of the same community (and the names of their camps were the same).[1] The left camps in New York State stressed the importance of "combating ethnic and racial bigotry, promoting interethnic and interracial cooperation, and teaching children to support the labor movement."[2] As in Canada, the communist influence was more direct in the US camp in the 1920s, in the early years. By the late 1930s, Yiddish culture and the history of East European and US working-class Jews were stressed.

Proletarian Camps for Children and Adults

In 1928, the Canadian Worker's Circle (Kanader Arbeter Ring) Loan Association in Montreal, part of the group that pulled out of the Arbeter Ring, put up the money to buy land in the Laurentians to create a co-operative camp, Nitgedayget. It was inspired by the adult resort organized in 1922 by garment workers in upstate New York.[3] The founders of Nitgedayget proclaimed it the first co-operative workers' camp for adults in Canada, a not-for-profit venture, in which workers could buy shares. Its opening day was chaotic because four hundred people showed up instead of the one hundred and fifty that the organizers expected. However, the mandolin orchestra played, various guests spoke, and the evening ended with a huge campfire with the children from nearby Camp Naivelt. The writer for *Der Kamf* was so

Mary Winer at Camp Nitgedeiget (Camp not to worry). The camp was at Fourteen-mile Lake in the Laurentians. Across the road was the children's camp. Quebec, late 1920s or early 1930s.

Courtesy of the family of Honey and Oscar Ross (Mary was Honey's mother).

moved that he/she could not begin to express the community's gratitude for the work of the women who made the camp possible or convey on paper the beauty of the scene.[4]

The children's camps were to be an extension of what was taught in the shules in the city: *Fun shul tsu kemp fun kemp tsu shul* (from school to camp, from camp to school). They attempted to instil a radical outlook on the world, emphasizing the struggles of workers, inter-ethnic solidarity, and opposition to racism. On Sunday, the children, dressed in white, with kerchiefs around their necks, marched, singing, to the dining hall. The kerchiefs resembled the red scarves worn by the communist young pioneer groups, and the white dress made this weekly event, called Sunday Salutes, special.[5] On Saturday night, the children put on entertainment for the adults.

While the programs included political issues, most of the campers remember the fun. Four old friends who had been campers in Kindervelt in Long Branch, Toronto, from the very first year, 1925, continued to get together all their lives. One meeting was in Toronto in 2000. At the time of the interview, they were in their eighties, born between 1917 and 1920, the Canadian children of immigrants. The conversation and laughter, and eating, of course—we sat around the dining room table with the hostess running back and forth to the kitchen—was interspersed with reminiscences of political events and concerts

Sunday white salutes, Kinderland, 1940s. The white salutes were a feature of the camp for most of its existence.

York University Libraries, Clara Thomas Archives and Special Collections, Sam and Manya Lipshitz fonds, FO444, ASC06331.

with mischief and anecdotes. Al Soren remembered the day the Italian anarchists Sacco and Vanzetti were executed, charged with a murder that was considered a frame-up by the left: "It was almost like a day of mourning—all the kids were so sad." Bessie (Chicofsky) Grossman recalled the children putting on a play about the Scottsboro boys, five young black boys aged twelve to nineteen who were charged with rape in the southern United States. The left supported the young men's case, believing they were unfairly charged. Bessie was supposed to play a prostitute who had accused the boys, but because that was considered inappropriate for a child, she was a "floozy" instead. It was years before the boys were freed and vindicated.

Leybl Basman, the teacher and dramaturge, became director of the children's camp in Toronto in 1931. He arrived in Winnipeg from Lithuania in 1928 and found himself in the midst of the political battles in the Freiheit Temple shule. After two years, he left to organize a shule in Windsor but felt isolated. His friend Joshua Gershman wrote him, "Why young man should you sit there in Windsor and be troubled? We need you in the shule and in the summer in the camp."[6] Philip Halperin, the editor of *Der Kamf,* also encouraged him. Basman arrived at the camp, which was then called Kindervelt, in 1931 to take over from Shmuel Davidovich of New York. Itche Goldberg, director of the national network of shules associated with the International Workers Order, came to help.

It is not clear whether the leaders from New York were there to give the Canadians the benefit of their experience in running a summer camp or to ensure that the correct line was followed.

Along with Basman, the staff included Tuvieh Levine, Jimmy Meslin, Avrom the artist, and Saide Gerrard, the dancer. The concert at the end of the summer offers a sense of the camp's politics—in close alignment with the Communist Party's emphasis on proletarianism. The concert, attended by five hundred campers and guests, took place on August 9, 1931, and included song, dance, recitations, and a play. The program began with "The Internationale" conducted by Riegelhaupt, who was the first leader of the Freiheit Gezang Fareyn. The children's choir performed, standing on two platforms set up between two rows of trees. Then came "March, March, Red Army," "Hold the Fort," and other workers' songs. Twenty children with red kerchiefs around their necks

Leybl Basman was director of the camp at various times since 1931 when it was still Kindervelt.

Archives of Ontario, 1405 23-113.

from the Finnish camp, who were members of the Young Pioneers, came to greet the Kindervelt children, marching in a disciplined row past the campers. A group of children recited the "Paris Commune" and one recited *In Birger Krig* (In the Civil War) by Soviet poet Itzik Feffer and *Royte Donershtik* (Red Thursday) by Yiddish poet Moyshe Nadir, a visitor from New York. Moyshe Mindes, reporting on the event for *Der Kamf,* noted that most of the children did not understand the recitations. Then came the greeters, Sam Lapedes for the Labour League, and Joshua Gershman, national organizer of the Industrial Union of Needle Trades Workers, who spoke about the dressmakers' struggle in the Schiffer and Hillman shop in Toronto.[7]

The second part of the program impressed the *Kamf* writers—the children did gymnastic exercises, making a pyramid. The audience was delighted with the "light, joyous, lively children staying in symmetrical rows, red flags in their hands which they waved in rhythm." The day ended with a play, *Vos der tog dertseylt* (What the day tells us), by A. Platner. The background set, a garden symbolizing the joy of work in a free socialist society, was drawn by Jimmy Meslin. In the middle stood a tall spire, with the red star of the USSR and a giant five, for the Soviet Union's five-year plan. "All in all, it was a beautiful spectacle in content and revolutionary spirit," declared a reviewer.[8]

Der Kamf writers in the 1930s considered the children's and adult camps in Quebec and Ontario important because they were "proletarian camps." The Quebec children's camp, Naivelt, opened in 1927, two years after the camp in Ontario. It is not clear how long it lasted, as an article in 1937 described the preparations for a new children's camp, now to be called Kinderland, in the same place, on Fourteen-mile Lake in the Laurentians. It was supported by the seven branches of the Montreal Kanader Arbeter Ring, but there were still financial concerns.[9]

A. Silverberg, one of the managers of Nitgedayget, the camp for adults, wrote that as a proletarian camp the main thing was not to "waste time as in the various hotels but for the workers who come for a short vacation to participate in their manner in lectures about unemployment, a government that starves, antiwar activities, in particular preventing a war with the Soviet Union."[10] They certainly didn't want the guests to waste time. A 1937 description by Yakhnes, the cultural director of Nitgedayget (a teacher in the New York shules in the winter), listed the extensive nature of the activities.[11] Throughout the eight weeks of the camp season, there were lectures every other day, twenty-six in all in summer 1937. Topics included Spain and the Spanish Civil War, Trotskyist espionage, the Canadian Workmen's Circle, the shules, Birobidjan (the Jewish autonomous republic in the USSR), the Congress against anti-Semitism, trade unionism, and the Altveltlekher Kultur Kongress (International Congress for Jewish Culture) held in Paris earlier that year. Thankfully the planners did allow time for an afternoon snooze.

Invited lecturers included Communist Party officials such as Stanley Ryerson and leaders in the left Jewish community. Three banquets were held, attended by about seven hundred guests in all—one for the Scottsboro boys, one for a comrade *Khaver* Mayov, and a peace banquet.[12] Yakhnes regretted that the Yiddish class did not take place, and although there was a library with books and newspapers, he said it was scarcely used. The highlights, in both *Der Kamf* articles and personal reminiscences, were the Friday night campfires where the children and adult campers came together for an evening of singing, a living newspaper (theatrical reenactments of current events), and discussions.

One wonders how the worker, weary after a week in the shop, could sit through such an exhaustive program. The surroundings no doubt helped. Both the Montreal and the Toronto sponsored camps were beautiful places, the first in the mountains of the Laurentians, the latter surrounded by farmland and woods. An article by I. Entin talks about the importance of the setting in Quebec. His eloquent description in Yiddish is somewhat lost in translation:

It's no wonder that the Khaverim [comrades] feel so good, are so loving and good-humoured. One sees the cabins in the valley. The wooden huts stand as if an orchard, the stones cluster as if laced, with a joyous lusty group in the midst. And from afar, there are mountains on all sides. This peacefulness alone allows the closeness comrades feel with one another that gets submerged in the drabness of everyday living in the city to emerge. There in camp Nitgedayget one opens up and feels free.... Each worker in this welcoming place feels at home. One can feel this at the lectures and at the game table and eating. And food is generously provided. Some ask for double portions, but I can hardly eat one portion. Let our enemies see how we run an enterprise! ... Rested, after an afternoon nap, one then goes boating, swimming, luxuriating in the beauty of nature.... The sun glistens on the water. The best poets can't find the precise wondrous words to describe the beauty of the chain of surrounding mountains and the skill in which Khaver Wolinski skilfully guides the boat round clumps of stones to the lilies.

Camp Kindervelt, Rouge Hills, late 1920s.

After a "hard" day comes supper and the evening concert. And even in camp Nitgedayget there are those who worry, in particular the executive of the cultural centre. We need a good concert, raffle, dance—to make a few dollars, and inform those who don't know about the cultural centre. The troubles of the organization are on their shoulders. If the lecturer is interesting, people sit still, listen and ask questions. They enjoy themselves and learn something.[13]

However, Entin complained that the cultural work was overloaded with lectures and discussions. Above all, he argued, people come to rest. There should be more time for relaxation and concerts should be held during the week and not just on weekends. The writer ends his friendly criticism with a suggestion that subsidies be provided for people who contribute a lot to the organization but can't afford the $8–$10 weekly fees.[14]

Rae Watson, who was one of the founders of Camp Kindervelt, purchased a share for $5.00 to help buy the camp in Brampton.

UJPO Archives.

The camp had an important place in the left community and despite the harsh rhetoric emphasizing the sharp differentiation between the pro-communist left and the social democratic Arbeter Ring, personal interactions between the groups could be respectful and considerate. When the Industrial Union of Needle Trades Workers (IUNTW) sent Max Dolgoy of Winnipeg to Toronto in 1931 to be an organizer, he was able to buy a ticket costing $25 for his wife, Annie, and their two children. They went directly to Kindervelt in Rouge Hills. Annie worked there, which helped pay the $3.50 a week charged for the children. But Max, unable to find work in Winnipeg, finally rode the rails to Toronto. He then took a bus to Rouge Hills to join his family. Arriving in the middle of the night and lost, he wandered into the Arbeter Ring Camp Yungvelt by mistake. They put him up for the night, and the next day helped him find the nearby Kindervelt.[15] The bitterness between the two organizations apparently did not extend to how one treated a penniless union organizer en route to his family.

By the early 1930s, the Toronto Labour League camps for children and adults in Rouge Hills were so successful that a larger and more permanent setting was needed. After much searching, they found the perfect place. The Canadian National Railways had an amusement park called Eldorado on the outskirts of Brampton, and it was up for sale. But no Jews were allowed in the amusement park; a large sign at the entrance declared "Gentiles Only." The Labour League got around this restriction with the help of a Ukrainian comrade who negotiated the deal. They set up a corporation called Eldorado Camp and Amusements Limited (ECAL), and people bought shares

The Dolgoy family: Max, Annie, Lenny, and Mitzi (Sid). This photo would have been taken before they left Winnipeg for Toronto.

Archives of Ontario, F1412 J11.

in the camp for $5.00. David Abramowitz remembers that some had to take a loan from the Labour League credit union to buy their share. They repaid it at twenty-five cents a week. It was impressive that these poorly paid workers, through a generous sharing of time and money, managed to purchase and build the camp.

Dozens of Jewish societies held their picnics in the park, the best in the Toronto vicinity where Jews were welcome. Harry Holtzman, a member of the camp's board of directors, estimated that 40,000 people visited the camp the first year it opened in 1936, with as many as three hundred children at a time in the Children's Colony, called Kinderland.

Recreation, Canadian Anti-Semitism, and Class

Particularly after Hitler's rise to power, there were not many places where Jews were welcome. A wave of anti-Semitism coursed through Canada. In Victoria Park in Toronto someone planted a huge sign, "England gave you Jerusalem, for God's sake leave the beach for us."[16] And "Gentiles only" signs were common in summer places and bathing spots. Italian-Canadian broadcaster Johnny Lombardi as a boy had tried to go swimming in the Sunnyside pool in Mimico but was stopped by a man at the gate pointing to the sign "Gentiles only." "But I'm Italian," protested Lombardi. He was chased away.[17]

Signs such as "No Jews Wanted" were common on the Toronto Islands and other resorts along Lake Ontario. Jackson's Point north of Toronto, the Lakeside Point in Scarborough, and Highland Park in Rouge Hills were some of the other places where Jews were not welcome. Resorts as far away as Grand Bend near London, Peterborough, Bronte, and Gravenhurst restricted their clientele. In the Cawthra Mansions Tearoom in Toronto, a visiting British civil servant asked about all the restaurants and hotels "for Christians only." He was assured that the restrictions were not meant for him, although he was an avowed atheist; they only applied to Jews.[18] As a result, the headline of a 1937 article in *Der Kamf* read "Camp Naivelt—an Answer to the Anti Semitism."[19]

There was clearly a class dimension to this exclusion. The Jewish population grew with the influx of East European Jews in the first decades of the twentieth century and unlike the earlier arrivals of Sephardic and German origins, they were poor. A respondent in a study by Esther Einbinder in 1933 declared: "The very appearance of Jews as they went about the streets with their rags or appeared slouching about the doorways of their dirty second-hand

Racist signs at Fallingbrook Beach, June 27, 1938. Anti-Semitic signs were ubiquitous in many parts of Canada. This was an added reason for Jews to have a place of their own.

Toronto Reference Library Picture Collection, Can-On-Toronto-Hist, 1938, CTA G&M SC 266 52350.

stores filled me with dislike."[20] The Jew was not only a threat to Christian society but a radical as well. The *Telegram* asserted, "Jews of all countries should be discriminated against as a race by a poll tax so high that friends in Montreal and Toronto and Winnipeg would have their resources strained to the utmost to lend their tribesmen through foreign post more than enough to bring a baker's dozen per annum."[21]

The stereotype of the Jew was pervasive but contradictory. They were all revolutionaries, and they were all rich and greedy. A 1944 novel by Gwendolyn Graham depicted a love affair between Erica, a well-born daughter of a Montreal English industrialist, and a Jewish lawyer. Her father is intransigent and refuses even to meet the man. The lawyer, Marc Reiser, from a small town in Northern Ontario, is principled and well educated—he's also tall, dark and handsome, contrary to the stereotype—but in her father's eyes, Erica sees that,

> He always came out as a nightmare figure, a crazy conglomerate of a shyster lawyer, quick, insinuating, and tricky; a fat clothing merchant with a cigar in his mouth ... a loud voiced flashy young man pushing his way to the head of the queue, a skull capped figure muttering incantations in a synagogue, a furtive greasy individual setting fire to his own house in order to collect the insurance ... who was perpetually turning up where he was not wanted, over-running hotels, beaches, clubs, and practically every place he was permitted to enter.[22]

The situation described in the novel was commonplace. People were judged and excluded without a second thought. Montreal-born Evelyn Shapiro, who later chaired the Manitoba Health Services Commission, recalled a skiing trip in the Laurentians with other university students in the 1940s. When they were planning to go out for a drink one evening, Evelyn was told she'd better not join them because she would not be allowed in.[23]

Class divisions influenced where camps were located. Northern Ontario was for the upper middle class and the wealthy. *Crestwood Heights*, a 1956 study of "the culture of suburban life" in Forest Hills, Toronto, provides a full description:

> Summer camps like clubs are ranked by status. Those camps catering to wealthy children are generally some greater distance to the north and are equipped with elaborate permanent buildings—flotillas of canoes, rowboats and sailboats and stables of riding horses. At the other end of the scale are the camps sponsored by urban welfare agencies which are apt to be much closer to the city, with fewer permanent buildings ... less elaborate recreational facilities, and a conspicuous policy of "back to nature"—though, even then, not too far.[24]

The artist Avrom and his son Zalman (later of Lovin' Spoonful fame) at Camp Naivelt, circa 1940s. The little cottages in the background were on King's Row.

Photo courtesy of Anna Yanovksy.

Naivelt was located about thirty miles from the city. People who wanted to visit for the weekend could get a ride on the back of a truck for twenty-five cents. Hard-to-get-to "wilderness" may have been the ideal for the well off, but the accessibility of Naivelt made weekend visits possible. While the green nature was admired, the focus in the left Jewish camps was on culture, health, and food. The notion of camping for these immigrants was quite at variance with the idealization of the benefits of "roughing it" in the camps of the bourgeoisie. Like the "Fresh Air" camps for the poor, described by Sharon Wall in her book about camping, notions of camping as good for children revolved around being in the "fresh air" and having enough food.[25] Not surprisingly, the prices also reflected class differences. In 1929, two of the ritzier camps were charging $250 for an eight-week stay.[26] Kindervelt's fees at the time were $5.50 weekly for children 7–10 years of age and $6.00 for the older children. The parents could rent a tiny shack on Kings Row for $12 a week, stay in their own cottages, or pitch a tent. If people couldn't afford to rent a cottage and didn't have a tent, they could always sleep on the floor of the dance hall. Although the camp had a deficit by summers' end, running a proletarian camp meant ensuring that it was affordable to working people.[27] Some years later, in 1937, prices were reduced for Labour League members and children from the shule to $4.50 and $5.00 weekly. Adult members were charged $10.00 weekly.[28] B. Bernard recalls going out to camp from Toronto:

> That ride was an event, no matter if we were riding out for two weeks, a week, or just a Sunday picnic. There were always songs and always singers. Many trucks left the corner of Ulster and Markham St. but lucky was the group that travelled with Lutsky in the rear to lead the singing and Mirsky up front to drive the truck.[29]

Montreal writer Mirl Erdberg-Shatan described Naivelt after the first year. The former amusement park, Eldorado, was immense, with woods, fields, valleys, hills, and the Credit River running through it:

> One winds one's way up a hill, and one comes to a large wide gate, beautifully and artistically built from wood by the counsellors and the children. Through the gate one sees a monument carved from wood, also by the counsellor and the children. It is of a man and a woman with a hammer and sickle, evoking the Russian Revolution from 1917 to 1928, and the fruits of the first five year plan.

Erdberg goes on to describe Kinderland. The bunks for the small children are around the statue. There is a doctor's office, with a room with beds for the "little patients" and an examining room. Nearby is a large pavilion for concerts, presentations, dance recitals, and singing. Just as in a real theatre, there is a large modern stage. A newly built dining room holds four hundred people. And on the hill just above is Kings Row, the cottages and bungalows for the adults. Erdberg continues: "Surely the plan to accommodate 500 children and 500 adults will soon be realized. The streets that will be built are laid out with names like Lenin Street, October Street, and so on."[30]

Davidovich, from New York, became the first director of the new children's camp renamed Kinderland. He had taught in the Toronto shule that year. *Der Kamf* offers a sense of his priorities—culture, health, and food: Davidovich "planned a model camp both physically and in spirit." The program included games, studies, wonderful concerts with the singing director Ringelhaupt, and a dance teacher. Doctor (Khaverte) Rosenblat oversaw camp cleanliness. She went from bunk to bunk "like a devoted mother attending to every corner." When they

Sign above the camp office. It reads:

"Become a member of the Labour League,

The biggest Jewish fraternal organization in Canada.

14 branches, 800 members

1,000 members by the 10th anniversary

At the labour league there are

2 children's shules, Camp Naivelt, wind orchestra

Jewish socialist library, credit and loan treasury

For the period of the campaign, the first quarter is free, the first bill is $2.55

Become a member now

Archives of Ontario, F1405-23-113.

go to see the doctor, the children "know they will be greeted with a loving smile, and the best will be done for them. The Labour League can be proud of the camp which is an example for all the cities in Canada."[31]

Ben Shek was sent to camp Naivelt's predecessor Kindervelt at Rouge Hills after he arrived in Canada from Poland in 1934, and then Naivelt's Kinderland, on the outskirts of Brampton from 1936 to the early 1940s. His memories linked recreation and sports with culture and politics. The politics were expressed through songs and plays and how games were played. When they played Steal the Flag, they called it CLDL after the Canadian Labour Defence League, the organization that defended union leaders and civil libertarians against the arbitrary violence of the police during the Depression years. The principle of "sharing" was important. When parents brought goodies to their children, they were put in a "casa," a collective pool for each bunk, and then shared.

In the 1930s, volunteers in the Spanish Civil War came to Camp Naivelt before they went off to fight with the Mackenzie-Papineau Battalion. While the war was on, the children's competing teams at the camps in Toronto and New York pitted the Republicans against Franco's fascists. One of the campers from New York's Kinderland remembered these battles. He was in a bunk assigned

Janusz Korczak platform, Camp Naivelt, on the occasion of the visit of the Polish visitor, Mirsky, 1946. He was one of a delegation of three representatives of Polish Jewry visiting Canada in 1946. In the back is the Sholem Aleichem monument built by Avrom.

York University Libraries, Clara Thomas Archives and Special Collections, Sam and Manya Lipshitz fonds, FO444, ASC34281.

to the enemy side—Franco's nationalists, called Loyalists—and to the dismay of the camp director his side was winning. His bunkmates were told this was unacceptable, and a compromise was reached, declaring a draw for the competing teams.[32]

When the veterans returned from Spain in 1938, the Friends of the Mackenzie-Papineau Battalion prepared a weekend carnival in their honour. The veterans dug a series of trenches in the camp to give the children and visitors an idea of their experience in Spain.[33] *Der Kamf* featured it on page one, and the editor deemed the event the most interesting of the entire summer season.

Visiting dignitaries sometimes attended the Sunday Salutes, when all the children gathered Sunday mornings, dressed in white. Three Polish visitors, Mikhail Mirsky, Anatol Wertheit, and Mark Bitte, arrived in the summer of 1946 just after the end of the Second World War. The campfire that weekend was the biggest ever. Avrom drew a huge picture for the occasion—a teapot and a hammer and a big X. The idea was to let the visitors rest: *Hak nisht kayn tchaynik* (don't bang like a loud samovar), a popular expression for "don't annoy." The three gave moving speeches, bringing greetings from the survivors of the Holocaust. The choir, under the direction of Emil Gartner, sang for the first time the song that was to become the anthem of the left, Hirsh Glik's "Zog nit Keynmol," written in the Vilna Ghetto when he heard news of the Warsaw Ghetto uprising of 1943.[34]

Yiddish continued to be used in concerts, plays and songs, but the children's everyday language was English. This was the case even in the early years when most of the children were fluent in Yiddish because it was spoken at home. In the 1940s and after, prominent leaders such as Sholem Shtern pleaded for the importance of Yiddish:

We have not reached the young element. Many of them, fully progressive, think only about Canada and consider Yiddish, the Jewish culture as a superfluous burden, a matter for their parents, grandparents.... The camp provides an opportunity to "enlighten" the youth on the importance of the Yiddish language and culture.[35]

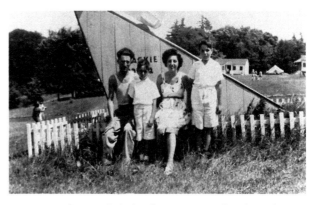

Monument in honour of Blackie, the sports counsellor whose plane was shot down in the Second World War.
UJPO Archives.

During the difficult war years in the 1940s, cultural events continued in the children's camps in Quebec and Ontario. The project for one of the weeks in the summer of 1942 was "army-week," in which thirty officers and soldiers from nearby Brampton visited Naivelt. Cookie Papeski, a young shule teacher originally from Winnipeg, led the singing. On August 16, a monument was built to honour Blackie, the camp's former sports director, a pilot who had disappeared and was assumed dead in one of the flying raids over enemy territory. Mitzi Dolgoy grieved:

> Blackie was the one who really developed me as a very good athlete. Swimming, volleyball, gymnastics.... We were so upset that they couldn't find him. I cried for days. He was a very important person in my life, and others' too.[36]

Dolgoy and his friend, Ben Chud, built a model airplane in the children's colony and dedicated it to Blackie. Rejected by the army because of poor eyesight, Dolgoy worked in a factory during the war and became the sports director at Naivelt during the summer.

It was difficult to staff the camps during the war years. In Quebec, a *Kamf* article noted that there were difficulties; the name of the adult camp was changed from Nitgedayget to the "Laurentian Vacation Club." However, under the leadership of Michael Schneiderman, with the help of Yakhnes, they still managed to put on weekly concerts.[37]

In 1942, despite staffing difficulties with so many young people being in the armed forces, the Toronto children's camp was packed, with two hundred and fifty children at its opening. Director Korn listed the thirteen counsellors who looked after the children in camp—they were young teenagers, fourteen and fifteen years of age. Seven were graduates of the shules, training to be teachers of Yiddish. The adult camp under Ben Yomin's leadership as cultural director was also full.

Remembering the War

At the end of the Second World War, and the uniting of the left organizations into the United Jewish People's Order (UJPO), the summer camps thrived. While many survivors of the war may not have wanted to talk about what they had experienced, the children of the left learned about the terrible tragedy and the destruction of Jewish life in the war years. Some of their fellow campers had been through the war and came to Canada as orphans. The left honoured those who died and those who fought back through song, cultural productions and at Naivelt, a structure dedicated to one of the heroes of the Warsaw Ghetto.

A platform honouring Janusz Korczak was built at Naivelt. Janusz Korczak was a Polish children's author and educator who was the director of an orphanage in the Warsaw Ghetto. When the German soldiers came to collect the 192 orphans the Jewish Underground, Zegota, offered him sanctuary, but he refused to abandon the children. There is a moving description of Korczak accompanying the children to the death camp:

> Janusz Korczak was marching, his head bent forward, holding the hand of a child, without a hat, a leather belt around his waist, and wearing high boots. A few nurses were followed by two hundred children, dressed in clean and meticulously cared for clothes, as if they were being carried to the altar.[38]

The platform became a centre for Naivelt events. Yakhnes would present his living newspapers each Friday night at the Korzcak platform. It was also where the children's Sunday salutes took place.[39]

The war was remembered not just through monuments but through the presence of some of the children recently arrived from Europe. Camp Naivelt in Toronto welcomed the three Chojnacki boys from Belgium. They were orphans who had been cared for in a Belgian orphanage after their parents and two sisters and a brother were deported to Auschwitz where they died. The Queen of Belgium protected the Belgian orphanage for as long as possible. When the Nazis attempted to deport the children to Auschwitz, the Belgian resistance rescued them.

Naivelters took special pride in one of the boys, Marcel Chojnacki. He was born in Brussels in 1932 and arrived in Canada in 1947 with his two brothers,

Israel and Jakob. Marcel remembers Paul Robeson staying with the children one night when they first arrived. The three brothers found their way to the Jewish left through their friends at Harbord Collegiate, and eventually Camp Naivelt.[40] Through the Jewish left, Marcel was able to train as a dancer. He first performed with Nancy Lima's company, the New Dance Theatre, associated with the UJPO. He eventually became a member of the National Ballet. Marcel performed at Naivelt's seventy-fifth reunion in 2001.

The adults continued to place great importance on the food and cultural programming for both the adult and the children's camps. In response to criticisms directed at the Montreal camp, more recreation was included in the program. Hikes in the Laurentians were planned. Wednesdays were for lectures, but Thursdays were devoted to play—literature, social science, humorous games, and quizzes with prizes.[41]

A new camp, Husavik, was organized in 1946 by the Winnipeggers, four miles from Winnipeg Beach on Lake Winnipeg. As in Toronto and Montreal, the women played an important role in establishing and supporting the camp.[42] In Ontario in the late 1940s, there was new construction at Naivelt that included a bathhouse for the children, called the Ritz, a building for the youth and the construction of what Basman called the largest swimming pool in all the camps in Canada. The Winchevsky Centre, the new centre in Montreal, was almost completed. In Toronto, the community acquired a magnificent building on 83 Christie Street. The community was thriving, both in the summer camps and in the winter locations.

Gerry Cohen of Montreal attended the Winchevsky shule and spent summers in Camp Kinderland in the Laurentians in the period just after the war. He described the ideological package as a mixture of yiddishkayt (democracy) and leftism: "In July and August, Camp Kinderland, forty miles from Montreal," was a place "where yiddishkayt and leftism flourished together among the fir trees and the mosquitoes … in our childhood consciousness, being Jewish, being anti-Nazi, being democratic and being communist all went together."[43] The camp was a sign of the rebuilding of Jewish life in the wake of the most terrible catastrophe of all time.[44] In the Laurentians, the camp mobilized to help the striking longshoremen on the great lakes. The Canadian Seaman's Union was forced out on strike, sabotaged by an anti-union company aided and abetted by the federal government and the RCMP,[45] one of the most disgraceful incidents in Canadian labour history. In Toronto, the Naivelters also actively supported the seamen.

Politics, Culture and Fun in Ontario's Naivelt

In the beginning, the children and most of the adults slept in tents. Mollie Myers, who arrived in at the camp in 1939, fresh from Winnipeg, recalled that while no one objected to building cabins for the children, the appropriateness of private cottages was debated. Was private property in this socialist camp a violation of communal principles? A report on Camp Naivelt from October 1936 is unequivocal—the leadership took a "determined" stand not to allow private bungalows.[46] After a big storm in 1940 had blown most of the tents down, this position was rescinded—but to call the early structures "cabins" was a bit of a stretch. Mollie remembered how women with small babies pitched tents and stayed the whole summer; their men came out on weekends. The atmosphere was communal and congenial. Mollie says:

> One day in the early 1940s there was a big storm and tents were blown away. The few cottages on the hills sheltered mothers with very small children.... Hymie and his friend bought a crate from Malton Airport that had been used for airplanes. They put it on the roof of his car and brought it to Naivelt and they plunked the firmly sealed four-sided crate in place and remained inside, with no door, no window, just an open roof and no door and no way of climbing out. A carpenter working nearby heard their call for help and came over. After some teasing and negotiating he brought a ladder and got them out.... In that cottage we raised two children and three grandchildren.[47]

Years later, Mollie was still going to the camp and had wonderful memories of lasting friendships, political discussions, joys and sorrows: "I think of my grandchildren enjoying the beautiful surroundings and remembering 'Zeyde's khochmes' [Grandpa's wisdom—Molly, in typical Yiddish style is speaking with affectionate sarcasm] and the story of how he built the cottage and remained inside."[48]

Rita Bergman loved sleeping in a tent: "The nicest thing was to have your head hanging out of the tent watching the stars fall. Oh, that was gorgeous!" Rita had arrived at Naivelt in 1936, just one year after it opened. She remembered the "wonderful feeling" of the place. The rides—a merry-go-round and a gondola—from the days when it had been an amusement park were still there, but not in working condition. There was a railroad track and a swimming hole. Some of the kids would go skinny-dipping, but not Rita: "I was too much of a prude to do something like that! I was a camper from the time I was eleven years old and I absolutely loved camp."[49]

When Rita was a bit older and had to work, her parents bought a "cottage": "My father went to Simpson's where he bought a garage and had them put it up under a big tree on the second hill." In that small space, he made a kitchen and bedroom where her mother, father, Rita and her sister Honey slept in two three-quarter beds. "I remember at fifteen coming out with friends. Imagine bringing friends to sleep in this little cottage! I brought a friend, one friend … but another one showed up without a place to sleep so that night, four of us slept in that three-quarter bed, Honey, myself, and my two girlfriends." On the weekends she and her father would take the train and walk in from Steeles and Churchville, about a mile and a half, carrying food with them.

The lack of amenities in the adult camp was challenging. Helen and Izzy Fine bought Cottage 29 on Hill 3 in 1950. For Sandy, the oldest of the four Fine daughters (one was an infant, and one was not yet born), this was very exciting: "I didn't know anyone who had a summer cottage." She said, "We didn't have a car to transport us from the city and had to ask relatives to take us out to camp. We rented a U-Haul and attached it to the back of my uncle's car. We packed it up to the very top, and away we went."

Although the distance from Toronto to the camp is only about fifty kilometres, Sandy remembers that it seemed to take a very long time. At one point, a passing car stopped them to tell them that the diapers for the baby had flown away. Helen Fine had a tough time at first. She did all the washing by hand, and she worked hard keeping the cabin spotless, a real challenge with the children running in and out. Helen Fine remembered that when she first arrived, she took one look and cried.

> The first year we had a cabin when we came out with the kids. And then we had an offer to buy this cottage. I said "where are we going to get the money?" [The man] said "don't worry about the money." So we bought the cottage and we didn't even pay a penny and I was crying because I didn't know what a cottage looked like! … It was all open, but there was no light so it was dark. The kids were small, I didn't have any water—we had a pump. We had to have a hose that had a box and then we put in the water and that's the way we washed our dishes. I had to wash my own diapers. It was a hard life. We didn't have a fridge, we had an icebox … we used to buy the ice from a man in Brampton and you know … how long does ice last? It was hard but we were all

Camp Kinderland campers loved and admired Pete Seeger. Avrom made this sketch in honour of Seeger's first appearance after the Cold War blacklist was lifted.

happy. We were a whole community. People that we know used to sing and we'd have [camp]fires, big fires, a lot.... Everybody was anxious to come out here! … It was popular because it wasn't far, there was a pool, and the surroundings were beautiful.

How did Helen spend her days at the camp?

What would I do? Play the piano. (I'm joking!). I had to wash my own diapers, I had to make lunch, not only that but there was a lifeguard … oh one thing after another when you start to think what happened … so the lifeguard only had a right to stay here till the middle of August. So, where would the guy stay? Where would he eat? He had a place to sleep because there were a lot of cabins, but he had no place to eat. So we used to give him here! My daughters would say "Raymond has to eat here." So I said OK.[50]

Both Izzy and Helen remember the concerts and lectures:

Izzy: Saturday nights were concerts, like we had Pete Seeger. We had a big hall … every week we had a lecture.… Lectures would be about trade unions, or how trade unions worked in England, or politics in America, or Europe. In the 30's and the 40's the issue was fascism—what to do to prevent it—and this was before WWII.

Helen: Do you know the Travellers? Well they grew up here and they would entertain a lot of people here. They used to take out their guitars, and they used to sing. You know Sharon, Lois & Bram? That's the way they made their beginning—from here. Because they grew up here and this is where they performed a lot.[51]

As Izzy and Helen remind us, politics is rarely the first or most prominent memory about the camp. I asked one of the first campers at Kindervelt, the son of one of the founders, about the activities of the young people in the 1920s who soon gravitated to the camp in Rouge Hills. Influenced by the earnest articles in the newspaper *Der Kamf* and a group picture entitled the "royte kolnye" [red colony], I expected an answer describing lectures and discussions.

His reply: "Romancing, of course."[52] And there are many stories of these mostly young people, some of whom rejected the notion of bourgeois marriage, fooling around—sometimes with other people's husbands or wives.[53] One of the founders of the camp had an affair with a director hired from New York. When the summer was over, she and her friend decided to visit him. They hitchhiked to New York because they had no money. The trip was not a success.

> "Sonia" had an affair with him. And he gave me some compliments too. He had a big heart. So, she left her husband. But he [the camp director] wasn't serious, he was a womanizer. She came to New York, he said, "Nothin' doing." ... Anyway he was a big-city man and we were small country people.[54]

Nor were the communist positions, which many people supported in principle, necessarily followed at the camps. Even those Jews who in the 1920s went along with the attempts of the Communist Party to make the party more "Canadian" by emphasizing class and minimizing the importance of ethnic cultural identity did so in Yiddish. This period also saw the development of the left-wing Yiddish shules in which children learned both Yiddish and socialist politics. The language of the children in the camps may have been English, but they sang and performed in Yiddish.

The philosophy changed in the popular front period of the 1930s when the left encouraged co-operation between different movements in the Jewish community. The rivalry between Yungvelt, the Social Democratic Workmen's Circle Camp, and Camp Kindervelt became a friendlier one. In the 1920s, Lil Robinson remembered that when the two camps visited each other to compete in games, the children's friendships disturbed some of the adults who were still busy denouncing each other. In the summer of 1935, when the two camps got together, they each had large signs welcoming the other. The children played several games of volleyball. However, while the connection between the children's camps was applauded, a *Kamf* writer pointed out the score—a win for Kindervelt in the first game and a draw in the second! The next week, the Kindervelt children were to go to Yungvelt and the feeling was that this friendly unity would be lasting.

B. Bernard, on the occasion of the fiftieth anniversary of the camp in the 1970s, recalled the extent to which the children took advantage of a non-authoritarian approach to camping: "Goldberg, and Korn and Feldman and Basman [the directors at various times] wouldn't admit it, but some of us dropped out of camp for days, and hid in a tent just over the hill, or in a cottage that wouldn't be occupied until Friday [when the weekend visitors arrived]."[55]

In his book *Red Diaper Baby*, James Laxer provides a sense of how the serious purposes of the camp sometimes conflicted with children's own agendas. He recalls the chaos and the fun that he had in the camp and the UJPO in the 1950s. For Laxer, Camp Naivelt was a "left-wing Jewish nirvana."[56] Summer camps at other places involved canoe trips, camping in the woods, maybe horseback riding, swimming, and archery but "things were different at Camp Naivelt." In contrast to the descriptions in *Der Kamf,* Laxer recalls "Possibly those who ran the Colony [the children's camp] thought it would be a good idea to include some political education in our life there. In practice they never did anything about it.... Whether by design or by happy accident, there were no thought police at Camp Naivelt."[57]

Laxer's dad, the son of a rabbi, was an organizer for the Communist Party and had left his attachment to Judaism; his mother was of Anglican background. For Jim, hanging around the UJPO at 83 Christie Street and spending summers at Camp Naivelt were an escape from the serious political lessons his father attempted to instil in the Laxer children:

> I was acutely aware of what the Communist Party thought. At the age of
> ten, I knew what the Communists thought about every single subject....
> I knew all about the revolution.... I knew what Leninism was.... Terrorism
> is bad. It doesn't work. The working class has to rise, blah blah blah. I knew
> why Stalin was the Great Leader. I knew how sad it was the day he died,
> etcetera. So, I was very, very politically acute. So when I tell you that their
> [Naivelt's] ability to transmit their politics was just about utter failure—if
> they were trying to do it, it wasn't getting through to me or the kids I was
> there with in the camp, that is for sure. It just wasn't. I mean, we had this
> warm atmosphere. We all knew it was a Jewish camp and it felt very Jewish.
> Ninety-eight percent of the people were Jewish. And you had lots of singing,
> lots of Jewish cultural events going on, but there was no attempt to make
> you more Jewish.[58]

Laxer recalled Sundays at Naivelt in the 1950s as "a bustling town ... you had literally thousands of people who came up there ... a fantastic atmosphere of life and vitality and people, who are talking ... it was just astounding." He compared it to Sundays in Toronto, which was "such a Waspy dead city."[59] He irreverently described the aging activists in the adult camp, many of whom had been garment workers involved in union work in the 1920s and 1930s:

> The quintessential Camp Naivelt man was attired in dark, loose-fitting shorts that extended to just above the knee. Shirts, which varied from the button-up variety to undershirts, were always tucked in. Black dress shoes and dark socks completed the outfit. The typical man was short and balding, with a stooped posture, a large pot-shaped belly, thin arms and spindly hairless legs.[60]

Laxer really liked his counsellor Jerry Goodis, a founding member of the singing group the Travellers. Goodis was the son of a tailor who became a union organizer in the needle trades. Laxer lived a double life, with the politics at home and the neighbourhood kids on his street who knew nothing about his political household. The UJPO and the camp were a relief from the political intensity in his family, and he welcomed the inclusiveness of the camp:

> In the camp [I] could be completely honest with people ... you could be half-Jewish and you could be a Commie and you didn't have to lie. In what I would regard as the normal world, which is the world of my street where I had to lie all of the time ... you had to keep these things in water-tight compartments, because it was a very scary environment at that time ... the anti-Communism was very strong, and nobody knows that better than a kid.[61]

Although Laxer felt political lessons as such were not part of camp, he recognized "we were learning a kind of brotherhood of humanity ... that kind of stuff suffused you ... it was a set of values that was there. But it wasn't political in the narrow sense of some guy sitting down and lecturing you about politics. That did not happen."[62] Activist and singer Pete Seeger, who first went to Naivelt in 1947, made a lasting impression on Laxer:

> The closest thing to propaganda were the concerts performed for packed houses in the auditorium on the little island in the Credit River.... On hot summer evenings the kids from the Colony [the children's camp] would squeeze into seats among the adult campers from the three hills. I can still picture Pete Seeger carrying his stool and his banjo out onto the bare stage. He would talk and sing and tell stories of the political struggles of working people from many countries. In South Africa, he told us, the government

Singing at Camp Naivelt, 1950s.

Photo courtesy of the family of Honey and Oscar Ross.

would not let people hold meetings of protest. So they had to make use of songs with no overt political message. One of them was "Everybody loves Saturday night." … Seeger began to sing, first softly and with ever greater force, keeping time on the floor with his large right foot. Before long we were all singing, until the auditorium was alive with energy. We were a vessel bound for a better world. [63]

The folk culture that developed at Naivelt and in the UJPO in the 1950s, Laxer noted, were some ten years ahead: "all the folk culture of the 1960s, I felt like I'd lived through it all ten years before… the Weavers and Pete Seeger and the Travellers."[64]

For Mitzi and Lenny Dolgoy, singing was always a big part of camp life:

> At camp, when it came time for breakfast or dinner, we were a group of singers. We sang on our way down! I'll never forget when Pete Seeger came and we wanted him to come to camp. He hitchhiked to Brampton and we raised enough money to get him home. I still remember standing on the dining table, singing away. We raised enough money for him to get back to New York.[65]

In the early 1950s, in the midst of the Cold War, Pete Seeger was a frequent visitor. In that period, to sing songs using words like peace and freedom branded performers as communist. In the US, his leftist views subjected him to attacks, redbaiting, and blacklisting. Called before the House Committee on Un-American Activities (HUAC) he risked jail by refusing to answer questions. Seeger was a hero to the left, and his songs, his music, and his principled devotion to working people were legendary. With Pete Seeger's encouragement, five campers—Mitzi Dolgoy, Jerry Gray, Oscar Ross, Jerry Goodis, and Helen Gray—got together in 1953 to form the Travellers.

In memories of Naivelt, it is the songs and the natural world that predominate for many people. Many accounts describe the wonderful concerts and dance performances.[66] Robert Fiveson, who went to camp in the 1950s and 1960s, says:

> The only happy memories I have as a boy were at camp. To this day raspberries are my favorite fruit—which we used to pick in great abundance in the woods. The songs we sang then still echo in my heart and mind. The smells of the wet grass, verdant forest, the bathroom building, milk that came in large aluminum kegs with the cream on top, cleaning up the kitchen and dining area, the pool, Basman the Director, the fossils in the rocks on the path down the hill, the clay on the shore of the river … so much still remains a part of who and what my brother and I are to this day.[67]

Mollie Myers stayed in her cottage each summer almost until her last breath. However, she complained that the Naivelt of the twenty-first century did not mean the same to the children of these old timers. I sat near Mollie for the Travellers Concert at Naivelt in 2000, part of the celebration of the camp's seventy-fifth year. At one point during the concert, one of the Travellers

Pete Seeger singing with the Travellers, circa 1960s. The group formed because they so admired Seeger from his visits to Camp Naivelt.

Photo courtesy of the family of Honey and Oscar Ross.

Naivelt Hill 2, Cottage 17. In front of David Chudnovsky and Charna Gord's cottage. Charna Gord's grandfather was Sam Green. His farmhouse in Long Branch was the location of the first camp in 1925. This picture was taken around 2012. Naivelters are still singing.

UJPO Archives.

fell. He quickly recovered and, still on the floor, calmed the crowd, assuring them that it was just an inner ear problem, nothing serious. But as people flocked to the stage to help, Mollie remarked to me: "Take a look, there's more doctors running up there than you'll find at Toronto General Hospital." These were the sons and daughters of the garment workers who built the community. Mollie said:

> To me the camp always looked beautiful. The Credit River was nice and clear and we used to swim in it before we built the swimming pool. We would have a grand time just loafing, maybe talking about recipes, or talking about world affairs. In later years, when Sherri Bergman came on the scene, she used to take us on hikes to recognize certain plants that were useful. We used to do exercises, we would swim, we would gossip, but mainly we had a reading circle. There was always culture and education included in all our activities.
>
> The organization was quite large at the time. We were a very popular organization. We built it on a pro-Socialist philosophy and this was like a commune. The stipulation to buy a cottage in camp is that you have to become a member of the organization. But our own children failed to take over where we left off. Our aim as immigrants was to put all that we had into our children—to strive, to educate, to make doctors and lawyers and dentists and professionals. The result was that they couldn't find a niche so to speak in our organization.... The comradeship, the relationships, the closeness have been very, very dear to me. I enjoyed every moment of the time I have spent in this camp. If the camp is to survive we must have young, socialist-minded or at least progressive-minded people here. There are lots of issues right now that they can fight for ... and this is a beautiful place to raise children.[68]

The Montreal camps and the Ontario overnight children's camp, Kinderland, closed their doors in the 1960s. A number of factors—the redbaiting of the 1950s, the disillusionment with communism following the revelations of what had happened to Jews in the Stalin period, the emergence of a more affluent generation that wanted a different kind of camping experience—all contributed. Faced with growing debt, the camp committee in Toronto sold off the southern portion of the Naivelt property, which became a conservation area, Eldorado Park. The town of Brampton acquired the pool, dance hall, and swings. Some of the old-timers, such as Mollie, were pessimistic about its continued survival.

However, the camp is still going strong with a new generation, though they are not necessarily the children and grandchildren of the founders, and fewer and fewer of them are Yiddish speakers. The community's inclusiveness and progressive politics keep it going. In 2012, Brampton awarded Naivelt Cultural Heritage status in recognition of its rich cultural history.

CONCLUSION

The Legacy of a Dissident Community

In February 1956, at the Twentieth Party Congress of the USSR, three years after Stalin's death, President Nikita Khrushchev called a special closed session for the Soviet delegates and made a speech that shocked them. The speech describing Stalin's crimes was initially kept a secret. However, through the Polish Yiddish newspaper the *Folkstimmme* and eventually the *New York Times*, left-wing Jews in Canada learned what had become of the beloved Soviet Yiddish writers and artists who had disappeared from public view in 1948.

On July 1952, a secret trial was held—the poet Itzik Feffer, along with twenty-four Yiddish writers, theatre people, a trade union leader, and other distinguished members of the Soviet Union's literati, were convicted on charges of "nationalism." One month later, on what is now known as the "night of the murdered poets," thirteen people were shot in Moscow's Lubyanka prison on Stalin's order. Among them were Dovid Hofshteyn, Leyb Kvitko, Peretz Markish, and the novelist Dovid Bergelson. This was actually round two—round one had taken place in 1937, when Moyshe Litvakov, the writers Izzy Kharik and Moyshe Kulbak, along with other prominent Jews, the leadership of Birobidjan, and the leading Red Army officers returning from Spain became the victims of Stalin. The revered head of the Moscow Yiddish art theatre, Shloime Mikhoels, had died on January 13, 1948, in what we now know was a staged "accident." Then in the fall of 1956, Khrushchev ordered the invasion of Hungary to put down an uprising. These actions left communists and sympathizers who thought of the USSR as a socialist country reeling.

For progressive Jews in the United Jewish People's Order (UJPO) and the sister organization in the United States, these events were a body blow. How

Painting of Shloime Mikhoels, head of the Moscow Yiddish Art Theatre.

Given to the author by Ann Sargent Fishauf and Louis Fishauf.

could these things happen? Did these events invalidate the many years the left Jewish community had organized to help working people, to create a more humane society in Canada? The UJPO was an organization that had admired the Soviet Union as an example of "actually existing socialism," of what they were hoping to achieve in Canada. Throughout the chilly climate of the Cold War, they objected to the curtailment of civil liberties in North America in the name of "national security" and defended the Soviet Union. Many members suffered personally from the climate of polarizing positions—either you were pro-communist, or anti-communist—there was no middle ground. Now UJPO members found that they had been lied to. After Stalin had died, Khrushchev and the Politburo first held Beria, the Secret Police Chief [NKVD] and Stalin's right-hand man, responsible for the murders, but now they learned that it was Stalin himself.

After Mikhoels' "accident," which we now know was a murder, he was given a state funeral. Shloime Mikhoels was too popular a figure simply to be tried and convicted. Peretz Markish, who was soon to be tried and executed himself, wrote a poem in Mikhoels' honour. It gives a sense of how important Mikhoels was to Yiddish culture and how deeply his loss was felt.

"Sh Mikhoels—An Eternal Light at His Casket."

Your last appearance before your people
Among broken rocks bedecked with snow
But—without your word—without your voice.
Nothing but your frozen breath—
Yet we hear now too, as always,
The unseen rustle of your eagle wings.
In which our people clothed you.
To be its solace, echo, and its plea....
Somewhere in heaven, midst wandering gleaming shine,
A star lights up in your brilliant name;
Be not ashamed of your defilement and your pain
—Let eternity be ashamed!

The curtain does not descend
Nor ere death do your eyes now close,
A whole generation proud will carry your gift
As your people's golden heritage.

(translated by Herbert H. Paper)[1]

The poet and novelist Chaim Grade was one of the many who mourned the night of the murdered poets.

"Elegy for the Soviet Yiddish Writers" [an excerpt]

I weep for you with all the letters of the alphabet
That made your hopeful songs. I saw how reason spent
Itself in vain for hope, how you strove against regret—
And all the while your hearts were rent
 to bits, like ragged prayer books ...

Chaim Grade (translated by Cynthia Ozick)[2]

For much of its existence, the Jewish left had struggled to maintain its autonomy from the Communist Party while maintaining strong support for the Soviet Union and socialist principles. It also had to defend itself against charges that it was nothing more than a communist front organization controlled by the Communist Party, which in turn was controlled by decisions made by the Communist Party of the Soviet Union. The left maintained that a pro-Soviet organization was not the same as a communist front group; they did not take orders from anyone. It was their commitment to socialist principles that kept them sympathetic to the Soviet Union.

Particularly in the early years of the 1920s, the connection between the left organizations and the newly organized Communist Party was proudly proclaimed, and often a rather blurry line existed between the two. At that time, Communist Party membership was quite a different matter than it later became under Stalin. Morris Biderman, for example, described how his involvement in the Freiheit Gezang Fareyn (Freedom Singing League) and the Jewish Cultural Club led to his joining the Young Communist League in 1927. In the 1920s, the Communist Party of Canada consisted largely of the ethnic communities—in particular, the Finnish Organization of Canada and the Ukrainian Labour Farmer Temple Association (ULFTA). The Jewish section of the Communist Party was called the Kompartey. After Lenin's death, when Stalin took power, there were substantial changes and a much more centralized, rigid organization was imposed. Proletarian internationalism was transformed into a movement under the leadership of the Communist Party of the Soviet Union. The Comintern became a place the Soviets dominated, rather than an international forum to discuss common interests and build international socialism. In the 1930s, during the "class against class" period, the party became much more sectarian. Ethnic alliances and alliances with other political groups were suspected of being nationalist, of diluting a "pure" revolutionary approach. However, historian Ian McKay argues that even in this period Moscow could not really rule—there was far more diversity in positions and actions in a vast country like Canada.[3]

The relationship between the Communist Party (CP) and the ethnic groups was not always easy. While most people involved in the cultural activities and fraternal organizations of the Jewish left were not CP members, they admired the Soviet Union and saw it as a place where their socialist ideals of equality, support for Jewish culture, were being realized. The CP tried to keep the "mass" organizations in line and make sure they took "correct" positions. Those in the UJPO insisted that they were not following anybody's line.[4] They admired what the Soviet Union stood for, and CP members were respected for their dedication, discipline, and hard work. But participants who were part of both the CP and the Jewish left experienced the difference between membership in the CP and the progressive Jewish left. In the UJPO, the broader organization, they had no hesitation in questioning what they didn't like. Unlike CP membership, which demanded total commitment, in the UJPO, people felt free to argue, discuss, disagree and hold whatever positions they pleased. And their personal lives remained their own.[5]

In the Communist Party and its youth organization, the National Federation of Labour Youth (NFLY), people had to be very careful about expressing politically acceptable positions. One interviewee felt that as a young woman, she was always nervous about being criticized for saying something incorrect. The CP criticized Norman Penner in the early 1930s when he enrolled in his final year of high school which was not funded by the Manitoba government. He was denounced for trying to "rise above the working class."[6] In contrast, some interviewees described the welcoming, pleasant atmosphere of the left Jewish organizations where people relaxed and had fun. Even those who left the

UJPO after 1956 look back fondly on the joy and intensity of being among young people excited about everything—sports, sex, political events, singing, dancing, changing the world.

Particularly in the late 1940s and early 1950s, as Jewish institutions in the Soviet Union were shut down, there was much to question. People were well aware of the pervasiveness of anti-communist sentiment that frequently took the form of state repression when workers tried to organize to improve their situation. Questions about what Stalin was doing were not voiced publicly, as people feared that this would simply serve the forces of reaction. People had to take sides—and there seemed to be no middle ground. My father was one who was deeply distressed wondering what had happened to his beloved Soviet writers and upset with the party people he knew who kept coming up with excuses for their silence. However, he never asked me to leave my left-wing shule or not to attend Camp Kinderland in New York State. The choice seemed to be between a milieu that valued the same things my immigrant parents did, a non-materialistic world—my parents' friends mostly immigrants like themselves with whom they were comfortable—or enter the ranks of redbaiters. The unfairness of the red scare in the United States was evident. People they knew had lives destroyed, teachers thrown out of work. This had nothing to do with events in the Soviet Union. This harm was done in North America.

Some people became involved in the Communist Party while maintaining a strong sense of the importance of their ethnic identity. As one woman said, "I am a communist because I am a Jew."[7] They were Jewish communists, as opposed to communists who "happened" to be Jews and whose commitment to internationalism involved considering their Jewish origins irrelevant. However, sometimes theoretical positions and personal relationships blurred this categorization. For example, Annie Buller's organizing work and beliefs were rooted in the labour movement rather than in the Jewish community. But her husband Harry Guralnik was the director of the shule, and much of her personal life was lived in the Jewish left community. One of the women's lodges of the UJPO renamed themselves the Annie Buller Lodge because they felt she was one of them. Even internationalists such as Bob Laxer, the grandson of a rabbi and married to a woman of Anglican origin, whose children did not receive a Yiddish education, vacationed at Naivelt. His children only learned about their Orthodox grandfather later in life, but they remember with fondness the UJPO and Camp Naivelt where they spent their summers.[8] The leaders of the progressive Jewish organizations and prominent Jewish communists such as Sam Lipshitz, Morris

Biderman, J. B. Salsberg, Joe Gershman, and Joe Zuken were Yiddishists with deep connections in secular Jewish cultural life.

The early 1950s were difficult years as the Cold War was in full force and the grief over those murdered in the Holocaust was still fresh. Khrushchev's revelations of the Twentieth Party Congress were shocking, and responses varied. Debates raged within both the CP and the left organizations, in particular the UJPO. Lipshitz, Biderman, and Salsberg initially hoped that there would be a re-examination of the relationship between the Soviet Union and the Canadian Communist Party. However when the Communist Party of Canada relegated these terrible crimes to "errors" and "mistakes," rather than promoting a rethinking of how Communist parties operated, the disillusionment was profound and the three, along with Harry Binder of Montreal, resigned from the CP. Some people left the CP but remained in the UJPO, some ceased to be members of both organizations, and others abandoned their socialist ideals altogether.

J. B. Salsberg, a member of the Ontario legislature for the Spadina riding from 1942 to 1954, was on the Central Committee of the Labour Progressive Party (originally the Canadian Communist Party).[9] He travelled to Moscow in 1956, and a description of his conversations with Soviet leaders was published in Yiddish in the *Der Vochenblat*. His nine articles were translated and printed in *Jewish Life*, the left Jewish publication in the United States.[10] For both publications, airing these very critical views was a major first step in openly disparaging CP policy. In one article, Salsberg described meeting with Soviet officials, including Khrushchev. He asked what had happened to support for Jewish culture in the Soviet Union, why the Jewish Anti-Fascist Committee been disbanded, and what had happened to Jewish writers, cultural workers, and community leaders. Some of the crimes, termed "excesses" by Soviet officials, were laid at the feet of Beria, head of the Secret Police, while unsatisfactory explanations were given to other queries. For example, Salsberg was told that Jews were now so "integrated" into Soviet life that there was no need for Yiddish newspapers or Yiddish cultural activity. The anti-fascist committee that had visited Canada in 1943 had become a tool of "bourgeois nationalist influences." Even after Salsberg's articles were published, the Labour Progressive Party under Tim Buck refused to challenge the actions and policies of the Soviet leadership.[11]

Morris Biderman, National President of the United Jewish People's Order, was also a member of the Communist Party and gave his view of the struggle inside the UJPO at that time. He initially thought that it was possible for those who had left the CP to remain in the UJPO. What followed was a struggle inside the UJPO that became very personal and bitter and that went on for three years. At first, there was almost complete unanimity on a Statement of Principles for the UJPO that Biderman had drafted. The following are excerpts from the Statement:

> The Jewish community in Canada has undergone important transformation. Economic, geographic and social factors have changed the character of the community and have affected our own organization. We always viewed with sympathy the great social experiment in the U.S.S.R. and especially the granting of full and equal rights to the Jewish people. The recent revelations of crime and injustice committed against the Jewish people in the U.S.S.R. have shocked and deeply disturbed all of our members.
>
> Conscious of these developments and fully aware of their implications for the work of our organization, we find it necessary at this time to re-define our aims and purposes and the principles which shall guide the United Jewish People's Order in all of its future activity.

> The United Jewish People's Order
> The United Jewish People's Order is an independent fraternal and cultural organization. It is not affiliated with any political party. It welcomes into its ranks Jews of all beliefs and opinions. Every member has the full right and opportunity to express his views and to assist in the formulation of its policies. All actions of the organization shall be determined democratically by the membership in accord with the stated aims and purposes.[12]

The statement went on to address issues such as support for Jewish cultural expression in both Yiddish and English, support for the provision of health benefits to members, connections with the organized Jewish community in Canada, peace in the Middle East and a secure Israeli State, trade union support, and "peace and friendship among nations" and the outlawing of "war as a means of settling disputes."[13]

The battle within the UJPO about how it should change was painful. The political situation generated personal recriminations and attacks between people who had been friends and comrades for decades. Biderman thought that although initially most members were supportive of the move to distance themselves from the CP, the mood shifted during the internal battles from 1956 to 1959. The UJPO leadership in Montreal remained party loyalists, in Biderman's view, and as the only paid official in the UJPO—he was national president and the executive director in Toronto—he felt himself the target of much of the dissension and anger in the organization. It got to the point where members stopped showing up to meetings because the acrimony and the unpleasantness were so extreme. A formerly active member said to Biderman, "We are not prepared to have heart attacks at our branch meetings. That is not why we joined the UJPO."

One of the bones of contention was support for the newspaper, *Der Vochenblat*. For years, the paper had been treated as a UJPO publication, supported by UJPO members with fundraising drives in the branches throughout Canada. Some felt that because the UJPO did not control the content of the paper, the UJPO branches should not be supporting the fund drives. It didn't help that there was a long history of personal friction between Lipshitz and Gershman. Some of the leadership of the left Jewish community who had been party members—Lipshitz, Salsberg, and Biderman—left to form a new group, the New Jewish Fraternal Order. Sam Carr, Joe Gershman, Muni Taub, and Becky Lapedes remained with the UJPO. Joe Gershman, editor of the newspaper, also remained in the CP until 1977. His editorials became quite critical of the CP and when he was censured in the *Canadian Tribune*, he withdrew his party membership.[14] In his letter of resignation he maintained that "as editor of a non-party organ and as a leading member of the only progressive Jewish mass organization ... I should be guided by the policies of the board of the paper and the leadership of the mass organization."[15]

Sam Carr had been a Communist Party organizer and a UJPO member. First arrested in 1931 when the party was declared illegal, along with seven other communists, he later spent three and a half years in jail after being named by Gouzenko and charged under the Official Secrets Act with passport offences. When he was released from jail, the party distanced itself from him, and Carr became active in the UJPO. He was a capable, influential person and, to Biderman's surprise, sided with those in the leadership who chose to remain in the UJPO, despite his formerly close friendship with the Biderman family.[16]

Joe Zuken, the communist alderman in Winnipeg, remained in the party and the United Jewish People's Order. It was said in Winnipeg that whatever positions Joe took in City Council became CP civic policy. While others were eulogizing Stalin on his death in 1953, Joe's wife Clara recalls she was crying "as if I had lost my father." Clara adds, "And Joe is standing beside me and he says very quietly, 'It should have happened a few years ago.'"[17]

Zuken kept his seat in the Winnipeg City Council during the Cold War because of his reputation as someone who could be trusted to do his best for his constituents. Known as a person who did not take kindly to directives, by mutual agreement he did not play a central role in the Communist Party of Manitoba. Zuken's comments in the aftermath of 1956 are worth recounting. In an interview conducted in 1984, Zuken recalled that he considered resigning at the time of the twentieth congress revelations about Stalin but decided not to:

> The reason why I didn't was ... that basically with respect to Canadian problems, the party had the best program of any party. And I could not see any other alternative, any other party on the Canadian scene, including the CCF, that was committed to the socialist perspective, and the socialist road ahead, for Canada. So despite my own political reservations, that was it.

Joe went on to say:

> I make a distinction between those who left who left honestly, and those who used the events of the Khrushchev disclosures as an excuse for getting out and attacking the party. I understand those who felt a sense of betrayal and disillusionment. I also looked at the faces of the old timers ... who for 30, 40 years and more have given their hopes, their dreams, their activities ... for the party.... I think that those who left should have also thought of them. Because you don't spit in the face of the people who helped to do the work.
>
> When Annie Buller and Joe Forkin went up to help organize some workers in Manitoba with my brother [Cecil Ross] who put his freedom on the line and went to Flin Flon and went to jail for it and they are only examples. When people went on the picket line, when people went marching on the May Days, when people went demonstrating for peace, when people went out when Sacco and Vanzetti were railroaded; they were fighting for a cause....
>
> Stalin did some terrible things with his purges, his cult of personality and so on .... But you don't condemn your work or the work of your comrades in causes that were correct because of some very terrible things that were done by Stalin.... I made a distinction between those who grappled with their conscience because of what happened in the Soviet Union or felt they could no longer carry a party card. They left, but they left and then did not attack the party. There are others who left the party and then started to attack the party. For them I have only contempt.... I think they should look at their own role in

the party, did they ask questions.... And I know people in both camps. [Those] who have left and done it in an honest way. And others who have left and who while in the party were very bureaucratic so who are in effect also attacking themselves, or twenty to twenty-five years of themselves.[18]

Ben Shek, who had grown up in the Labour League and the United Jewish People's Order, maintained that those who left the UJPO were wealthier than those who remained behind—indeed some of those who left did very well economically, but it is not clear whether Shek's economic analysis provides an adequate explanation of events. What we have is a difficult, complicated story in which positions and personal politics mixed with the result sometimes of severing friendships that were decades old. Was the UJPO indeed an independent organization, and would it continue to follow the leadership of the Communist Party? While some people such as Izzy Fine of Toronto, active in the UJPO, remained friends with those who left, many did not. The daughter and son-in-law of Sam and Manya Lipshitz, May and Gerry Cohen, were physicians and described how the waiting room in their office was one place where those who left the UJPO and those who stayed would meet and talk and remember the life and the ideals they shared.[19]

A poignant interview with four of the first campers at Kindervelt demonstrates the range of reactions. These were four old and dear friends, all in their eighties, having a reunion. The afternoon at one of their homes was spent reminiscing, noshing, and telling funny stories about when they first went to Kindervelt in the 1920s. When I raised the question of the Twentieth Party Congress, their responses made me worry that a wonderful afternoon might be ruined.[20] The responses varied. Lil felt that she did not know enough historical materialism to analyze what happened with Stalin and why. However, she couldn't get over a CP cell meeting she attended when Joe Gershman's wife, Celia, was raked over the coals for trying to adopt a baby when "there was so much work to do." Lil found this shocking. Shirley admired the selflessness of party members who could never earn enough to own a home or raise a family. Lil felt the demands were excessive.

Bessie, however, said simply that the split in the UJPO took place because Russia was persecuting Jewish people: "So break away from them.... All I know is going out on the picket line and taking food and clothing to people who weren't working—I thought that was a wonderful thing and why couldn't we continue doing that?" Al, the one man present, said:

I was born and brought up in a revolutionary family going back to my grandparents. They fled to Canada because the police were after them. My father would take me to union headquarters on Sunday mornings and he would proudly stand me on a table and when asked what I would be when I grew up, I would say—"Ikh vel zayn a Bolshevik" (I will be a Bolshevik). My family were staunch communists. When the split came [in the UJPO] and my father heard that Salsberg went to the "other side" he always knew that Salsberg was no good. 1956 came and we heard about how the Soviet Union sent troops into Hungary, and then Czechoslovakia. Sent troops into a socialist country? I read George Orwell's *Animal Farm*, which my granddaughter gave me and boy [he breaks down crying] we were betrayed. We were the sheep in the animal farm. We were lied to.

"Not the Whole Story." Anna Yanovksy and Ruth Howard are cottage owners at Naivelt. Anna is the artist Avrom's widow. Ruth is the popular theatre producer of Jumblies and the creator of the play *Oy di velt*, which she produced at Naivelt in 2008 and for Toronto's Mayworks the following year. Anna's tags say "I do not agree," "I was there"—her comments on Ruth's play in which she participated. When we performed the play for Mayworks, Ruth included a table around which people could gather to argue in the downstairs of the community centre where the play took place.

Photo by Michaela Otto.

Bessie commented that it was a terrible stress in their lives but "We still have our feelings—our principles haven't been betrayed. We have no place to go with that." Lil thought that the people who split and formed the New Jewish Fraternal Order (NJFO) were those who had become affluent but Al wasn't so sure. Shirley felt that the NJFO group had become more right-wing. As the conversation turned to Sam Lipshitz (one of the people they were criticizing), it was clear how personal relationships and political positions were intertwined. They all were sad to hear that "he's on his last days."

Fortunately, the afternoon was not completely ruined. The four friends said that they live the memories of the Jewish left "every day of our life" and that their shared history is very special to all of them. Lil talked about becoming less rigid after she gave J. B. Salsberg the cold shoulder. He had approached her later and said, "You have to understand why people change." She thought about that and indeed became less judgmental. Like Zuken, however, these four friends remained critical of people who "saw the light" and became avid Zionists and rushed to join the Canadian Jewish Congress. Or of those who were so damning of the left. They pointed out that "These were the leaders who went to Russia every year."

Shirley reminded the group of the important things they had done which had nothing to do with the Soviet Union. She remembered their support for the Estevan strike in Saskatchewan in the 1930s when Annie Buller was jailed for one year, and the dreadful living conditions of those workers. She remembered the group's peace activism: "I was collecting signatures against the atom bomb." The group also recalled that some people were afraid to sign, and the RCMP were taking pictures at rallies in Massey Hall and Maple Leaf Gardens. As the group got ready to end their visit, the anecdotes started to fly—stories of the RCMP copying down licence plates at Naivelt and threatening people of the danger of associating with the left, stories of those who were not able to cross the border into the United States because of their politics.

These four people who were not part of the leadership articulated some of the many difficult issues that they had lived with—such as the redbaiting. They recalled the good things they had experienced and what they did as well as their very critical views of the Communist Party and the Canadian Jewish Congress. They talked about how they had grappled with the shocking revelations about Stalin's USSR, a country and a leader they believed to be socialist. It was a privilege to know these people and to get a sense of the strong ties that remained three-quarters of a century later. Their differing views of events did not affect the important connections.

Continuity and the Importance of Dissent

The United Jewish People's Order continues to exist, with organizations in Toronto, a growing membership in Winnipeg, a small group in Vancouver, and individual members from places throughout the country. Some of the personal rifts have lessened as people remember their rich common history. Virtually all of the major leaders who fought these fierce battles are no longer alive. Most of the secular shules from all the movements have closed their doors. The Winchevsky shule remains as a Sunday school and still attempts to provide a progressive outlook on the world. Camp Naivelt thrives as a multigenerational community, *unzer zumer heym* (our summer home) for a new generation who value the collective lives in the very modest cottages at the back of Brampton's Eldorado Park. We enjoy the programming put together each summer by volunteers that includes music, political discussions, art, and fun. Our peace tea each summer is a legacy of the antiwar activism following the Hiroshima deaths in 1945. Speakers at the peace tea and the Sunday bagel brunches have included a war objector from the United States, an activist with the garment unions in the wake of the Bangladeshi tragedy, a doctor who organized the doctors' movement against the elimination of health care to refugees—issues that continue

The United Jewish People's Order participates in a demonstration in support of Six Nations' struggle for land and treaty rights, 2012.
UJPO Archives.

the Naivelt tradition. In Winnipeg, the choir meets weekly and performs at a variety of events in the Jewish community. Forums are held on both national and international issues. Vancouver members are active in events held at the Peretz Centre. Both the Toronto and Winnipeg organizations hold celebrations for the Jewish holidays.

The United Jewish People's Order was invited back into the Canadian Jewish Congress in 1996, but that was shortlived. In 2007, Congress decided to eliminate membership of organizations—collective voices would no longer be heard. The next move, in 2011, was to get rid of the Canadian Jewish Congress altogether. The Canadian Council for Israel and Jewish Advocacy (CIJA) became the national voice of Canadian Jewry; its only function is to mobilize support for the Israeli government.

The United Jewish People's Order remains a dissenting community with no connection to the Communist Party, formal or informal. The statement of aims proclaims UJPO to be a non-partisan, independent, socialist-oriented, secular cultural and educational organization. Members are in virtually complete agreement with the organization's emphasis on gender equality, social justice, and the environment for Canada and internationally. They take part in social action and related community activities in pursuit of these goals. The official position on the Middle East states that the UJPO "supports a negotiated agreement between the Israelis and Palestinians, which would mutually determine the sharing of the land and in which both peoples would live peacefully, securely and prosperously. The debates about what this means in practice are perhaps where members express the widest range of views."

The United Jewish People's Order continues to face challenges in its acceptance as a legitimate part of Canada's Jewish community, particularly because of its views on the Middle East. However, the demonization of any organization expressing critical views on the Israeli government is not just a Canadian phenomenon. Anthony Lerman, a British Jew hounded from his position as head of the Jewish Policy Research think tank, articulates the strong interest the Israeli government has in maintaining uncritical diaspora support. One method of achieving this is to make it harder for Jews outside Israel to criticize the actions of the Israeli government by accusing them of disloyalty, succumbing to "Jewish self-hatred," and being "fellow travellers" or anti-Semites—spurious and groundless charges. Lerman describes the difficulties of maintaining a critical view of Israeli government policy:

> Jewish critics with radical ideas for resolving the Israeli–Palestinian conflict—
> particularly those who stress there is a Jewish moral obligation to support
> Palestinian rights and that this is in Israel's own interests if it wants to be
> a genuinely democratic state—are subjected to a process of vilification,
> demonization and marginalization. Since such Jews often describe themselves
> as being outside the organized Jewish community, ostracizing them has been
> somewhat effective.[21]

However, silencing Jews in the diaspora is getting less effective. The Yiddish actor and singer, 86-year-old Theodore Bikel, along with over 150 American and British artists including Ed Asner, Eve Ensler, Roseanne Barr, Frank Gehry, Tony Kushner, Mandy Patinkin, Harold Prince, Vanessa Redgrave, and Wallace Shawn, among others, signed a petition in September 2012 backing Israeli artists who were refusing to perform in the settlements in the occupied territories. The petition praised the Israeli actors who "have refused to allow their work to be used to normalize a cruel occupation which they know to be wrong."[22] Bikel reacted to critics who labelled him anti-Zionist: "They are plainly wrong. I think I am more Zionist than anyone who thinks you should accept everything they say in Jerusalem as truth."[23] The former head of the American Jewish Congress and former Executive Head of the Synagogue Council of America, Rabbi Henry Siegman has been outspoken in his critique of Israeli policies in the occupied territories.[24]

Some are questioning the notion of Israel as the "homeland" of the Jews and emigrating there as a return from "exile." In 2013, the Art Gallery of Ontario hosted an exhibit by Israeli artist Yael Bartana. She created an artistic movement she called the Jewish Renaissance Movement in Poland. In it she turns the idea of homeland on its head. Home is where Jews have lived for hundreds of years, not a mythical past from centuries ago. The exhibit included a poster declaring that Jews want to return to the promised land from whence they came—Poland:

We want to return! Not to Uganda, not to Argentina or to Madagascar, not even to Palestine. It is Poland that we long for, the land of our fathers and forefathers....

With one religion, we cannot listen.
With one color, we cannot see.
With one culture, we cannot feel.
Without you we can't even remember.

Join us, and Europe will be stunned!

Jewish Renaissance Movement in Poland[25]

Bartana's exhibit challenges the dominant Jewish history as the history of a people displaced from their homeland. Sander Gilman's theoretical work suggests that we examine Jewish history from a different starting point altogether. Instead of focusing on "diaspora," Gilman reimagines Jewish history as the story of people living on a "frontier"—with no centre and periphery. It is a place where all peoples, including Jews, interacted to define themselves and those they encounter in reality or fantasy.[26] This perspective leads to challenging fixed notions of authenticity and identity. Both authenticity and identity involve shifting ideas in time and place. Who are the "real" Jews will be defined quite differently depending on the time and what part of the world we are talking about. Authenticity and identity are constantly challenged.

Stuart Charme looks at the varying and contradictory notions of authenticity among Jews.[27] The "authentic" garb of the Chassidic Jew is related to the dress of seventeenth-century Polish nobility.[28] Even the question of who is a Jew is not such a simple business, as Isaac Deutscher described in the *Non-Jewish*

Jew. Deutscher would include those who have gone beyond the boundaries of Judaism: Spinoza, Heine, Marx, Luxemburg, Trotsky, and Freud. These are some who found Jewry too narrow, too archaic, and too constricting, "and they represent the sum and substance of much that is greatest in modern thought, the sum and substance of the most profound upheavals that have taken place in philosophy, sociology, economics, and politics in the last three centuries."[29] These ideas point to a valuation of Jewish history as more than the narrative of exile from the holy land and return. Jewishness cannot be reduced to support for "Israel."

One of the results of the reorganization in the Canadian community is to try and shut down the richness of a multicultural, diverse understanding of Jewish identity. The reorganization has led the community full circle back to the top-down control wielded by the "uptown" Jews, who are now of Ashkenazi origin. In 1919, when the Canadian Jewish Congress was first organized, the concern was to develop a body that would address Canadian issues and social policy concerns that were not limited to Zionism. There was widespread support for a parliament of Jews that would provide relief to the Jews in war-torn Eastern Europe. It would take power from the Federation of Zionist Societies of Canada who opposed the setting up of such a body, taking the position that the time was not "opportune." The Canadian Jewish Congress was set up as a democratic and inclusive body. One of their first actions was to set up the Jewish Immigrant Aid Society (JIAS) to assist Jewish settlers and refugees in Canada. Now, over ninety years later, CIJA, the Centre for Israel and Jewish Affairs dominated by a handful of wealthy Jews, has become the official voice of the Jewish Community. Their mandate is to "increase support for Israel," interpreted as support for the Israeli government. Frank Bialystok, the head of the Ontario section of the Canadian Jewish Congress, explained that the CJC still exists, but in name only as they now have no budget with which to operate. They lost all their funding in 2011 when CIJA took over the functions of the CJC.

According to Bialystok, the shift in emphasis from social justice issues to Israeli advocacy has really changed the nature of the community.[30] The mainstream Jewish community moved to the right under Stephen Harper as Prime Minister, and an estimated 52 percent of Canadian Jews supported the Conservative Party. Harper was viewed as a friend of Israel because of his government's uncritical support of Israeli government policy. This led to some strange contradictions. In November 2012 Jason Kenney, then Minister of Citizenship, Immigration and Multiculturalism, was awarded an "honorary" degree by

Israel's Haifa University. The Jewish Refugee Action Network was organized in response to Harper's bill limiting applications from so-called "bogus refugees" from Central European countries, a bill that Kenney defended. Members of the Network pointed out that this "draconian and heartless" legislation was leaving vulnerable Roma and Jews of Hungarian, Slovak, and Czech origin unprotected as they are all targeted by Nazi skinheads.[32] The Canadian Doctors for Refugees mobilized to protest the decision that refugees are no longer eligible for health care. Dr. Philip Berger was one of the two organizers, and a number of other Jewish doctors are active in that group. Given Canada's history of indifference to the desperate plight of Jewish refugees in the 1930s, Jewish support for Kenney and Harper, officials in a government implementing such measures, is very problematic. On December 1, 2013, the Jewish National Fund honoured Stephen Harper for being such a warm friend to Israel. In his speech, Harper praised Israel as "a light of freedom and democracy in what is otherwise a region of darkness."[33] On that same day there was a global "Day of Rage" in Israel and in countries around the world against the announced expulsion of up to 70,000 Bedouins from their ancestral homelands in Palestine.[34]

What constitutes ethnic identity and tradition is a contested terrain. Despite claims to the contrary, tradition, like identity, is rooted in history. It is fluid and shifting and continuously reinvented. Far from being eternally fixed in some essentialized past, cultural identities are subject to the continuous "play" of history, culture and power.

The left Jewish community described in this book defined their identity in terms of culture, rather than religion. They also put their traditions of social justice front and centre. In the attempts to destroy the left movement through redbaiting, unions, cultural groups, and political organizations were also damaged. In fact, critics such as Ellen Schrecker have argued that it was not the left who was silenced in the Cold War, but the liberal middle. A demonized view of communists led people to accept violations of civil liberties.

In 2015, the anti-terrorism Bill C51, containing with some serious limitations of our rights and freedoms, was passed in the last days of the Harper government. In 2016, the unrevised bill was still in effect and the Liberal government allowed the RCMP to use the "preventive detention" clause to arrest people the authorities thought "may" commit a terrorist offence. One commentator, Hereward Fenton of Australia, maintains that the "term anti-terrorism is a euphemism for anti-democratic." When the state abandons hard-won principles such as the presumption of innocence, the right to a fair trial, and the right to

The Naivelt
Community,
summer 2015.

*Photo by Shlomit
Alexander Segal.*

know the evidence against an accused person, basic human rights are under attack. We saw how the fear of subversion in Canada led to measures such as the War Measures Act of 1919, section 98 of the Criminal Code, the Padlock Law in Quebec, and the demonization of those wanting a peaceful solution to world conflict. For ideological reasons, in the name of battling the evils of communism, dominant forces in the Canadian Jewish community remained silent in protesting many violations of our civil liberties. But Canada is a long way from Moscow. I would maintain that the redbaiting that has been a constant during the twentieth century was damaging to Canada and the Canadian Jewish community. The panic over what those in power deemed subversive was actually a fear of the challenge to the dominant powers, or as Ian McKay puts it, the idea of reasoning otherwise, imagining a different kind of society.[35] As this manuscript goes to press, many are still feeling the optimism of a new Canadian government that promises an inclusiveness and a respect for the public sector, for human rights, refugees, and First Nations peoples that we sorely missed for many years. We need to ensure that these are not empty words.

Extinguishing activism and ideals leads to impoverished lives in an impoverished world. Jewish secularism emerged from throwing off passivity—waiting for the next world, or for a God to make things better. Their movement, influenced by an Enlightenment project of a universal humanism and combined with socialist beliefs, rejected anti-Semitism, racism, and class exploitation. What is impressive about this left Jewish community was its activism—if they wanted something, they made it happen. It was the interweaving of all facets of living— culture, knowledge, political activism, community, friendships, inclusiveness.

For many reasons, the health of a community and a society requires dissenting voices.

Ruth Borchiver described it well:

My group were the children of the depression. We sang, we danced—music, theatre, mandolin—there was nothing we couldn't do. You could take mandolin lessons for a quarter. We learned about injustice, about race antagonisms, that our parents were workers. We had a different outlook on the world.

UJPO members still sing, dance, protest injustices and continue to hold a different outlook on the world.

Appendix A: People

My connection with the left Jewish community comes from my early life in the United States, as well as activities in Canada. This is an informal introduction to a few of my Canadian friends—those I had the pleasure to know, and others I came to love and respect through learning about their lives in interviews done by others or what they wrote themselves. Not all were "leaders" in the left organizations. Some of them left the United Jewish People's Order in the late 1950s, others left the Communist Party but not the UJPO, and some were never Communist Party members. They are all mentioned a number of times throughout the book.

Avrom Yanovsky (1911–1979)

Avrom was known as the beloved artist of the left. Generations of children of the Winchevsky Shule and Camp Naivelt marvelled at his chalk talks, which began with a squiggle and ended with a cartoon that had a political message. He arrived in Winnipeg as a child and was part of the first graduating class of Winnipeg's Labour Zionist Peretz School in 1925. It is noteworthy that he and at least four of his classmates became leftists: Bill Ross, who later became head of the Manitoba Communist Party, Annie Ross, Joe Zuken, and Nekhama Gemeril, who Avrom married. After moving to Toronto in 1931, Avrom was a co-founder of the Progressive Arts Club and an active participant in the Jewish left as an artist and set designer. Nekhama became a kindergarten teacher in the Winchevsky Shule. After Nekhama's untimely death in 1958, he fell in love with Anna, a young woman singer in the National Federation of Labour Youth.

Anna collaborated with an art historian, Anna Hudson, to put together an exhibit of some of Avrom's political cartoons, which was presented at York University at Ashkenaz, the biannual celebration of Yiddish music, in the Unionville Art Gallery in Vancouver and Winnipeg. In a short video, people spoke to their memories of Avrom. He was a witty man who didn't just speak, but punned constantly, despite a lisp. Avrom had a hand that was always drawing and a mind that was always working. If his sketchbook was not nearby he would draw on whatever was handy—a napkin, the newspaper, an envelope. Anna's apartment was filled to overflowing with Avrom's drawings, his cartoons, and hundreds and hundreds of his quick sketches. She said had he had just a bit of the capitalist in him, he could have been a rich man. His ethic and his principles wouldn't allow him to capitalize his talents for monetary gain.

Basman, Leybl (1905–1975)

Leybl Basman was educated in the Yiddish Institute in Wilkomir, Lithuania and arrived in Canada in 1928 devoted to the Yiddish language and culture. His influence in many areas is legendary on the left. Basman was a talented actor and a wonderful teacher, with a tremendous amount of energy he used in organizing wherever he was. He taught in Winnipeg, Windsor, Montreal, Toronto, and Vancouver. One counsellor remembers how, as the director of Camp Naivelt, Basman participated in preparing to open the camp for the summer. Not bothering with a hammer, he pulled out the boards nailed on the bunks shuttered for the winter with his bare hands. Some of the older UJPO members had fond memories of Leybl at Camp Naivelt sitting under a tree, reading aloud to an assembled group.

Borchiver, Ruth Biderman (1927–2007)

Ruth Borchiver grew up in the left movement, attending the shules as a child and then later working in the camp. She became a social worker and the head of Jewish Child and Family Services. She left the organization in the late 1950s and later wrote a PhD thesis in psychology entitled "Study of Class and Political Identification." When invited by her old friend Ben Shek in the 1990s to be the narrator for a cantata performed by the choir, she felt that the organization had changed a great deal from the one she had left. When I interviewed her, she explained how performing with the choir made her feel like she was returning home. Ruth felt her life had been enriched by her experiences in the organization. Her quotes are interspersed throughout the book. Ruth had done interviews with many of the major players in the United Jewish People's Order, and after I had spent a wonderful few hours with her as she reminisced, she generously loaned me the handwritten transcripts of her interviews, which have been invaluable. Sadly Ruth died quite suddenly not a year after I met her.

Fishauf, Brenda Diamond (1914–2015)

My friend Brenda Diamond Fishauf's life story really embodies the finest and also the most painful part of this history. In 2014, Brenda was one hundred years old and by then her hearing sometimes made it difficult to communicate, but her mind remained just fine. I met Brenda and her husband Nathan when I joined a Leyen Krayz (reading circle) at the Winchevsky Centre in the early 2000s. Brenda was shorter than me by a few inches (and I am 5'1") and a clever, gentle, woman.

The people from our Leyen Krayz were sitting around my dining room table for a Chanukah celebration when Brenda's husband Nathan began to tell the extraordinary tale of his flight from Staszow when the Nazis arrived in Lvov (Lemberg in Yiddish) and eventually the far east of the Soviet Union and his even more miraculous survival after the war. (Two of his friends were murdered in the Kielce pogrom AFTER the war while changing trains en route to Staszow, a trip that Nathan was supposed to be on.) When it became time for Brenda's story, we sat in her back yard and she described her life before her marriage to Nathan. Brenda was for many years the co-ordinator of our Leyen Krayz. To hear Brenda read in her beautiful Yiddish was a pleasure.

Gartner, Emil (1914–1960)

Emil Gartner was born in Vienna and classically trained as a conductor. He came to Canada where he became conductor of the Freiheit Gezang Fareyn, which became the Toronto Jewish Folk Choir. Under his leadership, the choir increased in size to 130 voices by the late 1940s. Although many in the choir were workers who did not know how to read music, inspired by Gartner, the repertoire expanded to include not only Yiddish folk songs and cantatas, and international songs, but classical works as well. The choir performed often at Massey Hall, sometimes with the Toronto Symphony Orchestra with guest artists from New York's Metropolitan Opera. Gartner was a very demanding conductor, and I was told the women were all in love with him. Paul Robeson, who became a personal friend of Gartner, was a frequent guest until his passport was taken away.

Gershman, Joshua (1903–1984)

Joe Gershman was born in Sokolov in the Ukraine. In 1921, his family sent him to Winnipeg to search for his father, who Gershman then discovered had recently died. He became a fur dresser, a communist, and a founder of the Kompartey, the national Jewish committee of the Community Party. Gershman became a union organizer in Quebec for the Industrial Union of Needle Trades Workers. Except for short intervals around the time of the Second World War, Gershman, as he was known, was the editor of the left Yiddish newspaper, *Der Kamf*, from 1937 until the paper folded in 1972. *Der Kamf* was renamed *Der Vochenblat* in 1940. He travelled the country soliciting funds to keep the newspaper going. Although Gershman remained a communist until late 1977, he became increasingly critical of the Soviet Union's lack of support for Yiddish culture. I met Joe a few times not long before he died and asked why he stayed in the Communist Party for so long. He said that he felt that if things were going to change, he could be more effective making that happen from the inside.

Lapedes, Becky (1900–1993)

Becky Lapedes was one of the founders of the Yiddishe Arbeter Froyen Fareyn (Jewish Women's Labour League) in 1923. She remained an activist her entire life. She is credited with the founding of the children's camp in 1925. Becky, with her typical modesty, maintained that it was her friend Rachel (Rae) Watson who was the prime mover, but Rachel died early. Thanks to interviews and tapes Becky's daughter, Sheyndl (Cheryl), shared with me, I found myself feeling great affection and admiration for this feisty, warm-hearted woman who lived her ideals. When a tragedy occurred in the community—a teenaged boy had died in a terrible accident—Becky was there every day quietly washing the dishes at the Shiva (the seven days of mourning following a funeral). A hard worker all her life, she knew how to give help where it was needed. The boy's sister, Ruth Biderman Borchiver, remembered how warmed her family was by Becky's help as they grieved this tragic loss.

Lipshitz, Sam (1910–2000)

Sam Lipshitz was very prominent in the Jewish left and on the Central Committee of the Communist Party. He was an organizer, a journalist, and, in the 1940s, on the executive of the Canadian Jewish Congress. Thanks to his daughter May and son-in-law Gerry Cohen, all of his material, a wonderful treasure trove of left Jewish history, was donated to the York Library Archives. Gerry and May spent many hours helping to organize the material. Sam was a formidable intellectual, but like many men of his generation he was so busy travelling in the service of the party and his ideals that much of the work of home, family, and earning fell to his wife, Manya. Sam was born in Radom, Poland and came to Canada with his family in the early 1920s.

Lipshitz, Manya Kantorovitch (1906–1996)

Manya became a radical because of her experiences in the twelfth Jewish children's commune just after the Bolshevik revolution. As a teacher in the Winchevsky Shule, she was known as a learned, kind woman and a wonderful teacher. Out of respect to her parents, she was married to Sam Lipshitz by a rabbi. They were both communists and were called on the carpet by the party for engaging in such a reactionary act as having a religious ceremony. Sam reported that he apologized and promised "never to do that again." He and Manya were together until Manya's death many years later. She held the fort caring for the family while he travelled extensively for the Communist Party and the United Jewish People's Order.

Shek, Ben (1927–2011)

The Shek family was active in the Jewish left from the moment they stepped foot on Canadian shores. Ben's father Sol became the secretary of the Labour League and his mother Bella joined the choir. Ben's life was spent in the League, later called the Toronto Jewish People's Order. With two working parents, the UJPO was a second home to Ben. Ben was active in the choir and the youth organization of the Communist Party, becoming editor of their newspaper, the *Champion*. In later years, he sang bass in the choir and put a great deal of energy into promoting the Toronto Jewish Folk Choir to keep it a going concern. Ben trained to become a teacher but was not hired because of his left politics. So he got himself a PhD and a distinguished career as a Professor of French at the University of Toronto, becoming elected a Fellow of the Royal Society of Canada in 2002. His long involvement with the Order made him a walking repository of UJPO history.

Shtern, Sholem (1906–1990)

Sholem Shtern was the Director of the Winchevsky Shule in Montreal and a frequent contributor to *Der Kamf*. Shtern was a member of a prominent Yiddish literary family in Montreal. His greatest passion was writing. His three brothers, Jacob Zipper and Yehiel and Israel Shtern, his sister, Shifre Krishtalka, and his nephew, Aaron Krishtalka, were all Yiddish writers and poets. His family encompassed the range of political and religious views. Jacob Zipper (he had changed his name to Zipper when he became politically active in Russia) was a Zionist and head of the Peretz School. Shifra Krishtalka taught in the Peretz School but sent her son Aaron (known as Arele) to the Winchevsky School. The father was an observant Jew. Although they were all secular, the family kept a kosher home to honour their father.

Usiskin, Roz (Rosaline) Wolodarsky (1930–)

Roz has been an activist in Winnipeg's left Jewish community since the late 1940s. Her gracious hospitality is legendary. And the delicious food is always accompanied by wonderful conversation. When I visit Winnipeg, we can sit in her kitchen and talk all day. Roz has helped me in so many ways with this project—with materials she collected, the research she has done, and her stimulating ideas. The penultimate chapter in this book is based on work we did together and presented at a Canadian Jewish Studies Conference in Winnipeg. Roz's book, *The Wolodarsky Family*, consists of the translation of handwritten letters from her grandmother, her aunt left behind in Russia because of the First World War, and her father who came to Winnipeg. They provide a unique inside glimpse of the lived experience of that difficult time. When I got my first job in 1973, teaching a course at the University of Winnipeg, and attended my very first sociology department meeting, they were awarding the gold prize for that year to their very best student. It was Roz Usiskin! She had returned to university as an adult to begin her scholarly career.

Roz is central to the Winnipeg United Jewish People's Order, but her connections in the broader Jewish community are extensive. She served as Executive Director of the Manitoba Multicultural Resource Centre and president of the Jewish Historical Society of Western Canada and the Jewish Heritage Centre of Western Canada. Her (still) unpublished master's thesis is the pioneering work on radicalism in the Jewish community in the pre-1919 years. Roz became involved in the UJPO as a young woman, later serving as the president of the organization for many years until 2013. Her husband's uncle, Mike Usiskin, was one of the pioneer farmers in Edenbridge, Saskatchewan.

Zuken, Joe (1912–1986)

Joe Zuken has the longest record of holding public office in North America for a communist. He was first elected to the Board of Education in 1941 and then was a municipal alderman in Winnipeg from 1961 until his retirement in 1983. A classmate of Avrom and Nekhama in the Peretz School class of 1925, he soon turned to the left and became a communist. Devoted to Yiddish, he was also an actor in a theatre group and recited for the Jewish left. Joe kept his seat because of his reputation for looking after those who needed help in his constituency,

Winnipeg's North End. Joe was trusted—one knew where to go if one was in trouble. Soon after coming to Winnipeg, I was sitting in his waiting room for the (un)happy purpose of a separation agreement for the end of my marriage. It's Winnipeg, one frosty October day—and in Winnipeg the topic of discussion is often the weather. One older man started to say how it really wasn't so cold—his brother and he would be working without shirts in that kind of weather. It was in that office I learned about the Jewish pioneer settlements in Saskatchewan and Manitoba, a history that could still be touched. When the Winnipeg City Council wanted to honour aldermen with long service by placing their portraits in city hall, Joe Zuken voted against the motion. He said he didn't want to be hung just yet.

Appendix B: The Communist Party and the Jewish Left

While it is important to keep in mind the distinction between the members of the Communist Party (CP) and participants in the pro-Soviet left organizations, the leadership were CP members and until 1956 attempted to follow Comintern policy, at least in name.

1917 and the Bolshevik Revolution

Under Lenin, the idea was to counter great Russian chauvinism through support of the development of ethnic cultures. Soviet policy under Lenin's leadership was to support ethnic minorities in a fusion of socialist internationalism and anti-colonial nationalism. Jews benefited from this policy. Religion was not tolerated—Muslim, Christian or Jewish—but ethnic identity was both encouraged and supported.

1924 Stalin Comes to Power

The Comintern became a vehicle for Stalin rather than a forum for the Communist parties internationally. In 1929, the Canadian party was to be organized by workplace rather than ethnic community. Sometimes Communist leaders even Anglicized their names to make the party appear more "Canadian." In Canada, this affected the left Finnish and Ukrainian communities, the Finnish Organization of Canada and the Ukrainian Labour Farmer Temple Associations, and many left.

1928 "Class Against Class" and Labour Policies

In this period of sectarian politics, democratic socialists were denounced as fiercely as capitalists or fascists. The hostility was a two-way business, and the

Jewish left was denounced as energetically as the pro-communists denounced the Zionists and the members of the Workmen's Circle, whose politics had moved substantially to the right.

Initially, communist trade unionists were part of the Trade Union Educational League Unions but organized within the mainstream unions. In 1928, a policy of dual unionism was put in place. In Canada, the Workers Unity League (WUL) was set up, and the work of organizing garment workers was through building a separate union, the Industrial Union of Needle Trades Workers, part of the WUL. Almost all the leadership of the IUNTW were Jews, who were active in the mass Jewish organizations—for example the Labour League in Toronto and the Liberty Temple in Winnipeg.

1936 Popular Front

With the rise of fascism, ethnic identity, which had been downplayed in official policy, once again was considered important. One response to the threat of fascism was to value Jewish ethnic identity and Yiddish and to reach out to all others in the Jewish community.

The 1940s

In 1940, after the signing of a non-aggression pact between Nazi Germany and the Soviet Union, the state declared the Communist Party illegal. A number of Jewish Canadian communists were interned along with Germans and Italians suspected of being Nazis or fascists, while others in the Jewish leadership went into hiding. After 1941, when the USSR entered the war in alliance with the West, pro-Soviet sympathies become acceptable, and the Jewish left flourished.

The 1950s: The Cold War

The Cold War was a period of rabid anti-communism characterized by the redbaiting undertaken by Senator McCarthy in the United States. The left Jewish groups were kicked out of the Canadian Jewish Congress, and every effort was made to marginalize those with pro-Soviet sympathies. Unions in Canada "cleansed" their leadership of communists. Jewish leftists had trouble crossing the border into the United States.

1956: The Twentieth Party Congress in the USSR

Stalin's crimes became public, causing shock and dismay in the left Jewish community. In particular, the murders of the writers, poets, and artists who were creating a Soviet Yiddish culture were mourned. The leaders of the left Jewish community, who were also members of the Communist Party, left both the party and the community. The left communities retained their socialist politics and continued to be active in progressive issues.

Appendix C: Glossary

The transliteration follows the YIVO rules, except where it is commonly spelled differently in English. An example is the writer Sholem Aleichem, where the YIVO spelling would be Aleykhem. Freiheit would be spelled Frayhayt, using YIVO rules, but because it appears in printed form before those rules came into effect, I have used the original spelling.

Arbeter Ring—Workmen's Circle.

Arbeter Sport Fareyn—Workers' Sport Association.

Arbeter Teatre Farband (ARTEF)—Workers' Theatre League, a collective of theatre artists that began in 1927 in New York.

bavegung—political movement.

Der Fraynd—The Friend, the newspaper of the Arbeter Ring.

Der Freiheit—A communist Jewish newspaper published in New York.

Der Kamf—The Struggle, the newspaper of the left community (later named *Der Vochenblat*).

Di Arbeter Froy—"The Woman Worker," a column in *Der Kamf* in the 1920s.

di linke—the left.

di rekhte—the right.

Dos Yiddishe Vort—The Israelite Press, the Winnipeg paper written in Yiddish and published from 1921 to 1981.

elementar shule—elementary school.

Farband—name of a Zionist organization.

farbrente communist—burning or fervent communist.

Freiheit Gezang Fareyn—Freedom Singing League, the original name of many of the left Jewish choirs (sometimes referred to in English as the Freedom Singing Circle).

Freiheit Temple—Liberty Temple, Winnipeg.

gymnasia—high school in Eastern Europe.

Hashomer Hatzair—the Youth Guard, a left Zionist movement.

Hasidism—a form of Orthodox Judaism.

Haskalah—the Jewish enlightenment.

higer geboyrene—those born here.

Kanader Arbeter Ring—Canadian Worker's Circle, a Montreal left group that broke from the Arbeter Ring in 1926. It is sometimes called the Kanader Hilf Fareyn or Canadian Mutual Aid Association.

kapote—long old-fashioned coat.

khaver (male); khaverte (female)—Friend or Comrade. A respectful form of address used among the left. It did not necessarily mean membership in the Communist Party.

kheder—religious Jewish school.

Kinderland—Children's Land, formerly Kindervelt, in Ontario. Name of the left camps in New York, Quebec, and Ontario.

Kindervelt—Children's World, a left camp from 1925 to 1934.

Komsomol—Young Communist League. Bolshevik organization for youth in the Soviet Union.

landsmanshaftn—mutual aid societies based on a common birthplace.

Lemberg, or Lvov in Russian—a city in Western Russia, part of the Ukraine in early 1900s.

Leyen Krayz—Reading Circle.

Loshn Kodesh—the Holy Tongue, as Hebrew is referred to by observant Jews

mittlshul—secular Jewish high school.

Muter Fareyn—the Mother's League.

Nitgedayget (or Nitgedeiget)—Not to worry, a camp in the Laurentians. There was also one in New York State.

Pan—Polish for Mr.

Poale Tsion—Workers of Zion, a left socialist Zionist organization.

proste—ordinary folk, can also mean uncultured.

Radikaler shuln—radical schools.

Reb—Mr. in Yiddish.

Rosh Hashoneh—Head of the Year, Jewish New Year, which occurs in the fall.

Sephardim—Jews originating from Spain.

Shabbos—the Sabbath.

shener un beser velt—more beautiful and better world.

sholem bayis—a peaceful house, an expression used for a loving, happy home.

shtetl—small largely Jewish city in Eastern Europe (plural shtetlekh).

shule—secular school.

shund—trash.

tsedekah—righteousness, justice. Giving to the poor as justice rather than charity.

veltlekher—literally worldly, it means secular.

Vochenblat (also *Vokhenblat*)—Canadian Jewish Weekly.

Yiddish gas—the Jewish street, or ordinary people in the community.

Yiddishe Arbeter Froyen Fareyn—Jewish Women's Labour League.

Yiddishe Kultur—Jewish Culture, the name of a magazine launched in 1935.

Yiddishkayt (also Yiddishkeit)—Jewishness or Jewish identity.

Yom Kippur—Day of Atonement, which falls eight days after Rosh Hashoneh.

Zhenotdel—Women's Department of the Russian Communist Party in the 1920s devoted to improving women's lives.

Appendix D: Abbreviations

CJC—Canadian Jewish Congress

HCA—Housewives Consumer Association

HUAC—the House Un-American Activities Committee, a Committee of the United States Senate, which investigated left activists and organizations

IKOR—Yiddish Kolonizatsiye in Rusland, or Yiddish Colonization in Russia, an organization supporting Jewish colonization in Russia

IUNTW—Industrial Union of Needle Trades Workers

IWO—International Workers Order, a secular left organization in the United States

JAFC—Jewish Anti-Fascist Committee

JPFO—Jewish People's Fraternal Order, the Jewish section of the IWO

UJPO—United Jewish People's Order

YIVO—Yiddish Scientific Institute. Founded in 1925 in Vilna, Lithuania, and moved to New York in 1940

YKUF—Yiddish Kultur Farband, or Jewish Cultural Association, founded in 1936

Notes

Introduction

1 The journals were rediscovered in the 1970s. An article in *Yiddishe Kultur* by poet Isaac Ronch, "Yiddish Journal of a Children's Commune in the Soviet Union," described the commune and propelled Manya Lipshitz to write her memoirs, "Bletlekh fun a Shturmisher Tsayt." Her book was translated by Max Rosenfeld and Marcia Usisikin as *Time Remembered: A Jewish Children's Commune in the Soviet Union in the 1920s* (Toronto: Lugus Publications, 1991).

2 Manya Lipshitz's memoir, *Time Remembered*, reproduced some of the journals the commune children had written, so we had names and some characteristics of her communards. For others, we made up names and biographies.

3 Ruth Howard provided the resources through her work as artistic director of Jumblies Theatre, a community arts initiative funded by the Metcalf Foundation, the Ontario Trillium Foundation, and a Toronto Community Foundation Vital Ideas grant.

4 C. J. Sharpe, 15, Camp Naivelt, 2008 (his commune name was Joel Freedman).

5 Morris Biderman: *A Life on the Jewish Left: An Immigrant's Experience* (Toronto: Onward Publishing, 2000), 60.

6 See Arthur J. Sabin, *Red Scare in Court: New York Versus the International Workers Order* (Philadelphia: University of Pennsylvania Press, 1993).

7 1979 Kinderland Journal. I was in camp at the time. Another of the charges proving communist connections was that we had hammers and sickles on our tablecloths. We thought this was pretty funny, considering we ate in a very bare concrete building with no tablecloths!

8 See for example Michael Freedland, "Hunting Communists? They Were Really After Jews," *Jewish Chronicle Online*, August 6, 2009, www.thejc.com/arts/arts-features/17299/hunting-communists-they-were-really-after-jews.

9 Paul Buhle, "Jews and American Communism: The Cultural Question," *Radical History Review* 23 (1980): 9–33.

10 Ian McKay, "Joe Salsberg, Depression-Era Communism, and the Limits of Moscow's Rule," paper presented to the seminar in honour of Gerry Tulchinsky, University of Toronto, 2013.

11 Gerald Tulchinsky, *Joe Salsberg: A Life of Commitment* (Toronto: University of Toronto Press, 2013).

12 Norman Penner, *Canadian Communism* (Toronto: Methuen, 1977), 273.

13 Ellen Schrecker, *The Age of McCarthyism: A Brief History with Documents* (Boston: St. Martin's Press, 1994), chapter 3. www.english.illinois.edu.

14 Paul Gilroy, *Against Race: Imagining Political Culture Beyond the Colour Line* (Cambridge: Harvard University Press, 2000), chapter 1.

15 Gilroy, *Against Race*, 104.

1 Origins

1 The Pale of Settlement delineated where Jews in the Russian empire were allowed to live. It roughly comprised much of present-day Lithuania, Belarus, Poland, Moldova, Ukraine, and parts of western Russia, excluding certain cities such as Kiev, Sevastopol, and Yalta. In the nineteenth century, the Pale included a Jewish population of over five million, the largest concentration or 40 percent of the world Jewish population.

2 Her name is spelled Khave using the YIVO method, but she is published in English as Chave.

3 To be fair, Sholem Aleichem's book *Tevye*, on which the play and musical are based, is substantially grimmer than the cheerful musical.

4 Chava Rosenfarb, *Of Lodz and Love*, translated from the Yiddish by the author (New York: Syracuse University Press, 2000), 71–73. In her acceptance speech for an honorary doctorate from Lethbridge where she lived, Rosenfarb wrote: "My classroom was the Lodz Ghetto, my teachers were my fellow inmates there and especially the poets, painters and intellectuals of the doomed writer's community, incarcerated between the barbed-wire walls of the ghetto, who accepted me at a very early age as a member. So I am a graduate of the Holocaust, of the death camps of Auschwitz and Bergen Belsen. I have matriculated in one of the greatest tragedies known to man." Rosenfarb died in February 2011.

5 Reb or Mister is a term of respect. The use of the Polish "Pan" reflects the characters' identification with Polish rather than Jewish culture.

6 A 25th-anniversary book from the Sholem Aleichem shule, Winnipeg. Leybl Basman, *25 Years of Progressive Jewish Education*. Excerpted and translated by the author.

7 The literal translation of veltlekher is worldly; it has come to mean non-religious or secular.

8 Mendele Mokher Sforim (Mendele the Bookseller) lived from 1836 to 1917; Sholem Rabinovitsh (pen name Sholem Aleichem) lived from 1859 to 1916; I. L. Peretz lived from 1852 to 1915.

9 I found that my Yiddish has much in common with the Low German spoken by Mennonites who had settled in Russia. It is easy to converse with them and be understood.

10 The word "proste" has class connotations, and it is not exactly translatable.

11 Dovid Katz, *Words on Fire: The Unfinished Story of Yiddish* (New York: Basic Books, 2004).

12 Jeffrey Shandler, "Imagining Yiddishland," *History and Memory* 15, no. 1 (Spring/Summer 2003): 123–49.

13 Dovid Katz, paraphrasing the paper by Matisyohu Mieses at the Chernowitz Conference of 1906 establishing Yiddish as a language of the Jewish people. Katz, *Words on Fire,* 273.

14 Gramsci uses the term "organic intellectuals" to denote the intimate bond between intellectuals and the class of which they are a part. Antonio Gramsci, *Selections from the Prison Notebooks* (New York: International publishers, 1971), 5–23.

15 Sholem Aleichem's *Tevye and His Daughters* was first published in Yiddish in 1894. He has six daughters, Tzeitel, Hodel, Chava Shprintze, Beylke, and Teibel, all of whom he loved dearly. When Shprintze runs off with a Gentile boy, Tevye, heartbroken, sits Shiva for her as if she were dead. The musical, *Fiddler on the Roof*, airbrushed the poverty with nostalgia.

16 C. Bezele Sherman, *The Jew Within American Society: A Study in Ethnic Individuality* (Detroit: Wayne State University Press, 1961), 86. Quoted in Shloime Perel, "The Jewish Communist Movement in Canada: Mid 1920s to Early 1950s" (Unpublished draft of PhD diss., McMaster University, chapter 4).

17 Louis Rosenberg, *Canada's Jews: A Social and Economic Study of Jews in Canada in the 1930s* (Montreal: McGill University Press, 1993), 31–35. First published by the Canadian Jewish Congress in 1939.

18 Mordechai Richler, *The Apprenticeship of Duddy Kravitz* (Montreal: Andre Deutsch, 1959), 13.

19 Joshua Gershman, in Irving Abella, "Portrait of a Jewish Professional Revolutionary: The Recollections of Joshua Gershman," *Labour / Le Travail* 2 (1977): 185–213.

20 Roz Usiskin, "Towards a Theoretical Reformulation of the Relationship Between Political Ideology, Social Class and Ethnicity: A Case study of the Jewish Radical Community, 1905–1920 (master's thesis, University of Manitoba, 1978), 121.

21 Doug Smith, *Joe Zuken: Citizen and Socialist* (Toronto: James Lorimer, 1990), 11.

22 John Marlyn, *Under the Ribs of Death* (Toronto: McClelland & Stewart, 1964), quoted in Jim Silver, "Winnipeg's North End," *Canadian Dimension,* January 2010, 5.

23 Harvey Herstein, "The Growth of the Winnipeg Jewish Community and the Evolution of its Educational Institutions" (master's thesis, University of Manitoba, 1964), 186, Table IV.

24 Roz Wolodarsky Usiskin, *The Wolodarsky Family* (Winnipeg, 2005). Published as a family project. Roz translated the handwritten letters to her father, Joseph Wolodarksy.

25 Ruth Borchiver, interview with Sam Lipshitz (1980s).

26 Sam Kagan, interview with Karen Levine, February 28, 1978, MHSO Jew-1004-Kag, Multicultural History Society, Toronto, Canada.

27 Sam Kagan, interview with Karen Levine.

28 When she went to get her immigration papers, the immigration officer offered to list her as the "twin" of her sister born in 1911.

29 Brenda Fishauf, interview with the author (in Yiddish), July 2004.

30 The estimated population of Staszow was 8,368 in 1921. See the Jewish genealogical website www.jewishgen.org.

31 Moses Kligsberg, "The Jewish Youth Movement in Interwar Poland, A Sociological Study," Yiddish, quoted in *Studies of Polish Jewry, 1919–39,* ed. Joshua A. Fishman (New York: YIVO, 1974), 165, quoted in *Awakening Lives: Autobiographies of Jewish Youth in Poland before the Holocaust*, ed. Jeffrey Shandler (New Haven: Yale University Press, 2002), xxix. The Yiddish Scientific Institute was founded in Vilna, Poland in 1924. Lacking any money, YIVO developed innovative methods of doing research, including contests in which young people wrote autobiographies. Adolescents from all over Eastern Europe, but primarily Poland, wrote their life stories in whatever language they chose. They came from all social classes, and from the entire spectrum of Polish Jewry—Orthodox, Bundists, Zionists. The

originals are in New York. Jeffrey Shandler translated some of these. See Shandler, *Awakening Lives*, xxix.

32 Kligsberg, "The Jewish Youth Movement in Interwar Poland," in Shandler, *Awakening Lives*, xxix.

33 Adele Wiseman, *The Sacrifice* (Toronto: Macmillan of Canada, 1956), 5.

34 Adele Wiseman attended the left-wing Sholem Aleichem Shule in the Liberty Temple in Winnipeg. Roland Penner, in his memoir *A Glowing Dream,* comments on his friendship with Wiseman and their common politics. Canadian novelist Margaret Laurence was a close friend of Wiseman. In *The Diviners*, the protagonist, Morag, goes to Winnipeg and is warmly welcomed by her friend's mother, a left-wing Jew, a character that appears to be modelled after Wiseman's mother.

35 Wiseman, *The Sacrifice*, 23.

36 Wiseman, *The Sacrifice*, 47.

37 Rosenberg, *Canada's Jews*, 177 (Table 117).

38 Sid Bagel, interview with Roz Usiskin, July 1981, Master tape no 259, Jewish Archives of Western Canada, Winnipeg.

39 Lil Himmelfarb Ilomaki, interview with the author, March 1996.

40 During the Eaton's Strike of 1912, male cloakmakers struck in support of the women making buttonholes, whose jobs were threatened. This is described in Ruth Frager, "Sewing Solidarity: The Eaton's Strike of 1912," in *New Essays in Women's History*, ed. Franca Iacovetta and Mariana Valverde (Toronto: University of Toronto Press, 1992), 189–228.

2 Revolutionary Values and the Jewish Left

1 Brenda Fishauf, interview with the author (in Yiddish), July 2004.

2 Emma Goldman, *Syndicalism: The Modern Menace to Capitalism* (New York: Mother Earth Publishing Association, 1913), theanarchistlibrary.org.

3 Arthur Liebman, *Jew and the Left* (New York: John Wiley & Sons, 1979), 289.

4 Nora Levin, *While Messiah Tarried: Jewish Socialist Movements, 1871–1917* (New York: Schocken Books, 1977), 167.

5 The transliteration would be Der freyheyt, but as the paper used the old spelling, Der Freiheit, that's the spelling used here.

6 "A Tale of Four Cities: 60 years of UJPO," *Outlook,* December 1986, 12–13.

7 Isaac Deutscher, "The Russian Revolution and the Jewish Problem," in *The Non-Jewish Jews and other Essays* (London: Oxford, 1968).

8 Gerald Tulchinsky, "Family Quarrel: Joe Salsberg, the 'Jewish' Question and Canadian Communism," *Labour / Le Travail* 56 (Fall 2005): 149–73.

9 Itche's account of his turn to the left was an interesting one. As a young man, and Yungvelt's director, he had organized a day commemorating Sacco and Vanzetti, the Italian anarchists who the left believed were murdered by the state. Emma Goldman, who was well known, arrived in the camp and announced that the program was too heavy for the children. The leadership of the Arbeter Ring ordered Itche's plans halted, and Itche left in disgust. Itche Goldberg, interview with the author, New York, May 1995. The story was also recounted at Itche's 100th birthday celebration.

10 Itche Goldberg, interview with the author, May 1996.

11 Joan Sangster, *Dreams of Equality: Women on the Canadian Left, 1920–50* (Toronto: McClelland & Stewart, 1989).

12 Ben Shek, interview with the author, May 2005.

13 Bella Shek, interview with the author, March 2006.

14 M. Olgin, *Der Internazionale Arbeiter Ordn* (The International Workers Order) (New York: Farlag/Internazaionale Arbeiter Ordn, 1931), 15.

15 S. Shek, "Der Ordn in dinst fun zayne mitglider" (The Order in the Service of its Members), UJPO Second National Convention, Montreal, 1947.

16 M. Biderman, "Fun der ershter biz der tsveyter Natsionaler Convention" (From the first until the second National Convention), UJPO Convention Book, June 1947.

17 H. Guralnik, "Faroys tsu a freydikn morgn" (Forward to a joyful morning), First National Convention United Jewish Peoples Order, April 27–29, Toronto, 1945.

18 Roz Usiskin, interview with the author, Winnipeg, 2008. Joe Zuken served as school trustee for twenty years until 1961. He was elected as city alderman from Winnipeg's North End and served from 1961 until his retirement in 1983.

19 Letter from Joseph Wolodarsky to his sister Polya, also called Pesel or Pauline, circa 1930s, translated by Roz Wolodarsky Usisikin.

3 Cultural Initiatives and the Politics of Everyday Life

1 Sol Shek provides statistics on the class background of members in the 1936 10th anniversary book of the Labour League. At the time, there were 803 members in Toronto. Shek, *Souvenir Book of the Ten Years of the Labour League* (Toronto: Supreme Printing Company, 1936).

2 *On Our Forerunners—At Work Epilogue: Notes on the Twentieth Century.* Compiled by David Rome. Canadian Jewish Congress, Serial Publication. New Series, No. 10, 117.

3 Antonio Gramsci, *Selections from Prison Notebooks* (New York: International Publishers, 1972).

4 Paul Buhle, in "Jews and American Communism," *Radical History Review* 23 (Spring 1980): 9–33, articulates this eloquently in his review of Liebman's book, *Jews and the Left* (New York: John Wiley & Sons, 1979).

5 Louis Rosenberg, *Canada's Jews: A Social and Economic Study of Jews in Canada in the 1980s* (Montreal: McGill Queens, 1993), 136. Originally published in 1939 by the Canadian Jewish Congress.

6 M. Nadir, "Der Vakenalia," *Morgn Freiheit,* September 14, 1929. Quoted in Bat-Ami Zucker, "American Jewish Communists and Jewish Culture in the 1930's," *Modern Judaism* 14 (1994): 177. Many Canadian leftists subscribed to *Freiheit*, and Nadir's work was also published in *Der Kamf.*

7 Raymond Williams, *Keywords* (New York: Oxford, 1983), 87–93.

8 See Michael Denning, *The Cultural Front* (London: Verso, 1997), 63 and footnote 21.

9 1947 UJPO Convention Book (Toronto: United Jewish People's Order, 1947).

10 Paul Freire, *The Politics of Education: Culture, Power and Liberation* (Westport, Connecticut & South Hadley, Massachusetts: Bergin & Garvey, 1985). See chapter 7, "Culture, Action and Conscientization," 67–120.

11 Paulo Freire, "The Adult Literacy Process as Cultural Action for Freedom," *Harvard Educational Review* (Summer 1970): 205–25.

12 Stuart Hall, "Cultural Identity and Diaspora," reprinted in *Social Theory,* 2nd ed., ed. Roberta Garner (Toronto: University of Toronto Press, 2010), 563.

13 Denning, *Cultural Front,* 497.

14 M. J. (Moissaye) Olgin, *Kultur un Folk: Ophandlungen un essayen vegn kultur un vegn shrayber* (Culture and People) (New York: YKUF, 1949), 134 ff.

15 Labour Zionists were socialists intent on building a socialist homeland in Israel (or Mandate Palestine). Some, such as Halperin, inspired by the success of the Soviet Revolution, became communists, hoping to build socialism in the country in which they lived.

16 *Der Kamf* 1, January 1926, 1.

17 *Der Kamf.* Not signed, January 1, 1932, 4. See also Charles N., "Yiddishe arbeter farshtarkt di proletarishe kultur front" (Jewish workers strengthen the proletariat cultural front), *Der Kamf*, January 25, 1935, 10.

18 M. Pearlman, "Fir Yor Abeter Kultur Tsentr" (Four Years of the Workers Cultural Centre), *Der Kamf*, October 31, 1930.

19 Gershman is listed as editing the magazine from 1936 on. The Archives of Ontario collection of Gershman's papers, however, shows that in 1936, Guralnik wrote an article as editor of *Der Kamf* for the tenth anniversary book of the Labour League, and Sam Lipshitz edited the paper for a while in 1945. Guralnik later became director of the School and Culture Committee of the UJPO and principal of the Winchevsky shule.

20 Roz Usiskin's interview with Fayvl Simkin is in the archives of the Western Canada Jewish Heritage Centre, Winnipeg.

21 The periods were ideological concepts adopted by the Communist International or Comintern in 1928. They believed the widespread economic collapse of the late 1920s and early 1930s would revolutionize the working class and that proletarian revolution was imminent. This period, known as the Third Period, changed in the mid-1930s to what is known as the Popular Front.

22 Izzy Kharik was a victim of Stalin's purges in the 1930s.

23 Gerry Kane, interview with the author, May 2000.

24 Mendele the Bookseller, known as the grandfather of Yiddish literature, is the pseudonym of Sholem Yankev Abramovich. Sholem Aleichem, the pen name of Sholem Rabinovitsh, is known as the father, and I. L. Peretz the son (although Sholem Aleichem and Peretz lived during the same period).

25 Olga Eizner Favreau, personal conversation with the author, July 2012.

26 Emil Gartner, "Our Life—Our Art," June 1947, UJPO Convention Book.

27 This was known by the left as the "sha shtil policy" (be quiet), where, fearing an anti-Semitic backlash, the CJC restricted itself to influencing Canadian policy by lobbying government for political interventions. See, for example, Frank Bialystok, *Delayed Impact: The Holocaust and the Canadian Jewish Community* (Montreal: McGill Queen's University Press, 2000), chapter 1.

28 The UJPO was organized by city and branch. The branches were numbered and named by occupation or hometown, for example, the Needle Workers, Branch 5, the Radomer Branch 12 (people from the town of Radom, Poland). The women had their own branches, e.g. Rosa Luxemburg Branch 6, although a few of the women joined mixed branches.

4 Fighting Class Exploitation and Fascism

1 Desmond Morton, *A Short History of Canada* (Toronto: McClelland & Stewart, 1997), 166.

2 James Struthers, "How Much is Enough?: Creating a Social Minimum in Ontario, 1930–44," *Canadian Historical Review* 72, no 1 (1991): 42.

3 Ian Mosby, "Food Will Win the War: The Politics and Culture of Food and Nutrition During the Second World War" (PhD diss., York University, 2011), 48–49.

4 Mercedes Steedman, *Angels of the Workplace: Women and the Construction of Gender Relations in the Canadian Clothing Industry, 1890–1940* (Toronto: Oxford University Press, 1997), 142–44.

5 "Cloakmakers Choose Busy Time to Tie Up Industry Here, Investigator Finds," *Winnipeg Free Press*, July 18, 1934. See also Ruth Frager, *Sweatshop Strife: Class, Ethnicity and Gender in the Jewish Labour Movement of Toronto, 1900–1939* (Toronto: University of Toronto Press, 1992). Fanny Levine, Eva Newmark, and Jean Sable recalled in a CBC interview on June 24, 1979, the deplorable conditions in Toronto and Montreal in the 1930s. www.cbc.ca/archives.

6 Di Arbeter Froy (The Woman Worker), "Di shklaferishe badingunden fun di farkoyferins" (The slavelike situation of the sales lady), *Der Kamf*, March 21, 1930, 3.

7 Steedman, *Angels of the Workplace*, 82.

8 "A beyzer foreman, finstere shop, arbeterins, un shmutz bizn holz" (An angry foreman, a worker's dark shop and dirt up to the neck), *Der Kamf*, January 29, 1926.

9 See, for example, Daniel Katz, *All Together Different: Yiddish Socialists, Garment Workers and the Labor Roots of Multiculturalism* (New York: NYU Press, 2011).

10 Katz, *All Together Different*, 185–223.

11 The Catholic Church was very conservative and young Quebec women who were Catholic faced the disapproval of the priests. This was not the case in the Jewish community, where the rabbis did not play this role. See Irving Abella, "Portrait of a Jewish Professional Revolutionary: The Recollections of Joshua Gershman," *Labour/Le Travail* 2 (1977): 201, based on interviews conducted by Irving Abella, David Chud, and Elaine Mitchell in 1973, 1974, and 1975.

12 Abella, "Portrait of a Jewish Professional Revolutionary," 201.

13 Bessie Schachter, "Froyen in dem Strike" (Women in the Strike), *Der Kamf*, August 6, 1926.

14 Schachter, "Froyen in dem Strike."

15 Mike Buhay [Montreal], "Klasn Kamf un Yiddishkayt," *Der Kamf*, August 6, 1926.

16 Max Dolgoy, interview with Mercedes Steedman, 1980s. See Steedman, *Angels of the Workplace*.

17 "Arrest 10 after Riot by Girls on Strike," *Toronto Star*, January 16, 1931.

18 Others of the ten had Jewish names and may also have been Labour League members.

19 Becky Lapedes, interview with her daughter Cheryl Tallan, 1980s.

20 Quoted in *Jewish Life and Times*, ed. Sharon Chisvin, vol. 7, *Women's Voices: Personal Recollections* (Winnipeg: Jewish Historical Society of Western Canada, 1998), 27.

21 Steedman, *Angels of the Workplace,* 131.

22 Roz Usiskin, "Winnipeg's Jewish Women," in *Jewish Radicalism in Winnipeg, 1906–1860*, ed. Daniel Stone (Winnipeg: Jewish Heritage Society of Western Manitoba, 2003), 118. See

also Jodi Giesbrecht, "Accommodating Resistance: Unionization, Gender, and Ethnicity in Winnipeg's Garment Industry, 1929–1945, *Urban History Review* 39, no. 1 (2010): 5–19.

23 L. Vasil, "Freda Coodin—a korbn fun klas kamf, [a victim of class struggle]," *Der Kamf*, April 16, 1935, 3. Vasil is a pseudonym for Guberman (personal communication with Perry Coodin, Freda's nephew).

24 L. Vasil, "Freda Coodin—a korbn fun klas kamf."

25 Details of the trial are in the Strike and Lockouts files of Canada. "Girl Striker Gets 6 Months on 9 Charges," *Winnipeg Tribune*, January 12, 1934; "Woman Strike Agitator Goes to Jail," *Winnipeg Free Press*, January 11, 1934; "Crown Evidence Ends in Strike Riot Case," *Winnipeg Free Press*, January 11, 1934. Perry Coodin, a cousin, said that Mottl's children told him that Hurtig had threatened the family with a lawsuit.

26 Fanny Levine, Eva Newmark, and Jean Sable, CBC interview, June 24, 1979. The minimum wage established in 1938 by the Fair Labor Standards Act was $2.50 an hour, or $11 for a 44-hour week. www.dol.gov. This was in the period of Roosevelt's New Deal. It doesn't seem that there was a minimum wage in Canada at the time (there was a minimum wage for women, but it was very low). Bennett finally began to introduce some measures in 1935. See Government of Canada, Labour Program, *Minimum Wage Database Introduction*, srv116.services.gc.ca.

27 Evelyn Dumas, *The Bitter Thirties in Quebec* (Montreal: Black Rose Books, 1975), 48–49.

28 Andrée Lévesque, *Red Travellers: Jeanne Corbin and her Comrades* (Montreal: McGill Queen's University Press, 1996), 146.

29 Rose Shanoff, interview with Mercedes Steedman, 1980s.

30 Sol Shek, "Der Labour league in tsifern" (The Labour league in numbers), *10th Anniversary Book of the Labour League* (Toronto: Labour League, 1936).

31 Ester Reiter, "My Neighbour, Red Lil the 'Rabble Rouser' and the Sixtieth Anniversary of the On to Ottawa Trek," *Outlook Magazine*, May 1995. Stephen Endicott indicates that Moscow opposed the formation of a National Unemployed Workers' Association as part of the Workers' Unity League. Leading communists such as Sam Carr, Tom Ewen, and Tim Buck were furious. They carried on their activities under a new name, the Relief Camp Workers Association. Endicott, *Raising the Workers' Flag: The Workers' Unity League of Canada, 1930–1936* (Toronto: University of Toronto Press, 2012), 274.

32 Izzy and Helen Fine, interview with Michelle Cohen, Naivelt, June 2004.

33 Sid Dolgoy, interview with the author, November 2007.

34 Ruth Frager, *Sweatshop Strife* (Toronto: University of Toronto Press, 1992), 39.

35 Frager, *Sweatshop Strife*, 209.

36 Mercedes Steedman, "The Promise: Communist Organizing in the Needle Trades, the Dressmakers' Campaign, 1928–1937," *Labour/Le Travail* 34 (Fall 1994): 37–73; Giesbrecht, "Accommodating Resistance."

37 I. Strashuner, "Der veg fun Labour League" (The path of the labour league), *10 Years Labour League Souvenir Book* (Toronto, 1936), unpaged.

38 Gerald Tulchinsky, *Branching Out* (Toronto: Stoddart, 1998), 176–99.

39 Hugh Garner, *Cabbagetown*, 2nd ed. (Toronto, McGraw Hill, 1968), 201 ff.

40 Rose Betcherman, *The Swastika and the Maple Leaf: Fascist Movements in Canada in the Thirties* (Pickering, Ontario: Fitzhenry & Whiteside, 1978), 79.

41 www.historyofrights.com, reconfigured as HistoryOfRights.ca in February 2015.

42 Celia Ceborer, interview with Frances Patai, n.d.

43 Freddy Rotter told me this story about her dad, Julian Rotter, who was a lovely man in every way. Personal communication, October 2013.

44 *Globe and Mail*, May 2, 1935, 1.

45 *Time*, April 17, 1933.

46 H. M. Caiserman, "Pampered Children Disdain their Parents: A Challenge to the Community," *Canadian Jewish Chronicle*, September 28, 1934. Quoted in David Rome, *Clouds in the Thirties: On Anti Semitism in Canada, 1929–39* (Montreal: National Archives; Canadian Jewish Congress, 1978), 7, 14.

47 Caiserman, "Pampered Children Disdain their Parents."

48 Rome, *Clouds in the Thirties*, 12.

49 Rome, *Clouds in the Thirties*, 17.

50 This is a complex and controversial story. I am providing the position that makes the most sense to me, one presented by Paul Preston in *The Spanish Civil War*, revised and expanded edition (New York: Norton, 2006). He synthesizes many different points of view in his analysis.

51 Albert Prago, *Jewish Currents,* February 1977, 6.

52 This was in addition to their support for Fred Rose's candidacy for parliament, the shules, the *Clarion, Der Kamf*, building a children's camp in the Laurentians, and lectures on various subjects (given by men).

53 "Jim" (Myrtle Eugenia) Watts was the Communist Party reporter in Spain and also had a radio program reporting from Spain. Less is known about Florence Pike. It seems she went to Spain after hearing Norman Bethune speak. She left three children with relatives in Canada and when Frederika Martin, the head nurse and archivist of the medical brigade contacted one daughter years later, she had no idea why her mother had gone to Spain or even which side she had been supporting.

54 Her correspondence is housed at the Tamiment Library in New York City. Unfortunately, she died before completing the history of the medical brigades.

55 Peter Carroll, interview with Esther Silverstein (Blanc), 1991.

56 Peter Carroll and James Fernandez, *Facing Fascism in New York* (New York: Museum of City of New York; NYU Press, 2007), 44, 50.

57 M. Muni, "Hilf far Shpanye af der Yiddisher Gas" (Help for Spain on the Jewish Street), *Der Kamf*, May 7, 1937, 4.

58 See, for example, Becky Ewen, "Women Tireless Helping Canuck Boys in Spain," *Clarion*, July 24, 1938, 3. She says, "One of the most outstanding and inspiring factors in the help that has been given for the boys in Spain, has been that afforded by hundreds of women throughout Canada."

59 *Der Kamf*, October 23, 1936, 1.

60 Henry Beattie, quoted in "Cigarettes for Boys in Spain," *Clarion*, July 9, 1937, 1. He went on to say, "I've not yet met an American or Canadian who could smoke those Spanish cigarettes. We thought they were terrible but we treasured a Canadian or American cigarette. When anyone was lucky to get one, he would take one puff then pass it around to his buddies."

61 Girls' Brigade Assists Spain," *Clarion*, March 25, 1938, 4.

62 Victor Hoar and Mac Reynolds, *The Mackenzie-Papineau Battalion* (Toronto: Copp Clark, 1969), 252.

63 Ruth I. Davidow, quoted in *Into the Fire: American Women in the Spanish Civil War*, directed by Julia Newman (USA: First Run Features, 2002).

64 *Lebns farn Lebn* (Lives for Life), (New York: Bronx mittlshul of the International Workers Order, 1939).

65 *Lebns farn Lebn*, 16.

66 *Lebns farn Lebn*, 16.

67 Preston, *The Spanish Civil War*, 109.

68 "Yiddishe froyen organizirn far Kanader frayvilike in Shpanie " (Jewish women organize help for Canadian volunteers in Spain) (A letter from Winnipeg), *Der Kamf*, August 6, 1937, 4.

69 Harry Prize (Hamilton), "Unzer Hilf far Shapnia" (Our help for Spain), *Der Kamf*, September 3, 1937, 3.

70 Jean Watts, "Two Canadians Visit a Colony: Canada's Adopted Children," *Clarion*, March 5, 1938, 2.

71 Malcolm Ross (Executive Secretary, Canadian Committee to Aid Spanish Democracy), "Tzu Hilf di Spanisher Kemfer" (To Help the Spanish Fighters), *Der Kamf*, July 15, 1938, 7.

72 Malcolm Ross, "Tzu Hilf di Spanisher Kemfer."

73 "Veteranen fun Shpanie ba groysn Carnival in Kemp Naivelt" (Veterans of Spain at a big Carnival at Camp Naivelt), *Der Kamf*, August 26, 1938, 1.

74 Michael Petrou, *Renegades: Canadians in the Spanish Civil War* (Toronto: UBC Press, 2008), 181.

75 Sam Lipshitz interview with Ruth Borchiver, Toronto, 1980s. Ruth generously gave me her handwritten transcriptions of interviews she did for her PhD dissertation, "A Social-psychological Analysis of Millennial Thought in the Communist Party of Canada: 1921–1957 (PhD diss., University of Toronto, 1991).

76 Samuel Lipshitz, "A Great American Gathering Greets Jewish Delegates from Russia," *Canadian Jewish Review*, July 6, 1943, 7. Note that the translation from the Yiddish is literally Lifshitz, but the family uses the name Lipshitz. Sholem Aleichem is probably the most well known of all the Yiddish writers (see chapter 4). His son-in-law B. Z. Goldberg was editor of the Yiddish newspaper *Der Tog* (the day).

77 Lipshitz, "A Great American Gathering Greets Jewish Delegates from Russia," 7.

78 In his short life, Izzy (Israel) Kharik (1898–1937) was a significant and powerful Yiddish writer, a poet whose work engaged aesthetic movements as varied as expressionism and socialist realism and who, despite his position of power as a celebrated poet, member of the prestigious Belorussian Academy of Science, and editor of the Minsk literary journal, expressed ambivalence about the consequences of the Bolshevik Revolution. Kharik was at the peak of his career in June 1937 when he was arrested and later killed as part of the Great Purges. From David Shneer, Yivoencyclopedia, www.yivoencyclopedia.org.

79 "Sholem Shtern, Der bazukh fun Sholem Asch, Shloime Mikhoels and Itzik Feffer in Montreal" (The meeting of Sholem Asch, Shloime Mikhoels and Itzik Feffer in Montreal), *Shrayber vos ikh hob gekent: memuarn un essayn* (Writers I have known: memoirs and essays) (Montreal, Adler Printing, 1982), 73–74.

80 Isroel Tsinberg was another of the Soviet Jewish literati murdered by Stalin.

81 Sholem Asch was a celebrated Yiddish writer well known in Europe as well as North America. He was one of the participants in the Czernowitz Yiddish language conference. Born in Poland, he moved to the United States in 1910 where he became a citizen. Asch accompanied Mikhoels and Feffer on their visit to North America for the Jewish Anti Fascist League.

82 Ben Lappin, "When Mikhoels and Feffer Came to Toronto," *Viewpoints* 2 (1972): 43–63.

83 Lappin, "When Mikhoels and Feffer Came to Toronto," 46.

84 Lappin, "When Mikhoels and Feffer Came to Toronto," 52.

85 Lappin, "When Mikhoels and Feffer Came to Toronto," 52.

86 Brenda recalls: "There was just one Jewish woman with two children on the boat. Her husband was in Toronto and owned a butcher shop. She was coming to him. That was the only Jewish immigrant. She was one and I was the other. On the boat, the others were all farmers from Czechoslovakia or from Ukraine. People that either bought farms or worked on the farms. They were the only immigrants who could come these days. No Jews." Brenda Fishauf, interview with the author, in Yiddish, Toronto, July 2004.

87 Brenda Fishauf, interview with the author, 2004.

88 Anna Reid, *Leningrad, Tragedy of a City Under Siege* (New York: Bloomsbury, 2011), reviewed in the *Observer*, September 25, 2011.

89 Dos goldene bukh [the golden book] is in the Archives of the Jews of Western Canada, located in Winnipeg. It was donated by Lissa Donner, the granddaughter of Fred Donner, an activist and a founder of the UJPO in Winnipeg.

90 Sam Lipshitz, interview with Ruth Biderman, 1980s.

91 Sylwia Szymanska translated these letters when she was assisting May and Gerry Cohen in organizing their father's archives donated to York University.

92 H. M. Caiserman, "Report from Poland."

93 Voyewodisher Yiddiesher Commitet, January 6, 1946, Milenczkego 10, Kattowitz ZA 1945, Canadian Jewish Congress Archives.

94 Voyewodisher Yiddiesher Commitet, January 6, 1946.

95 See for example, Caiserman's "Report from Poland."

5 *Arbeter Froyen Vakht Oyf* (Working Women Awake!)

1 Itche Goldberg, interview with author; Sam Kagan, interview with Karen Levine, 1970s, Multicultural History Society of Ontario; and the Memoirs of Manye Lipshitz, *Bletlekh fun a Shturmisher Tsayt* (Time Remembered), trans. Max Rosenfeld and Marcia Usiskin (Toronto: Sam Lipshitz; Diversified Publicity Bureau; Lupus Publications, 1977).

2 Alexandra Kollontai, "Communism and the Family," first published in *Komunistka* 2 (1920), and in English in *Selected Writings of Alexandra Kollontai*, trans. Alix Holt (London: Allison & Busby, 1977).

3 Manye Shur, Secretary, Exeketiva fun Yiddish Arbeter Froyen Fareyn, "5 yor Yiddishe Arbeter Froyen Fareyn" (Five years of the Jewish Women's Working League), *Der Kamf*, February 24, 1928, 5. Joan Sangster in *Dreams of Equality* discusses the Women's Labour Leagues and the role of Florence Custance, the Director of Women's Issues for the Communist Party. It is interesting that while Becky Buhay published articles regularly in

Der Kamf, there is no mention of Custance in any of the articles I read in *Der Kamf,* nor does there seem to be any formal affiliation with other Leagues or direction from above. The women organized May Day celebrations with Women's Labour Leagues from other ethnic organizations. The CP may have approved of these women's activities, but they were clearly not directing them, at least not for the Jewish women, who were supporting the shules, the camps, and the choirs. The left Jewish women seem similar to the Ukrainian women, whose ties were with their ethnic organization, the ULFTA, rather than with the CP.

4   Mary McCune, "Creating a Place for Women in a Socialist Brotherhood: Class and Gender Politics in the Workmen's Circle, 1892–1930," *Feminist Studies* 28, no. 3 (Fall 2002): 585–610.

5   Wendy Z. Goldman, "Industrial Politics, Peasant Rebellion and the Death of the Proletarian Women's Movement in the USSR," *Slavic Review* 55, no. 1 (Spring 1996): 46–77.

6   Richard Stites, *The Women's Liberation Movement in Russia: Feminism, Nihilism, and Bolshevism, 1860–1930* (New Jersey: Princeton University Press, 1990).

7   Kollontai spent four and a half months touring the United States where she attempted to find a US publisher for her English translation of Lenin's pamphlet "Socialism and War." She attended a memorial rally for Joe Hill in Seattle and spoke from the same platform as Eugene Debs in Chicago. In all, she spoke at 123 meetings in four languages.

8   This is the name of a well-known book by Christopher Lasch written in the 1970s, *Haven in a Heartless World: The Family Besieged* (New York: Basic Books, 1977). The haven, in Lasch's history of the family, is created by women for their men.

9   Rokhl (Rachel) Holtman, Di Arbeter Froy (The Woman Worker), "Di Heym un Kooperativa Virtshaft" (The home and cooperative household economy), *Der Kamf,* March 12, 1926, 4.

10 Holtman, "Di Heym un Kooperativa Virtshaft."

11 Rachel Watson, "Di Froy in di Kapitalistisher lender un in Sovyetn Farband" (The Woman in the Capitalist lands and in the Soviet union), Di Arbeter Froy, *Der Kamf,* May 14, 1926, 4.

12 Watson, "Di Froy in di Kapitalistisher lender un in Sovyetn Farband," 4.

13 Watson, "Di Froy in di Kapitalistisher lender un in Sovyetn Farband," 4.

14 Watson, "Di Froy in di Kapitalistisher lender un in Sovyetn Farband," 4.

15 See for example Meg Luxton, *More than a Labour of Love: Three Generations of Women's Work in the Home* (Toronto: Women's Press, 1980); S. Bonnie Fox, ed., *Hidden in the Household: Women's Domestic Labour Under Capitalism* (Toronto: Women's Press, 1980); and Roberta Hamilton and Michele Barrett, *The Politics of Diversity: Feminism, Marxism, Nationalism* (Montreal: Book Center, 1987).

16 Fox, *Hidden in the Household;* Hamilton and Barrett, *The Politics of Diversity.*

17 Watson, "Di Froy in di Kapitalistisher lender un in Sovyetn Farband," 4.

18 Watson, "Di Froy in di Kapitalistisher lender un in Sovyetn Farband," 4.

19 The promise that technology would lighten women's burden has never been fulfilled. These potentially labour-saving devices have been transformed into a consumption opportunity through the demand for one in every household, along with higher standards of cleanliness. See Susan Strasser, *Never Done: A History of American Housework* (New York: Pantheon Books, 1982); Ruth Cowan, *More Work for Mother: The Ironies of Household*

Technology from the Open Hearth to the Microwave (New York: Basic Books, 1983); and Stuart Ewen, *Captains of Consciousness: Advertising and the Social Roots of the Consumer Culture* (New York: McGraw Hill, 1976).

20 See McCune, "Creating a Place for Women in a Socialist Brotherhood." McCune references three articles by Holtman in *Der Fraynd* from 1922 and 1923: "Di Froy un der industri" (The woman and industry), March 14, 1923, 17–18; "Di antshtelung fun der moderner froyen-bavegung" (The rise of the modern women's movement), August 14, 1923, 20–21; and "Froye clubn in Amerike" (Women's clubs in America), November 13, 1922, 21–23.

21 F. Frumes, "Vilde shtik: unzer sivilizatsiye un di froyen" (Wild events: our civilization and the women), Di Arbeter Froy, *Der Kamf*, April 2, 1926, 4.

22 Frumes, "Vilde shtik: unzer sivilizatsiye un di froyen," 4.

23 See, for example, Ruth Frager and Carmela Patrias, *Discounted Labour: Women Workers in Canada, 1870–1939* (Toronto: University of Toronto Press, 2005).

24 Rachel Watson, "Darfn Arbeter Froyen nutzn kinstleche sheynkayt-mitlen?" (Do Working women need to use artificial beauty products?), *Der Kamf*, May 28, 1926, 4.

25 Sam Kagan, interview with Karen Levine.

26 Bess Schockett, interview with author, July 17, 2006.

27 Bess Schockett, interview with author, July 17, 2006.

28 There is a debate about how to characterize these movements. Sylvia Paletschek would call them "women's emancipation movements," while Karen Offen would use the term "feminist" to characterize political movements that challenge male hegemony. See Sylvia Paletschek and Bianka Pietrow-Ennker, eds., *Women's Emancipation Movements in the Nineteenth Century: A European Perspective* (Stanford: Stanford University Press, 2004).

29 Jennifer Guglielmo, "Transnational Feminism's Radical Past: Lessons from Italian Immigrant Women Anarchists in Industrializing America," *Journal of Women's History* 22, no. 1 (Spring 2010): 10.

30 Kate Weigand, *Red Feminism: American Communism and the Making of Women's Liberation* (Baltimore: Johns Hopkins Press, 2001). Although Weigand's history is based on the US and is limited to Communist Party members, in the Jewish left, as noted earlier, the boundary between Canada and the United States was very permeable and the American women's Canadian counterparts were also engaged in radical challenges in an earlier period.

31 See the excellent thesis by Nancy Butler, "Mother Russia and the Socialist Fatherland: Women in the Communist Party, 1932–1941," with special reference to the activism of Dorothy Livesay and Jim Watts (PhD diss., Queens University, Kingston, 2010).

32 B. Schachter, "Di arbeter froy vert aktiv" (The women workers become active), *Der Kamf*, December 28, 1928.

33 Schachter, "Di arbeter froy vert aktiv."

34 These were Mary McCune's findings in "Creating a Place for Women in a Socialist Brotherhood." The left women celebrated their activities and prided themselves on their separateness. There is no indication that they wanted to be integrated with the men.

35 Becky Lapedes, interview with her daughter, Cheryl Tallan, Toronto, 1984.

36 Too often, the movement is referred to (and dismissed) as the Jewish communist movement, ignoring the distinction between those who were actually Communist Party members and those who embraced communist ideals. Paul Buhle articulates this well in "Jews and American Communism: The Cultural Question," *Radical History Review* 23 (Spring 1980): 9–33.

37 Florence Custance was on the first Central Committee of the Communist Party and was elected Secretary of the Women's Bureau. After Tim Buck gained the upper hand, Custance was removed from the National Executive Committee in 1929 and died shortly after. www.socialisthistory.ca.

38 Becky Buhay and Annie Buller started the Labour College in Montreal after attending the Rand School in New York. Andrée Lévesque, *Red Travellers: Jeanne Corbin and Her Comrades* (Montreal: McGill-Queen's, 1996).

39 Although her brother, Mike Buhay, was the first editor of *Der Kamf* in 1924, it is not clear whether Becky wrote in Yiddish, or whether the articles under her name were translated. She and her brother were born in England.

40 See Mariana Valverde, *The Age of Light, Soap, and Water: Moral Reform in English Canada, 1885–1925* (Toronto: University of Toronto Press, 1991).

41 Rebecca Buhay, "Di Laydn fun der froy unter Kapitalism" (The suffering of the woman under capitalism), *Der Kamf*, December 1924, 18.

42 Buhay, "Di Laydn fun der froy unter Kapitalism."

43 Alice Kessler Harris discusses attitudes toward women workers and the question of protective legislation for women in her essay "Where are the Organized Women Workers?" in *Gendering Labor History* (Urbana: University of Illinois, 2007).

44 Becky Buhay, "Vos darf zayn di foderungen fun der arbeter froy?" (What should be the demands of the working woman?), Mit Der Arbeter Froy (With the working woman), *Der Kamf*, September 1925, 14–16.

45 *Der Kamf*, February 11, 1927.

46 Executive of the Toronto Yiddishe Arbeter Froyen Fareyn, "Groysn degraykhungen fun Toronto Yiddishn Arbetn Froyen Fareyn." (Important accomplishments of the Toronto Jewish Working Women's League), Di Arbeter Froy, *Der Kamf*, February 11, 1927.

47 B. Berkowitz, "De fayerung fun dem froyen tog in Montreal" (The Celebration of Women's Day in Montreal), *Der Kamf*, March 21, 1930, 3.

48 Berkowitz, "De fayerung fun dem froyen tog in Montreal," 3.

49 *Der Kamf*, February 24, 1928, 5.

50 *Der Kamf*, February 24, 1928, 5.

51 "A krivde fun an arbeter-froy" (A grievance from a woman worker), *Der Kamf*, June 11, 1926, 4.

52 *Der Kamf*, February 1927.

53 Becky Lapedes, interview with her daughter Cheryl Tallan, Toronto, 1984.

54 Executive of the Toronto Yiddishe Arbeter Froyen Fareyn, "Groysn degraykhungen fun Toronto Yiddishn Arbetn Froyen Fareyn."

55 Becky Lapedes, interview with her daughter Cheryl Tallan, Toronto, 1984.

56 Becky Lapedes, interview with her daughter Cheryl Tallan, Toronto, 1984.

57 Becky Lapedes, interview with her daughter Cheryl Tallan, Toronto, 1984.

58 Becky is no doubt referring to the internal struggles in the Canadian Communist Party, where Maurice Spector was ousted because he took Trotsky's position on questions of how to build socialism.

59 Becky Lapedes, interview with her daughter Cheryl Tallan, Toronto, 1984.

60 Ella May Wiggins was a union organizer in Gastonia, in the US south, who was killed in 1929 in a strike at a textile mill. She lived in an African American neighbourhood and was organizing African Americans and Whites into the communist-led National Textile Workers Union.

61 Gina Medem was a Polish Jewish journalist. She and her husband Vladmir were Bundists. After the Soviet Revolution she became pro-Soviet. She travelled to Spain during the Spanish Civil War.

62 "Toronto Froyen Branches 3 un 6 fun Labour-League organizirn fleysh strike" (Toronto women's branches 3 and 6 organize a meat strike), *Der Kamf*, March 31, 1933, 10; "Fleysh strike in Toronto geendikt mit a gevins" (Meat strike ends with a victory), *Der Kamf*, April 7, 1933, 1.

63 Manya Lipshitz, "Di froyen muzn farnemen zeyer platz inem algemeynem kamf" (Women must take their place in the united struggle), *Der Kamf*, May 13, 1936, 19.

64 *Der Kamf*, October 31, 1935, 1.

65 Moyshe Katz, "Glaykhe recht far froyen in dem praktic" (Equal rights for women in practice), *Der Kamf*, March 25, 1935, 3.

66 Katz, "Glaykhe recht far froyen in dem praktic," 3.

67 Lindor Reynolds, "Mount Carmel Clinic: An Oasis of Acceptance in a Judgmental World," *Winnipeg Free Press*, May 18, 2013. www.winnipegfreepress.com.

68 Annie Buller, "Di rol fun der froy in der milkhomeh un in der nokh-milkhomeh velt" (The Role of the woman in the War and in the Post-War World), *Der Vochenblat*, March 8, 1945, 5.

69 United Jewish People's Order, *First National Convention Jubilee Book* (Toronto: UJPO, 1945).

70 United Jewish People's Order, *First National Convention Jubilee Book*.

71 Olga Eizner Favreau, conversation with the author, March 2012.

72 Annie Buller, "International Women's Day Highly Significant," "Canadian Jewish Weekly" (English section of *Der Vochenblat*), March 7, 1946.

73 Becky Lapedes, *Di Ordn Froyen Farnemen zeyer platz* (The women of the Order take their place). Booklet for the United Jewish People's Order Second National Convention, June 20–22, 1947, unpaged. Becky is described as an important activist of the Women's Council of the Toronto United Jewish People's Labour League.

74 See Julie Guard's work for an in-depth history of this movement. Guard, "Canadian Citizens or Dangerous Foreign Women? Canada's Radical Consumer Movement, 1947–1950," in *Sisters or Strangers? Immigrant, Ethnic, and Racialized Women in Canadian History*, ed. Marlene Epp, Franca Iacovetta, and Frances Swyripa (Toronto: University of Toronto Press, 2004), 161–89.

75 Guard, "Canadian Citizens or Dangerous Foreign Women?"

76 Becky Buhay, "Vos konen di froyenh ton tsu farzikhern dem fridn?" (What can the women do to secure the freedom?), *Der Kamf*, February 24, 1949.

77 Ruth Frager, *Sweatshop Strife* (Toronto: University of Toronto Press, 1992), 160.

78   Lil Robinson, Shirley Fistell, Bessie Grossman, and Al Soren, interview with author. Videotaped by B. H. Yael, Toronto, 2000.

6 Democracy and Dissent

1   Minutes of a meeting of the National Executive Committee, Sunday, April 29, 1951, at the Royal York Hotel, Toronto, Ontario. Marked Confidential. Canadian Jewish Archives, Montreal.

2   See for example, "The Struggle For Democracy in Canadian Jewish Life," *Outlook* 18, no. 5 (May 1980): 7.

3   Donald Avery, *Dangerous Foreigners: European Immigrant Workers and Labour Radicalism in Canada* (Toronto: McClelland & Stewart, 1979).

4   Gerald Tulchinsky, *Taking Root: The Origins of the Canadian Jewish Community* (Toronto: Stoddart, 1997), 40–95.

5   Tulchinsky, *Taking Root*, 261–75.

6   David Rome, compiler, *On Our Forerunners—At Work. Epilogue: Notes on the Twentieth Century* (Montreal: Canadian Jewish Archives, New Series no. 10, 1978), 188.

7   Rome, *On Our Forerunners*, 188.

8   Gerald Tulchinsky, *Branching Out: The Transformation of the Jewish Community* (Toronto: Stoddart, 1998), 123.

9   W. D. C., "Cosmopolitan Winnipeg: IV. The Hebrew People," Special Section, *Manitoba Morning Free Press*, Saturday, December 28, 1912, 1. This quote is from Henry Trachtenberg, "The Winnipeg Jewish Community and Politics: The Inter-War Years, 1919–1939," *MHS Transactions*, Series 3, no. 35 (1978–79), Manitoba Historical Society. www.mhs.mb.ca.

10   Trachtenberg, "The Winnipeg Jewish Community." Almazov left Winnipeg after 1919, moving to New York, where he wrote for the left newspaper *Der Freiheit*.

11   Trachtenberg, "The Winnipeg Jewish Community."

12   Police Chief Draper ignored Mayor Stuart's warning that there was going to be trouble between Nazi hooligans and the largely Jewish baseball team, called the Harbord Playground. He did nothing. The result was the Christie Pits (then known as Willowvale Park) riot. *Yiddishe Zhurnal*, August 13, 1933. See Cyril H. Levitt and William Shaffir, *The Riot at Christie Pits* (Toronto: Lester & Orpen Dennys, 1987) for a fuller description of the incident.

13   "Police Board Usurp Power Given Council, *Toronto Star*, January 16, 1931, 1–2.

14   Irving Abella, interview with the author, April 2006.

15   Isador Koulack, personal communication with the author, 1964.

16   Roland Penner, *A Glowing Dream, A Memoir* (Winnipeg: Gordon Shillingford, 2007), 34.

17   See Irving Abella and Harold Troper, *None is Too Many* (Toronto: Lester & Orpen Dennys, 1982) and Frank Bialystok, *Delayed Impact: The Holocaust and the Jewish Community* (Montreal: McGill-Queens, 2000) for a critical examination of the Canadian government and the Congress in efforts to save the lives of European Jewry. Amy Katz analyzes the community's insistence on proving its legitimacy and loyalty to Canada. Amy Katz, "Canadian Jewish mythology in mainstream histories" unpublished paper, April 2004.

18 One example of this is the full-page Eaton's ad placed in the program of the Toronto Jewish Folk Choir for its annual concert. See Ester Reiter, "Secular Yiddishkait: Left Politics, Culture and Community," *Labour/Le Travail* 49 (Spring 2002): 121–46.

19 See for example, Bernard Knox, "Premature Anti-fascist," www.english.illinois.edu or John Gerassi, *The Premature Antifascists: North American Volunteers in the Spanish Civil War, 1936–39: An Oral History* (New York: Praeger, 1986).

20 Irving Abella, personal interview with the author, May 2003. Abella indicated that his father, a prominent Labour Zionist, opposed the expulsion. Although Abella's father disagreed with the views of the left, he thought it important for the Congress to be an inclusive body.

21 Reg Whitaker and Gary Marcuse, *Cold War Canada: The Making of a National Insecurity State, 1945–1957* (Toronto: University of Toronto Press, 1994), 71. Of the thirteen people charged with violating the Official Secrets Act, seven were convicted. Fred Rose was found guilty of conspiracy to violate the Official Secrets Act and the Labour Progressive Party. Organizer Sam Carr was sentenced for offences related to procuring a false passport.

22 Whitaker and Marcuse, *Cold War Canada*, 71.

23 Sam Carr, interview with Ruth Borchiver, 1980s.

24 Whitaker and Marcuse, *Cold War Canada*. See also Wikipedia, "Socialism and Social Democracy in Canada," en.wikipedia.org.

25 See for example, David Levy, *Stalin's Man in Canada: Fred Rose and Soviet Espionage* (New York: Enigma Books, 2012). The author's disparagement of his subject is constant. For example, he refers to Rose as "Freddy," a jarring note throughout the book.

26 The Supreme Court Justices on the Royal Commission were Roy Lindsay Kellock and Robert Taschereau, who later participated in the Supreme Court's decision to deny an appeal.

27 See Merrily Weisbord, *The Strangest Dream* (Montreal: Vehicle Press, 1984), in particular chapter 14, "The Fred Rose Case." In addition to her research, the book has the advantage of the author's personal knowledge of key interviewees who knew the case.

28 Weisbord, *The Strangest Dream*, 11.

29 Ruth Borchiver, interview with Sam Carr, 1980s.

30 Victor Huard, "Armageddon Reconsidered: Shifting Attitudes Towards Peace in English Canada, 1936–1953" (PhD diss., Queen's University, 1995).

31 Walter Schneir, *Final Verdict: What Really Happened in the Rosenberg Case* (New York: Melville House, 2010).

32 A. Rosenberg, "Der Ordn in Montreal," *United Jewish People's Order Fourth National Convention Book* (Montreal: UJPO, 1954).

33 Elizabeth Schulte, "The Trial of Ethel and Julius Rosenberg," *International Socialist Review* 29 (May–June 2003). www.isreview.org.

34 "Save the Rosenbergs Conference," *Canadian Tribune*, October 27, 1952.

35 Lucy Dawidowicz, "The Rosenberg Case: Hate America Weapon," *New Leader*, 1951. See also "Anti-Semitism and the Rosenberg Case: The Latest Communist Propaganda Trap," *Commentary Magazine*, 1951, www.commentarymagazine.com.

36 Lucy S. Dawidowicz, "Anti-Semitism and the Rosenberg Case" *Commentary*, July 1952, 41–45; Arnon Gutfeld, "The Rosenberg Case and the Jewish Issue," *Antisemitism Worldwide* 2002/3 (2004): 29–53. www.tau.ac.il.

37 Arnon Gutfeld, "The Rosenberg Case and the Jewish Issue." See also Edward S. Shapiro, "Julius and Ethel Rosenberg," reprinted from Shapiro, *A Time for Healing: American Jewry Since WWII* (Baltimore: John Hopkins University Press, 1992), mobile.myjewishlearning.com. Jewish leftists had also been disproportionately targeted by McCarthy. American Jewish organizations refused (or were afraid) to consider that this had anything to do with their Jewishness. They remained silent when HUAC in 1947 started investigations in Hollywood. The careers of ten prominent Hollywood screenwriters, six of them Jewish, were destroyed when they refused to co-operate with the committee and implicate their friends and acquaintances. They were sent to prison for contempt of Congress in 1950 and were blacklisted for years afterwards. The AJC denounced those who resorted to the Fifth Amendment, deeming them unpatriotic. They feared such challenges would provoke a wave of anti-Semitism.

38 See Gary Kinsman, Dieter K. Buse, and Mercedes Steeman, eds., *Whose National Security?: Canadian State Surveillance and the Creation of Enemies* (Toronto: Between the Lines, 2000).

39 Whitaker and Marcuse, *Cold War Canada*, 301–3.

40 Bess Schockett, interview with the author, July 2006.

41 "The Truth Cannot Be Padlocked," *Montreal Gazette*, January 28, 1950, 1, file 107, box 11, ZA 1950, CJC Archives.

42 *Saturday Night*, February 7, 1950. See also February 21, 1950 editorials, file 107, box 11, ZA 1950, CJC Archives.

43 *Civil Liberties Bulletin* 3 and 4, February and March 1950; *Canadian Tribune*, February 13, 1950, file 107, box 11, ZA 1950, CJC Archives.

44 Letter from Mrs. Sahila M Bordo, President, Jewish Junior Welfare League to Saul Hayes, Executive Director, CJC, February 8, 1950, file 107, box 11, ZA 1950, CJC Archives.

45 Letter from Saul Hayes, National Executive Director, CJC to Mrs. Saila M Bordo, President, Jewish Junior Welfare League, March 2, 1950, file 107, box 11, ZA 1950, CJC Archives.

46 Letter from H. Frank, Executive Director, CJC Western Division to Saul Hayes, February 22, 1950, file 107, box 11, ZA 1950, CJC Archives.

47 Letter from H. Frank, Executive Director, CJC Western Division to Saul Hayes, February 22, 1950.

48 *Jewish Post*, February 9, 1950, 2, file 107, box 11, ZA 1950, CJC Archives.

49 Letter from Morris Biderman, Secretary, National Executive Board, United Jewish Peoples Order, addressed to all members of the Dominion Council of Canadian Jewish Congress. n.d., but circulated between March 15 and April 20, 1950, file 10, box 11, ZA 1950, CJC Archives.

50 Tulchinsky, *Branching Out*, 275.

51 See Grant Purves, "War Criminals: The Deschenes Commission." Prepared for the Library of Parliament. www.parl.gc.ca.

52 See Tulchinsky, *Branching Out*, 324–26.

53 "United Jewry Will Fight Rearmament of Germany Despite Congress Diktat," *Canadian Tribune*, June 18, 1951.

54 "United Jewry Will Fight Rearmament of Germany Despite Congress Diktat."

55 See Whitaker and Marcuse, 397–401. They refer to "the monstrous effects on Korean civilians of the methods of warfare adopted by the United Nations—the blanket

fire-bombing of North Korean cities, the destruction of dams and the resultant devastation of the food supply, an unremitting aerial bombardment more intensive than anything experienced during the Second World War" (391). See also www.globalresearch.ca/the-korean-atrocity-forgotten-us-war-crimes-and-crimes-against-humanity/.

56 Statement of the National Executive Committee of the United Jewish Peoples Order to the Jewish People in Canada. Virtually all UJPO members understand this to be the reason for the later expulsion. Personal communication, David Abramowitz, National President, UJPO; Ben Shek, National Secretary, UJPO. See also "The Struggle for Democracy in Canadian Jewish Life," reprinted in *Canadian Jewish Outlook* 18, no. 5 (May 1980): 7; Albert Abramowitz, "UJPO: Our Genesis in Toronto 1926–86," in *UJPO 60th Anniversary Book* (Toronto: UJPO, 1986), 2; Maurice Zeilig, "UJPO: Our Winnipeg History," in *UJPO 60th Anniversary Book*.

57 Estimates of the number of signers vary. David Adams, *The American Peace Movements* (New Haven: Advocate Press, 1985); "Stockholm Peace Appeal Writes of 500 Million Signers," 12. en.wikipedia.org. The International Association of Democratic Lawyers' "Declaration of the International Conference to Celebrate the 60th Anniversary of the Stockholm Appeal: 1950–2010" declares that hundreds of millions of people signed the appeal. Signatories included Jorge Amado, Louis Aragon, Pierre Benoit, Marcel Carné, Marc Chagall, Maurice Chevalier, Jacques Chirac, Frank Marshall Davis, Duke Ellington, James Gareth Endicott, Ilya Ehrenburg, Lionel Jospin, Robert Lamoureux, Thomas Mann, Yves Montand, Pablo Neruda, Noël-Noël, Gérard Philipe, Pablo Picasso, Jacques Prévert, Pierre Renoir, Armand Salacrou, Dmitri Shostakovich, Simone Signoret, Michel Simon, and Henri Wallon.

58 *Shalom Aleichem: Peace—It's in Your Hands* (Toronto: Canadian Peace Congress Jewish Committee, 1950). Kenney Collection, Thomas Fisher Rare Book Library, University of Toronto.

59 *Shalom Aleichem: Peace—It's in Your Hands.*

60 Memo from the Anti Defamation League of B'Nai Brith, August 30, 1950; Jewish Telegraphic Agency, "American Jewish Organizations Denounce Procommunist Stockholm Peace Appeal," August 21, 1950.

61 September 1950 statement, file 61, box 6, ZA1951, CJC Archives.

62 Stephen Endicott, *James G. Endicott: Rebel Out of China* (Toronto: University of Toronto Press, 1980), 267.

63 Stephen Endicott, conversation with the author, Toronto, November 25, 2012.

64 Confidential memo, no 967, from Saul Hayes to the National Executive, September 25, 1950, file 61, box 6, ZA1951, CJC Archives.

65 Confidential Minutes of a Meeting of the National Executive Committee, April 29, 1951 at the Royal York Hotel, Toronto, Ontario, file 61, box 6, ZA1951, CJC Archives.

66 Confidential Minutes of a Meeting of the National Executive Committee, April 29, 1951.

67 Morris Biderman, *A Life on the Jewish Left: An Immigrant's Experience* (Toronto: Onward Publishing, 2000).

68 Confidential Minutes of a Meeting of the National Executive Committee, April 29, 1951.

69 Memo dated May 23, 1951 for the Eastern Region, and June 13, 1951, for the Central Region, file 61, box 6, ZA1951, CJC Archives.

70 Michael Benazon, interview with the author, April 2004, Montreal.

71 Letter from Saul Hayes to H. Frank, May 10, 1951, file 61, box 6, ZA1951, CJC Archives.

72 Letter from H. Frank to Saul Hayes, May 14, 1951, file 61, box 6, ZA1951, CJC Archives.

73 Selchen's abstention is particularly noteworthy because in an editorial, he supported Congress' opposition to the Stockholm petition. *Dos Yiddishe Vort* (The Israelite Press), n.d.

74 "Preserve Democracy and Freedom in Jewish Life: Do Not Permit the Exclusion of a Part of Congress." Flyer for meeting to be held June 19, 1951, file 61, box 6, ZA1951, CJC Archives.

75 Letter from Frank to Hayes, June 25, 1951. Also *Jewish Post*, June 28, 1951, 1, file 61, box 6, ZA1951, CJC Archives.

76 *Jewish Post,* April 5, 1951, 2, file 61, box 6, ZA1951, CJC Archives.

77 *Jewish Post,* April 5, 1951, 2.

78 Letter from Saul Lipshitz to Saul Hayes, June 29, 1951, file 61, box 6, ZA1951, CJC Archives.

79 Biderman, *A Life on the Jewish Left*. Biderman left the UJPO in 1958.

80 In "The Canadian Jewish Polity," Harold Waller describes Bronfman as "the best Canadian example of behind the scenes power" in the Jewish Community. Waller, in *The Jews in Canada*, ed. Robert J. Brym, William Shaffir, and Morton Weinfeld (Toronto: Oxford University Press, 1993), 259.

81 B. Z. Goldberg, "The Events of the Day," *Der Tog*, May 16, 1952. Translated by the author.

82 Letters from Sam Lipshitz to Sam Bronfman and Saul Hayes, both dated October 18, 1951. Reply from Hayes to Bronfman, October 21, 1951, file 61, box 6, ZA1951, CJC Archives.

83 Allan Kent and Clem Shields, *The Telegram*. The nine articles were reprinted in a pamphlet published in 1951. Kenny Collection, Thomas Fisher Rare Book Library.

84 Michelle Cohen, interview with Mary Winer at Camp Naivelt, July 1994.

85 G. A. Cohen, *If You're an Egalitarian, How Come You're So Rich?* (Boston: Harvard University Press, 2000).

86 *The Israelite Press,* March 28, 1950.

87 *The Israelite Press*, April 3, 1953.

88 *The Israelite Press*, April 3, 1953.

89 Roz Usiskin reported that the account of the second memorial appeared on page one of the *Israelite Press* later that month.

90 www.dcd.ca/exhibitions/limadent/newdancepop/tourtwo11.html.

91 Personal communication with Olga Eisner, April 2012.

92 Charles Law, "A Signpost to Jewish Youth," United Peoples' Order Fourth National Convention, May 1954.

93 Charles Law, "A Signpost to Jewish Youth."

94 A. Rosenberg, "Der Ordn in Montreal."

7 Language and the Education of a New Generation

1 A shul is a synagogue or place of worship. Shule is the Yiddish word for a secular Yiddish school.

2 See Benny Mar, "A Hell Whose Name is School," *Ha'aretz*, February 5, 2010. Here is the description from a review of Maimon's autobiography, *The Heder*: "The school," writes Maimon, "is usually a small hut filled with smoke, in which some of the pupils sit on benches, and some on the ground. The rabbi sits on the table wearing a filthy shirt.... The 'helpers,'

each in his corner, drill the pupils in their studies, bullying them like little despots, not unlike the *melamed* [teacher] himself." Maimon draws the reader's attention to the curses of the heder's instructional methods: haphazard and unsystematic teaching of the Torah and Hebrew grammar; jumbled teaching of the common parlance, Yiddish; reliance on "all sorts of hard-to-understand commentaries"; teaching by the "pilpul method," which "is completely contrary to systematic and purposeful study," and more. In sum, writes Maimon, "Since the children are sentenced to suffer at the early stage of their childhood in a hell that is called school, it is easy to understand the joy and cheerfulness with which they anticipate their salvation from it."

3   Chava Rosenfarb, *Bociany* (Israel: I. L. Peretz Press, 1983), 112 ff. [Yiddish].

4   Chassidism arose in the eighteenth century as a movement against a legalist practice of Judaism, a class-based revolt against the scholarly elite. It attempted to emphasize spirituality and honour the unlettered common folk rather than scholars who could devote themselves entirely to study. That is why Peretz talks about "toyre or torah for everybody." The Torah is the five books of the Hebrew bible.

5   Speech at the 1908 Czernowitz Conference. czernowitz.org/peretz.html.

6   Dovid Katz, *Words on Fire: The Unfinished Story of Yiddish* (New York: Basic Books, 2004), 240.

7   It is important to keep in mind that Ultra Orthodox Jews retained Yiddish as their language and still do. However, they were not allowed to read secular Yiddish writers. It was considered "treyf"—not kosher.

8   Katz, *Words on Fire*, 240.

9   In the early years, most of the labour Zionists were socialists of some sort. There were also differences in orientation between left and right. Some of the left Zionists, such as Emmanuel Ringelblum, historian and archivist of the Warsaw Ghetto, were pro-communist. Zionism in this period meant support for the establishment of a Jewish state in Palestine or the land of Israel. Views on the form that state should take varied enormously.

10 H. Noweck, "Battles for the Secular Yiddish School" in the Dr. Chaim Zhitlowksy Jubilee Book on his seventieth birthday. David Rome, compiler, *The Education Lesson of the Migration,* Canadian Jewish Archives, n.s. 45 (Montreal: Canadian Jewish Congress, 1991), 44–47. Chaim Zhitlovsky (1865–1943) was born in Vitebsk in Eastern Europe and went to the United States before World War I. A revolutionary socialist and a nationalist, Zhitlowsky was a central figure in the progressive Russian and American Jewish intelligentsia and a leading theoretician of secular Jewish culture and thought. Zhitlowsky took part in the 1908 Czernowitz conference on Yiddish.

11 Rome, *The Education Lesson of the Migration*, 66.

12 Saul L. Goodman, "Khaim Zhitlowsky and Simon Dubnow: Architects of American Jewish Secularism," *Humanistic Judaism* 17, no. 1 (Winter 1989), 27–33.

13 Leybl Basman, *25 Years of Progressive Jewish Education* (Winnipeg: Sholem Aleichem Shule, 1946), 5–12. Translated from the Yiddish by the author. A kheder is a religious school for little boys. Some go on to the Yeshiva for advanced religious study.

14 A. Glantz, "Natsionale Radikaler Shules" (National Radical Schools), *Der Keneder Yid* (The Israelite Press), February 12, 1914, 1.

15 Rome, *The Education Lesson of the Migration*.

16 Naomi Prawer Kadar, "Fun di kinders veg (From the children's way), Yiddish Periodicals for American Children" (PhD diss., Columbia University, 2007), 98.

17 I. Gurevitch, "Jewish Youth and Education," *Dos Yiddishe Vort* (The Israelite Press), July 25, 1952. Quoted in Harvey Herstein, *The Growth of the Winnipeg Jewish Community and the Evolution of its Educational Institutions* (master's thesis, University of Manitoba, 1964), 98.

18 Louis Rosenberg, *Canada's Jews: A Social and Economic Study of Jews in Canada in the 1930s* (Montreal: McGill-Queen's Press, 1993) [originally published in 1939]. This is the only comprehensive study of its kind in the period I am researching.

19 Rosenberg, *Canada's Jews*, 174.

20 Rebecca Margolis's book *Jewish Roots, Canadian Soil* (Montreal: McGill-Queens, 2011) does not mention the Winchevsky shule in Montreal in her chapter on Montreal's secular Jewish schools. The left shules are discussed in Fradle Pomerantyz Freidenreich, *Passionate Pioneers* (Teaneck, New Jersey: Holmes & Meter, 2010).

21 Saul Shek, "The Labor League in Numbers," *10 Years Labour League* (Toronto, 1936), no page numbers.

22 Statistics compiled from Herman Frank, *Shule Almanac: The Modern Yiddish Shules Throughout the World* (Philadelphia: Workmen's Circle Schools, 1935), 348–64.

23 Freidenreich, *Passionate Pioneers*, 198.

24 David Rome, compiler, *On Our Forerunners—At Work. Epilogue: Notes on the Twentieth Century,* Canadian Jewish Archives, n.s. 10 (Montreal: Canadian Jewish Archives, 1978), 134.

25 Rome, *On Our Forerunners*, 136.

26 Paulo Freire, *Pedagogy of the Oppressed* (New York: Continuum, c2000). It was first published in 1970.

27 Day schools developed in the 1920s in Montreal and Winnipeg. Winnipeg's Liberty Temple also had a day school for a short period. The Winchevsky shule in Montreal had a full-day school in the late 1940s and early 1950s. The only secular day school teaching Yiddish still survives in Montreal, a reuniting of the folk shule (Jewish People's School and the I. L. Peretz Shule) in 1971. See jppsbialik.ca.

28 *Di Fareynikte Froyen Leyenkrayz in Detroit* (The United Women's Reading Circles in Detroit) n.d., n.p. The pamphlet was printed in honour of their fifth anniversary in 1939. Archives of the Secular Yiddish Schools in America (SYSA), Stanford, California.

29 Sonia Levin, "The YKUF in Canada and Around the World," *Der Vochenblat* (Canadian Jewish Weekly), January 23, 1941, 2.

30 Basman taught in Winnipeg from 1929 to 1931 (see chapter 4).

31 Levin, "The YKUF in Canada and Around the World," 2.

32 H. Sandler, "On the Cultural Front in Winnipeg," *Der Vochenblat,* February 2, 1940, 1.

33 Sandler, "On the Cultural Front in Winnipeg," 2.

34 Sandler, "On the Cultural Front in Winnipeg," 2.

35 Molodovsky was born in Belarus, taught in the Ukraine, and lived in Warsaw, Poland before immigrating to the US in 1935. She moved to Israel in 1948 and lived there until 1952. Much of her poetry is the poetry of exile.

36 *Di Fareynikte Froyen Leyenkrayz in Detroit.*

37   Gittl Simkin, "A fertl yor hundert muter fareyn" (Twenty five years of the mother's league), *25 year yor Yubl—Bukh, 1921–46* (25 Year Anniversary Book, 1921–46) (Winnipeg, 1946), 26–28.

38   Roz Usiskin, interview with Fayvl Simkin, Jewish Heritage Centre of Western Canada Archives, 1970s.

39   Simkin, "A fertl yor hundert muter fareyn," 26. M. Bloshtein's full name was Moyshe Mordechai but I prefer to refer to him the way she did.

40   B. Nozhnitsky, "Zikhroynes" (Memories), *25 year yor Yubl—Bukh, 1921–46* (25 Year Anniversary Book, 1921–46) (Winnipeg, 1946), 21.

41   Khaver, which means friend or comrade, was used by the left as a form of respectful address. The feminine is Khaverte. Books printed in an earlier period may spell it Chaver.

42   Faygl Kirk, "Mazel Topve tsu undzer zilberner Khasens" (Congratulations on our 25th anniversary), *25th Year Anniversary Book, Sholem Aleichem School* (Winnipeg, 1946), 39.

43   Nozhnitzki, "Zikhroynes," 18.

44   M. Bloshtein, "20 yor yubilee funem Arbeter Ring, 10 yor yubiley funem Freiheit Temple un 6 yor yubiley fun der Arbeter Ring shule" (To the 20th anniversary of the Workmen's Circle, 10th anniversary of the Liberty Temple and 6th anniversary of the Workmen's Circle Shule), *Dos Yiddishe Vort*, October 7, 1927, 4.

45   Although the left had separated from the Workmen's Circle in Montreal and Toronto in 1926, in Winnipeg they were still together. There were, however, tensions between the left and the social democratic right.

46   Steiman's Hall, a community gathering place in the 1920s, became the Merchant's Hotel in the 1930s. In the 1970s, it developed a terrible reputation as the site of much violence. In late 2012, the Province of Manitoba bought the hotel as part of an urban renewal project; the planning included a satellite university campus, social service offices, and a housing complex. One of my grandsons, a student at the University of Winnipeg, took a course on the site. Half the class consisted of Aboriginal students.

47   "Freyd un bagaysterung baym graduir yontev in Vinnipeg" (Joy and spirit at the graduation holiday in Winnipeg), *Der Kamf*, October 14, 1927, 1.

48   S. Lapedes, "Dos arbeter kind farn arbeter klas" (The worker's child for the working class), *Der Kamf*, April 24, 1931, 7.

49   International Workers Order, "Di Shul far ayer kinder" (The school for your children). Pamphlet, December 1935, 9–10.

50   R. Zaltsman, *Tsu der geshikhte fun der arbiter bavegung* (To the history of the workers' movement) (New York: International Workers Order, 1936), 180.

51   M. Bakal, "Di umparteyisher Arbeter shuln darfn zayn proletarish, nit yiddishist" (The non aligned schools need to be proletarian, not yiddishist), *Der Kamf*, May 31, 1929, 4.

52   Sh. Nepom, "Minimaturn," *Der Kamf*, July 5, 1929, 4.

53   P. Halperin, "Farvos shuln fun Kanader Arbeter ring?" (Why shules of the Canadian Labour Circle?), *Der Kamf*, August 17, 1929, 3, 6.

54   Halperin, "Farvos shuln fun Kanader Arbeter ring?" 3, 6.

55   Secular Jewish Schools of North America Archives (SYSA), Stanford, California, n.d., probably 1950s.

56 Leybl Basman, probably the most revered teacher in the left wing shules, was the subject of criticism when he left Winnipeg to teach in Windsor. He was denounced by Branch 3 of the Windsor Labour League as a "reformist liberal" not capable of running a revolutionary shule. H. Berne, Sec., "Far a Proleterisher shule" (For a proletarian shule), *Der Kamf*, February 20, 1931, 4. The denunciation did not prevent Toronto or Montreal from hiring him. The next year, Basman, now teaching in Montreal, wrote an article, "Unzer Shul programme," praising the project system and criticizing those who "pretend to be radical, but distance themselves from the daily struggles of the working class." He named Yakov Levin in the United States and M. Bloshtein in Winnipeg. Levin, part of the nonaligned left movement, wanted children to be exposed to all positions and make up their own minds. His ideology was denounced as liberal.

57 Freiheit Temple Shule Almanac, Winnipeg Temple School Almanac, May 1937, 3. Using the now standard Yivo spelling, Freiheit would be spelled Frayhayt.

58 Moyshe Miller, "A shmues mit der fargangenhayt" (A conversation with the past), *Der Pen*, Oxford, 1990. Thanks to Roz Usiskin of Winnipeg for bringing this wonderful article to my attention.

59 *Sholem Aleichem Shule 25th Year Anniversary Book, 1921–1946* (Winnipeg: Sholem Aleichem Shule, 1946).

60 Dora Rosenbaum, interview with the author, Winnipeg, March 2006.

61 Itche Goldberg, interview with the author, May 1994, New York.

62 Betzelel Friedman, ed., *Arbeter Shul Teaching Book for the First Year*, illustrated by B. Gropper and A. Fastovski (New York: International Workers Order, 1934), 18.

63 Friedman, *Arbeter Shul Teaching Book for the First Year*, 105.

64 Friedman, *Arbeter Shul Teaching Book for the First Year*, 76.

65 www.tagnwag.com/dick_and_jane_titles.html.

66 Friedman, *Arbeter Shul Teaching Book for the First Year*, 112.

67 Moyshe Shifris, writer of story. Maisel and Betzelel Friedman, eds. *Arbeter Shul Teaching Book for the Second Year* (New York: International Workers Order, 1933), 14.

68 Lil Ilomaki, conversation with the author, 1996.

69 Recollections of Lenny Dolgoy, Jewish Heritage Centre of Western Canada Archives, n.d., n.p.

70 A. Kamenetzki and Moishe Shifris, *Arbeter Shul Teaching Book for the Fourth Year* (New York: International Workers Order, 1934), 107. Note that the polite term for African Americans at the time was "Negro."

71 Kamenetzki and Shifris, *Arbeter Shul Teaching Book for the Fourth Year*, 122.

72 Description of contents of some of the books in the *Arbeter shule: Mir lernen un kemfn* series of the 1930s.

73 *Memories of Esther: Dedicated to the lasting memory of the Yiddish Teacher Esther Codor Cohen* (Stanford: SYSA Archives, 1990), 33.

74 I heard Mildren Gutkin do this twice, once in a reading circle before she began her reading, and then again when I was interviewing her in her home in April 2003.

75 Ben Shek, interview with the author, May 1995.

76 Ruth Borchiver, born in 1928, attended the shules in the 1930s and early 1940s and taught in the late 1940s and 1950s. She died in 2007.

77 It isn't appropriate to name the informant or the teacher, both of whom are dead. Unfortunately, it was not possible to elicit details on what was meant by "liking the girls a bit too much." The respondents' reference to this gave the impression of discomfort rather than overt actions. She also described visiting him years later with her friends, which made him so happy that he cried. Another student in the shule at the time confirmed her account of this teacher.

78 "Julius comes to the defense of his people," *Yungvarg*, Jan–Feb, 1947, 4–5.

79 I. Kleinshtein, "Unzere Kinder—Unzer Shtoltz" (Our children, our pride), *Der Vochenblat*, June 21, 1945, 3.

80 See Pierre Berton, "No Jews need Apply," *Maclean's*, November 1948.

81 "Der Metzav fun di Yidish-Veltlekhe shuln" (The Status of the Jewish Secular Children's Schools), *Der Vochenblat*, July 2, 1942, 7.

82 I. Kleinshtein, "Unzere Kinder—Unzer Shtoltz" (Our children, our pride), *Der Vochenblat*, June 21, 1945, 3.

83 "Yiddishe Kinder in der Yiddisher Shul" (Jewish Children in the Jewish school), *Der Vochenblat*, December 5, 1946, 7.

84 P. Bloomstone, "Shul un Heym" (School and Home), *Der Vochenblat*, June 19, 1947, 6.

85 Hirsh Glik, *Lider fun di ghettos un lagern* (Songs of the ghettos and concentration camps), compiled by Sh. Kacjzerginski (New York: Congress for Jewish Culture, 1948), 3. Translation adapted by the author from Ruth Rubin, *A Treasury of Yiddish Song* (New York: Schocken Books, 1950), 185.

86 Helena Khatskills, *Yungvarg*, December 1945. The story was also very popular in the North American shules, underlining the transatlantic nature of the culture.

87 Mirl Erdberg-Shatan "Problemn fun Unzer Shuln" (The problems of our shules), *Der Vochenblat*, April 20, 1944, 6.

88 "The Background of Our School Conference," *Der Vochenblat*, Aug. 19, 1943, 7.

89 "To the Children of the Winnipeg Sholem Aleichem School," *Der Vochenblat*, April 15, 1948, 7.

90 Rebecca C. Margolis, "Yiddish Literary Culture in Montreal, 1905–1940" (PhD diss., Columbia University, 2005), 340–48.

91 Margolis, "Yiddish Literary Culture in Montreal, 1905–1940," 340–48.

92 J. Mamelak, "To the Program of Our Order Schools," *Der Vochenblat*, August 2, 1945, 3.

93 "Twenty Years of Jewish Progressive Education," *Der Vochenblat*, December 19, 1946, 7.

94 "A Big School Holiday in Montreal," *Der Vochenblat*, May 7, 1942, 7.

95 Olga Eizner Favreau, interview with the author, February 2013.

96 Leybl Basman, "The Progressive Spirit of our Schools," *Der Vochenblat*, May 19, 1949, 3.

97 "Morris Winchevsky School in Toronto," *Der Vochenblat*, September 16, 1948.

98 Ruth Borchiver, personal interview with the author, May 2006.

99 Gerald A. Cohen, "Politics and Religion in a Montreal Communist Jewish Childhood," in *If You're an Egalitarian, How Come You're So Rich?* (Cambridge: Harvard University Press, 2000), 222–24.

100 Gerry Cohen remembers that this happened in 1952, on a Friday. However, lots of evidence, including a report in *La Presse*, January 28, 1950, indicates he was right about the Friday, but off by a few years. I don't know what the weather was that day. This is a good example of the perils of uncorroborated oral testimony.

101 Curriculum Outline for Workmen's Circle Schools (n.d., but most likely 1960s), folder 27, box 20, SYSA Archives.

102 Dr. Shloime Simon, "Fifty Years of the Sholem Aleichem Folk Institute," in *Our First Fifty Years*, ed. Saul Goodman (New York: Sholem Aleichem Folk Institute, 1972), 109–16.

103 Leybl Basman, "Vegn zikh aleyn un vegn mayn dor" (About myself and my generation). Notes for a retirement speech, 1970. Label Basman Papers MU 9093, Series 85, Archives of Ontario.

104 Manya Lipshitz, "Return after 35 Years," in *Time Remembered*, trans. Max Rosenfeld and Marcia Usiskin (Toronto: Lugus, 1991), 70–71.

105 Mordechai Miller, Moyshe's father, had died in 1946. *Sholem Aleichem Shule 25th Year Anniversary Book, 1921–1946* (Winnipeg: Sholem Aleichem Shule, 1946).

106 See for example Ellen Schrecker, *Many are the Crimes: McCarthyism in America* (Boston: Little Brown, 1998).

107 Gerald Bain, interview with the author, May 2009.

108 I include my own experiences, as the more I learn about the Ordn linke (left wing) shules in Canada, the more resemblance there is to my experiences in New York. Even many of our teachers were the same.

109 See, for example, "Philosophy and Curriculum of the Sholem Aleichem Folk Shules," n.d. (Because it is written in English, it likely comes from the 1960s), folder 13, box 2, SYSA Archives; "Curriculum of the Jewish Secular School, 1962," prepared by the teachers of the Los Angeles Kindershules.

8 Cultural Life

1 Mollie Myers, interview with the author, March 1996.

2 Ben Shek, born in 1927. Interview with the author, 2005.

3 Philip Halperin, "Alhambra Hall," *Der Kamf,* March 12, 1937, 6 (reprint from Mar. 29, 1929).

4 J. Gershman, *Der Kamf,* February 24, 1945, "Observations on the 20th Anniversary of the Jewish Folk Choir," 41. Translated by Gloria Bruner. Joe Gershman was editor of *Der Kamf* for most of the years between 1936 and the paper's demise in 1978.

5 The performers included singer Yitskhak Levin, violinist A. Goodman, and dancers Eva Daynev and Saide Gerrard. The program also included speeches by Morris Spector from the newly formed Communist Party and Philip Halperin, editor of *Der Kamf*. Advertisement for a concert and fundraiser for *Der Kamf*, April 30, 1926, 1.

6 "Unzer Firer" is most likely homage to Lenin. "All Workers are Coming Saturday Evening to the Jubilee Concert of Kamf," *Der Kamf,* December 31, 1926, 1.

7 Books from 1908 were found at Camp Naivelt. The Montreal date is from a web description.

8 Sam Kagan, interview with Karen Levine, February 28, 1978, Multicultural History Society of Ontario (MHSO), Jew-1004=Kag 1978.

9 The cards from the library were in the United Jewish People's Order. Sharon Power went through them listing the holdings in the library.

10 Halperin, "Alhambra Hall"; M. Mindes, "Di arbeter bibliotek: a vikhtiker ring fun proletar-ishe kultur-front" (The Worker's Library: an important element in the proletarian cultural front), *Der Kamf,* April 19, 1929, 4.

11 Halperin, "Alhambra Hall"; M. Mindes, "Di Arbeter Bibliotek."

12 M. Pearlman, "Fir Yor Abeter Kultur Tsentr" (Four years of the Workers Culture Centre) *Der Kamf*, October 31, 1930.

13 A. Rosenberg, "Tsen Yor Arbeter Kultur Tsentr in Montreal" (Ten years of the Jewish Workers Culture Centre in Montreal), *Der Kamf*, January 9, 1936, 2.

14 Pearlman, "Fir Yor Abeter Kultur Tsentr."

15 Rosenberg, "Tsen Yor Arbeter Kultur Tsentr in Montreal."

16 Sholem Shtern, "Elf Yor Yiddisher Arbeter Kultur Tsenter in Montreal" (Eleven years of the Workers Culture Centre in Montreal), *Der Kamf*, February 5, 1937, 5.

17 Shtern, "Elf Yor Yiddisher Arbeter Kultur Tsenter in Montreal."

18 Sholem Shtern, *The White House: A Novel in Verse*, translated from Yiddish with foreword by Max Rosenfeld (Montreal: Warbrooke Publishers, 1974).

19 Shtern, *The White House*, 132.

20 Shtern, *The White House*, 134.

21 Although the Canadian party had been organized as an amalgamation of different groups and funded primarily by the Finnish Organization of Canada and the Ukrainian Labour Farmer Temple Association, they were no longer party members through their participation in their ethnic organizations.

22 See Andrée Lévesque, *Red Travellers: Jean Corbin and Her Comrades*, translated by Yvonne M. Klein (Montreal: McGill-Queens, 2006) for an excellent description of the sectarianism of this period. Social Democrats were branded as Social Fascists and an attempt was made to "Canadianize" the Party.

23 Morris Biderman, *A Life on the Jewish Left: An Immigrant's Experience* (Toronto: Onward Publishing, 2000), 84. Biderman wrote this book after he left the UJPO.

24 See Jim Mochuruk, "'Pop & Co' vs Buck and the 'Lenin School Boys'" in *Reimagining Ukrainian Canadians: History, Politics, Identity*, ed. Rhonda L. Hinther and Jim Mochuruk, 331–75 (Toronto: University of Toronto Press, 2011).

25 Y. B., "Unzer dertsiyung kursn" (Our educational courses), *Der Kamf*, September 30, 1932.

26 Pearlman, "Fir Yor Abeter Kultur Tsentr."

27 Rosenberg, "Tsen Yor Arbeter Kultur Tsentr in Montreal."

28 "Workers Culture Centre in a Clear Class Way," *Der Kamf*, October 31, 1930, 1.

29 "Workers Culture Centre in a Clear Class Way"; Rosenberg, "Tsen Yor Arbeter Kultur Tsentr in Montreal."

30 "Tsum fusbol sezon in Montreal" (To the soccer season in Montreal), *Der Kamf*, May 8, 1936, 4.

31 A. Sheikovitz, "Mitglider campanye fun arbeter sport fareyn in Montreal" (Members Campaign of the Workers' Sport Association in Montreal), *Der Kamf*, January 15, 1935, 10.

32 N. Brenska and A, Sheikovitz, "Zig far Montrealer Sportsler" (Victory for Montreal Sportsmen), *Der Kamf*, October, 1931.

33 Brenska and Sheikovitz, "Zig far Montrealer Sportsler."

34 M. B. "The Great Jubilee of the Toronto Cultural Centre," *Der Kamf*, May 8, 1936, 4.

35 Benjamin Katz, "On the First Anniversary," *Der Kamf*, May 13, 1932, 5.

36 Katz, "On the First Anniversary."

37 M. Biderman, *Freiheit Gezang Fareyn un der Labour League* (10 Years of the Labor League) (Toronto: Supreme Printing 1936); "With the Sections of the Cultural Centre," *Der Kamf*, May 13, 1932, 6.

38 R. Bruner, "Activity of the Toronto Cultural Centre," *Der Kamf*, Jan. 25, 1932, 10.

39 Bruner, "Activity of the Toronto Cultural Centre," 10.

40 Bruner, "Activity of the Toronto Cultural Centre," 10; "The Jewish Workers' Cultural Centre and the Kamf," *Der Kamf*, January 1, 1932, 4.

41 "With the Sections of the Cultural Centre."

42 "With the Sections of the Cultural Centre."

43 Bruner, "Activity of the Toronto Culture Centre," 10.

44 Charles N., "Improve Our Culture Activity Amongst the Jewish Workers," *Der Kamf*, January 25, 1935, 10.

45 Ben Itzhak, "Kultur Tsentr in Winnipeg" (Cultural Centre in Winnipeg), *Der Kamf*, January 1, 1932, 9.

46 Itzhak, "Kultur Tsentr in Winnipeg."

47 H. Zaretsky, "In Arbeter Yugnt Klub" (In the Workers' Youth Club), *Der Kamf*, November 4, 1927, 4.

48 "Kamf Yubilee Fayerung in Winnipeg" (Kamf anniversary celebration in Winnipeg), *Der Kamf*, January 1, 1933, 9.

49 Joe Zuken, interview with Doug Smith, May 29, 1984. A series of interviews with Joe Zuken were used to write the book *Joe Zuken, Citizen and Socialist* (Toronto: Lorimer, 1990). Doug Smith generously allowed me to look at the original interviews.

50 Sybil Cherniak and Saul Cherniak, interview with Doug Smith, n.d. 1980s (courtesy of Doug Smith).

51 For example, Emanuel Ringelblum, a left labour Zionist and the archivist of the Warsaw Ghetto, also supported the Soviet Union and Jewish settlement in Birobidjan. Samuel D. Kassow, *Who will Write Our History: Emanuel Ringelblum, the Warsaw Ghetto and the Oyneg Shjabes Archive* (Indiana: Indiana University Press, 2007), 1–48.

52 Section 98 criminalized and allowed for the imprisonment or systematic deportation of agitators, radicals, or activists or anyone belonging to an "unlawful organization." It was enacted in 1919 following the Winnipeg General Strike and targeted foreign-born radicals in particular. Tim Buck and seven other leaders of the CPC were incarcerated under Section 98 in 1931. The law was finally changed in 1936.

53 ARTEF or the Arbeter Teatr Farband, the Workers Theatre Collective, was first organized as a left artists' drama collective in New York and included prominent actors such as Joseph Opatoshu.

54 M. Mesy, "With Faster Steps, Let Us Go Forward," *Der Kamf*, January 25, 1935, 10.

55 The following are some examples of the performances. September 4, 1928: Second Jubilee in Monument National Theatre, with performances by both mandolin orchestras, the choir, the drama section, a ballet, and men's and women's groups from the sport league. Sam Lipshitz, "Jubilee Celebration from the Montreal Workers' Cultural Centre," *Der Kamf*, September 14, 1928, 3. September 29, 1928: a literary-musical evening at the Workmen's Circle House, with performances by a New York fiddler, a mandolin quartet, a dramatization of Sholem Aleichem's *Presnice* by Levin and Khazanov, a comic play, plus games and

a comic magazine. Lipshitz, "Jubilee Celebration from the Montreal Workers' Cultural Centre," 3. November 2, 1930: Fourth Jubilee in Prince Arthur Hall, with performances by the choir, the mandolin orchestra, the wind orchestra, and the dramatic section (tickets 35 cents). Pearlman, "Four Years of the Workers Cultural Centre," 2. September 24, 1932: banquet to celebrate the JWCC's new home at 4093 Lawrence. Schedule included singing of "The Internationale," speech by chairman Pearlman, greetings from other organizations, and performances by a trio, Comrade Wexler, and "The Believers" (Isaac Afres) from the drama circle. M. S. "The opening of our new home," *Der Kamf*, September 24, 1932, 2. May 1936: banquet for the opening of the 1936 soccer season with speaker Fred Rose. February 1937: performance of "Artef" at the concert of the Young Men's Hebrew Institute.

56 Rebecca Margolis, "Negotiating Jewish Identity," *Shofar: An Interdisciplinary Journal of Jewish Studies* 27, no. 4 (Summer 2009): 29–48.

57 Ida Maza, "Shener fun der zun" (More beautiful than the sun), *Der Kamf*, April 3, 1941, 5.

58 Miriam Waddington, "Mrs. Maza's Salon," in *The Canadian Jewish Studies Reader*, ed. Richard Menkis and Norman Ravvin, 216–23 (Calgary: Red Deer Press, 2004).

59 Sholem Shtern, "We Must Centralize Our Work," *Der Kamf*, October 16, 1935, 3.

60 Shtern, "We Must Centralize Our Work."

61 Charles N., "Farbesern unzer kultur tetikayt tsvishn di yiddisher arbeter " (Improve our culture activity amongst the Jewish workers), *Der Kamf*, January 25, 1935, 10.

62 "The Fate of Yiddish Culture," *Der Kamf*, June 16, 1941, 5.

63 Matthew Hoffman, "From Czernowitz to Paris: The International Yiddish Culture Congress of 1937." Unpublished paper presented at the 100th anniversary of Cznernowitz conference, York University, 2008.

64 M. B., "The Great Jubilee of the Toronto Cultural Centre."

65 M. B., "The Great Jubilee of the Toronto Cultural Centre"; S. Lipshitz, "The Toronto Cultural Centre Carries Out a Successful Jubilee," *Der Kamf*, May 15, 1936, 3; S. Shtern "The Toronto Cultural Centre," *Der Kamf*, November 6, 1936, 3.

66 Benita Wolters-Fredlund, "We Shall Go Forward With Our Songs Into the Fight for Better Life: Identity and Musical Meaning in the History of the Toronto Jewish Folk Choir 1925–59" (PhD diss., University of Toronto, 2005).

67 Oral historians have noted that firsthand accounts often provide a version of the truth that can change over time. A good example is the excitement and honour accorded Jacob Schaefer when he was invited to conduct in Toronto in 1935. According to Melech Epstein, Schaefer is an "involuntary communist" and Epstein attributes his early death at forty-eight from heart attacks due to the "strain" caused by the Communist Party's emphasis on "proletarian" music. He dismissed the cultural activities as "completely dominated by the party, communist controlled" and "communist dominated." Epstein, *The Jew and Communism* (New York: Trade Union Sponsoring Committee, 1959), 210–14. The memoirs of Morris Biderman, *Life on the Jewish Left,* which include Schaefer's visit to Toronto, contradict Epstein's claims.

68 P. Podoliak, "In the Mandolin Symphony Orchestra," *Der Kamf*, October 22, 1937, 3.

69 M. B., "The Great Jubilee of the Toronto Cultural Centre."

70 "Five Years of the Mandolin Orchestra," *Der Kamf*, November 6, 1936, 3.

71 Podoliak, "In the Mandolin Symphony Orchestra."

72 Lipshitz, "The Toronto Cultural Centre Carries Out a Successful Jubilee."

73 August Bridle, "Jewish Culture Club Program is Exciting," *Toronto Star,* May 11, 1936, 7.

74 Podoliak, "In the Mandolin Symphony Orchestra"; "Five years of the Mandolin Orchestra."

75 Podoliak, "In the Mandolin Symphony Orchestra"; "Five years of the Mandolin Orchestra."

76 Podoliak, "In the Mandolin Symphony Orchestra"; "Five years of the Mandolin Orchestra."

77 Sid (Mitzi) Dolgoy, interview with the author, October 2007.

78 Avrom Yanovksy, "The Toronto Jewish Folk Choir was My School," *Twenty-fifth Anniversary Book of the Toronto Jewish Folk Choir* (Toronto: UJPO/Morris Printing, 1945), unpaged.

79 The poem appears in Yiddish and English in the *25th Jubilee Book of the Toronto Jewish Folk Choir*. The translation was done by M. Weinstein. By May 1935, it had been performed four times in New York, three times in Chicago, twice in Cleveland, twice in Detroit, twice in Los Angeles, and in Boston, Philadelphia, Newark, Paris, and Warsaw. "A revolutzier muziker in Toronto" (A revolutionary musician in Toronto), *Der Kamf,* May 10, 1935, 1.

80 Ben Shek, interview with the author, April 1996.

81 http://www.yadvashem.org/yv/en/exhibitions/music/images/notes/vilna_shtiler_shtiler.pdf. This translation is by Eliyahu Mishlovin. It was sung in Yiddish.

82 Claire Klein Osipov, interview with the author, May 1996.

83 Mollie Klein Goldsman, interview with the author, May 1996.

84 Ruth Borchiver, interview with the author, May 2006.

85 Ishike, "The Concert from the Labour League Schools," *Der Vochenblat,* May 10, 1940, 3.

86 Toronto Jewish Choir concert program, May 1944.

87 Mollie Myers, interview with the author, April 1996.

88 S. Kirk, "We are Young and Vigorous," *UJPO Convention Book*, 1947.

89 The concerts were on May 25, 1946, March 25, 1947, November 19, 1947, December 4 and 6, 1948, and December 3 and 5, 1949. Wolters-Fredlund, "We Shall Go Forward With Our Songs," 255 note 89.

90 Toronto Jewish Folk Choir Archives at the United Jewish People's Order, Winchevsky Centre, Toronto.

91 Wolters-Fredlund, "We Shall Go Forward With Our Songs," 256.

92 Mollie Klein, interview with the author, March 1996.

93 John Steward, *Jubilee Book of the Toronto Jewish Folk Choir*, 1950. Steward includes in his list *The Crucible* by the US playwright Arthur Miller. For Steward, Canadian culture included all he thought of value for Canadians.

94 Typed speech found in Sam Lipshitz archives, York University. The date of the speech is not listed but from references in the speech it would be 1954. At the time, Lipshitz was the head of the Committee of Progressive Jewish Organizations as well as on the Central Committee of the Communist Party. It was clearly addressed to "comrades" in the CP. It reads as a defence of the UJPO's cultural activities and "how best to bring the party program to bear on our work among Jewish Canadians."

95 Brochure of Toronto Dance Theatre, Toronto 1949/50. Collection of Pearl Blazer who danced with the theatre group.

96 Brochure of the New Dance Theatre (Toronto) 1952/53. Collection of Pearl Blazer.

97 New Dance Theatre of Toronto advertisement. Collection of Pearl Blazer.

98 Claire Klein Osipov, interview with the author, March 2006.

99 Joan Orenstein, *UJPO Convention Book*, 1954.

100 S. Simkin, "The Order in Winnipeg," *UJPO Convention Book*, 1947.

101 S. Zarkin, "The Progressive Voice in Vancouver," *UJPO Convention Book*, June 1947. The speakers included the pro-communist left rabbi from New York and prominent members of the Jewish left based in Toronto—Joshua Gershman, Sam Lipshitz, Harry Guralnik, Morris Biderman, and Sol Shek.

102 Harry Gulkin, "Montreal Jewish Folk Choir Does a Jubilee Panorama," *Canadian Jewish Weekly*, March 8, 1956, 4.

103 Gary Cristall, CBC Radio series on the history of folk music in English Canada, folk-musichistory.com, first aired summer 2008.

104 Some of the ideas were inspired by Paul Buhle's article "Jews and American Communism: The Cultural Expression," *Radical History Review* 25 (Spring 1980): 9–33. Buhle is not responsible for how I have adapted his insights.

9 Summer Camps

1   See the souvenir books produced in Camp Kinderland for the 1978 reunion and the 1999 reunion.

2   Paul Mishler, *Raising Reds: The Young Pioneers, Radical Summer Camps and Communist Political Culture in the United States* (New York: Columbia University Press, 1999), 88.

3   The housing co-operative in the Bronx was inspired by Finnish co-operative houses in Brooklyn. The co-ops were on a much larger scale. See the film *At Home in Utopia* about the co-operative houses in the Bronx.

4   "Unzere proletarishe kemps" (Our proletarian camps), *Der Kamf*, July 13, 1927, 2.

5   Campers in the Zionist camps dressed in white on Friday nights for Oneg Shabat, a ceremony marking the beginning of the Sabbath.

6   Basman recalled his experiences at the camp in a memoir called *Shtralinke zikhroyes* (Shining memories).

7   There was a general strike in the industry at that time led by the Industrial Union of Needle Trades Workers.

8   Moyshe Mindes, *Der Yorlekher Kindervelt Kontsert* (the Annual Kindervelt concert), *Der Kamf*, August 14, 1931, 7.

9   L. Basman, "Beste arbet fun kemp Kinderland" (Best work of Camp Kinderland), *Der Kamf*, May 7, 1937.

10 A. Silverberg, "Oyfn shvel fun fiftn yor kemp Nitgedayget" (At the threshold of the fifth year of Camp Nitgedayget), *Der Kamf*, June 24, 1932, 2.

11 While Yakhnes undoubtedly had a first name, he was known by his last name.

12 The Scottsboro boys, teenagers charged with rape in racist Alabama in 1961, were found guilty. Appeals were supported by the American Communist Party. The cases were tried three times in what was widely considered a miscarriage of justice. In 2013, the Alabama parole board granted the Scottsboro boys a posthumous pardon.

13 I. Elbin, "In Nitgedayget," *Der Kamf*, July 24, 1936.

14 Elbin, "In Nitgedayget."

15 Max Dolgoy, interview with Mercedes Steedman, 1980s.

16 Harry Holtzman, Secretary of Camp Naivelt, "Camp Naivelt: An Answer to the Anti Semitism," *Der Kamf*, August 13, 1937, 1.

17 Paul Townsend, "Portrait of the Street: Documentary by Sandra Danilovic," en.wikipedia.org/wiki/Johnny_Lombardi.

18 Stephen Speisman, "Antisemitism in Ontario: The Twentieth Century" in *Antisemitism in Canada: History and Interpretation*, ed. Alan Davies (Waterloo: Wilfred Laurier Press, 1992), 121.

19 Holtzman, "Camp Naivelt: An Answer to the Anti Semitism."

20 Esther Einbinder, "An Exploratory Study of Attitudes Towards Jews in the City of Toronto, 1934" (master's thesis, University of Toronto, 1934), 19–24.

21 Einbinder, "An Exploratory Study of Attitudes Towards Jews," 118. Quote from the *Evening Telegram*, September 22, 1924.

22 Gwethalynn Graham, *Earth and High Heaven* (Toronto: Cormorant Books, 2003), 162. The book, originally published in 1944, won the Governor General's Award and became a best seller in Canada.

23 Personal communication with the author, Winnipeg, 1980s.

24 John R. Seeley, R. Alexander Sim, Elizabeth W. Loosley, and David Riesman, *Crestwood Heights: A Study of the Culture Of Suburban Life* (Toronto: University of Toronto Press, 1956), 310.

25 Sharon Wall, *The Nurture of Nature: Childhood, Antimodernism, and Summer Camps, 1920–55* (Vancouver: UBC Press, 2009), 51.

26 Wall, *The Nurture of Nature*, 68.

27 "Faroys tzu eygenem proletarishn kemp in Toronto! Finfter sezon kemp 'Kindervelt'" (Forward to our own proletarian camp in Toronto! Fifth season of Camp 'Kindervelt'), *Der Kamf*, June 28, 1929, 3.

28 "Farkhapt nokh di vokhn far fargenign in Kemp Naivelt" (Take weeks of pleasure in Camp Naivelt). Ad, *Der Kamf*, August 20, 1937.

29 B. Bernard, "A Storehouse of Memories: 50 years Camp Kinderland and Naivelt," *Der Vochenblat* (Canadian Jewish Weekly), July 9, 1975, 4.

30 Mirl Erdberg Shatan, "Ayndrukn funem sheynem Toronto Kemp 'Naivelt'" (Impressions of the beautiful Camp Naivelt), *Der Kamf*, June 18, 1937, 5.

31 Shatan, "Ayndrukn funem sheynem Toronto Kemp 'Naivelt'."

32 Personal communication, Camp Kinderland, Tolland Massachusetts visiting day, July 2011. I didn't receive permission for this informal exchange, so I won't identify the informant.

33 *Der Kamf*, August 26, 1938, 1 See also discussion in chapter 5.

34 Sholem Shtern, "Tsu der derefenung fun di kemps" (To the opening of the camps), *Der Vochenblat*, June 25, 1942, 2.

35 Shtern, "Tsu der derefenung fun di kemps."

36 Sid Dolgoy, interview with the author, November 2007.

37 G. Bresko, "A sezon arbet fun "Laurentian Vacation klub," *Der Vochenblat*, September 28, 1944, 3.

38 Joshua Perle, "Holocaust Chronicles," in *Holocaust Chronicles: Individualizing the Holocaust Through Diaries and Other Contemporaneous Personal Accounts*, ed. Robert Moses Shapiro (KTAV Publishing House, 1999), quoted in Wikipedia, "Janusz Korczak," en.wikipedia.org.

39 Leybl Basman, "Shtralinke Zikhroynes: Kemp Naivelt un Kinderland—a halber yorhundert fun likhtiker vunder" (Shining memories: Camp Naivelt and Kinderland—fifty years of light filled memories), *Der Vochenblat*, July 5, 1975, 4–5.

40 Phone conversation with the older brother, Israel Chojnacki, October 2013.

41 "Vos di Montrealer konen dervartn hayntikn zumer in Laurentian Vacation Club" (What the Montrealers can expect this summer in Laurentian Vacation Club), *Der Vochenblat*, June 16, 1949, 6.

42 L. Guberman, "Mir Boyen Undzer Kemp in Vinipeg" (We Build our Camp in Winnipeg), *Der Vochenblat*, Sept 12, 1946, 3.

43 G. A. Cohen, "A Montreal Communist Jewish Childhood," in *If You're An Egalitarian, How Come You're So Rich* (Boston: Harvard University Press, 2000).

44 Leybl Basman, "Kemp 'Naivelt' far yung un alt far kleyn un groys," *Der Vochenblat*, July 3, 1947, 6.

45 George Vair called this "a story about anti-union shipping companies, who demonstrated a blatant disregard for the law, about a corrupt rival International union that was known for its unlawful violent activities, about a federal government and the RCMP, who aided and abetted these forces and about a Canadian labour movement, who yielded to the pressures of the American labour movement, and betrayed their Canadian brothers." His description may sound extreme but in testimony before the Canadian parliament in 1996, David Broadfoot of the Canadian Merchant Navy Association recalled that in 1946, "Our government imported a thug, a real heavy-duty gangster from Brooklyn (Hal C. Banks), to smash our union and bring in the Seafarers' International Union.... They came on our ships with baseball bats and bicycle chains. That's how they introduced their union to Canada." Testimony, June 18, 1946. A powerful National Film Board documentary called *Canada's Sweetheart: The Saga of Hal C. Banks* relates this disturbing history.

46 Report on Camp Naivelt—Toronto, October 1, 1936. Winchevsky Centre Archives.

47 Mollie Myers, interview with Michelle Cohen, July 1994.

48 Mollie Myers, interview with Michelle Cohen, July 1994.

49 Rita Bergman, interview with Michelle Cohen, July 1994.

50 Helen and Izzy Fine, interview with Michelle Cohen, July 1994.

51 Helen and Izzy Fine, interview with Michelle Cohen, July 1994.

52 I do not want to identify my source because this information was relayed informally.

53 Bessie Grossman remembered as a little girl telling a man that his wife had gone up the hill with Mr. X. She often wondered later if the marriage had survived whatever happened "up the hill."

54 Becky Lapedes told this story to her daughter, Cheryl [Sheyndl] Tallan. Interview with Sheyndl Tallan, 1980.

55 Bernard, "A Storehouse of Memories."

56 James Laxer, "At Camp Without a Paddle" in *Red Diaper Baby: A Boyhood in the Age of McCarthyism* (Toronto: Douglas & McIntyre, 2004), 121.

57 Laxer, *Red Diaper Baby*, 127.

58 James Laxer, interview with the author, March 2003.

59 Laxer, interview with the author, March 2003.

60 Laxer, *Red Diaper Baby*, 124.

61 Laxer, interview with the author, March 2003.

62 Laxer, interview with the author, March 2003.

63 Laxer, *Red Diaper Baby*, 127–28.

64 Laxer, *Red Diaper Baby*, 127–28.

65 Sid (also known as Mitzi) Dolgoy, interview with the author, May 2007.

66 "Fartsvaygte kultur un gezelshaft tetikaytn vern ongefirt in undzer progresiver kemps" (Various cultural and social activities are conducted in our progressive camps), *Der Vochenblat*, July 21, 1949, 2.

67 Robert Fiveson, "Memories of Naivelt." Booklet prepared for fiftieth anniversary of Naivelt, 1975.

68 Mollie Myers, interview with Michelle Cohen, 1994.

Conclusion

1 R. Saivetz and Sheila Levin Woods, editors and compilers, *August 12 1952. The Night of the Murdered Poets*, rev. ed. (New York: National Conference on Soviet Jewry, 1973), 25.

2 Saivetz and Woods, *August 12 1952*, 1.

3 Ian McKay made this argument when he presented a paper at a seminar in honour of Jerry Tulchinsky, Toronto, November 2013.

4 For example, in Ruth Borchiver's interview with Morris Biderman, head of the United Jewish People's Order from 1945 to 1957, he complained that the Communist Party expected the UJPO to do its bidding, a position that neither he nor the UJPO were happy with. Collection of the author.

5 A friend, who was an only child, thought that the only reason her communist parents decided to have a child was because the party had decided that it would help in connecting with non-Party people and their families. It must be said, that whatever the reason for her conception, the child was adored.

6 Ruth Borchiver, interview with Norman Penner, Toronto 1984. The "denouncing" would have occurred in the 1930s.

7 Interview with Ruth Frager in *Sweatshop Strife: Class, Ethnicity, and Gender in the Jewish Labour Movement of Toronto, 1900-1939* (Toronto: University of Toronto Press, 1992).

8 Jim Laxer, *Red Diaper Baby: A Boyhood in the Age of McCarthyism* (Toronto: Douglas and McIntyre, 2005).

9 The Communist Party had been renamed the Labour Progressive Party or LPP in 1943. They renamed themselves the Communist Party in 1959.

10 J. B. Salsberg, "Talks with Soviet Leaders on the Jewish Question," *Jewish Life,* May 1957.

11 "Four Leading LPP Members Resign from Party," Press release, Sam Lipshitz Papers, no. 151, York Archives.

12 J. Gershman Papers, box 25, Ontario Archives.

13 J. Gershman Papers, box 25, Ontario Archives.

14 Personal conversation with Joe Gershman, June 1981. Joe was in a seniors' residence and I would visit him from time to time. He told me that on a visit to the USSR just after the war, he asked for help in finding out if his mother and sister had survived. There was no response. Then he remained in the USSR longer than planned because he was ill. While

he was in hospital, his sister read an article that he had written for the Soviet press and contacted him. He felt that the Party had known all along how to find his family but hadn't told him.

15   *Canadian Tribune* clipping given to me by Anna Yanovksy, dated November 10, 1977.

16   Morris Biderman, *Life on the Jewish Left* (Toronto: Onward Publications, 2000), 141.

17   Doug Smith, *Joe Zuken, Citizen and Socialist* (Toronto: James Lorimer, 1990), 159.

18   Joe Zuken Interview #8 with Doug Smith. Some of this interview is in Smith's book *Joe Zuken, Citizen and Socialist*, 162–63.

19   Informal conversation with May and Gerry Cohen. Gerry's parents stayed in the UJPO but the Lipshitzes and May and Gerry left.

20   I was the interviewer. I've used pseudonyms for the four people. Two of them have since died, and the others might not want to comment publicly on this sensitive topic.

21   Anthony Lerman, "The Abuse of Dissenting Jews is Shameful," *Guardian*, August 20, 2012, www.theguardian.com.

22   Nathan Guttman, "Why Some Jewish Stars Support Israeli Artistic Boycott," *Forward*, September 8, 2010. forward.com. For a full list of the signers of the petition see jewishvoiceforpeace.org.

23   Bikel, named Theodore after Theodore Herzl, was born in 1924 in Austria. His family fled to mandate Palestine in the late 1930s. A singer of Yiddish (and twenty-six other languages) and known for his performance of Tevye in *Fiddler on the Roof*, Bikel was honoured at the age of eighty-nine at the seventy-fifth anniversary of Kristallnacht in Austria in November 2013. He performed Yiddish songs and the anthem of the Jewish resistance "Zog nit Keynmol." Tom Tugend, "Austria Honoring Vienna Native Theodore Bikel at Kristallnacht Commemoration," www.jta.org.

24   See *Democracy Now* broadcast, July 30 and 31, 2014, www.democracynow.org.

25   Yael Bartana, "And Europe will be Stunned," AGO exhibit, January 25–April 1, 2012.

26   Sander Gilman, *Jewish Frontiers: Essays on Bodies, Histories, and Identities* (New York: Palgrave Macmillan, 2003).

27   Stuart Charme, "Varieties of Authenticity in Contemporary Jewish Identity," *Jewish Social Studies* 6, no 2 (Winter 2000): 133–55.

28   Steven W. Lowenstein, *The Jewish Cultural Tapestry* (New York: Oxford University Press, 2000), 170.

29   Isaac Deutscher, *The Non-Jewish Jew and Other Essays* (London: Oxford University Press, 1968).

30   Frank Bialtstok expressed these views at a conference he organized honouring the historian Gerald Tulchinksy, Toronto, November 17, 2013.

31   See, for example, Julian Sher, "By the Numbers: The Jewish Vote," *Globe and Mail*, April 22, 2011. The IPSOS Reid exit poll also indicated that 52 percent voted Conservative. Dennis Gruending, "Stephen Harper's Majority, One Year Later," April 27, 2012, www.dennisgruending.ca/2012/04/stephen-harpers-majority-one-year-later/.

32   Joanne Hill, "Arab Group Challenge to Funding Decision in Judge's Hands," *Jewish Tribune*, June 4, 2013, www.jewishtribune.ca, "Conservative Refugee Reforms Put Party At Odds With Jewish Group," *Huffington Post*, July 7, 2013. www.huffingtonpost.ca.

33 www.cjnews.com.

34 http://morallowground.com/2013/12/01/worldwide-day-of-rage-protest-against-israels-expulsion-plan/.

35 Ian McKay, *Reasoning Otherwise: Leftists and the People's Enlightenment in Canada, 1890–1920* (Toronto: Between the Lines, 2008).

Index

Hirshbein, Peretz, 54

Hitler, Adolf, 40, 54, 59, 73, 75–76, 78, 80, 85, 90, 127, 183, 188, *189*, 208–9, 239

Hofshteyn, Dovid, 24, 220, 257

Holocaust, 5–6, 41, 59, 85–91, 146–47, 184, 219, 262

Holtman, Rokhl (Rachel), 100, 102; *Mayn Lebns Veg* (My Life's Path), 99

Holtzman, Harry, *40*, 238

Housewives Consumer Association (HCA), 117, 120

Howard, Ruth, 3, *267*

HUAC (House Un-American Activities Committee), 7–8, 130, 254, 308n37

Hudson, Anna, 277

Hurtig, Adolph, 68–69

identity: ethnic, 10–11, 51, 202, 251, 261, 273, 284–85; production of, 50; Yiddish, 49. *See also* Jewish identity

IKOR (Yiddish Kolonizatsiye in Rusland), 10, 34, 84, 203

Ilomaki, Lil Himmelfarb, 30, *31*, 70–71, 179

Industrial Union of Needle Trades Workers (IUNTW), 63–66, 68–70, 72, 203, 235, 238, 280, 285

International Conference on Yiddish Culture, 127

International Democratic Women's Federation, 119

International Federation Against Racism and Anti-Semitism: 1937 Paris Congress, 77, 84

internationalism: revolutionary commitment to, 48; socialist, 24; vs. Zionism, 127

International Ladies Garment Workers Union (ILGWU), 62, 64–66, 73, 80

International Workers Order (IWO), 80, 83, 160, 183, 210; and Communist Party, 38; cultural contributions of, 51; disbanding of, 6; Emma Lazarus clubs, 7; history of, 39–40; Jewish People's Fraternal Order (JPFO), 5–6; schools, 162–63, 168,

170, 172, 177, 231, 234; as "subversive organization," 6

International Yiddish Cultural Congress, 210

Israel, 188, 192, 270–73, 296n15, 311n9

Italy, fascist, 59, 76, 78

Jewish Anti-Fascist Committee. *See under* Soviet Union

Jewish Children's (Work) Communes: Minsk, 29; Vitebsk, 1–3, 29

Jewish Cultural Clubs and Societies, 6, 259

Jewish Cultural League, 123

Jewish culture, 37, 220, 260, 262; proletarian, 52–53; secular, 18–20, 54. *See also* cultural life

Jewish holidays, 188–89, 269

Jewish identity, 5, 11, 18, 48, 51, 59, 229, 272–73, 285; and Canadianness, 55

Jewish Immigrant Aid Society (JIAS), 272

Jewish International Cultural Congress, 54

Jewish Labor Committee, 66, 138

Jewish left: and anti-racism, 180; "communist," 4; and Communist Party, 37–42, 284–86; and culture, 49, 55–56, 210; important dates affecting, 43–45; mainstream discomfort with, 123; progressive, 48, 96, 123, 260; pro-Soviet, 53, 86; and revolutionary values, 33–45; secular, 4–12, 16, 47, 59, 97, 130–31, 160, 195, 208, 228, 232; and women's equality, 109, 114, 119

Jewish Mutual Aid League (Yiddisher hilfs fareyn), 37, 98

Jewish National Fund, 273

Jewish People's Committee, 91

Jewish People's Fraternal Order (JPFO), 36; Cultural Division, 172

Jewish radicalism, 47–48, 156; emergence of, 33

Jewish Refugee Action Network, 273

Jewish Renaissance Movement in Poland, 271

Jewish Socialist Library, 198

Jewish socialists, making of, 15–32